ETERNITY GIRL

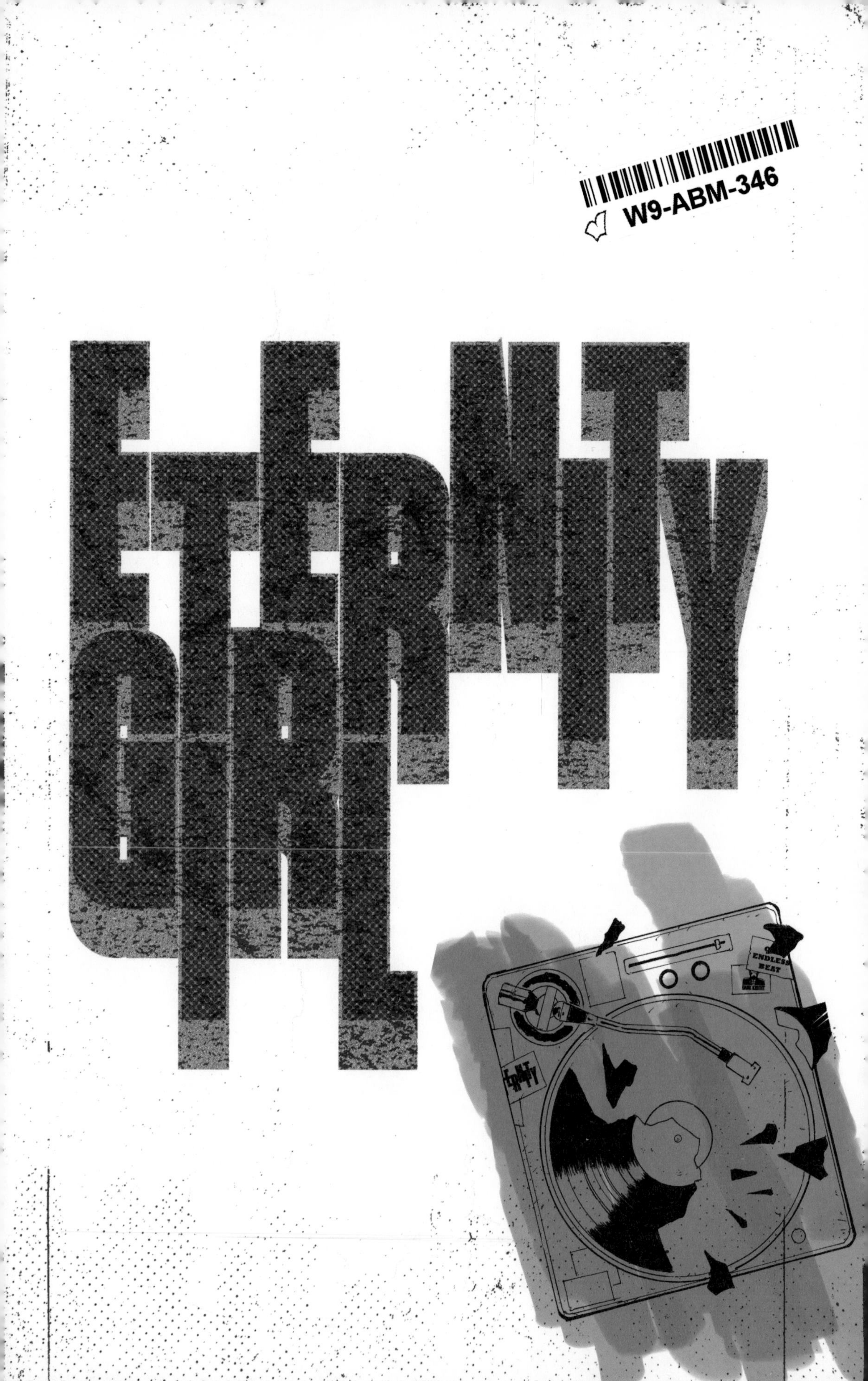
ENDLESS BEAT

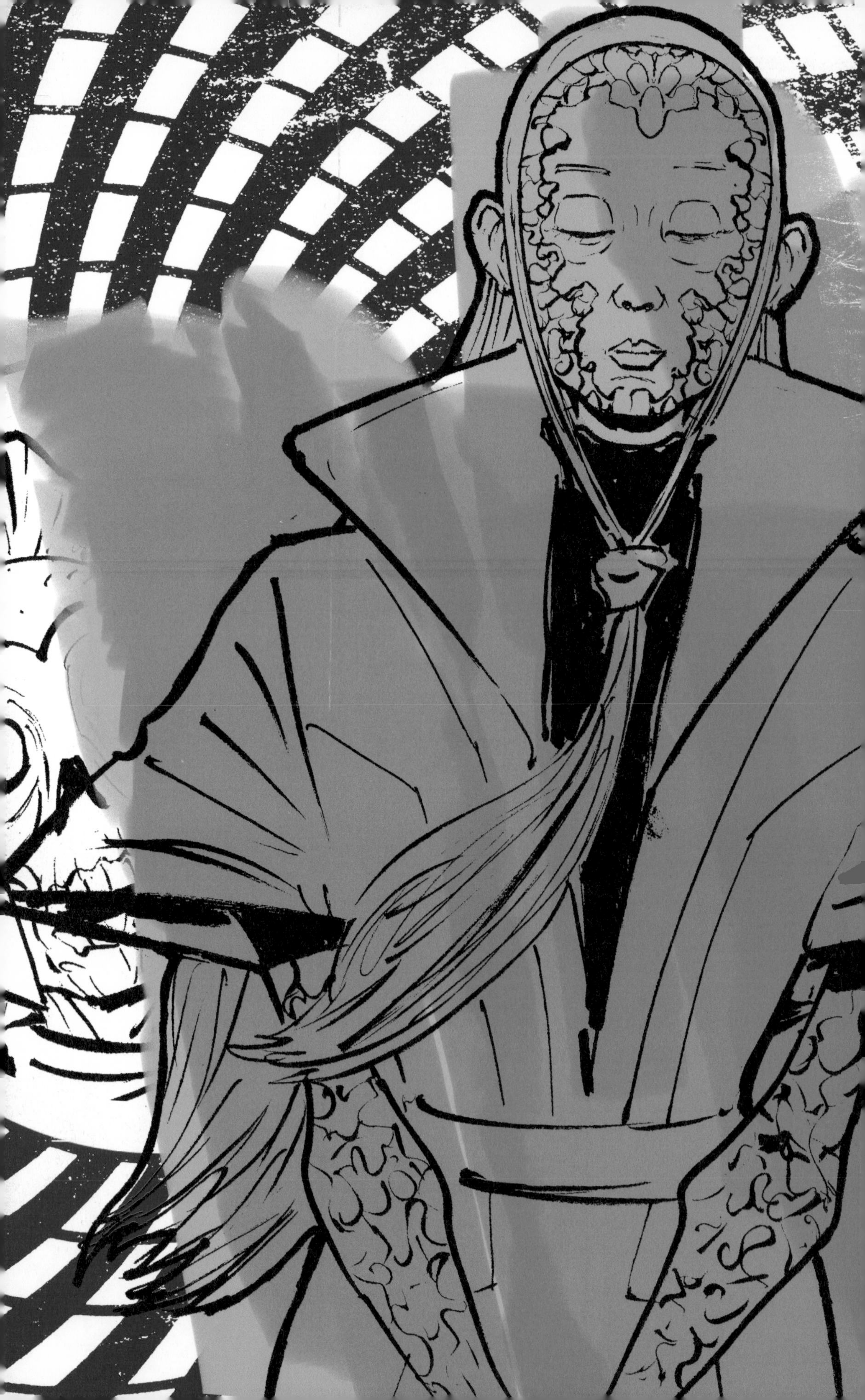

ETERNITY GIRL

MAGDALENE VISAGGIO Writer
SONNY LIEW Artist
CHRIS CHUCKRY Colorist
TODD KLEIN Letterer
SONNY LIEW Cover Art and Original Series Covers
GERARD WAY DC's Young Animal Curator

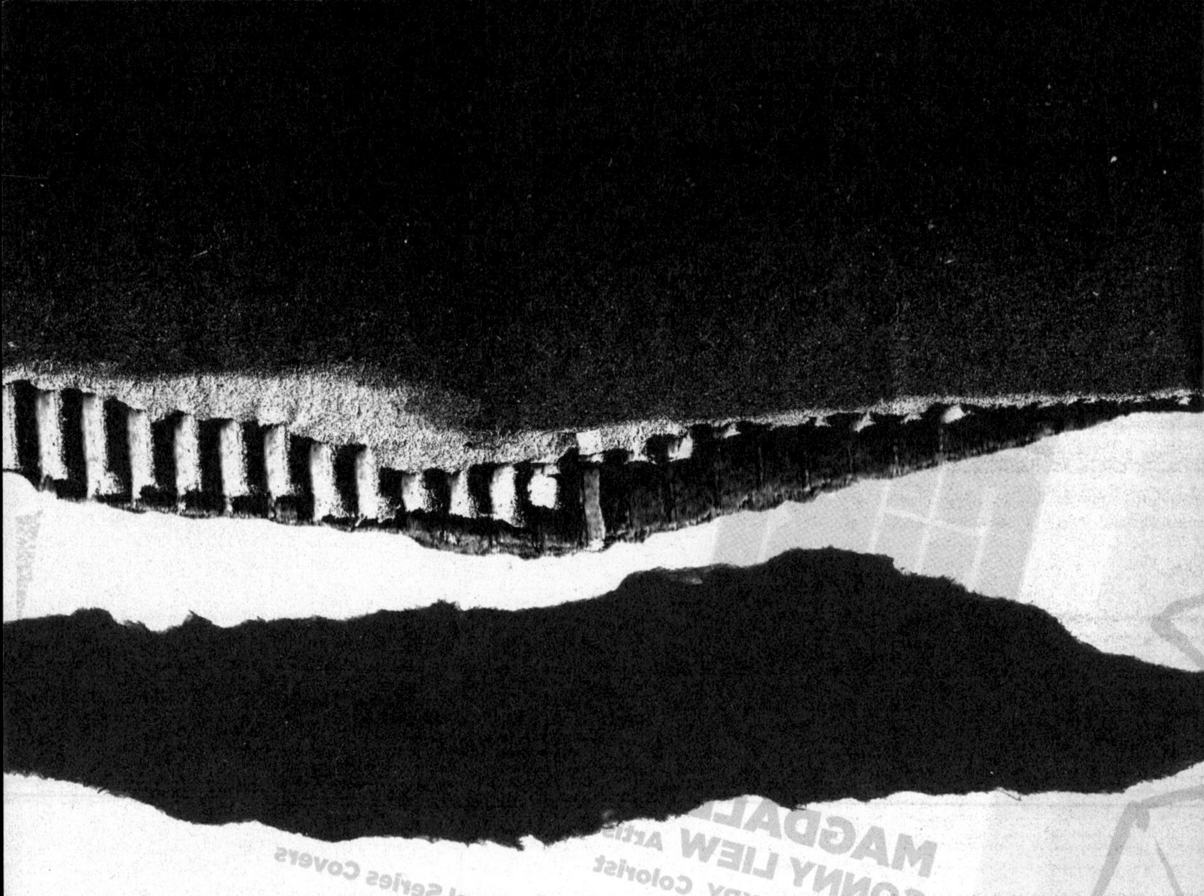

MAGDALENE VISAGGIO Writer
SONNY LIEW Artist
CHRIS CHUCKRY Colorist
TODD KLEIN Letterer
SONNY LIEW Cover Art and Original Series Covers
GERARD WAY DC's Young Animal Curator

ANDY KHOURI Editor – Original Series
MAGGIE HOWELL Assistant Editor – Original Series
JEB WOODARD Group Editor – Collected Editions
SCOTT NYBAKKEN Editor – Collected Edition
STEVE COOK Design Director – Books
LOUIS PRANDI Publication Design

BOB HARRAS Senior VP – Editor-in-Chief, DC Comics
MARK DOYLE Executive Editor, Vertigo & Black Label

DAN DiDIO Publisher
JIM LEE Publisher & Chief Creative Officer
AMIT DESAI Executive VP – Business & Marketing Strategy, Direct to Consumer &
Global Franchise Management
BOBBIE CHASE VP & Executive Editor, Young Reader & Talent Development
MARK CHIARELLO Senior VP – Art, Design & Collected Editions
JOHN CUNNINGHAM Senior VP – Sales & Trade Marketing
BRIAR DARDEN VP – Business Affairs
ANNE DePIES Senior VP – Business Strategy, Finance & Administration
DON FALLETTI VP – Manufacturing Operations
LAWRENCE GANEM VP – Editorial Administration & Talent Relations
ALISON GILL Senior VP – Manufacturing & Operations
JASON GREENBERG VP – Business Strategy & Finance
HANK KANALZ Senior VP – Editorial Strategy & Administration
JAY KOGAN Senior VP – Legal Affairs
NICK J. NAPOLITANO VP – Manufacturing Administration
LISETTE OSTERLOH VP – Digital Marketing & Events
EDDIE SCANNELL VP – Consumer Marketing
COURTNEY SIMMONS Senior VP – Publicity & Communications
JIM (SKI) SOKOLOWSKI VP – Comic Book Specialty Sales & Trade Marketing
NANCY SPEARS VP – Mass, Book, Digital Sales & Trade Marketing
MICHELE R. WELLS VP – Content Strategy

MIX
Paper from
responsible sources
FSC® C132124

Perhaps the strangest creation of George Sumner, the Formless Girl debuted in "The Birth of the Formless Girl" in 1956's ASTOUNDING TALES #32. Originally conceived as a "horror superhero," Sumner was forced by his editors to fit the character of Caroline Sharp into the increasingly popular science fiction superhero mold. Still, Caroline Sharp would never stray too far from Sumner's original idea, a monster movie heroine struggling to maintain her humanity.

"The Birth of the Formless Girl," ASTOUNDING TALES #32. Story and art by George Sumner. 1956.

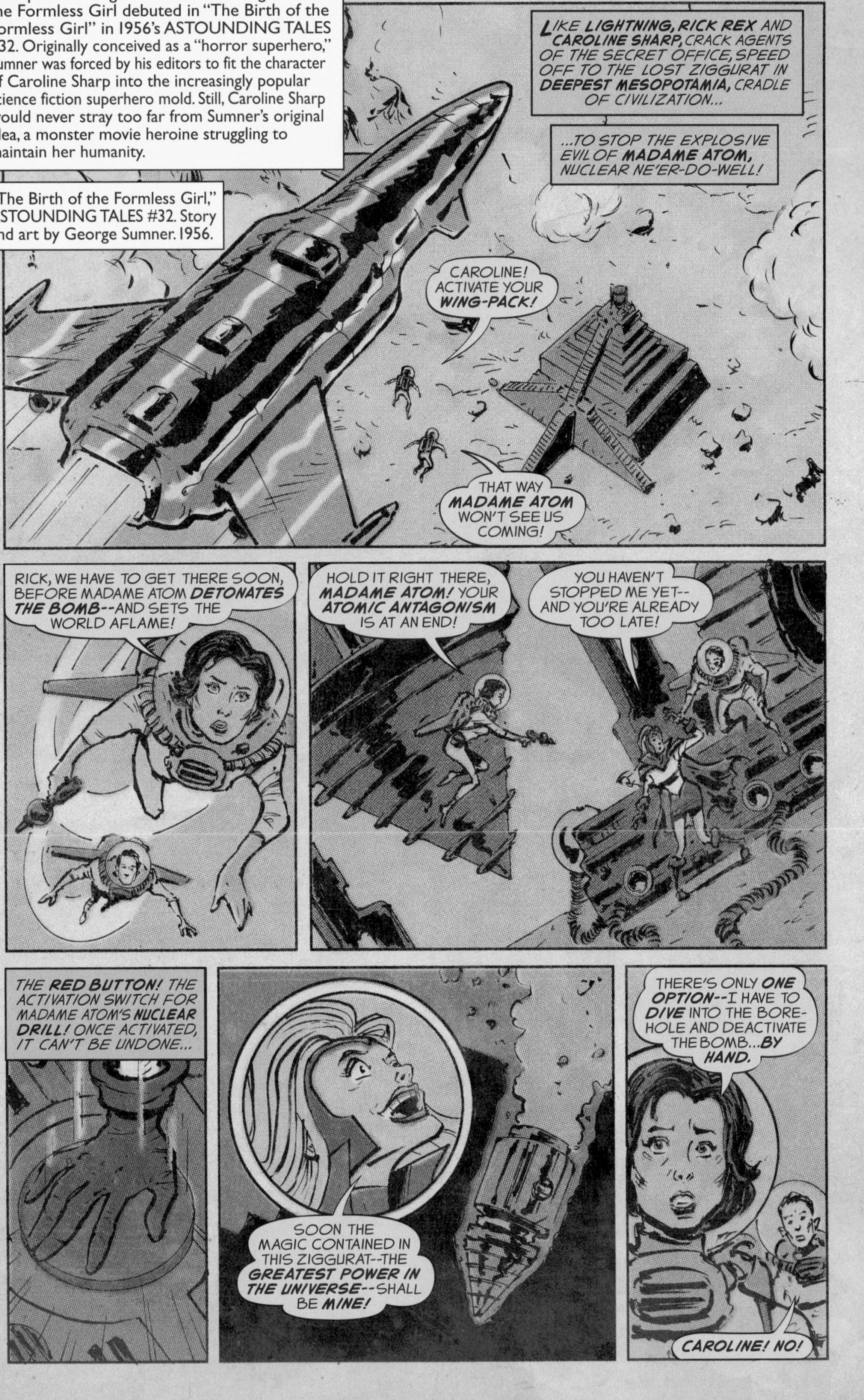
LIKE LIGHTNING, RICK REX AND CAROLINE SHARP, CRACK AGENTS OF THE SECRET OFFICE, SPEED OFF TO THE LOST ZIGGURAT IN DEEPEST MESOPOTAMIA, CRADLE OF CIVILIZATION...
...TO STOP THE EXPLOSIVE EVIL OF MADAME ATOM, NUCLEAR NE'ER-DO-WELL!
CAROLINE! ACTIVATE YOUR WING-PACK!
THAT WAY MADAME ATOM WON'T SEE US COMING!
RICK, WE HAVE TO GET THERE SOON, BEFORE MADAME ATOM DETONATES THE BOMB--AND SETS THE WORLD AFLAME!
HOLD IT RIGHT THERE, MADAME ATOM! YOUR ATOMIC ANTAGONISM IS AT AN END!
YOU HAVEN'T STOPPED ME YET--AND YOU'RE ALREADY TOO LATE!
THE RED BUTTON! THE ACTIVATION SWITCH FOR MADAME ATOM'S NUCLEAR DRILL! ONCE ACTIVATED, IT CAN'T BE UNDONE...
SOON THE MAGIC CONTAINED IN THIS ZIGGURAT--THE GREATEST POWER IN THE UNIVERSE--SHALL BE MINE!
THERE'S ONLY ONE OPTION--I HAVE TO DIVE INTO THE BORE-HOLE AND DEACTIVATE THE BOMB...BY HAND.
CAROLINE! NO!

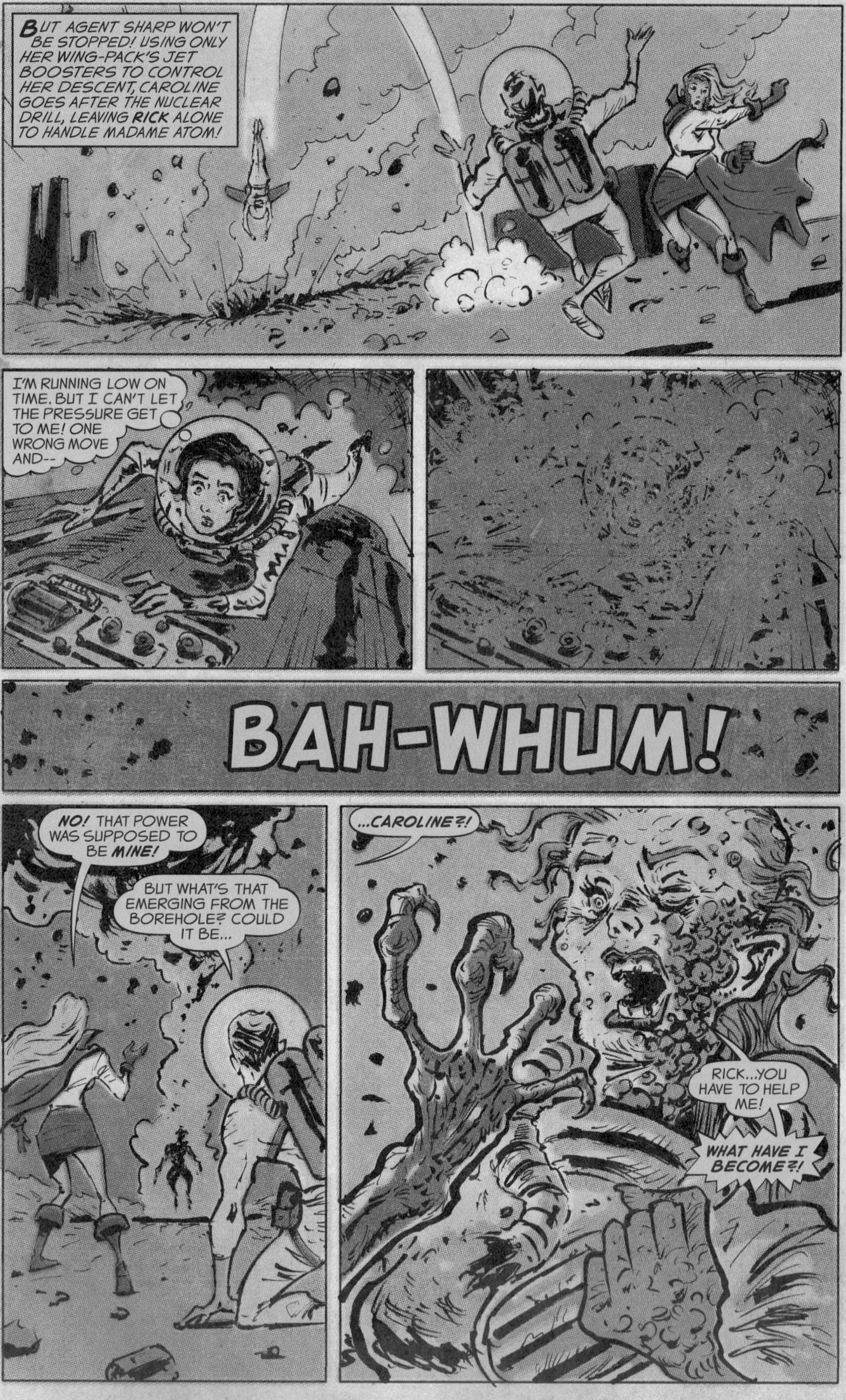
BUT AGENT SHARP WON'T BE STOPPED! USING ONLY HER WING-PACK'S JET BOOSTERS TO CONTROL HER DESCENT, CAROLINE GOES AFTER THE NUCLEAR DRILL, LEAVING RICK ALONE TO HANDLE MADAME ATOM!
I'M RUNNING LOW ON TIME. BUT I CAN'T LET THE PRESSURE GET TO ME! ONE WRONG MOVE AND--
BAH-WHUM!
NO! THAT POWER WAS SUPPOSED TO BE MINE!
BUT WHAT'S THAT EMERGING FROM THE BOREHOLE? COULD IT BE...
...CAROLINE?!
RICK...YOU HAVE TO HELP ME!
WHAT HAVE I BECOME?!

By the early 1960s, ASTOUNDING TALES had been canceled, and "the Formless Girl" with it. But in 1981, the writer-artist team of Fred Hand and Garry Streicher brought the book back to life as ALPHA 13. Hand's version named Caroline Sharp "Chrysalis" for the first time, the leader of a team of super-powered misfits working for a secret governmental organization to stop Madame Atom's plan to plunge the world into anarchy. A book without clear-cut heroes and villains, ALPHA 13 pitted anarchism against exploitative authorities, and struggled to maintain an audience.

"Nevermore, Never Man," ALPHA 13 #27. Story by Fred Hand, art by Garry Streicher. 1983.

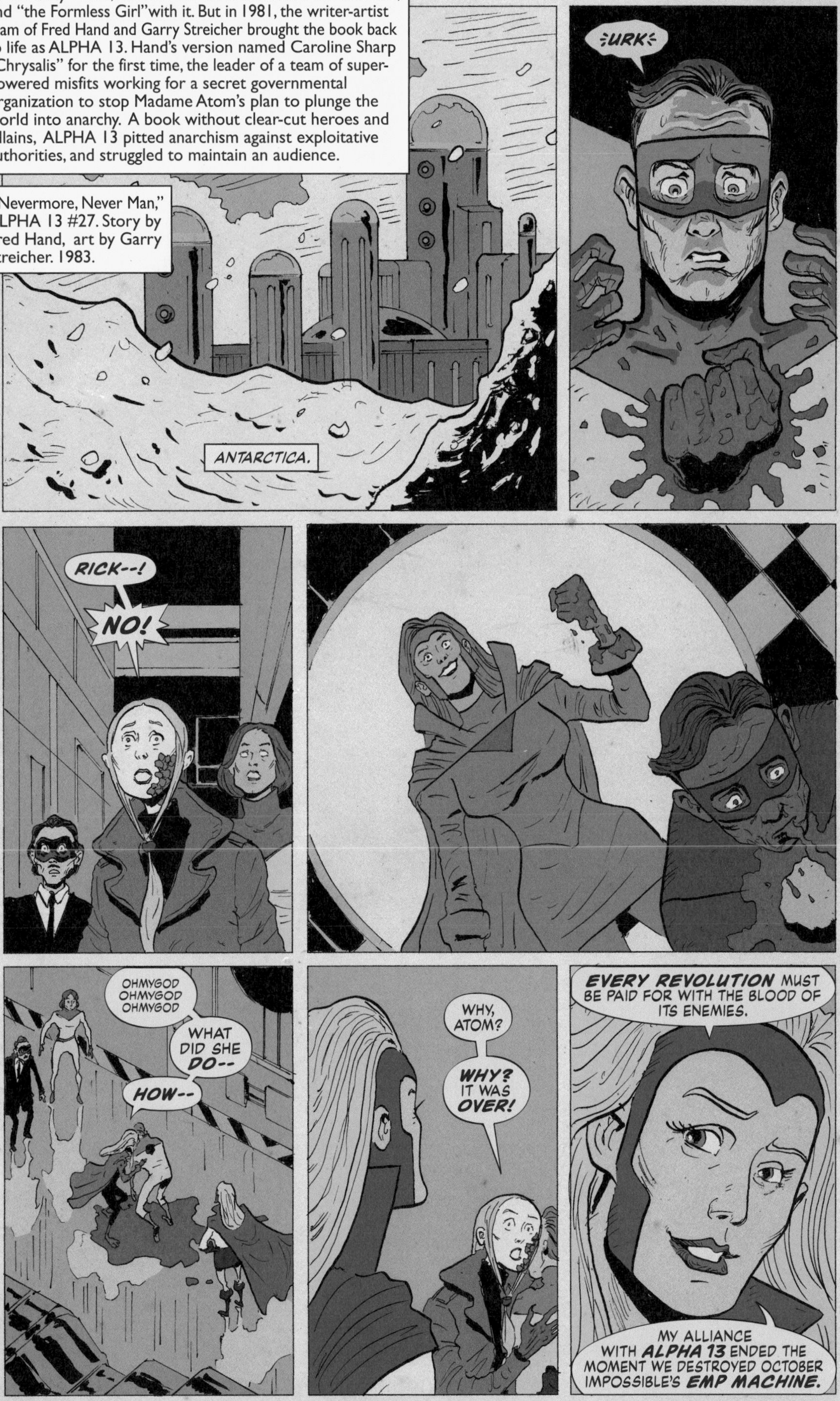

ANTARCTICA.
URK
RICK--!
NO!
OHMYGOD OHMYGOD OHMYGOD
WHAT DID SHE DO--
HOW--
WHY, ATOM?
WHY? IT WAS OVER!
EVERY REVOLUTION MUST BE PAID FOR WITH THE BLOOD OF ITS ENEMIES.
MY ALLIANCE WITH ALPHA 13 ENDED THE MOMENT WE DESTROYED OCTOBER IMPOSSIBLE'S EMP MACHINE.

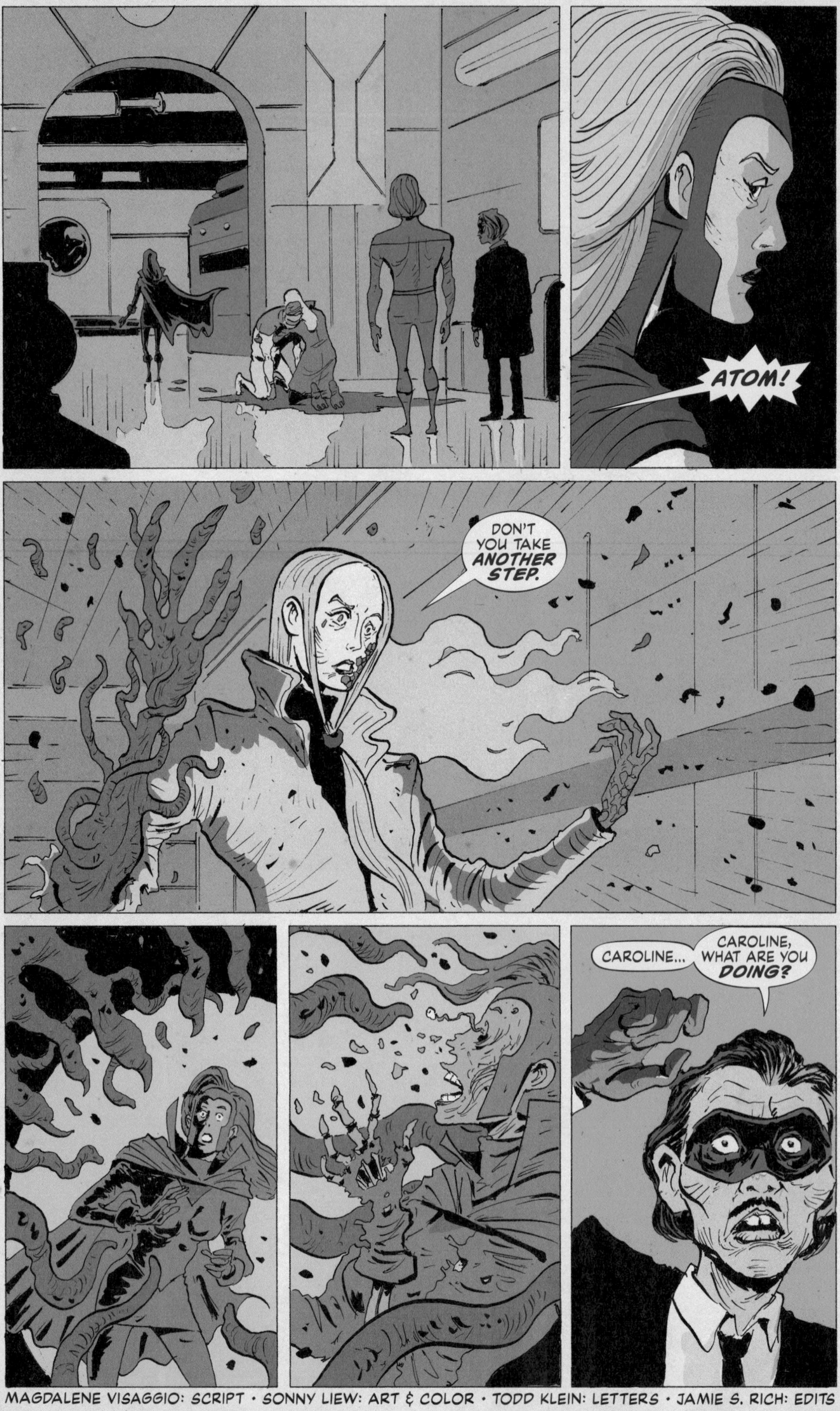
ATOM!
DON'T YOU TAKE ANOTHER STEP.
CAROLINE...
CAROLINE, WHAT ARE YOU DOING?

MAGDALENE VISAGGIO: SCRIPT • SONNY LIEW: ART & COLOR • TODD KLEIN: LETTERS • JAMIE S. RICH: EDITS

In 1990 Garry Streicher was able to convince the publisher to bring ALPHA 13 back, this time in a book entitled CHRYSALIS: THE ETERNITY GIRL. Fred Hand had passed away in a tragic car accident the year prior, so Streicher was teamed with writer Bev Wilson. Together, Wilson and Streicher crafted a psychedelic epic which took the anarchist themes of ALPHA 13 into the afterlife with a story about the eternal cycle of death and resurrection before ending after 35 issues in 1993.

"Unfortunate Souls," CHRYSALIS: THE ETERNITY GIRL #1. Story by Bev Wilson, art by Garry Streicher. 1990.

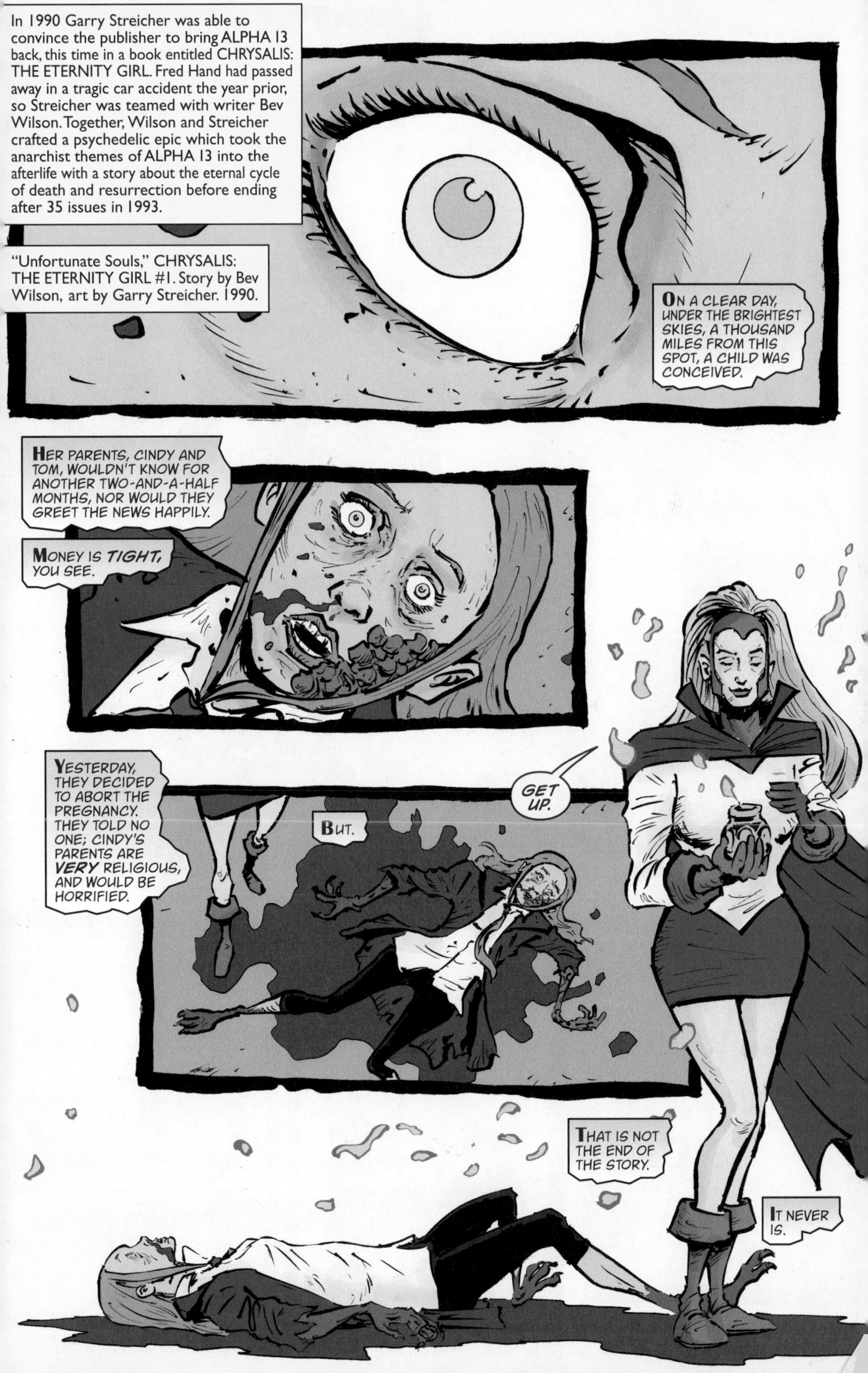
ON A CLEAR DAY, UNDER THE BRIGHTEST SKIES, A THOUSAND MILES FROM THIS SPOT, A CHILD WAS CONCEIVED.
HER PARENTS, CINDY AND TOM, WOULDN'T KNOW FOR ANOTHER TWO-AND-A-HALF MONTHS, NOR WOULD THEY GREET THE NEWS HAPPILY.
MONEY IS *TIGHT,* YOU SEE.
YESTERDAY, THEY DECIDED TO ABORT THE PREGNANCY. THEY TOLD NO ONE; CINDY'S PARENTS ARE **VERY** RELIGIOUS, AND WOULD BE HORRIFIED.
BUT.
GET UP.
THAT IS NOT THE END OF THE STORY.
IT NEVER IS.

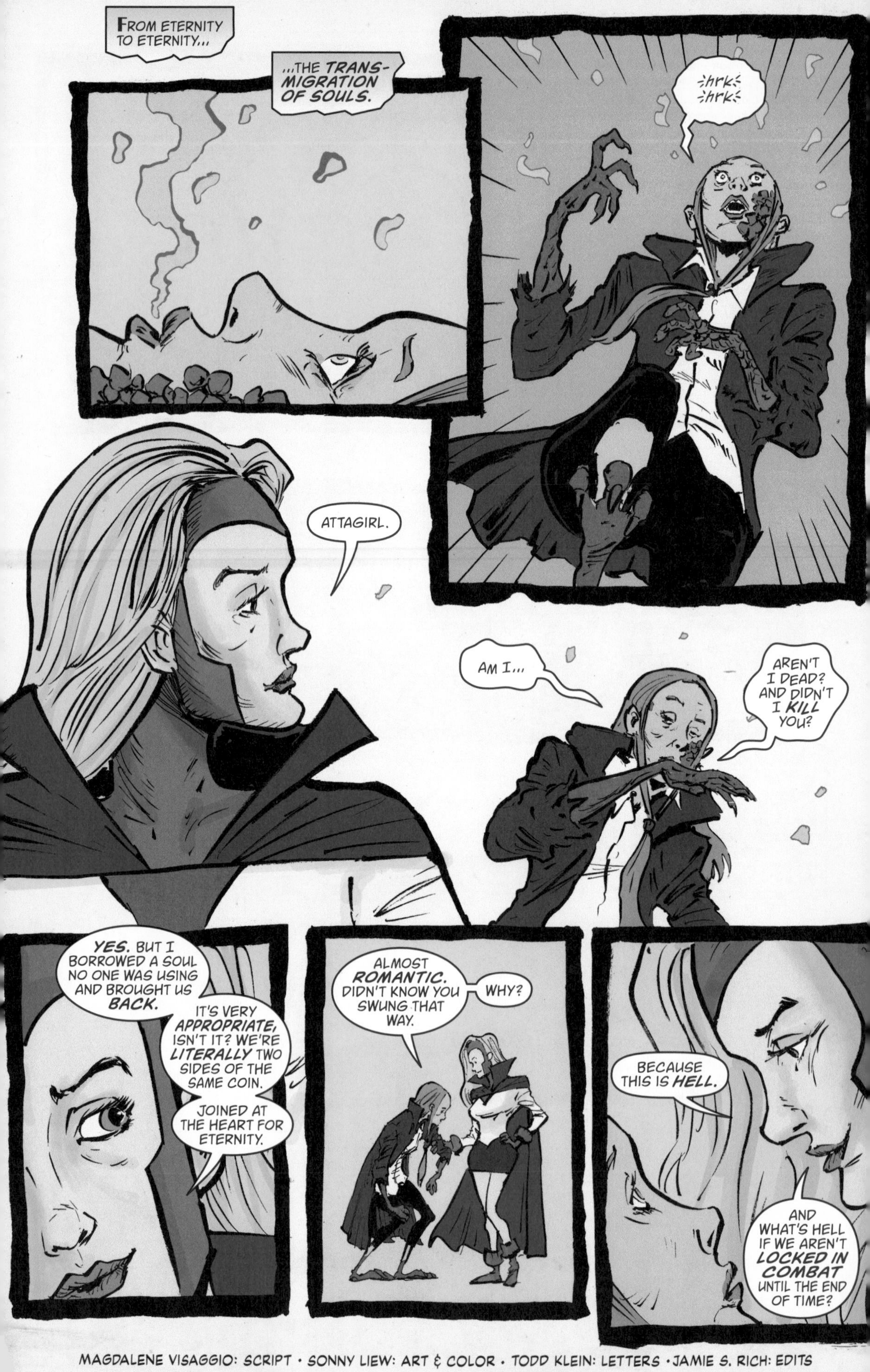
FROM ETERNITY TO ETERNITY...
...THE TRANS-MIGRATION OF SOULS.
hrk hrk
ATTAGIRL.
AM I...
AREN'T I DEAD? AND DIDN'T I KILL YOU?
YES. BUT I BORROWED A SOUL NO ONE WAS USING AND BROUGHT US BACK.
IT'S VERY APPROPRIATE, ISN'T IT? WE'RE LITERALLY TWO SIDES OF THE SAME COIN.
JOINED AT THE HEART FOR ETERNITY.
ALMOST ROMANTIC. DIDN'T KNOW YOU SWUNG THAT WAY.
WHY?
BECAUSE THIS IS HELL.
AND WHAT'S HELL IF WE AREN'T LOCKED IN COMBAT UNTIL THE END OF TIME?

MAGDALENE VISAGGIO: SCRIPT • SONNY LIEW: ART & COLOR • TODD KLEIN: LETTERS • JAMIE S. RICH: EDITS

In 2008, ALPHA 13 was revived again as a six-issue miniseries written by Paul Cruey with art by Ellie Keegan. A complete reimagining that ignored all existing continuity, this version focused on Caroline Sharp/Chrysalis' transformation and its effect on her, driving Caroline deep into an existential morass. Unlike previous incarnations, Cruey and Keegan's ALPHA 13 had little psychedelic imagery, preferring experimental storytelling that tried to capture Caroline's fractured experience of reality. Released to critical confusion, a promised ongoing series never materialized.

"Operation: Existence!," ALPHA 13 Vol. 2 #6. Story by Paul Cruey, art by Ellie Keegan. 2008.

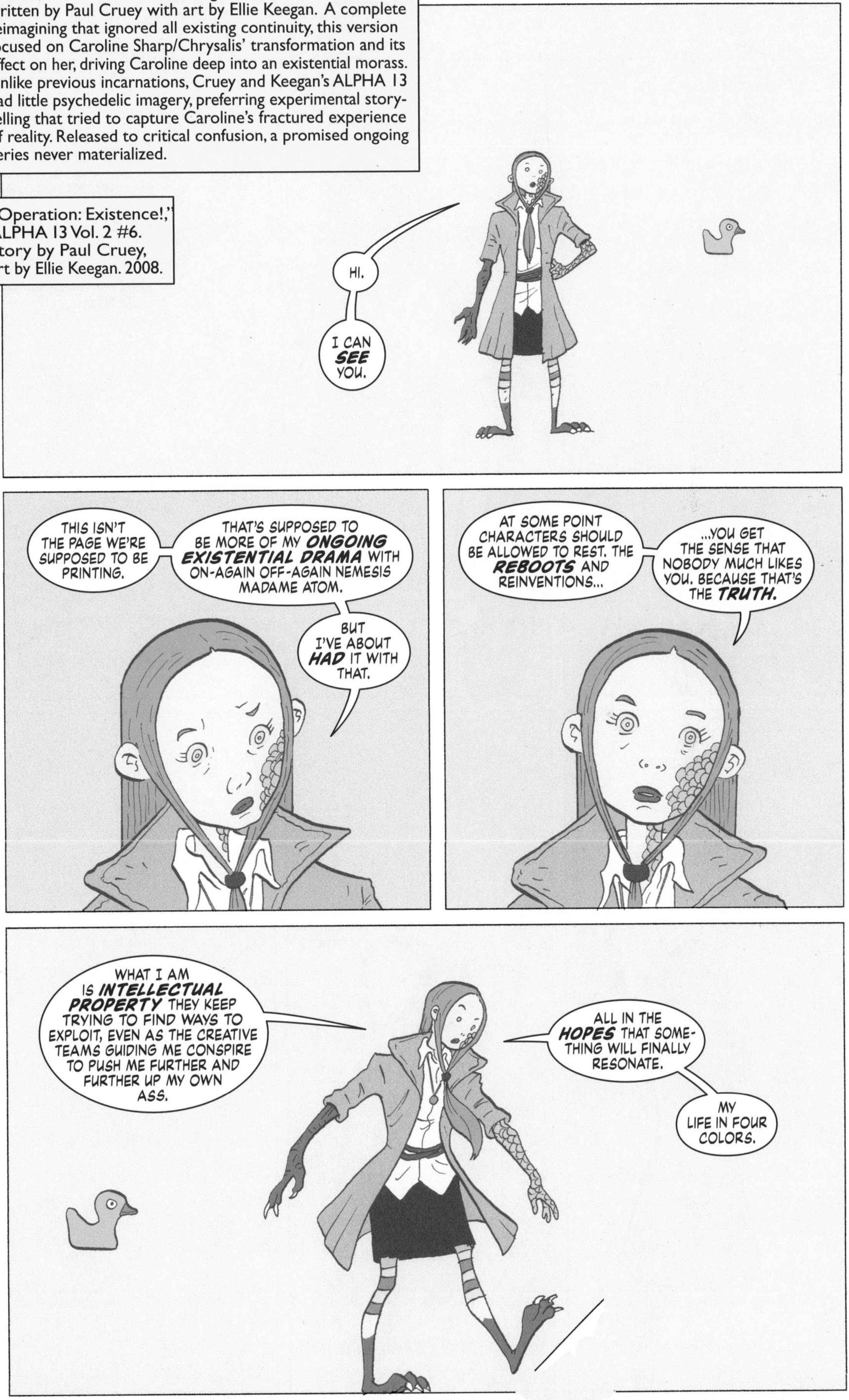
HI.
I CAN SEE YOU.
THIS ISN'T THE PAGE WE'RE SUPPOSED TO BE PRINTING.
THAT'S SUPPOSED TO BE MORE OF MY ONGOING EXISTENTIAL DRAMA WITH ON-AGAIN OFF-AGAIN NEMESIS MADAME ATOM.
BUT I'VE ABOUT HAD IT WITH THAT.
AT SOME POINT CHARACTERS SHOULD BE ALLOWED TO REST. THE REBOOTS AND REINVENTIONS...
...YOU GET THE SENSE THAT NOBODY MUCH LIKES YOU. BECAUSE THAT'S THE TRUTH.
WHAT I AM IS INTELLECTUAL PROPERTY THEY KEEP TRYING TO FIND WAYS TO EXPLOIT, EVEN AS THE CREATIVE TEAMS GUIDING ME CONSPIRE TO PUSH ME FURTHER AND FURTHER UP MY OWN ASS.
ALL IN THE HOPES THAT SOMETHING WILL FINALLY RESONATE.
MY LIFE IN FOUR COLORS.

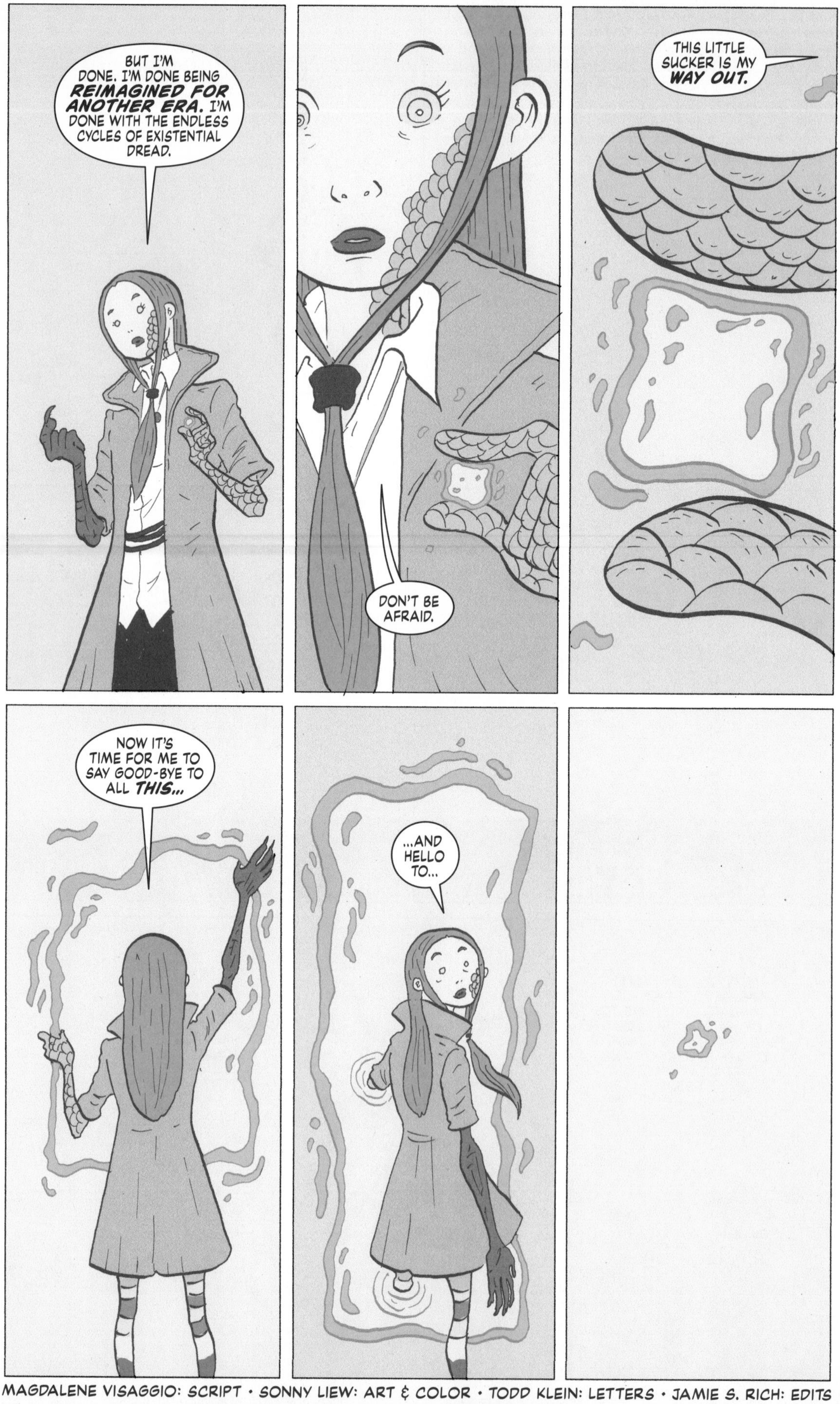
BUT I'M DONE. I'M DONE BEING **REIMAGINED FOR ANOTHER ERA.** I'M DONE WITH THE ENDLESS CYCLES OF EXISTENTIAL DREAD.
DON'T BE AFRAID.
THIS LITTLE SUCKER IS MY **WAY OUT.**
NOW IT'S TIME FOR ME TO SAY GOOD-BYE TO ALL **THIS...**
...AND HELLO TO...

MAGDALENE VISAGGIO: SCRIPT • SONNY LIEW: ART & COLOR • TODD KLEIN: LETTERS • JAMIE S. RICH: EDITS

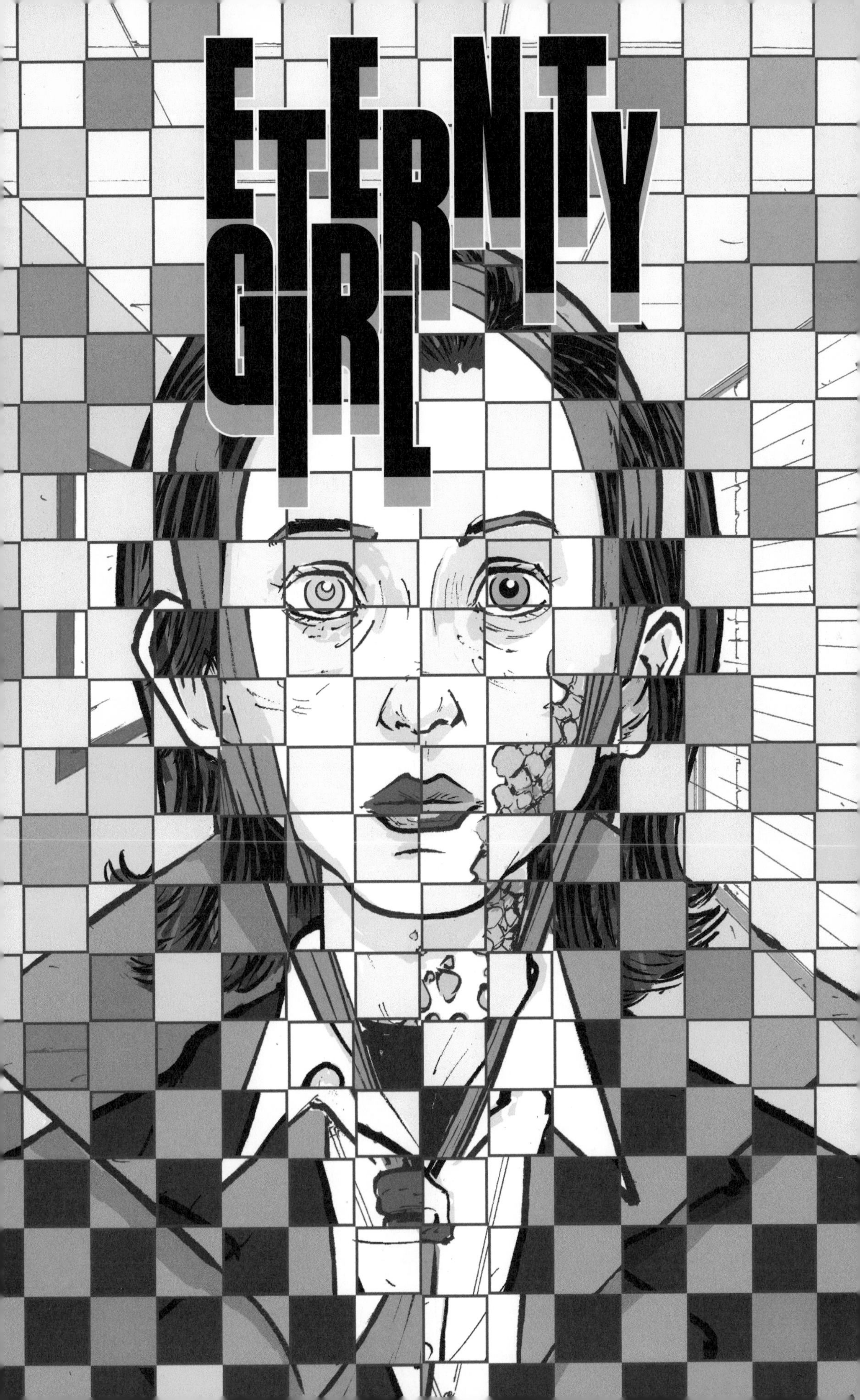
ETERNITY
GIRL

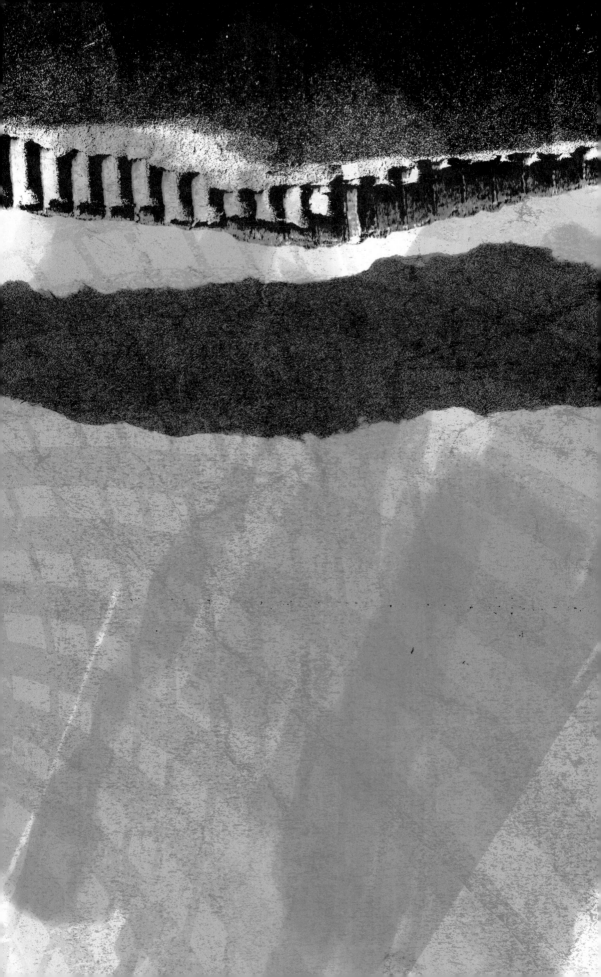

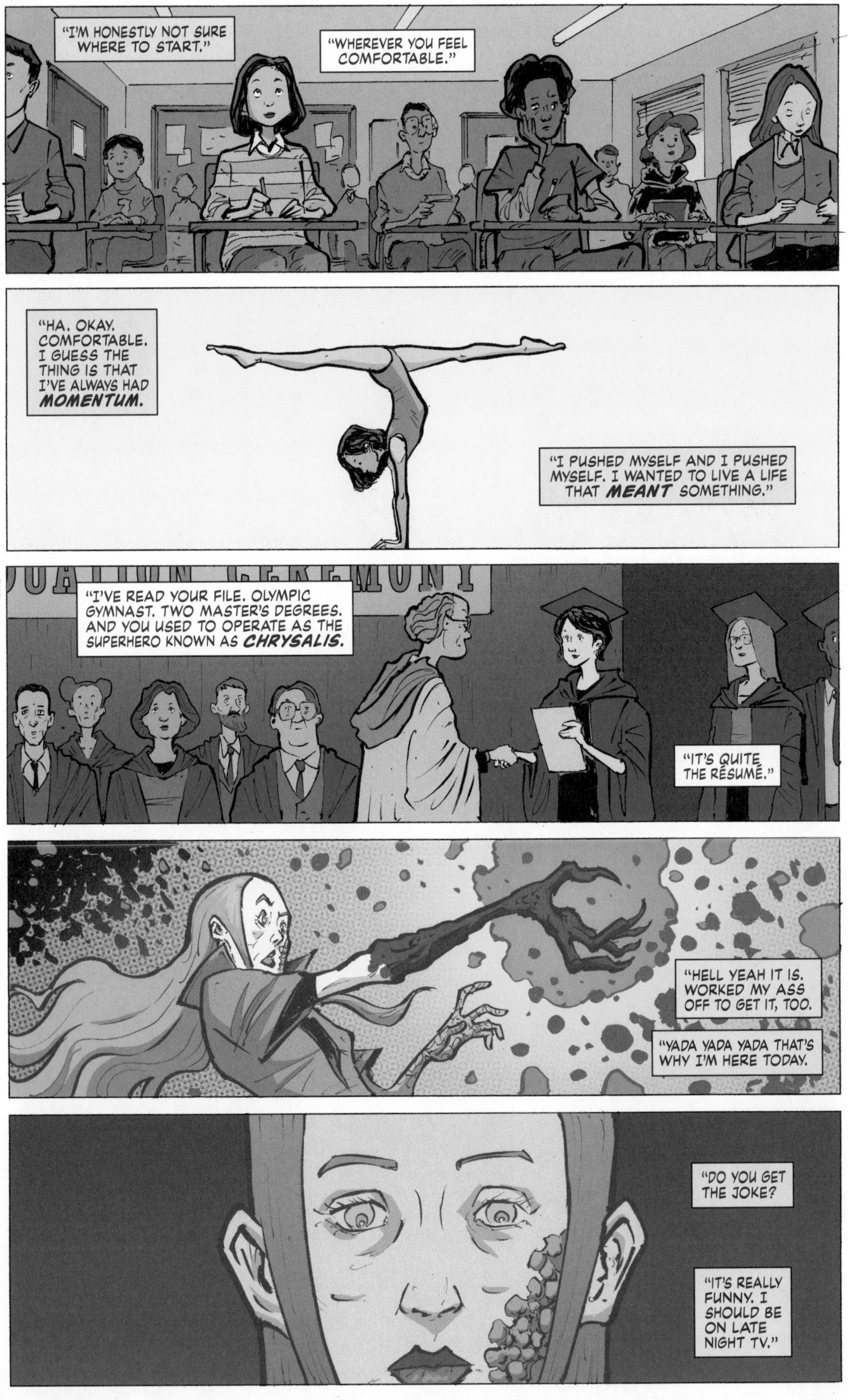
"I'M HONESTLY NOT SURE WHERE TO START."
"WHEREVER YOU FEEL COMFORTABLE."
"HA. OKAY. COMFORTABLE. I GUESS THE THING IS THAT I'VE ALWAYS HAD MOMENTUM.
"I PUSHED MYSELF AND I PUSHED MYSELF. I WANTED TO LIVE A LIFE THAT MEANT SOMETHING."
"I'VE READ YOUR FILE. OLYMPIC GYMNAST. TWO MASTER'S DEGREES. AND YOU USED TO OPERATE AS THE SUPERHERO KNOWN AS CHRYSALIS.
"IT'S QUITE THE RÉSUMÉ."
"HELL YEAH IT IS. WORKED MY ASS OFF TO GET IT, TOO.
"YADA YADA YADA THAT'S WHY I'M HERE TODAY.
"DO YOU GET THE JOKE?
"IT'S REALLY FUNNY. I SHOULD BE ON LATE NIGHT TV."

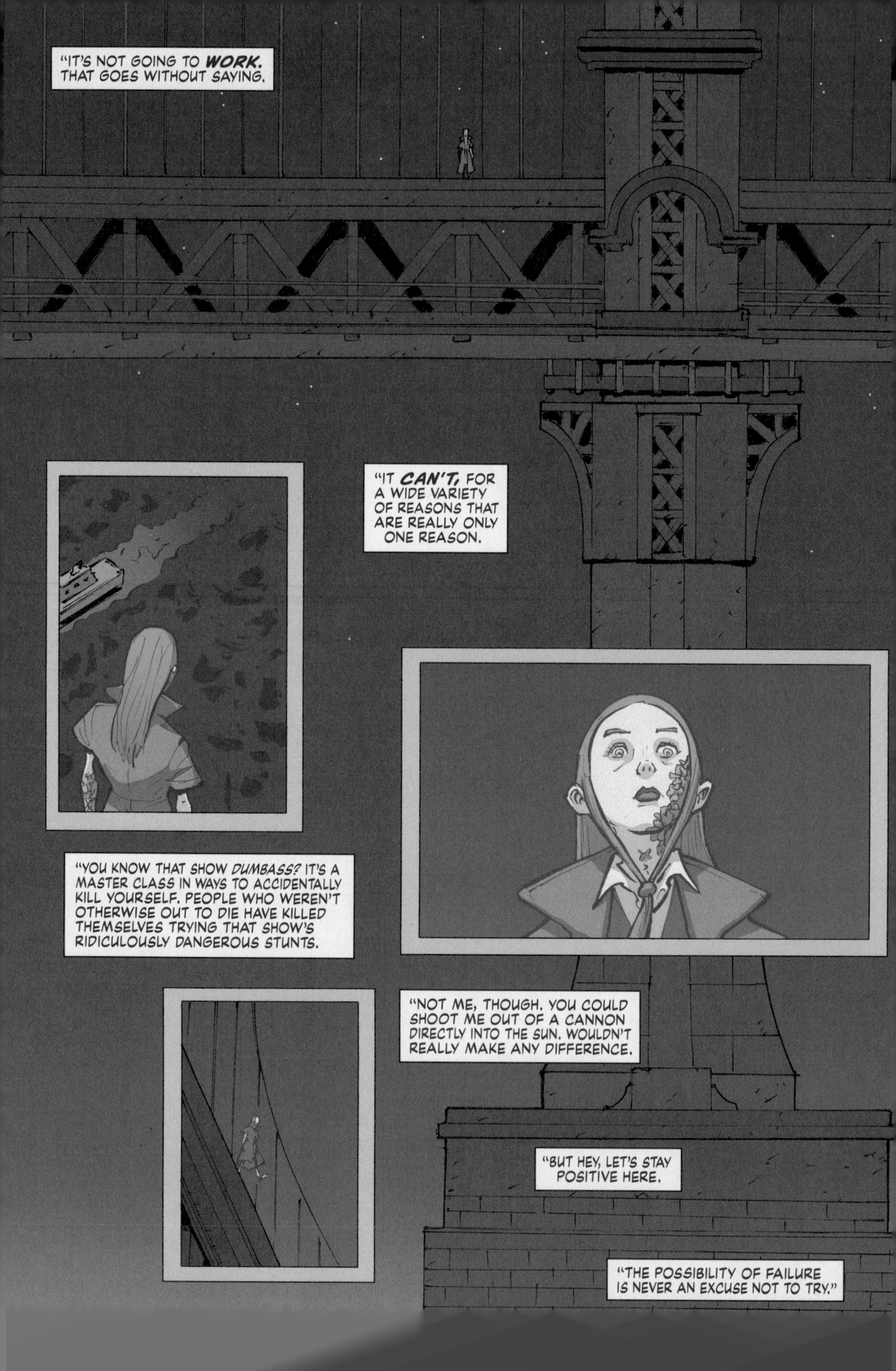
"IT'S NOT GOING TO **WORK.** THAT GOES WITHOUT SAYING.
"IT **CAN'T,** FOR A WIDE VARIETY OF REASONS THAT ARE REALLY ONLY ONE REASON.
"YOU KNOW THAT SHOW *DUMBASS?* IT'S A MASTER CLASS IN WAYS TO ACCIDENTALLY KILL YOURSELF. PEOPLE WHO WEREN'T OTHERWISE OUT TO DIE HAVE KILLED THEMSELVES TRYING THAT SHOW'S RIDICULOUSLY DANGEROUS STUNTS.
"NOT ME, THOUGH. YOU COULD SHOOT ME OUT OF A CANNON DIRECTLY INTO THE SUN. WOULDN'T REALLY MAKE ANY DIFFERENCE.
"BUT HEY, LET'S STAY POSITIVE HERE.
"THE POSSIBILITY OF FAILURE IS NEVER AN EXCUSE NOT TO TRY."

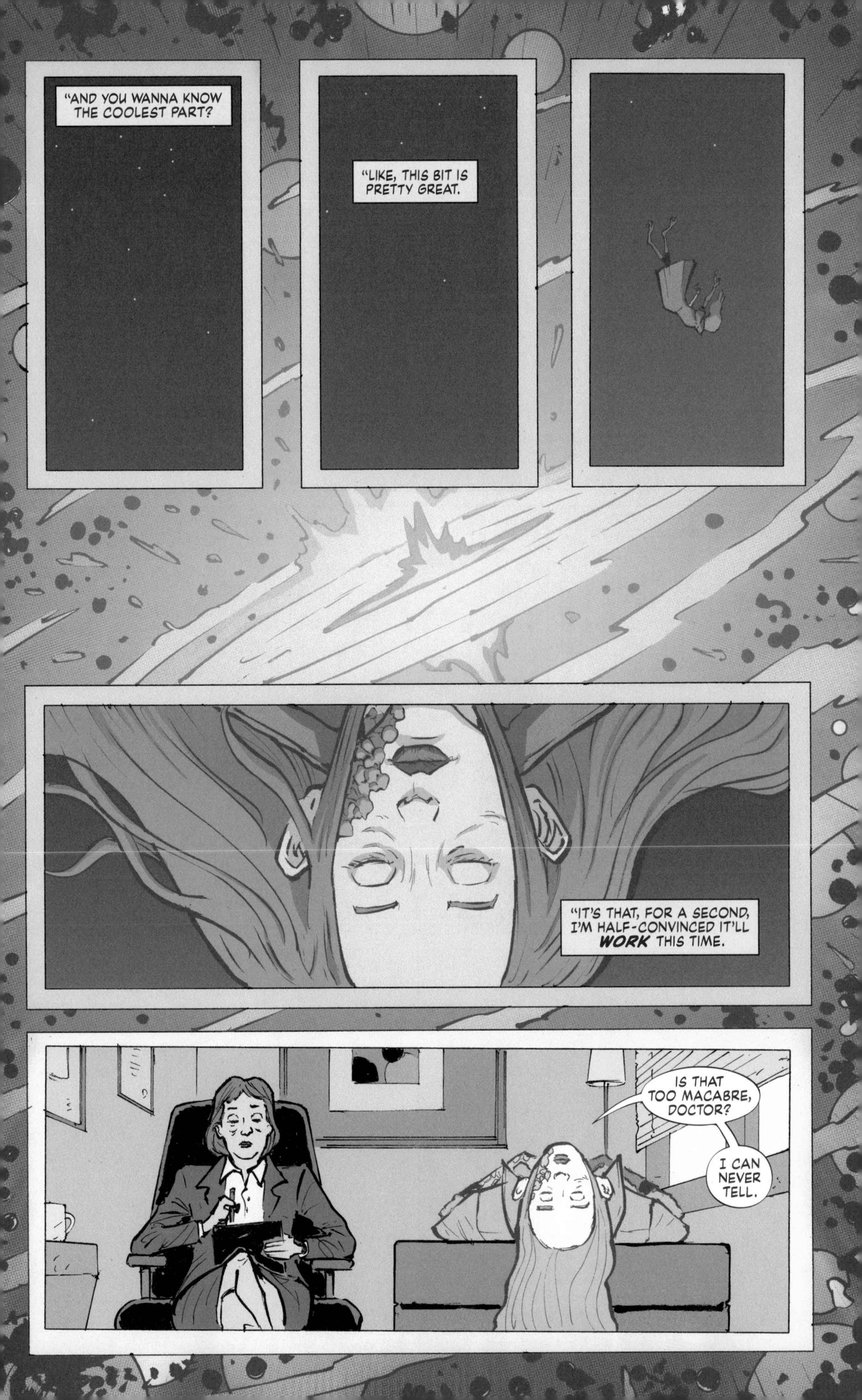
"AND YOU WANNA KNOW THE COOLEST PART?
"LIKE, THIS BIT IS PRETTY GREAT.
"IT'S THAT, FOR A SECOND, I'M HALF-CONVINCED IT'LL ***WORK*** THIS TIME.
IS THAT TOO MACABRE, DOCTOR?
I CAN NEVER TELL.

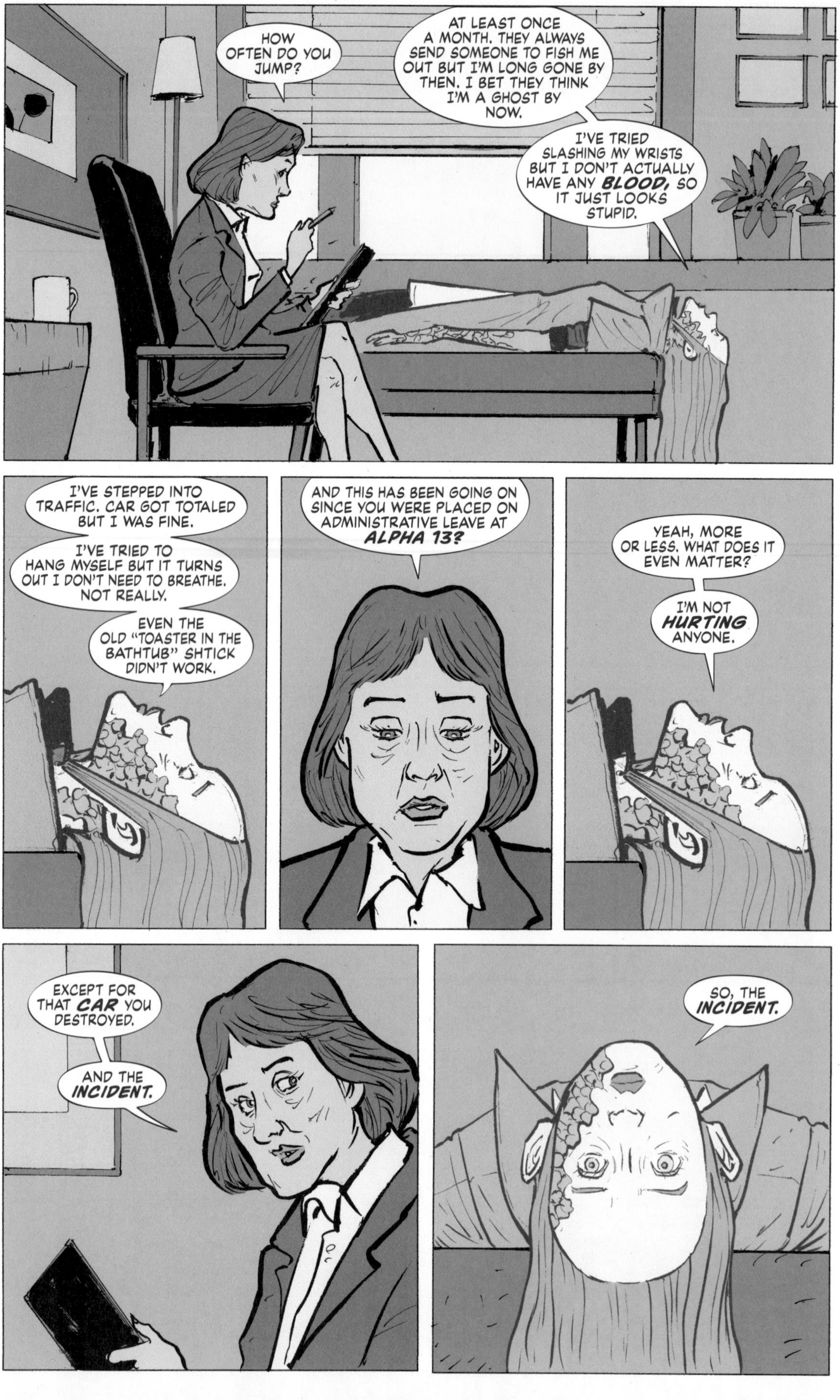
HOW OFTEN DO YOU JUMP?
AT LEAST ONCE A MONTH. THEY ALWAYS SEND SOMEONE TO FISH ME OUT BUT I'M LONG GONE BY THEN. I BET THEY THINK I'M A GHOST BY NOW.
I'VE TRIED SLASHING MY WRISTS BUT I DON'T ACTUALLY HAVE ANY BLOOD, SO IT JUST LOOKS STUPID.
I'VE STEPPED INTO TRAFFIC. CAR GOT TOTALED BUT I WAS FINE.
I'VE TRIED TO HANG MYSELF BUT IT TURNS OUT I DON'T NEED TO BREATHE. NOT REALLY.
EVEN THE OLD "TOASTER IN THE BATHTUB" SHTICK DIDN'T WORK.
AND THIS HAS BEEN GOING ON SINCE YOU WERE PLACED ON ADMINISTRATIVE LEAVE AT ALPHA 13?
YEAH, MORE OR LESS. WHAT DOES IT EVEN MATTER?
I'M NOT HURTING ANYONE.
EXCEPT FOR THAT CAR YOU DESTROYED.
AND THE INCIDENT.
SO, THE INCIDENT.

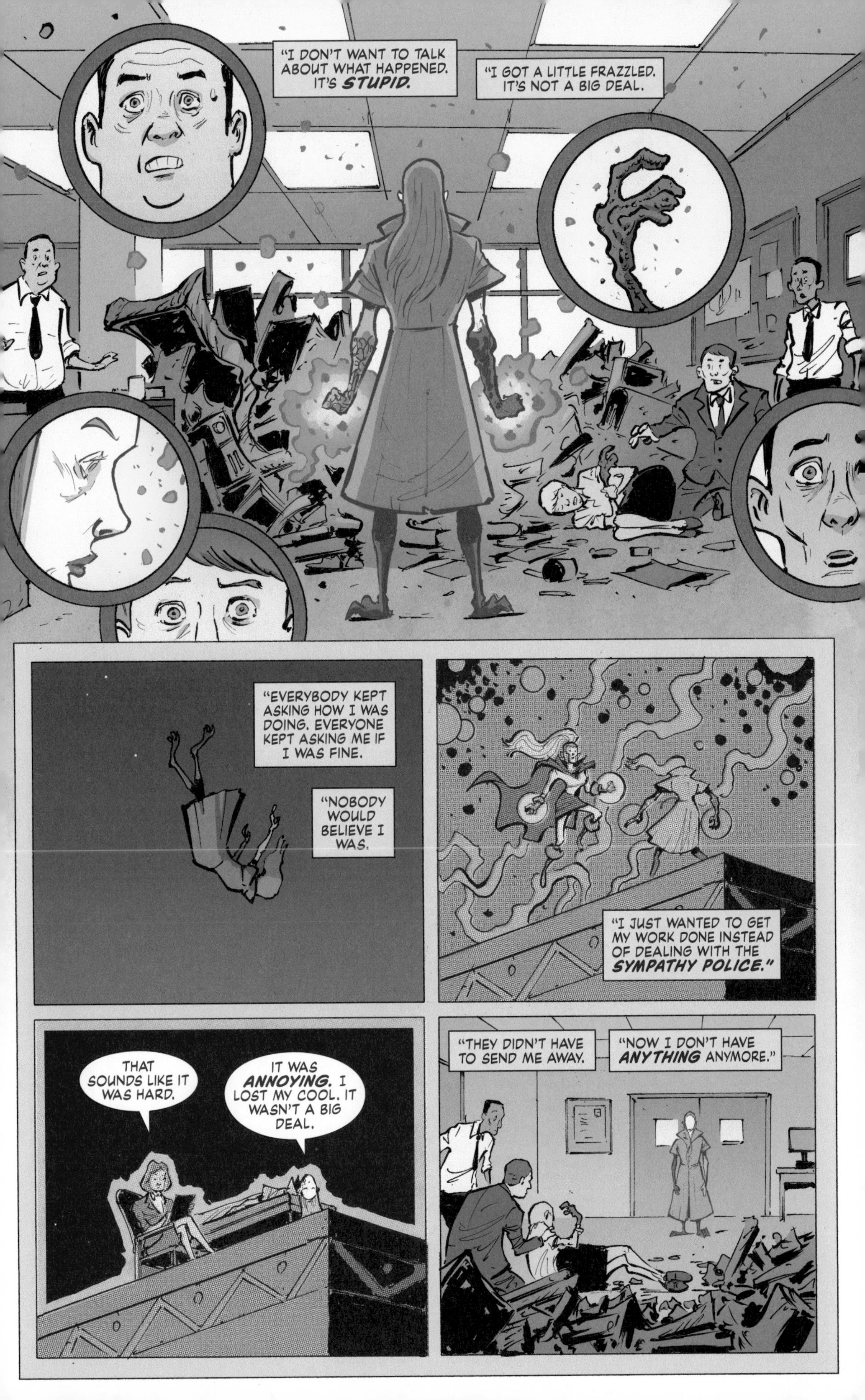
"I DON'T WANT TO TALK ABOUT WHAT HAPPENED. IT'S STUPID.
"I GOT A LITTLE FRAZZLED. IT'S NOT A BIG DEAL.
"EVERYBODY KEPT ASKING HOW I WAS DOING. EVERYONE KEPT ASKING ME IF I WAS FINE.
"NOBODY WOULD BELIEVE I WAS.
"I JUST WANTED TO GET MY WORK DONE INSTEAD OF DEALING WITH THE SYMPATHY POLICE."
THAT SOUNDS LIKE IT WAS HARD.
IT WAS ANNOYING. I LOST MY COOL. IT WASN'T A BIG DEAL.
"THEY DIDN'T HAVE TO SEND ME AWAY.
"NOW I DON'T HAVE ANYTHING ANYMORE."

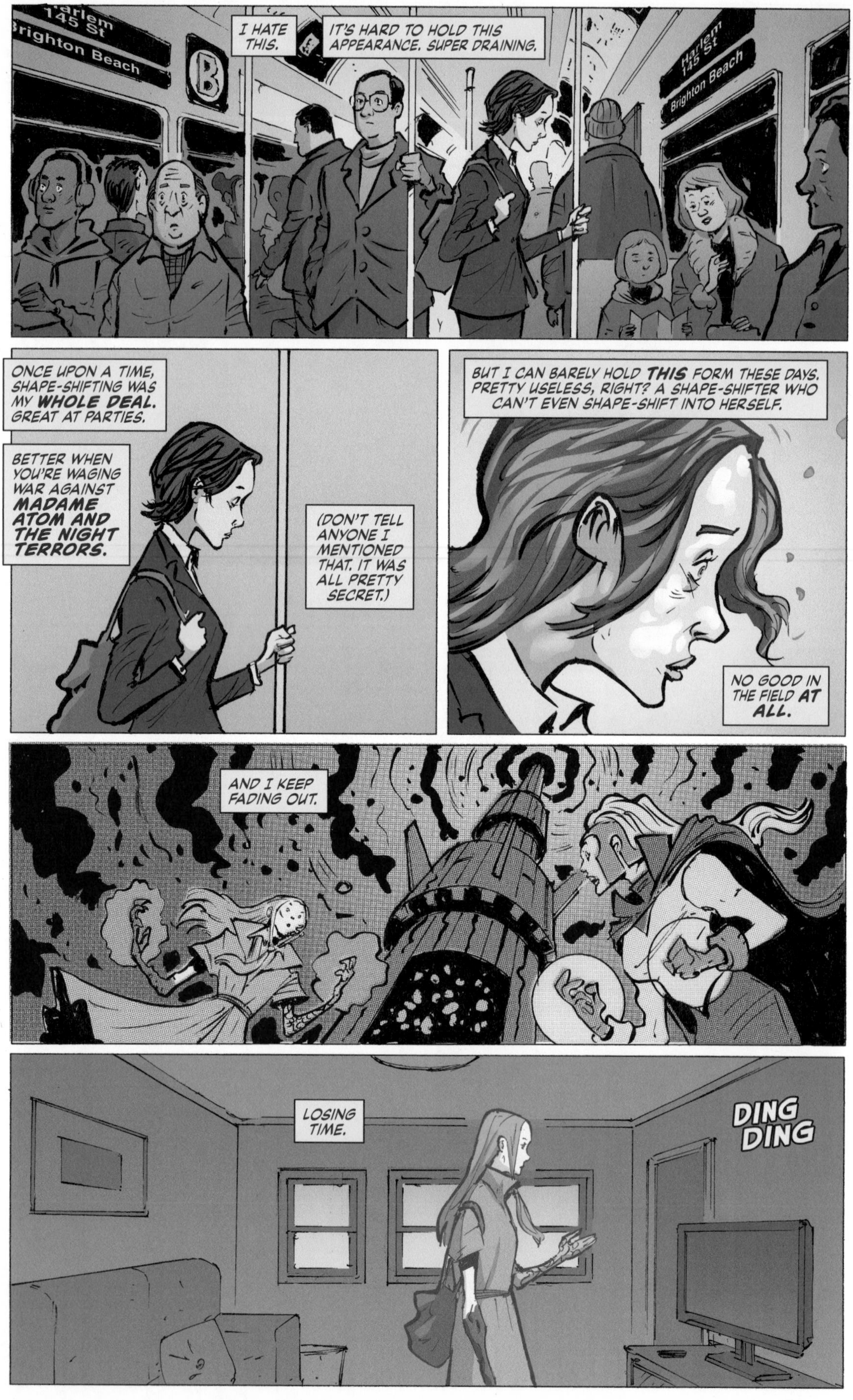
Harlem 145 St
Brighton Beach
B
I HATE THIS.
IT'S HARD TO HOLD THIS APPEARANCE. SUPER DRAINING.
Harlem 145 St
Brighton Beach
ONCE UPON A TIME, SHAPE-SHIFTING WAS MY **WHOLE DEAL.** GREAT AT PARTIES.
BETTER WHEN YOU'RE WAGING WAR AGAINST **MADAME ATOM AND THE NIGHT TERRORS.**
(DON'T TELL ANYONE I MENTIONED THAT. IT WAS ALL PRETTY SECRET.)
BUT I CAN BARELY HOLD **THIS** FORM THESE DAYS. PRETTY USELESS, RIGHT? A SHAPE-SHIFTER WHO CAN'T EVEN SHAPE-SHIFT INTO HERSELF.
NO GOOD IN THE FIELD **AT ALL.**
AND I KEEP FADING OUT.
LOSING TIME.
DING DING

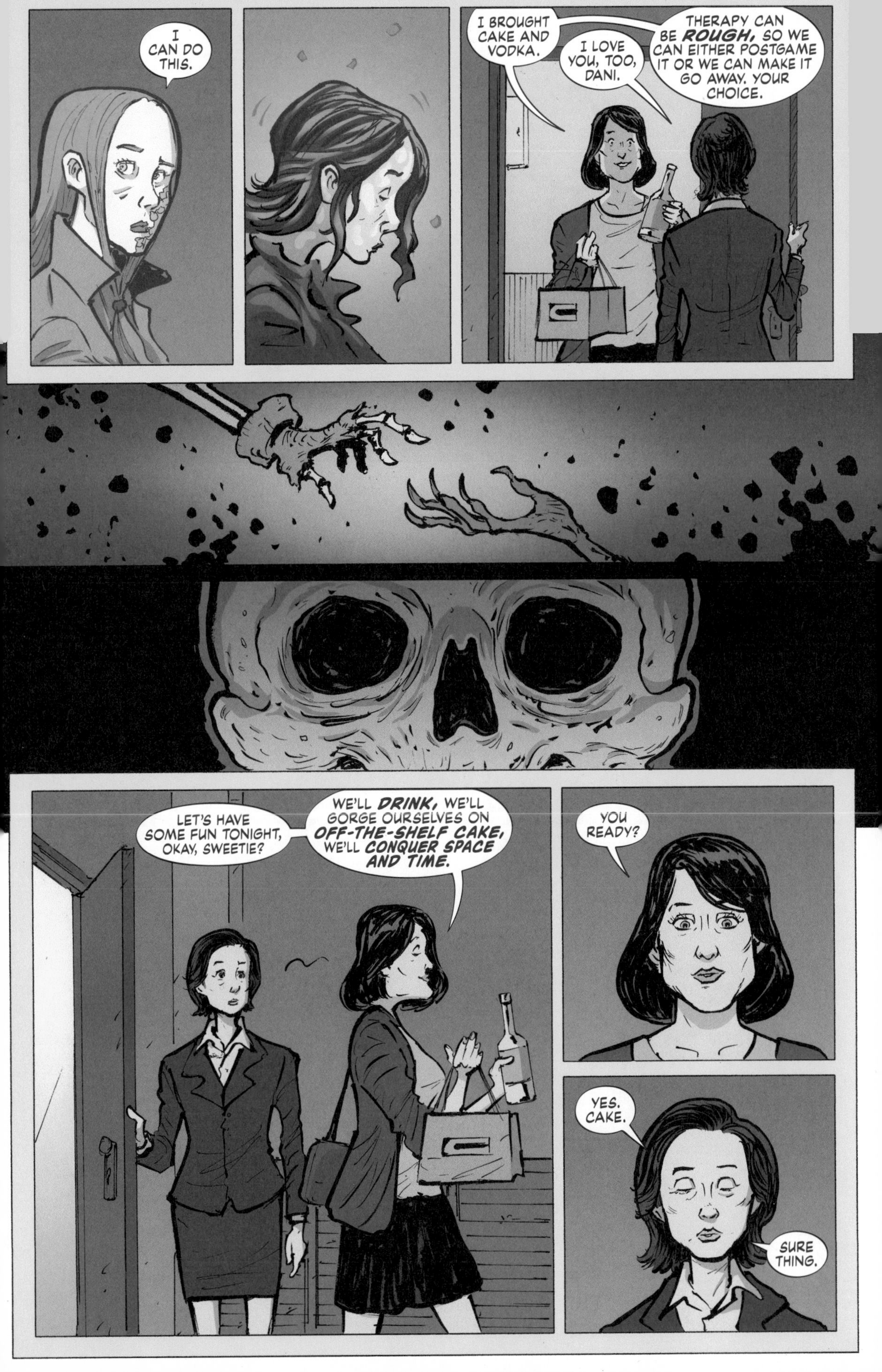
I CAN DO THIS.
I BROUGHT CAKE AND VODKA.
I LOVE YOU, TOO, DANI.
THERAPY CAN BE ROUGH, SO WE CAN EITHER POSTGAME IT OR WE CAN MAKE IT GO AWAY. YOUR CHOICE.
LET'S HAVE SOME FUN TONIGHT, OKAY, SWEETIE?
WE'LL DRINK, WE'LL GORGE OURSELVES ON OFF-THE-SHELF CAKE, WE'LL CONQUER SPACE AND TIME.
YOU READY?
YES. CAKE.
SURE THING.

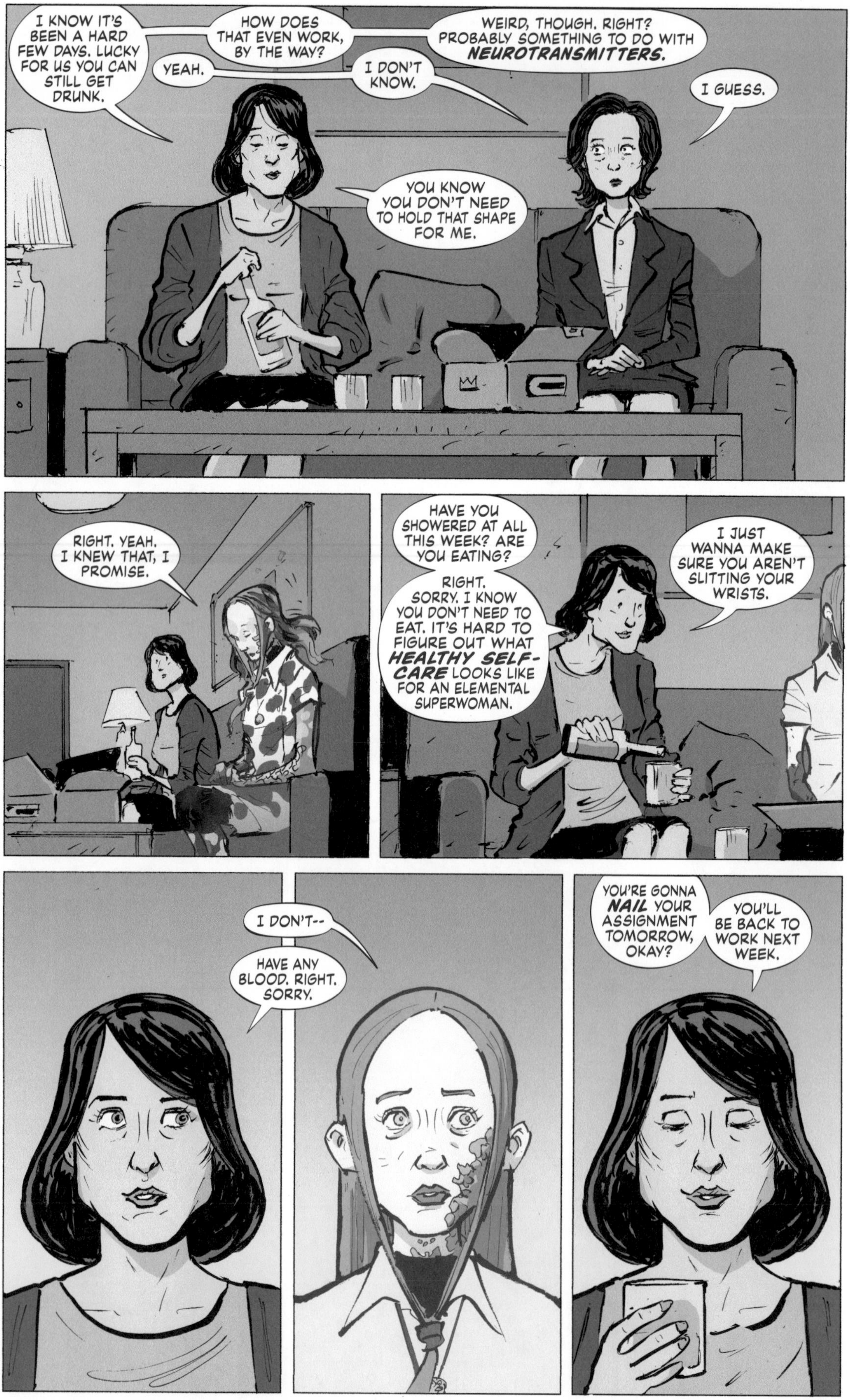
I KNOW IT'S BEEN A HARD FEW DAYS. LUCKY FOR US YOU CAN STILL GET DRUNK.
YEAH.
HOW DOES THAT EVEN WORK, BY THE WAY?
I DON'T KNOW.
WEIRD, THOUGH. RIGHT? PROBABLY SOMETHING TO DO WITH NEUROTRANSMITTERS.
I GUESS.
YOU KNOW YOU DON'T NEED TO HOLD THAT SHAPE FOR ME.
RIGHT. YEAH. I KNEW THAT, I PROMISE.
HAVE YOU SHOWERED AT ALL THIS WEEK? ARE YOU EATING?
RIGHT. SORRY. I KNOW YOU DON'T NEED TO EAT. IT'S HARD TO FIGURE OUT WHAT HEALTHY SELF-CARE LOOKS LIKE FOR AN ELEMENTAL SUPERWOMAN.
I JUST WANNA MAKE SURE YOU AREN'T SLITTING YOUR WRISTS.
I DON'T--
HAVE ANY BLOOD. RIGHT. SORRY.
YOU'RE GONNA NAIL YOUR ASSIGNMENT TOMORROW, OKAY?
YOU'LL BE BACK TO WORK NEXT WEEK.

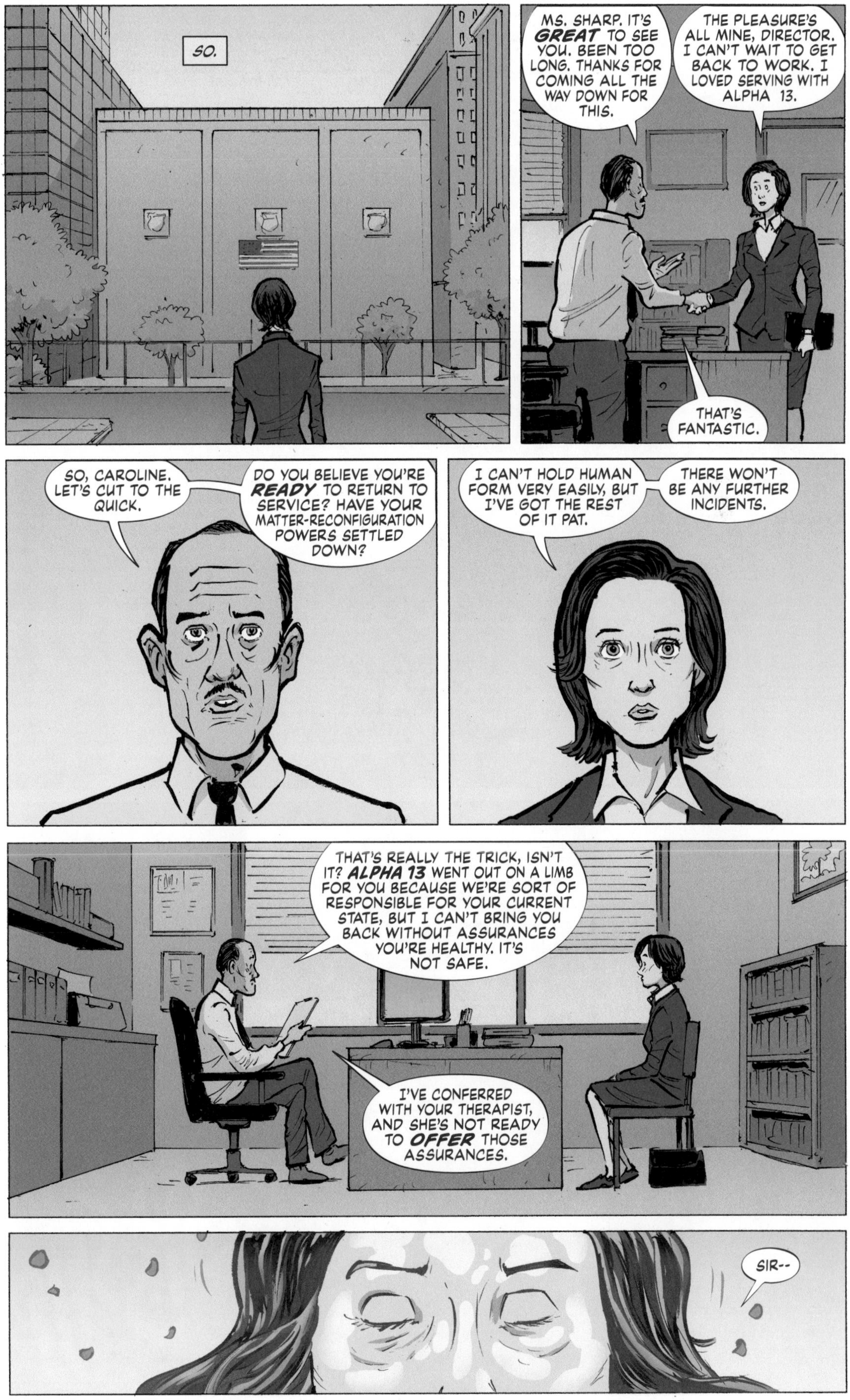
SO.
MS. SHARP. IT'S GREAT TO SEE YOU. BEEN TOO LONG. THANKS FOR COMING ALL THE WAY DOWN FOR THIS.
THE PLEASURE'S ALL MINE, DIRECTOR. I CAN'T WAIT TO GET BACK TO WORK. I LOVED SERVING WITH ALPHA 13.
THAT'S FANTASTIC.
SO, CAROLINE. LET'S CUT TO THE QUICK.
DO YOU BELIEVE YOU'RE READY TO RETURN TO SERVICE? HAVE YOUR MATTER-RECONFIGURATION POWERS SETTLED DOWN?
I CAN'T HOLD HUMAN FORM VERY EASILY, BUT I'VE GOT THE REST OF IT PAT.
THERE WON'T BE ANY FURTHER INCIDENTS.
THAT'S REALLY THE TRICK, ISN'T IT? ALPHA 13 WENT OUT ON A LIMB FOR YOU BECAUSE WE'RE SORT OF RESPONSIBLE FOR YOUR CURRENT STATE, BUT I CAN'T BRING YOU BACK WITHOUT ASSURANCES YOU'RE HEALTHY. IT'S NOT SAFE.
I'VE CONFERRED WITH YOUR THERAPIST, AND SHE'S NOT READY TO OFFER THOSE ASSURANCES.
SIR--

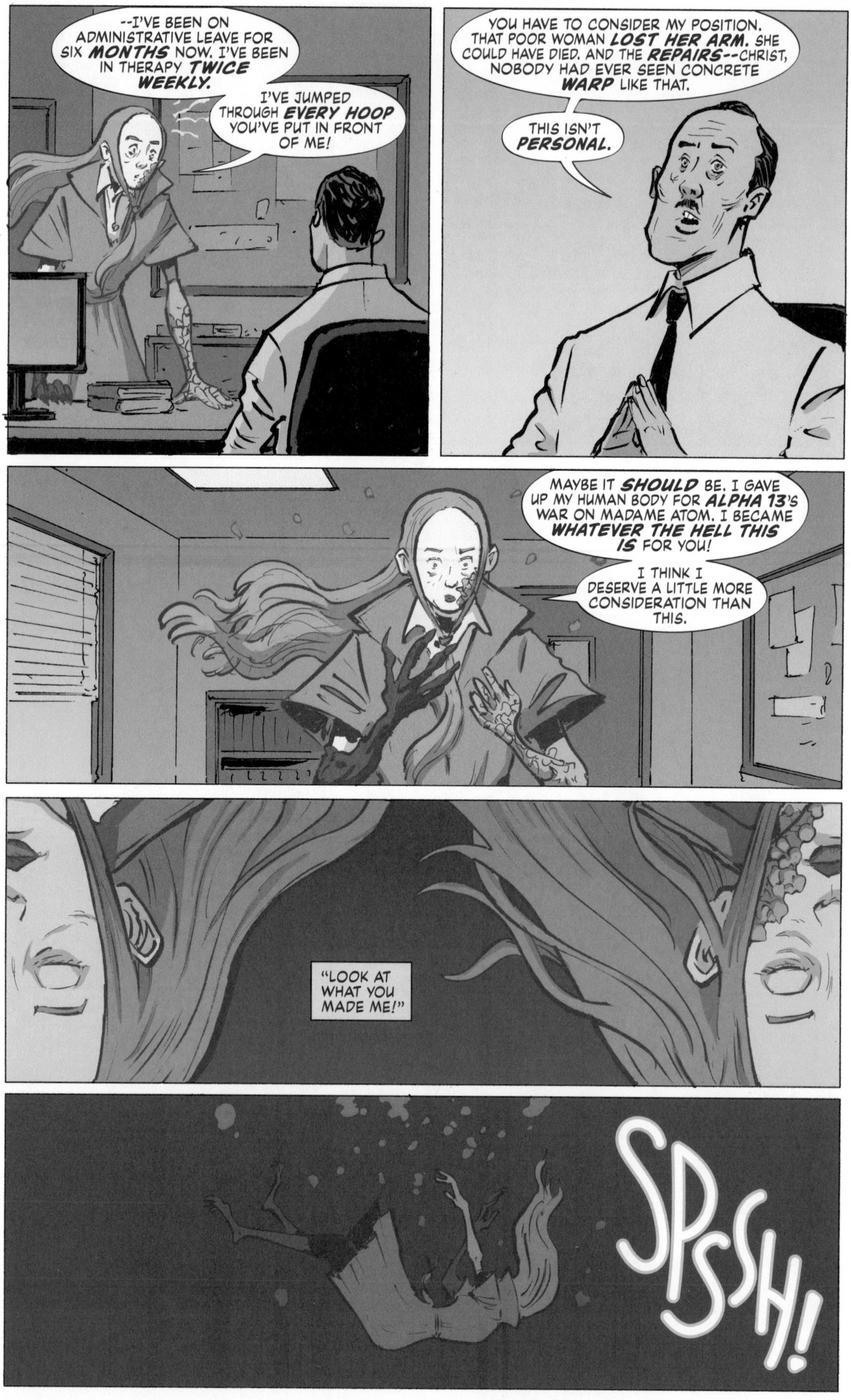
--I'VE BEEN ON ADMINISTRATIVE LEAVE FOR SIX MONTHS NOW. I'VE BEEN IN THERAPY TWICE WEEKLY.
I'VE JUMPED THROUGH EVERY HOOP YOU'VE PUT IN FRONT OF ME!
YOU HAVE TO CONSIDER MY POSITION. THAT POOR WOMAN LOST HER ARM. SHE COULD HAVE DIED. AND THE REPAIRS--CHRIST, NOBODY HAD EVER SEEN CONCRETE WARP LIKE THAT.
THIS ISN'T PERSONAL.
MAYBE IT SHOULD BE. I GAVE UP MY HUMAN BODY FOR ALPHA 13'S WAR ON MADAME ATOM. I BECAME WHATEVER THE HELL THIS IS FOR YOU!
I THINK I DESERVE A LITTLE MORE CONSIDERATION THAN THIS.
"LOOK AT WHAT YOU MADE ME!"
SPSSH!

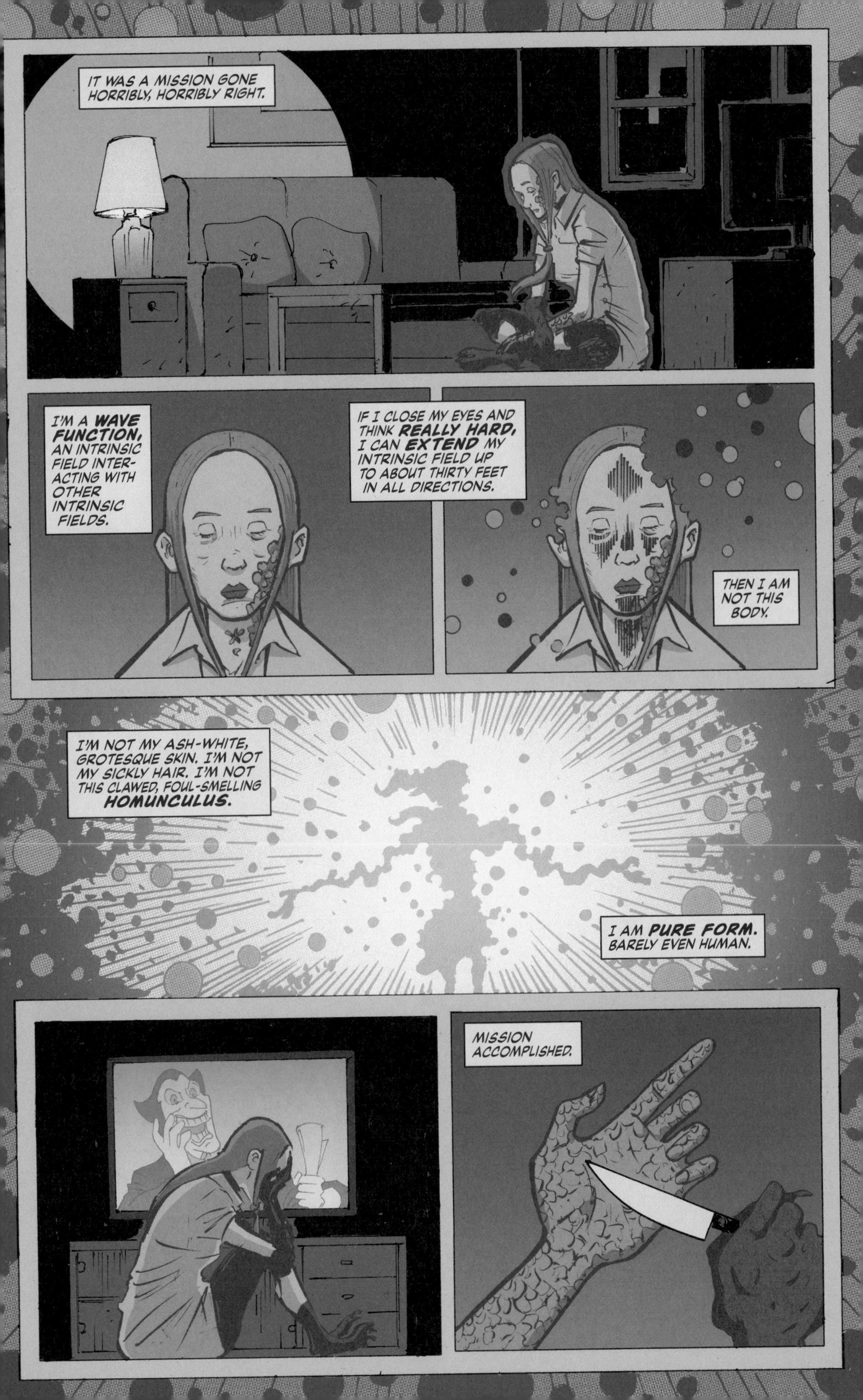
IT WAS A MISSION GONE HORRIBLY, HORRIBLY RIGHT.
I'M A **WAVE FUNCTION,** AN INTRINSIC FIELD INTERACTING WITH OTHER INTRINSIC FIELDS.
IF I CLOSE MY EYES AND THINK **REALLY HARD,** I CAN **EXTEND** MY INTRINSIC FIELD UP TO ABOUT THIRTY FEET IN ALL DIRECTIONS.
THEN I AM NOT THIS BODY.
I'M NOT MY ASH-WHITE, GROTESQUE SKIN. I'M NOT MY SICKLY HAIR. I'M NOT THIS CLAWED, FOUL-SMELLING **HOMUNCULUS.**
I AM **PURE FORM.** BARELY EVEN HUMAN.
MISSION ACCOMPLISHED.

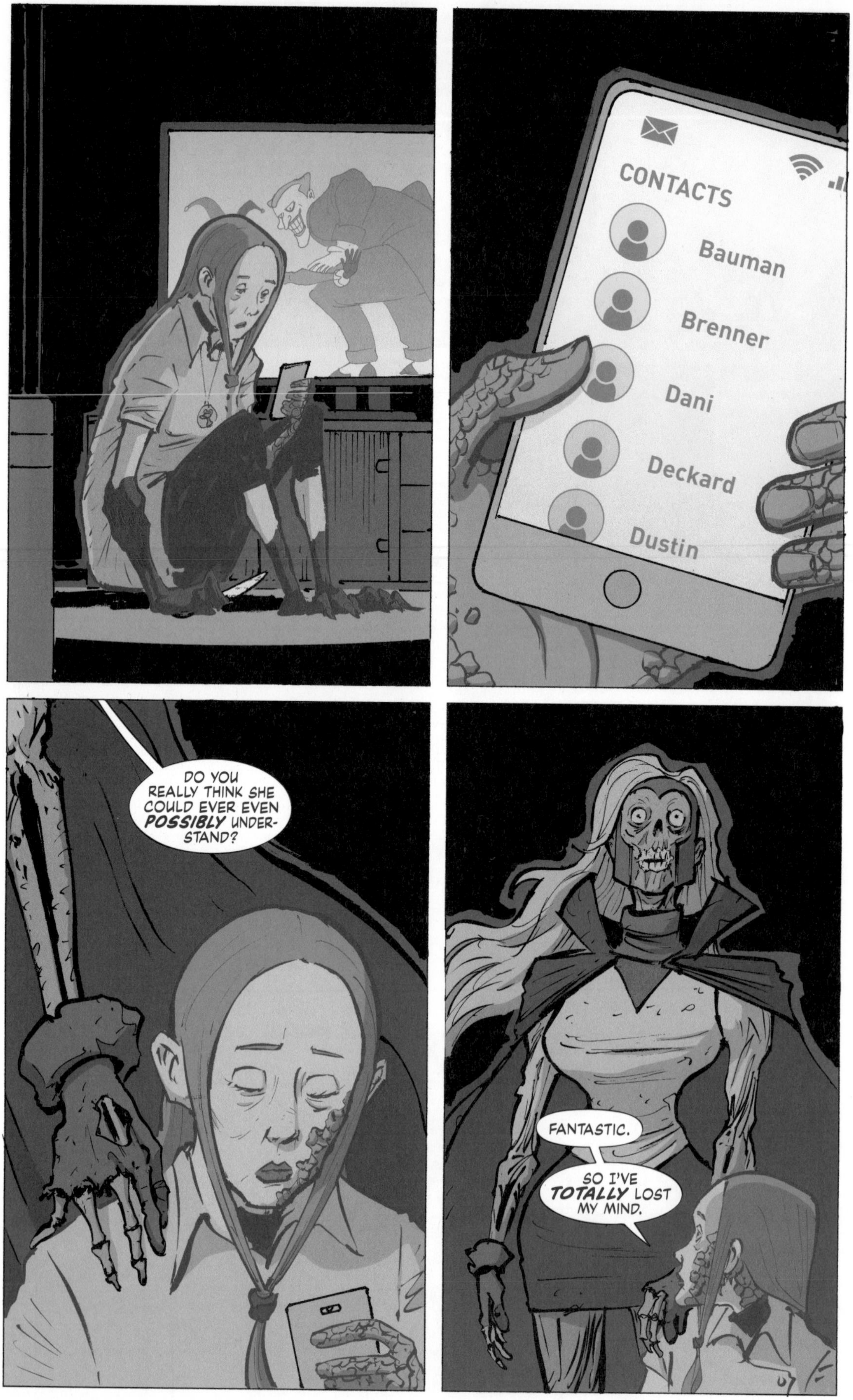
CONTACTS
Bauman
Brenner
Dani
Deckard
Dustin
DO YOU REALLY THINK SHE COULD EVER EVEN POSSIBLY UNDER-STAND?
FANTASTIC.
SO I'VE TOTALLY LOST MY MIND.

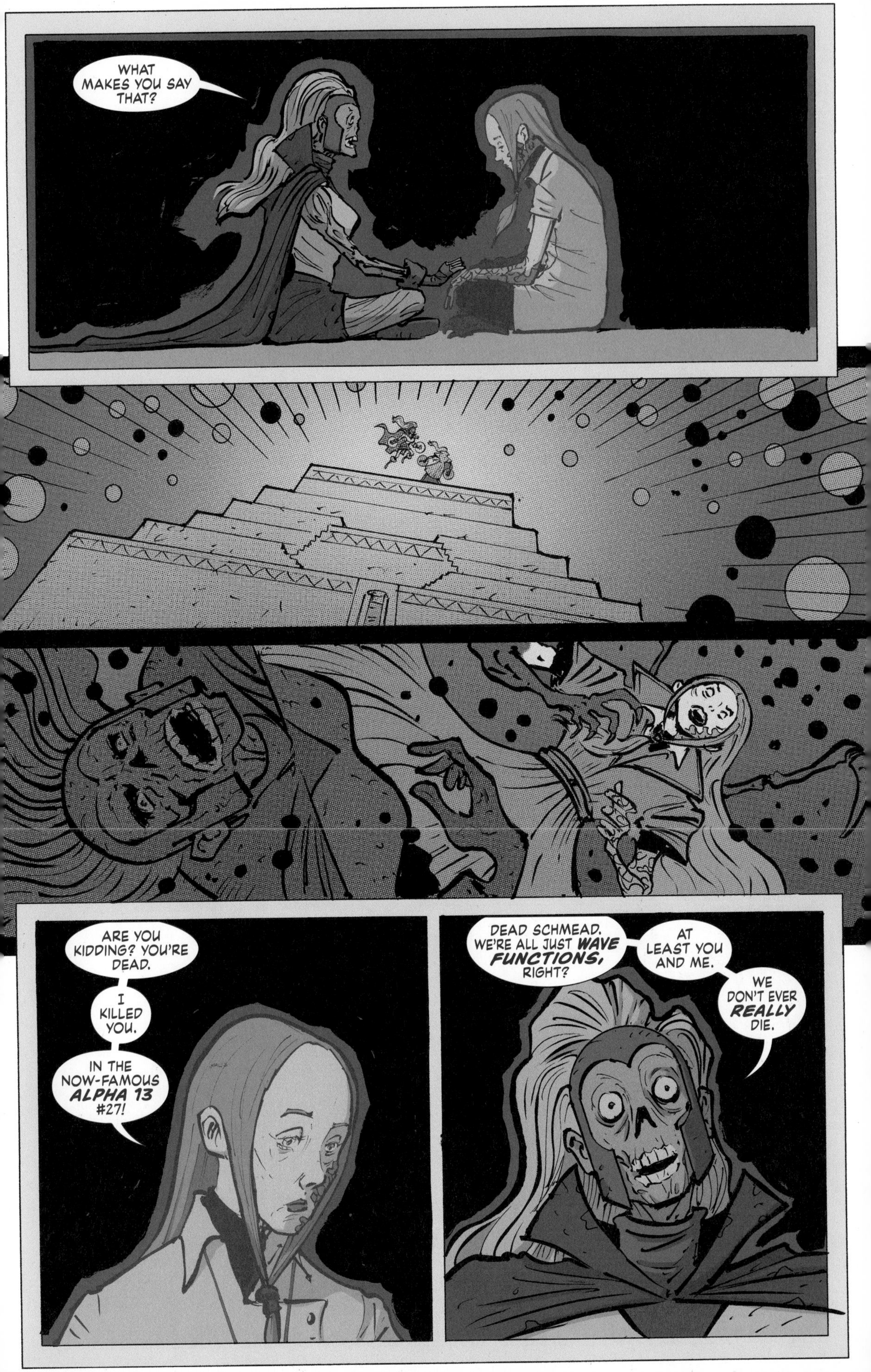
WHAT MAKES YOU SAY THAT?
ARE YOU KIDDING? YOU'RE DEAD.
I KILLED YOU.
IN THE NOW-FAMOUS ALPHA 13 #27!
DEAD SCHMEAD. WE'RE ALL JUST WAVE FUNCTIONS, RIGHT?
AT LEAST YOU AND ME.
WE DON'T EVER REALLY DIE.

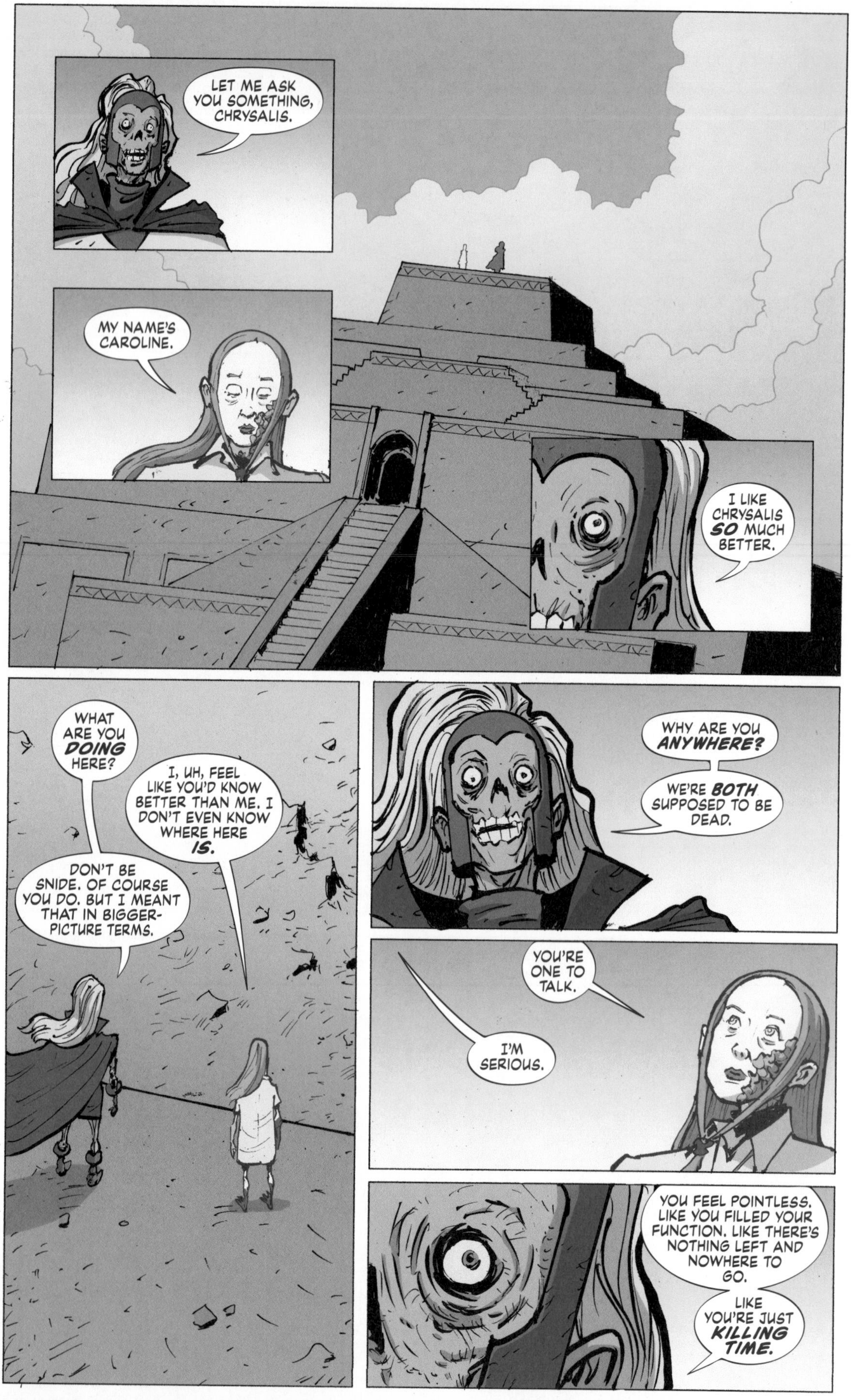
LET ME ASK YOU SOMETHING, CHRYSALIS.
MY NAME'S CAROLINE.
I LIKE CHRYSALIS SO MUCH BETTER.
WHAT ARE YOU DOING HERE?
I, UH, FEEL LIKE YOU'D KNOW BETTER THAN ME. I DON'T EVEN KNOW WHERE HERE IS.
DON'T BE SNIDE. OF COURSE YOU DO. BUT I MEANT THAT IN BIGGER-PICTURE TERMS.
WHY ARE YOU ANYWHERE?
WE'RE BOTH SUPPOSED TO BE DEAD.
YOU'RE ONE TO TALK.
I'M SERIOUS.
YOU FEEL POINTLESS. LIKE YOU FILLED YOUR FUNCTION. LIKE THERE'S NOTHING LEFT AND NOWHERE TO GO.
LIKE YOU'RE JUST KILLING TIME.

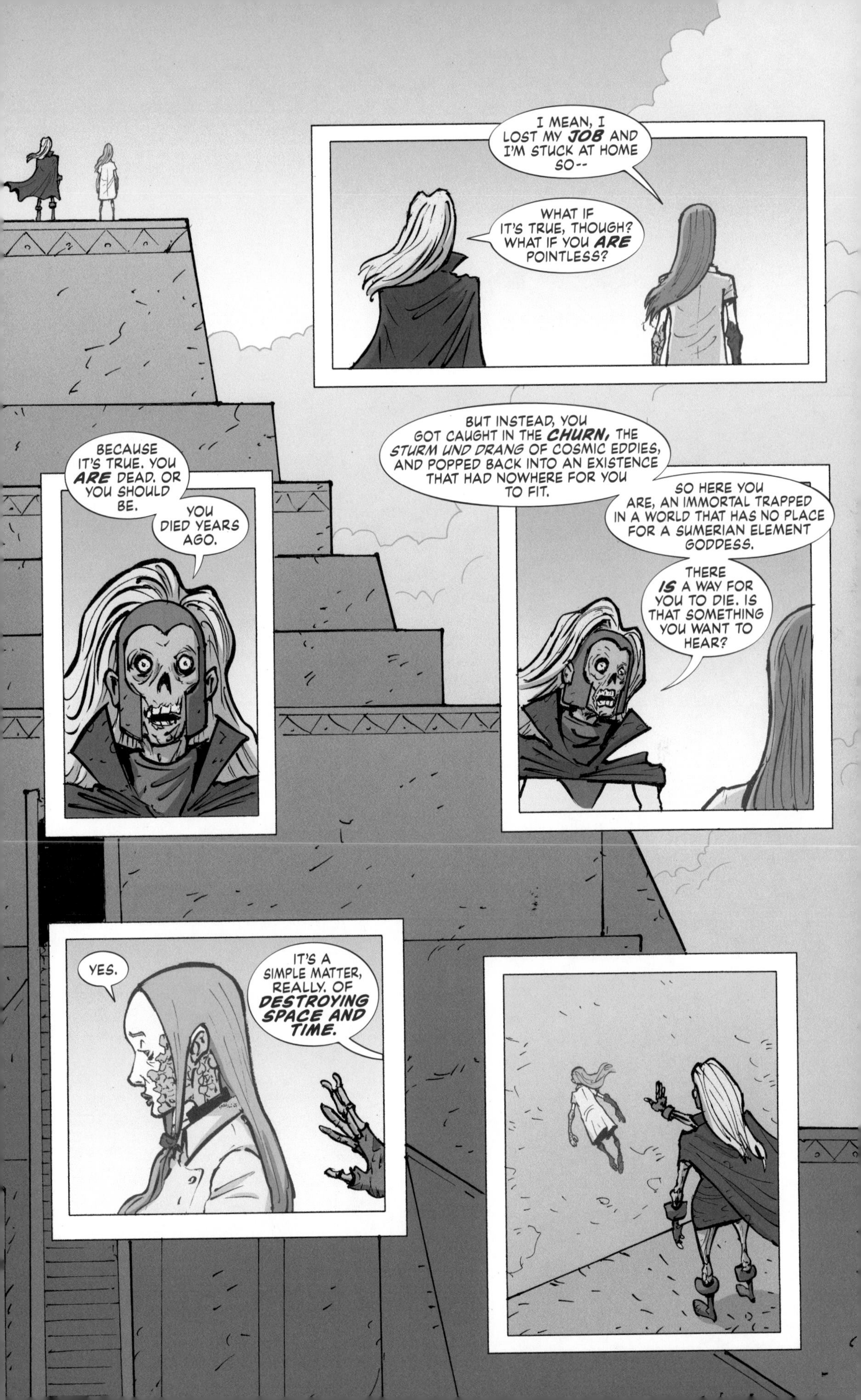
I MEAN, I LOST MY JOB AND I'M STUCK AT HOME SO--
WHAT IF IT'S TRUE, THOUGH? WHAT IF YOU ARE POINTLESS?
BECAUSE IT'S TRUE. YOU ARE DEAD. OR YOU SHOULD BE.
YOU DIED YEARS AGO.
BUT INSTEAD, YOU GOT CAUGHT IN THE CHURN, THE STURM UND DRANG OF COSMIC EDDIES, AND POPPED BACK INTO AN EXISTENCE THAT HAD NOWHERE FOR YOU TO FIT.
SO HERE YOU ARE, AN IMMORTAL TRAPPED IN A WORLD THAT HAS NO PLACE FOR A SUMERIAN ELEMENT GODDESS.
THERE IS A WAY FOR YOU TO DIE. IS THAT SOMETHING YOU WANT TO HEAR?
YES.
IT'S A SIMPLE MATTER, REALLY. OF DESTROYING SPACE AND TIME.

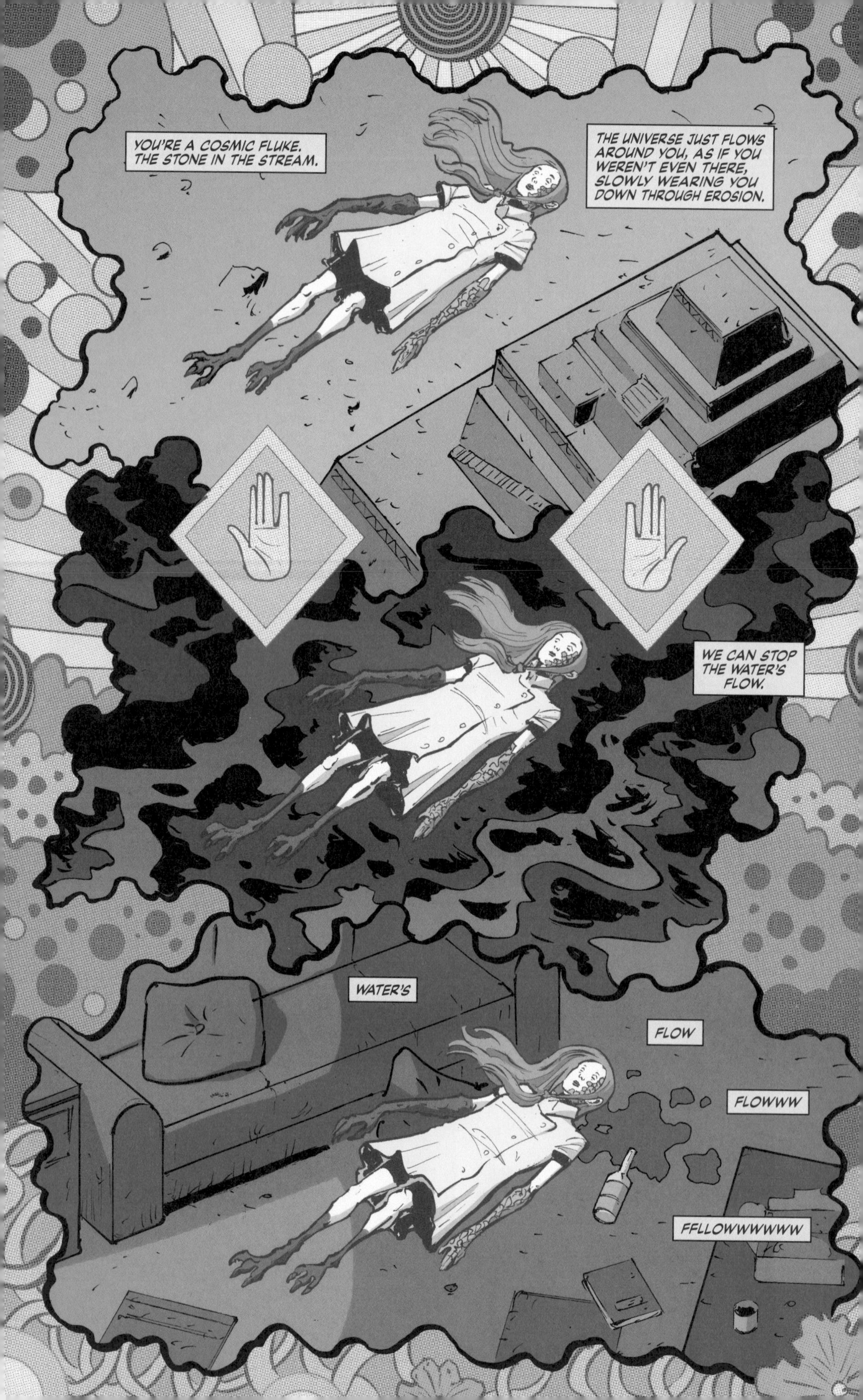
YOU'RE A COSMIC FLUKE. THE STONE IN THE STREAM.
THE UNIVERSE JUST FLOWS AROUND YOU, AS IF YOU WEREN'T EVEN THERE, SLOWLY WEARING YOU DOWN THROUGH EROSION.
WE CAN STOP THE WATER'S FLOW.
WATER'S
FLOW
FLOWWW
FFLLOWWWWWW

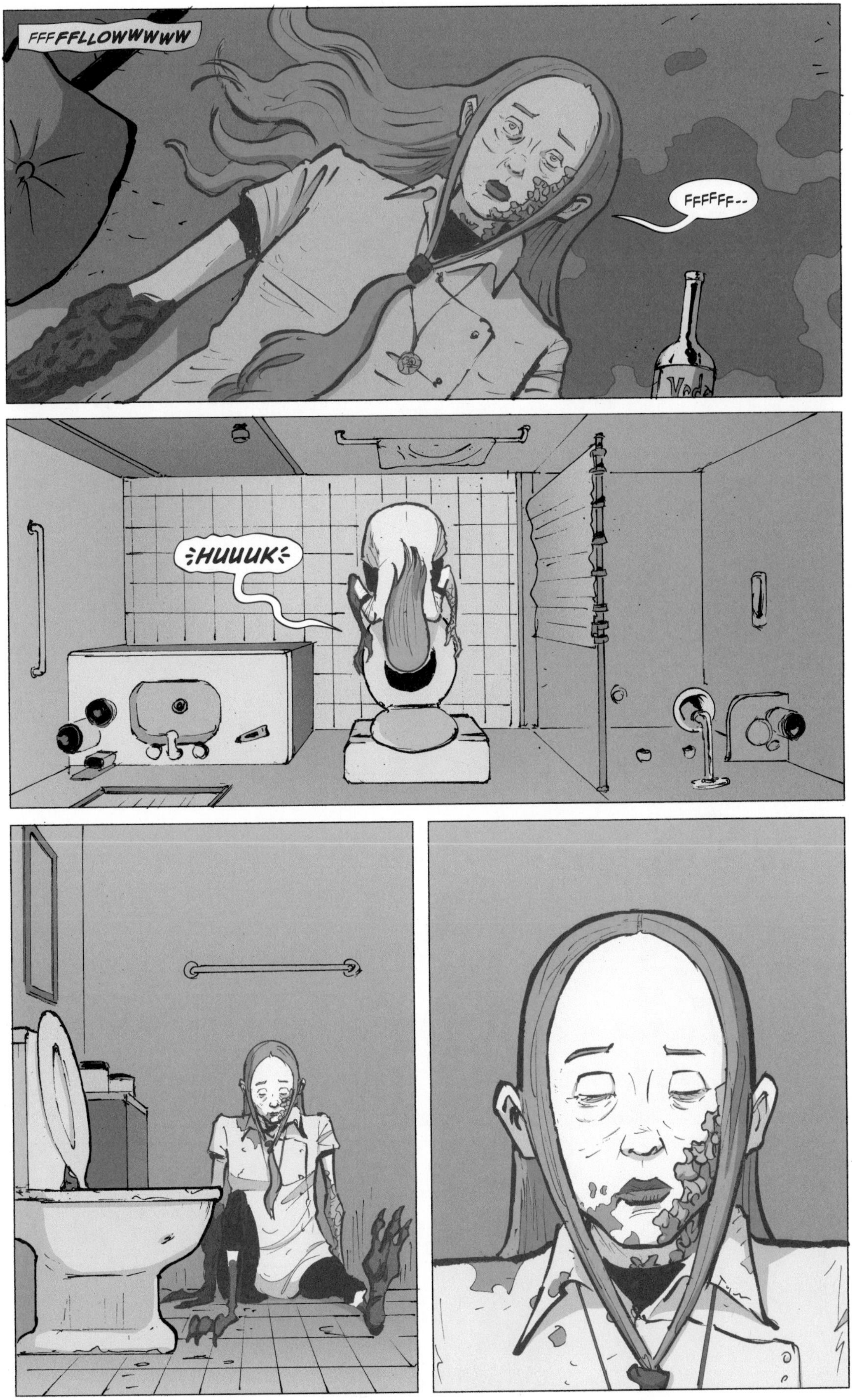
FFFFFLLOWWWWW
FFFFFF--
HUUUK

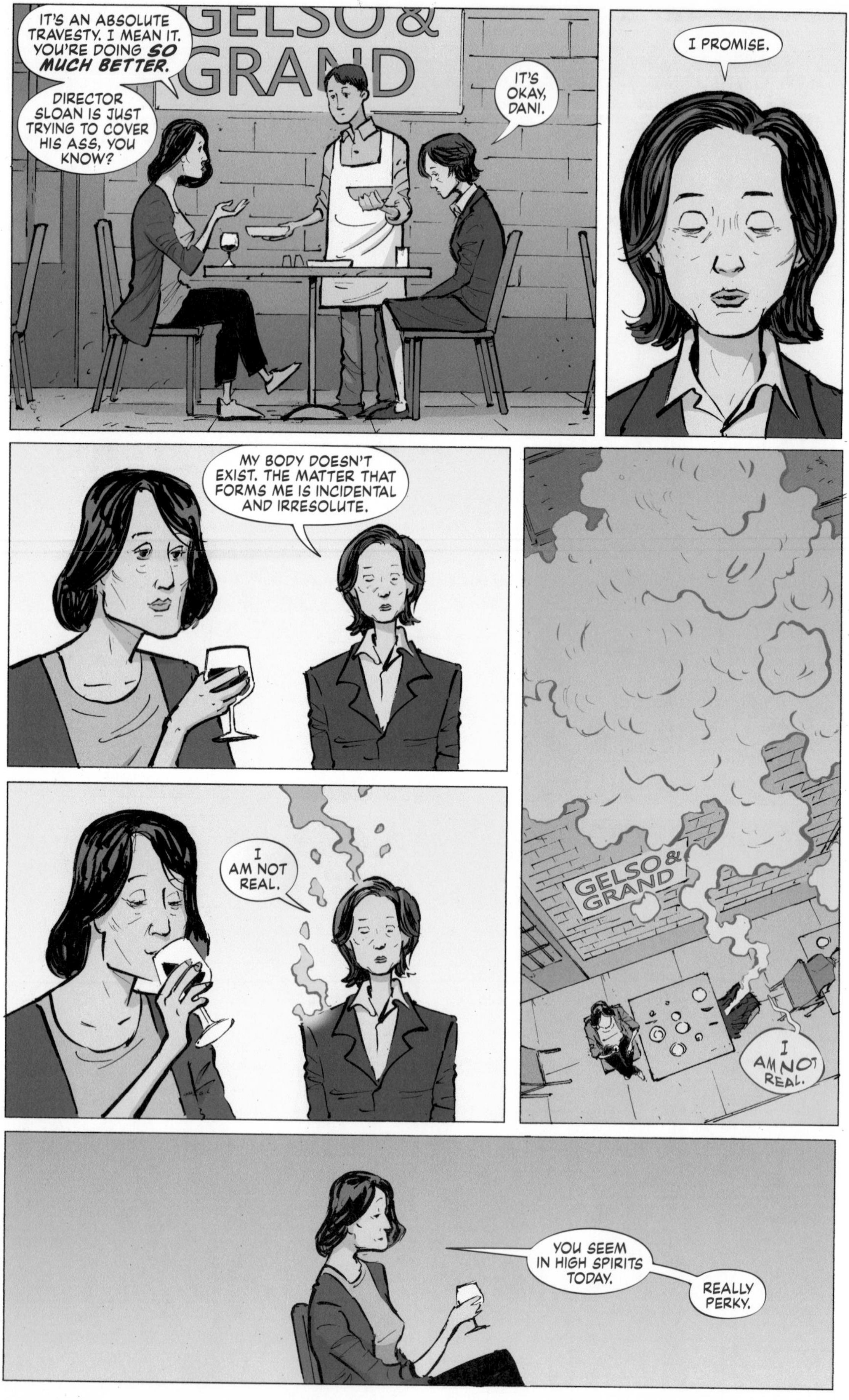
IT'S AN ABSOLUTE TRAVESTY. I MEAN IT. YOU'RE DOING SO MUCH BETTER.
DIRECTOR SLOAN IS JUST TRYING TO COVER HIS ASS, YOU KNOW?
GELSO & GRAND
IT'S OKAY, DANI.
I PROMISE.
MY BODY DOESN'T EXIST. THE MATTER THAT FORMS ME IS INCIDENTAL AND IRRESOLUTE.
I AM NOT REAL.
GELSO & GRAND
I AM NOT REAL.
YOU SEEM IN HIGH SPIRITS TODAY.
REALLY PERKY.

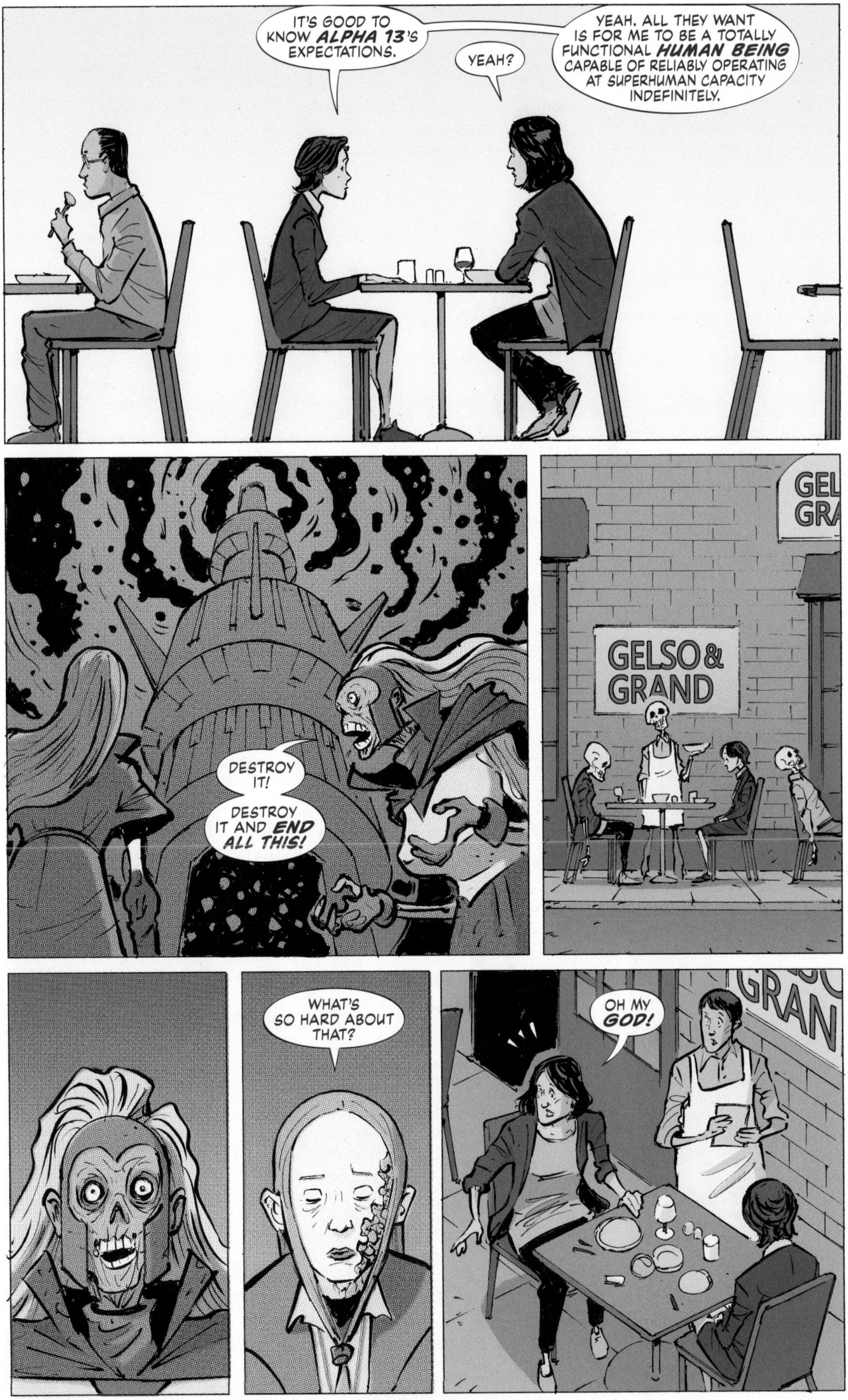
IT'S GOOD TO KNOW ALPHA 13'S EXPECTATIONS.
YEAH?
YEAH. ALL THEY WANT IS FOR ME TO BE A TOTALLY FUNCTIONAL HUMAN BEING CAPABLE OF RELIABLY OPERATING AT SUPERHUMAN CAPACITY INDEFINITELY.
DESTROY IT!
DESTROY IT AND END ALL THIS!
GELSO & GRAND
WHAT'S SO HARD ABOUT THAT?
OH MY GOD!

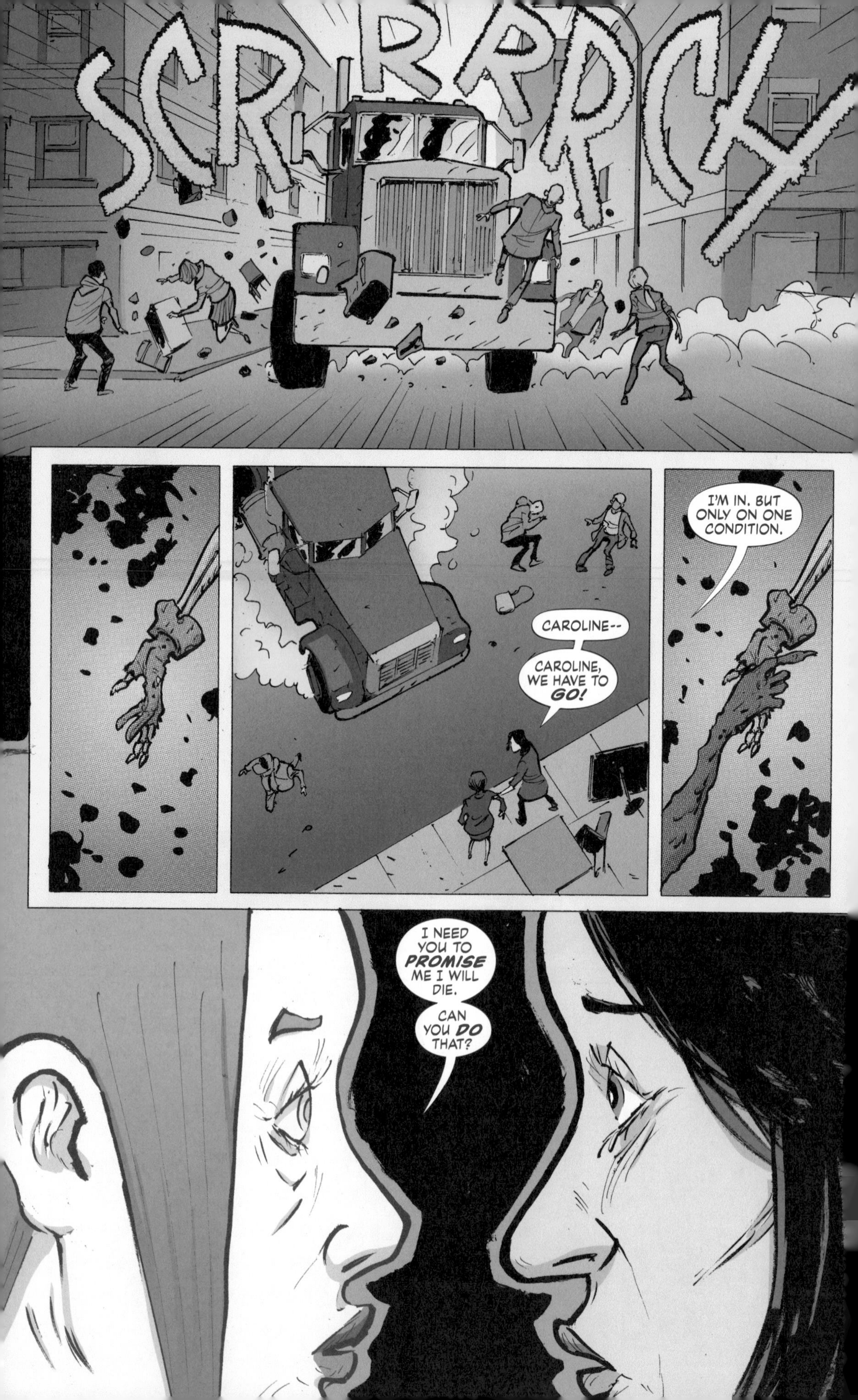
SCRRRCH
CAROLINE--
CAROLINE, WE HAVE TO GO!
I'M IN. BUT ONLY ON ONE CONDITION.
I NEED YOU TO PROMISE ME I WILL DIE.
CAN YOU DO THAT?

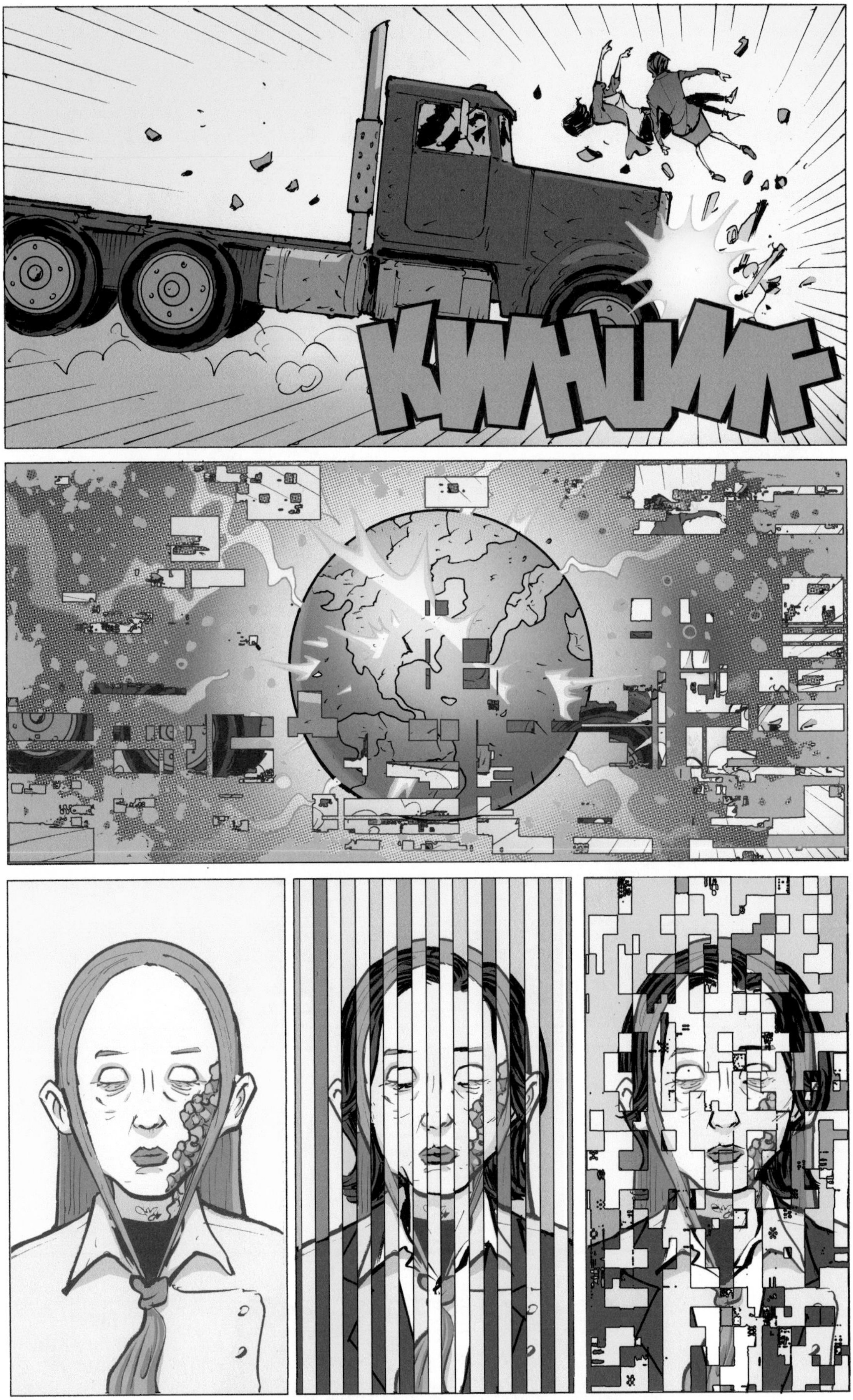
KWHUMF

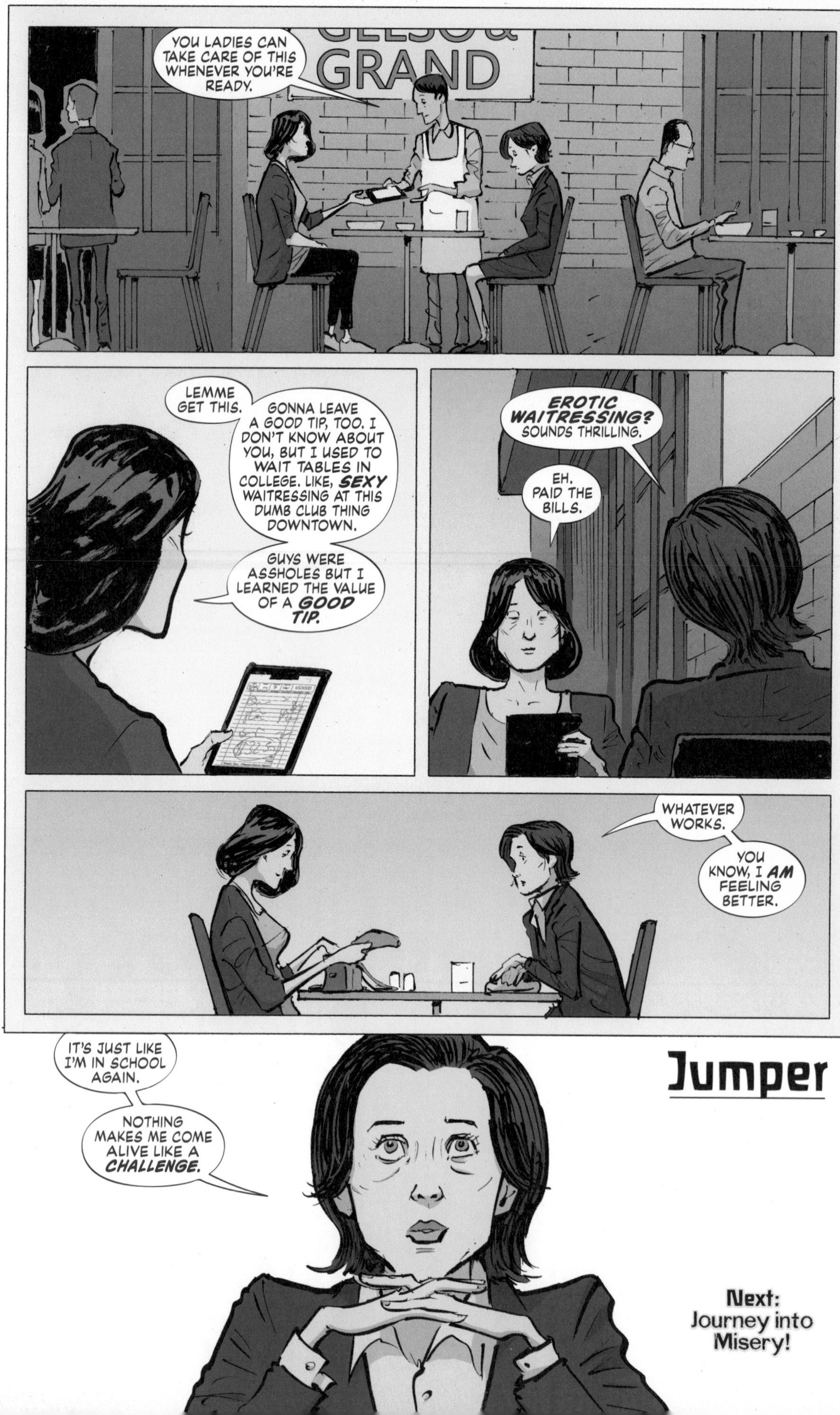

YOU LADIES CAN TAKE CARE OF THIS WHENEVER YOU'RE READY.
GRAND
LEMME GET THIS.
GONNA LEAVE A GOOD TIP, TOO. I DON'T KNOW ABOUT YOU, BUT I USED TO WAIT TABLES IN COLLEGE. LIKE, *SEXY* WAITRESSING AT THIS DUMB CLUB THING DOWNTOWN.
GUYS WERE ASSHOLES BUT I LEARNED THE VALUE OF A *GOOD TIP.*
EROTIC WAITRESSING? SOUNDS THRILLING.
EH. PAID THE BILLS.
WHATEVER WORKS.
YOU KNOW, I *AM* FEELING BETTER.
IT'S JUST LIKE I'M IN SCHOOL AGAIN.
NOTHING MAKES ME COME ALIVE LIKE A *CHALLENGE.*
Jumper
Next: Journey into Misery!

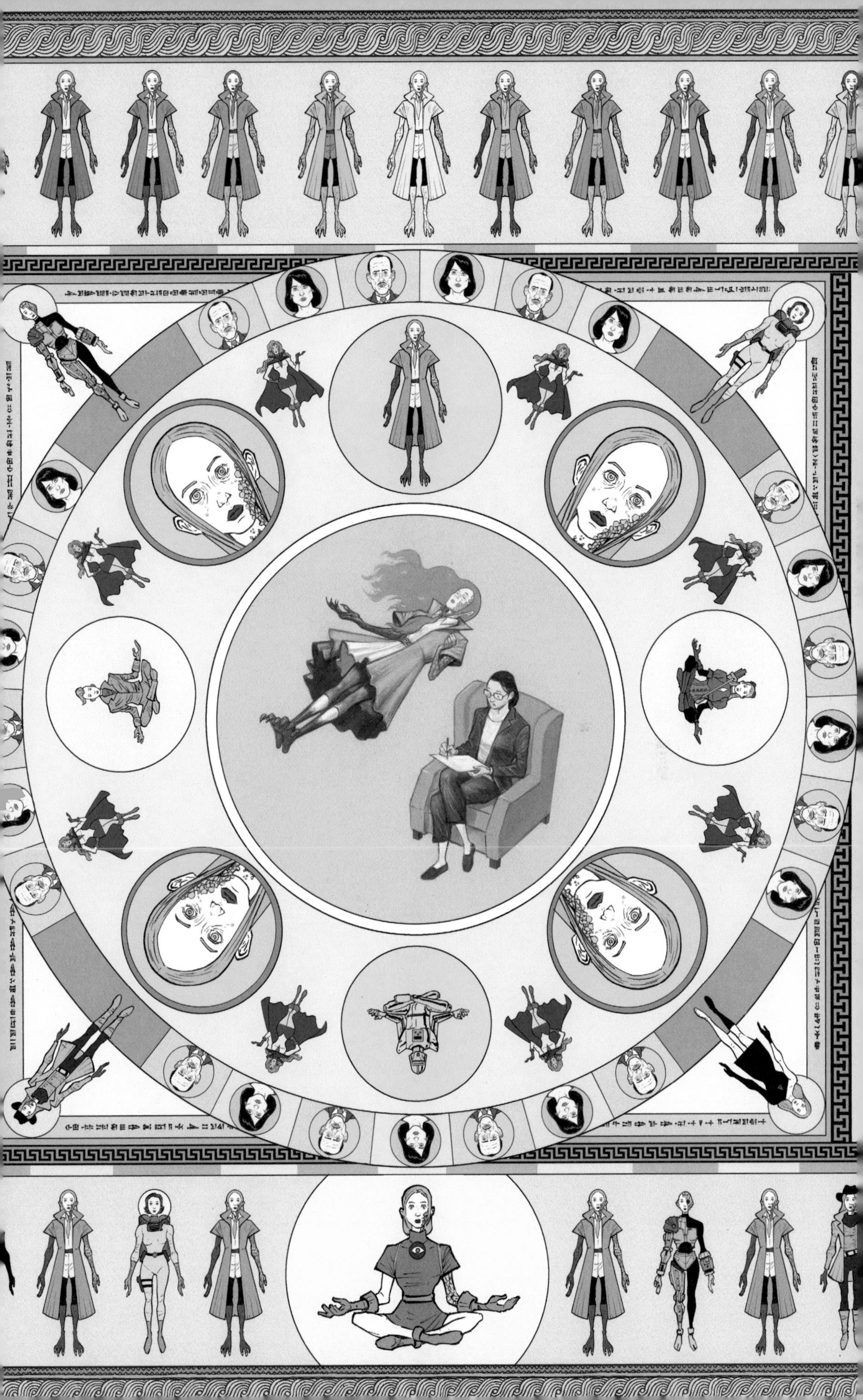

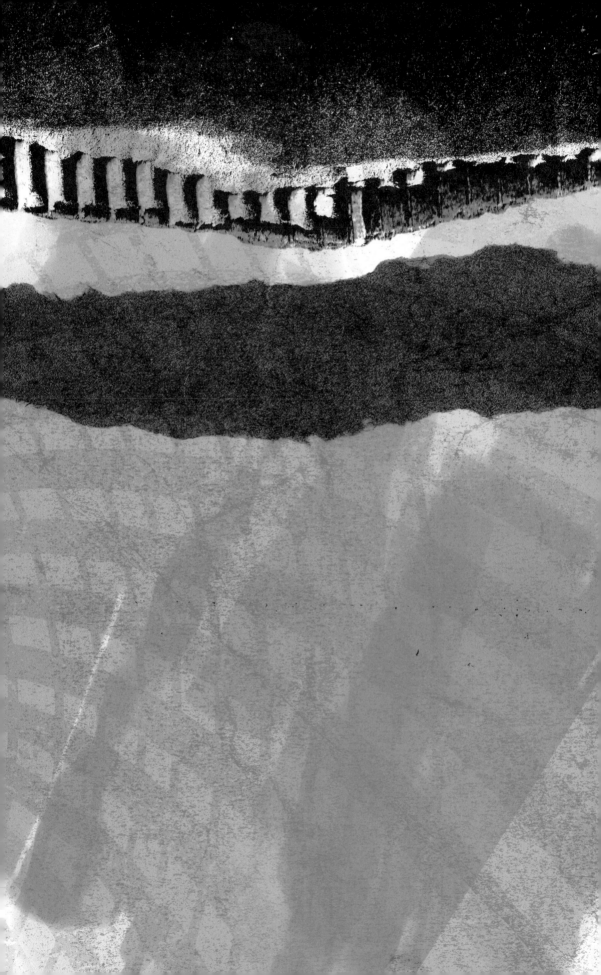

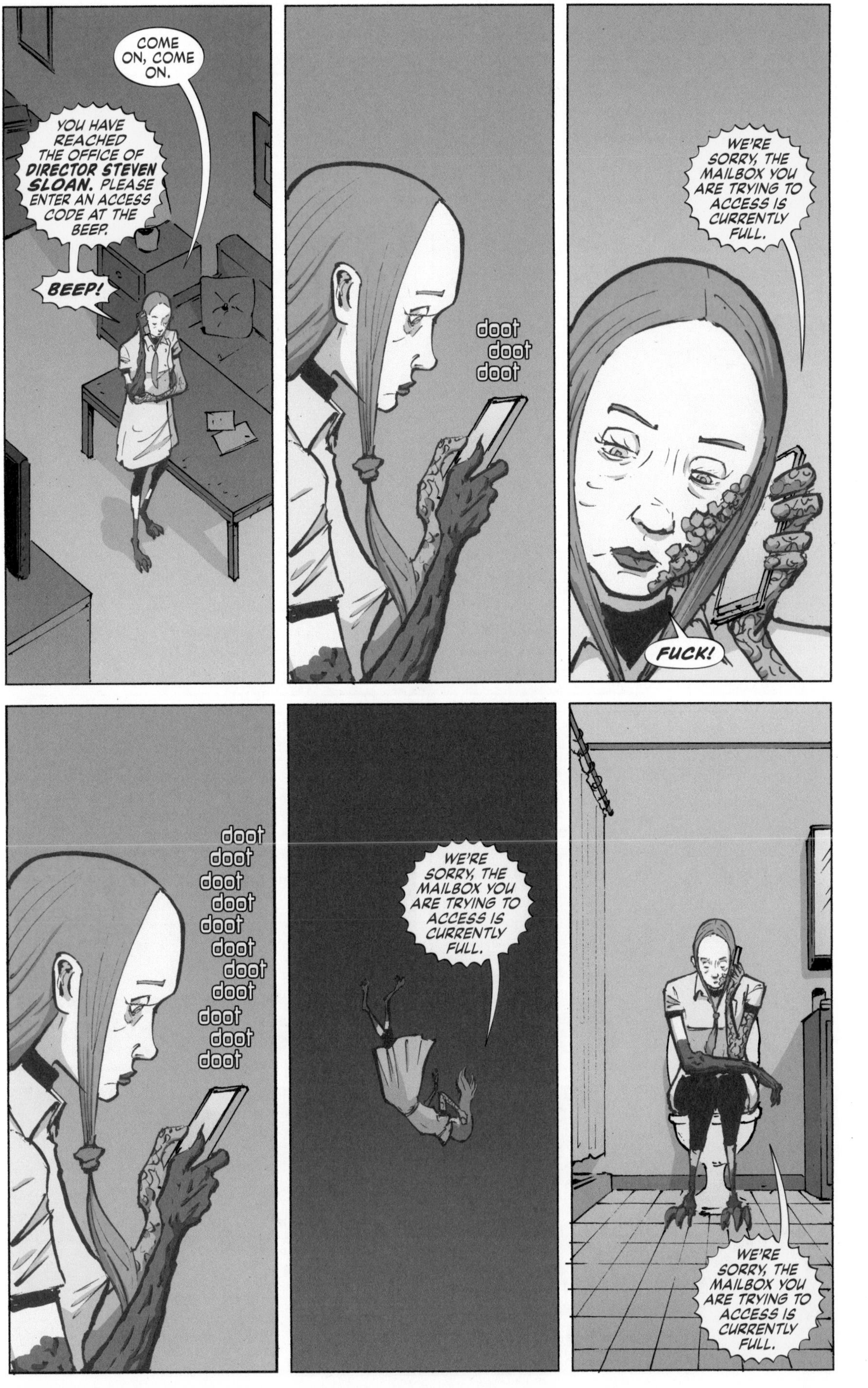
COME ON, COME ON.
YOU HAVE REACHED THE OFFICE OF DIRECTOR STEVEN SLOAN. PLEASE ENTER AN ACCESS CODE AT THE BEEP.
BEEP!
doot doot doot
WE'RE SORRY, THE MAILBOX YOU ARE TRYING TO ACCESS IS CURRENTLY FULL.
FUCK!
doot doot doot doot doot doot doot doot doot doot doot
WE'RE SORRY, THE MAILBOX YOU ARE TRYING TO ACCESS IS CURRENTLY FULL.
WE'RE SORRY, THE MAILBOX YOU ARE TRYING TO ACCESS IS CURRENTLY FULL.

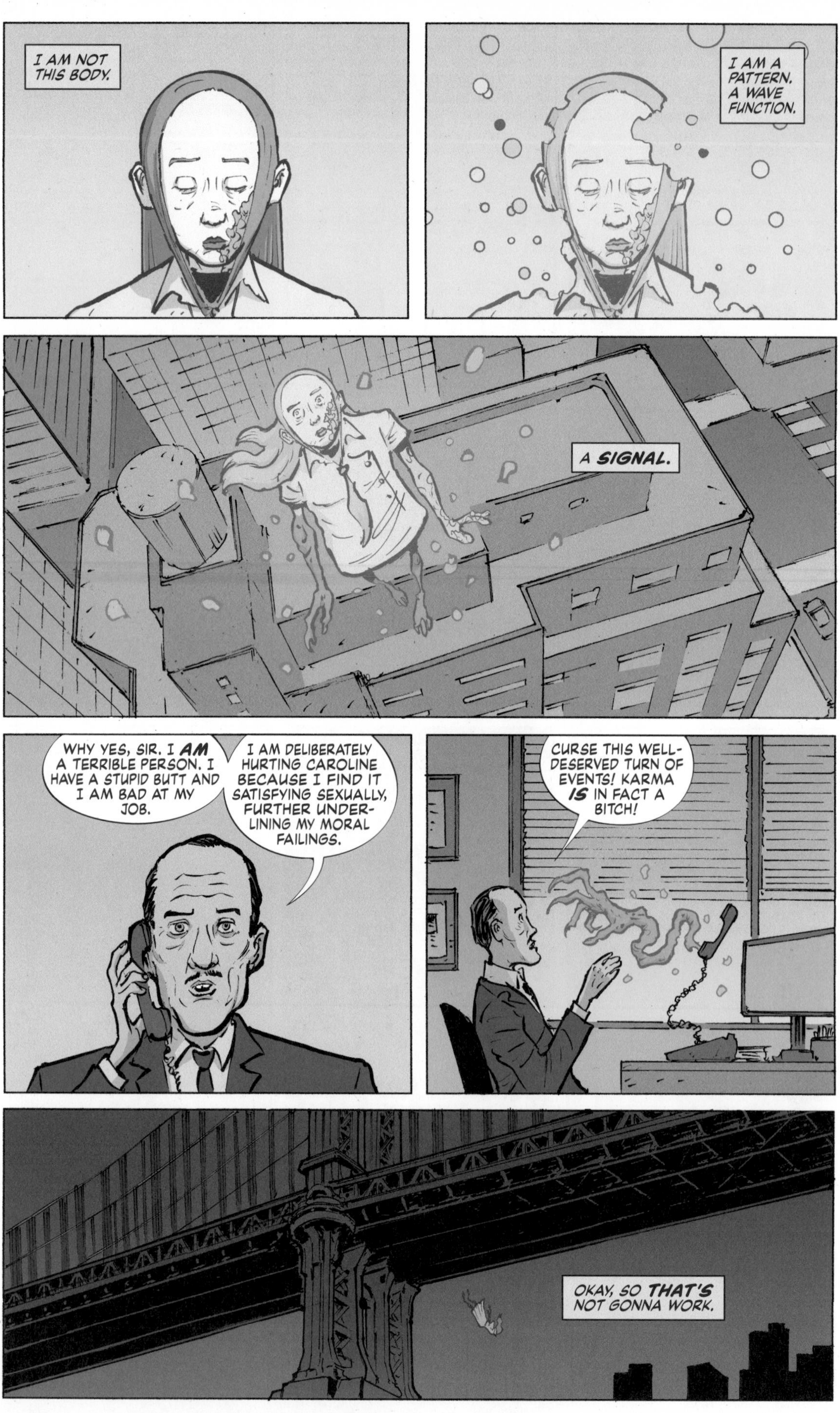
I AM NOT THIS BODY.
I AM A PATTERN. A WAVE FUNCTION.
A SIGNAL.
WHY YES, SIR. I AM A TERRIBLE PERSON. I HAVE A STUPID BUTT AND I AM BAD AT MY JOB.
I AM DELIBERATELY HURTING CAROLINE BECAUSE I FIND IT SATISFYING SEXUALLY, FURTHER UNDER-LINING MY MORAL FAILINGS.
CURSE THIS WELL-DESERVED TURN OF EVENTS! KARMA IS IN FACT A BITCH!
OKAY, SO THAT'S NOT GONNA WORK.

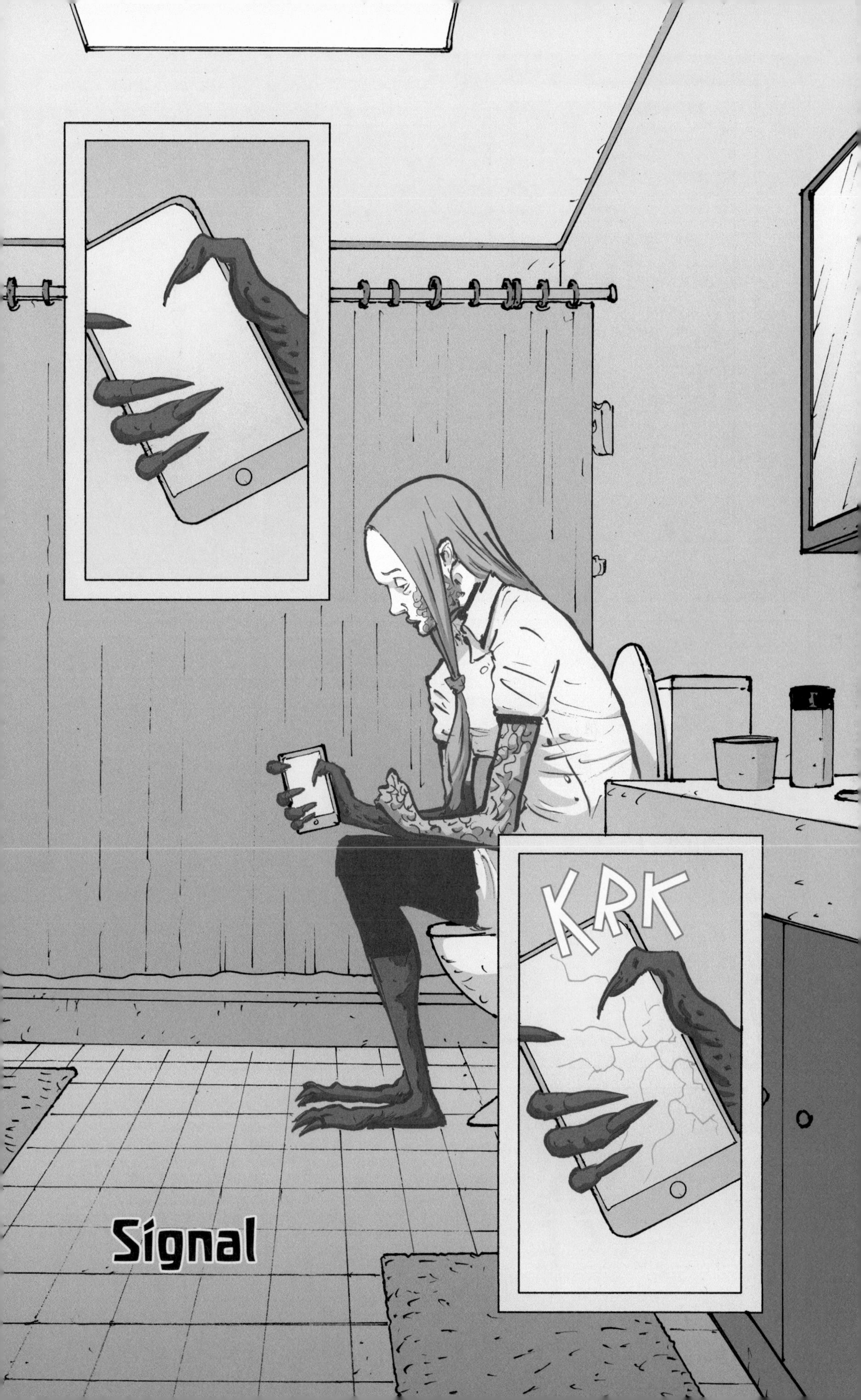
KRK
Signal

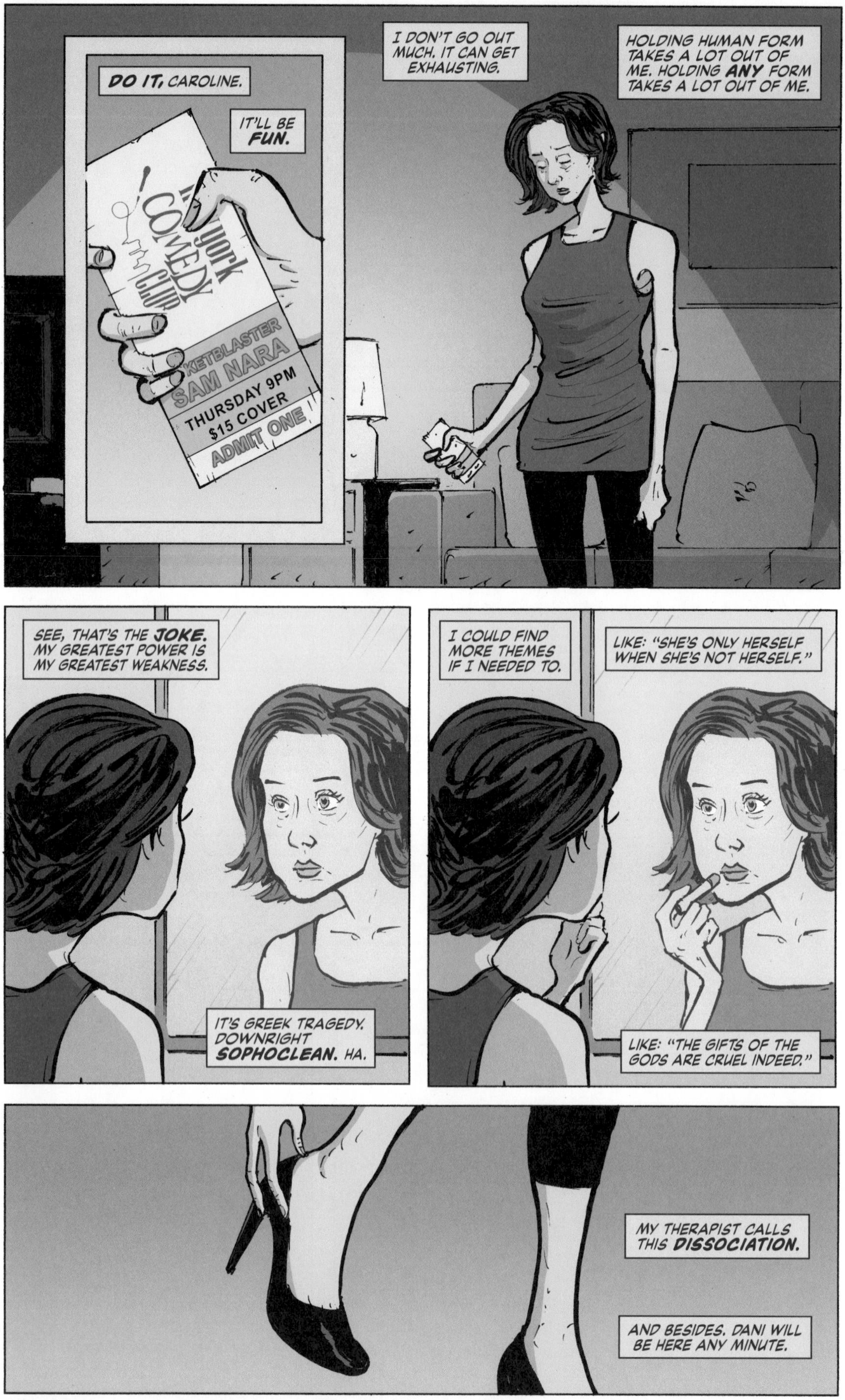
DO IT, CAROLINE.
IT'LL BE FUN.
COMEDY CLUB
SAM NARA
THURSDAY 9PM
$15 COVER
ADMIT ONE
I DON'T GO OUT MUCH. IT CAN GET EXHAUSTING.
HOLDING HUMAN FORM TAKES A LOT OUT OF ME. HOLDING ANY FORM TAKES A LOT OUT OF ME.
SEE, THAT'S THE JOKE. MY GREATEST POWER IS MY GREATEST WEAKNESS.
IT'S GREEK TRAGEDY. DOWNRIGHT SOPHOCLEAN. HA.
I COULD FIND MORE THEMES IF I NEEDED TO.
LIKE: "SHE'S ONLY HERSELF WHEN SHE'S NOT HERSELF."
LIKE: "THE GIFTS OF THE GODS ARE CRUEL INDEED."
MY THERAPIST CALLS THIS DISSOCIATION.
AND BESIDES. DANI WILL BE HERE ANY MINUTE.

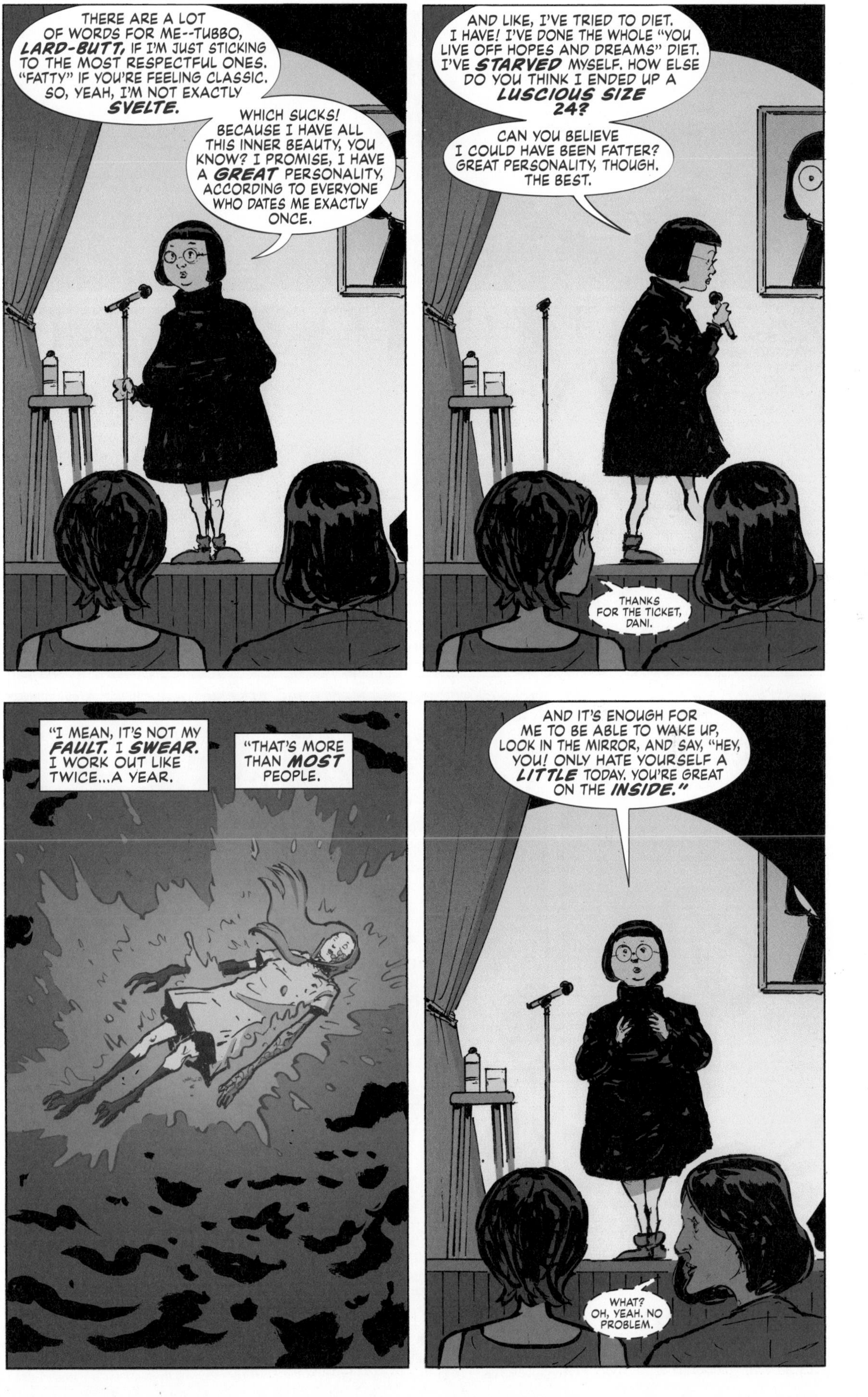
THERE ARE A LOT OF WORDS FOR ME--TUBBO, LARD-BUTT, IF I'M JUST STICKING TO THE MOST RESPECTFUL ONES. "FATTY" IF YOU'RE FEELING CLASSIC. SO, YEAH, I'M NOT EXACTLY SVELTE.
WHICH SUCKS! BECAUSE I HAVE ALL THIS INNER BEAUTY, YOU KNOW? I PROMISE, I HAVE A GREAT PERSONALITY, ACCORDING TO EVERYONE WHO DATES ME EXACTLY ONCE.
AND LIKE, I'VE TRIED TO DIET. I HAVE! I'VE DONE THE WHOLE "YOU LIVE OFF HOPES AND DREAMS" DIET. I'VE STARVED MYSELF. HOW ELSE DO YOU THINK I ENDED UP A LUSCIOUS SIZE 24?
CAN YOU BELIEVE I COULD HAVE BEEN FATTER? GREAT PERSONALITY, THOUGH. THE BEST.
THANKS FOR THE TICKET, DANI.
"I MEAN, IT'S NOT MY FAULT. I SWEAR. I WORK OUT LIKE TWICE...A YEAR.
"THAT'S MORE THAN MOST PEOPLE.
AND IT'S ENOUGH FOR ME TO BE ABLE TO WAKE UP, LOOK IN THE MIRROR, AND SAY, "HEY, YOU! ONLY HATE YOURSELF A LITTLE TODAY. YOU'RE GREAT ON THE INSIDE."
WHAT? OH, YEAH. NO PROBLEM.

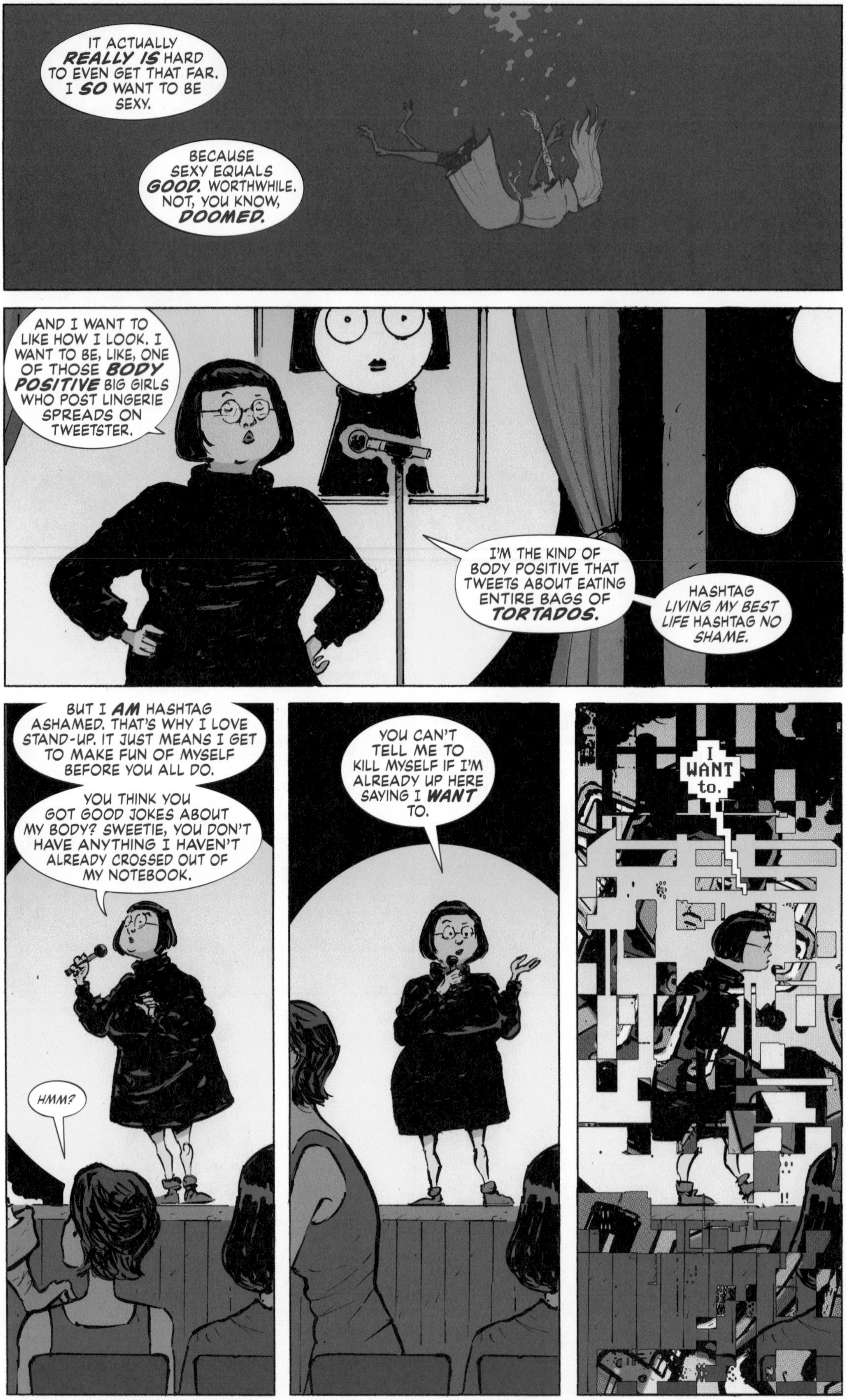
IT ACTUALLY REALLY IS HARD TO EVEN GET THAT FAR. I SO WANT TO BE SEXY.
BECAUSE SEXY EQUALS GOOD. WORTHWHILE. NOT, YOU KNOW, DOOMED.
AND I WANT TO LIKE HOW I LOOK. I WANT TO BE, LIKE, ONE OF THOSE BODY POSITIVE BIG GIRLS WHO POST LINGERIE SPREADS ON TWEETSTER.
I'M THE KIND OF BODY POSITIVE THAT TWEETS ABOUT EATING ENTIRE BAGS OF TORTADOS.
HASHTAG LIVING MY BEST LIFE HASHTAG NO SHAME.
BUT I AM HASHTAG ASHAMED. THAT'S WHY I LOVE STAND-UP. IT JUST MEANS I GET TO MAKE FUN OF MYSELF BEFORE YOU ALL DO.
YOU THINK YOU GOT GOOD JOKES ABOUT MY BODY? SWEETIE, YOU DON'T HAVE ANYTHING I HAVEN'T ALREADY CROSSED OUT OF MY NOTEBOOK.
HMM?
YOU CAN'T TELL ME TO KILL MYSELF IF I'M ALREADY UP HERE SAYING I WANT TO.
I WANT to.

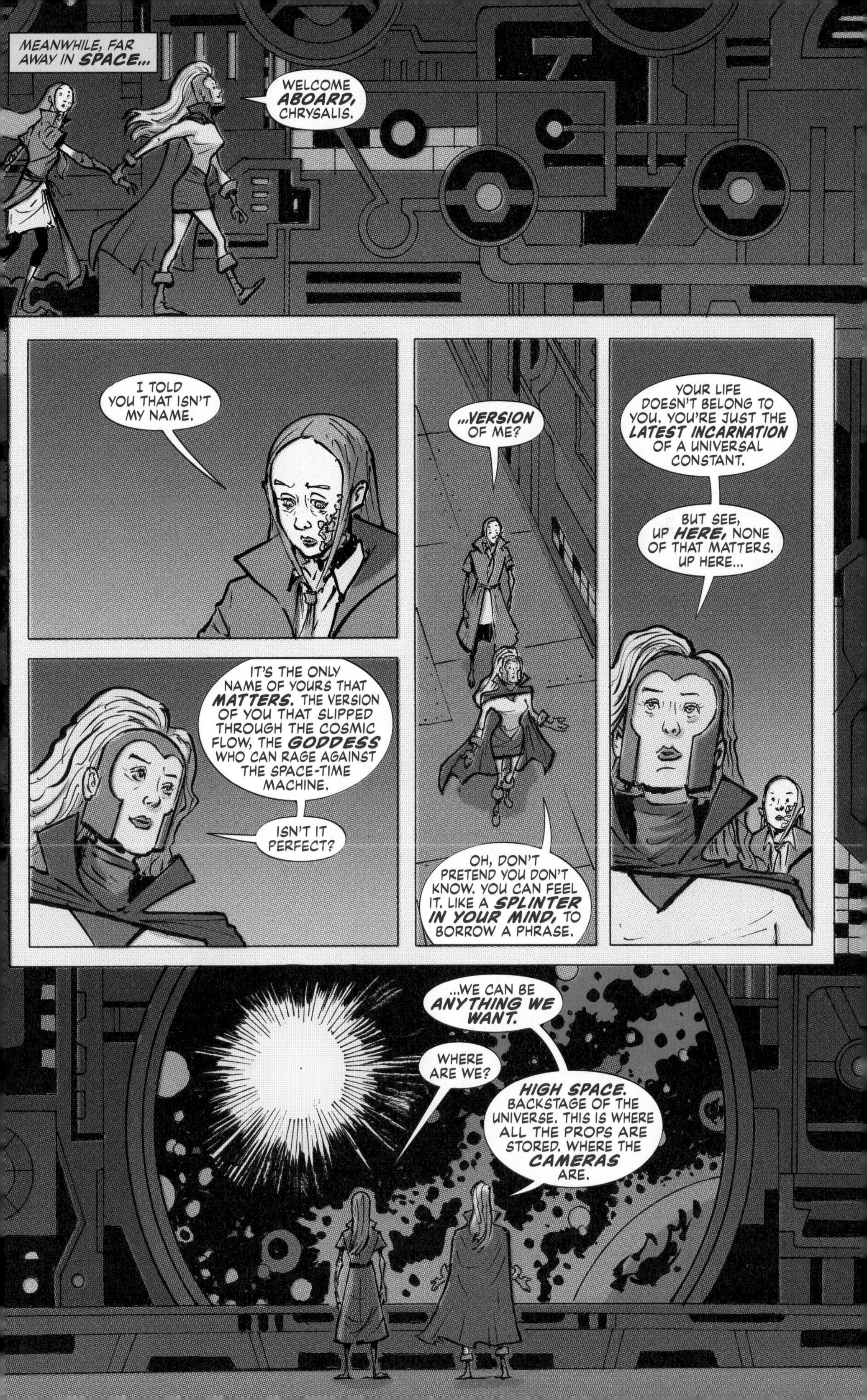
MEANWHILE, FAR AWAY IN SPACE...
WELCOME ABOARD, CHRYSALIS.
I TOLD YOU THAT ISN'T MY NAME.
IT'S THE ONLY NAME OF YOURS THAT MATTERS. THE VERSION OF YOU THAT SLIPPED THROUGH THE COSMIC FLOW, THE GODDESS WHO CAN RAGE AGAINST THE SPACE-TIME MACHINE.
ISN'T IT PERFECT?
...VERSION OF ME?
OH, DON'T PRETEND YOU DON'T KNOW. YOU CAN FEEL IT. LIKE A SPLINTER IN YOUR MIND, TO BORROW A PHRASE.
YOUR LIFE DOESN'T BELONG TO YOU. YOU'RE JUST THE LATEST INCARNATION OF A UNIVERSAL CONSTANT.
BUT SEE, UP HERE, NONE OF THAT MATTERS. UP HERE...
...WE CAN BE ANYTHING WE WANT.
WHERE ARE WE?
HIGH SPACE. BACKSTAGE OF THE UNIVERSE. THIS IS WHERE ALL THE PROPS ARE STORED. WHERE THE CAMERAS ARE.

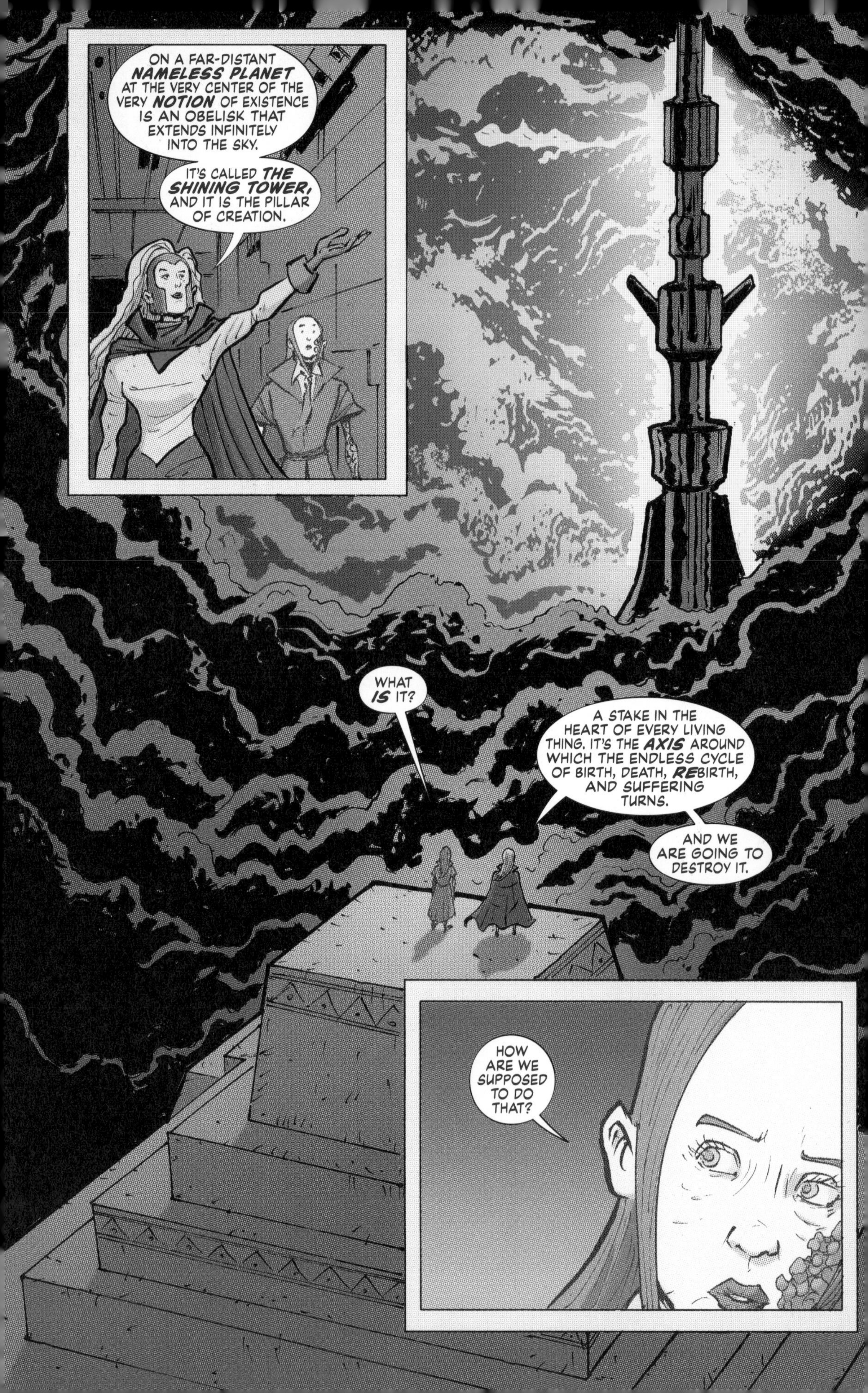
ON A FAR-DISTANT NAMELESS PLANET AT THE VERY CENTER OF THE VERY NOTION OF EXISTENCE IS AN OBELISK THAT EXTENDS INFINITELY INTO THE SKY.
IT'S CALLED THE SHINING TOWER, AND IT IS THE PILLAR OF CREATION.
WHAT IS IT?
A STAKE IN THE HEART OF EVERY LIVING THING. IT'S THE AXIS AROUND WHICH THE ENDLESS CYCLE OF BIRTH, DEATH, REBIRTH, AND SUFFERING TURNS.
AND WE ARE GOING TO DESTROY IT.
HOW ARE WE SUPPOSED TO DO THAT?

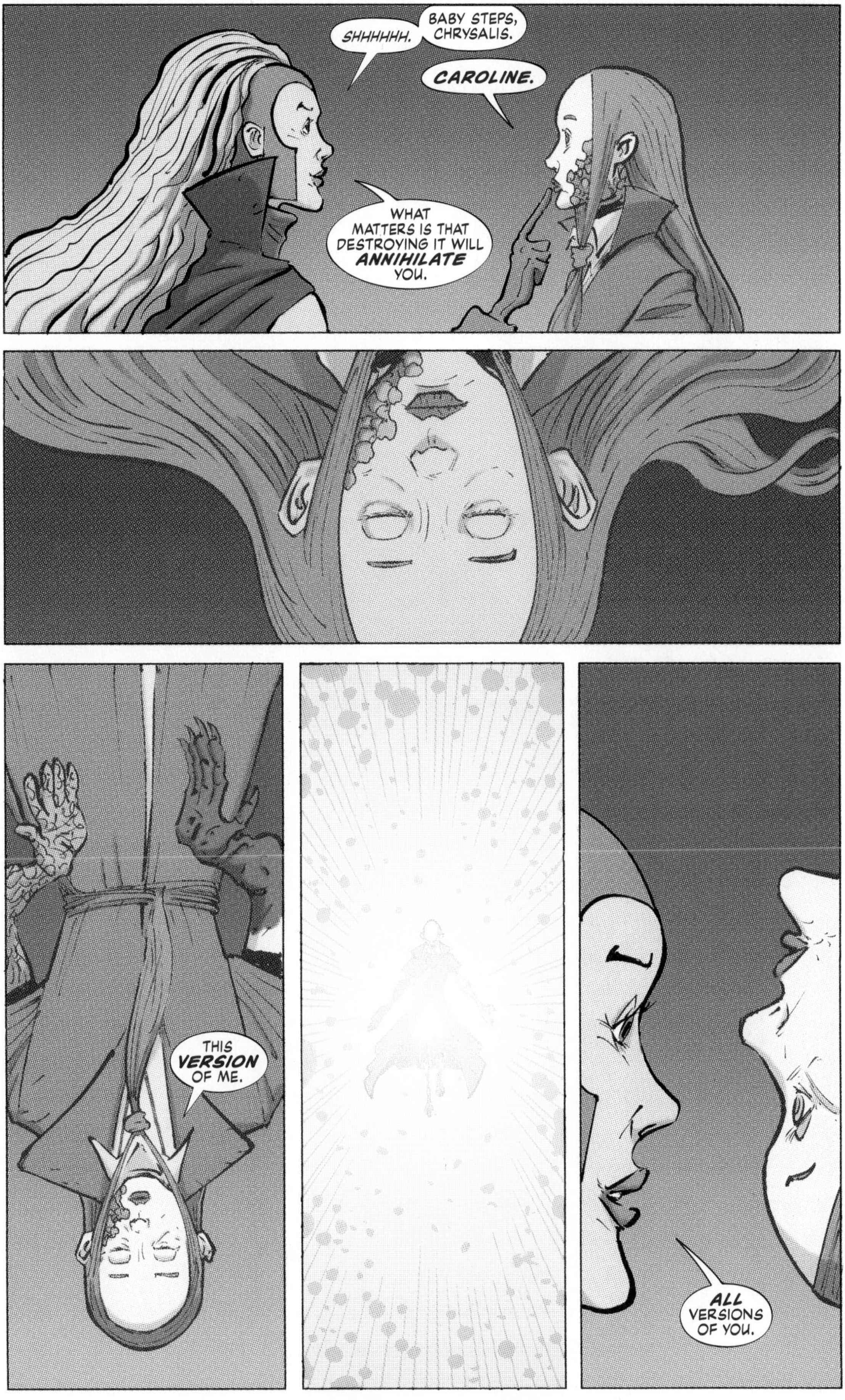
SHHHHHH.
BABY STEPS, CHRYSALIS.
CAROLINE.
WHAT MATTERS IS THAT DESTROYING IT WILL ANNIHILATE YOU.
THIS VERSION OF ME.
ALL VERSIONS OF YOU.

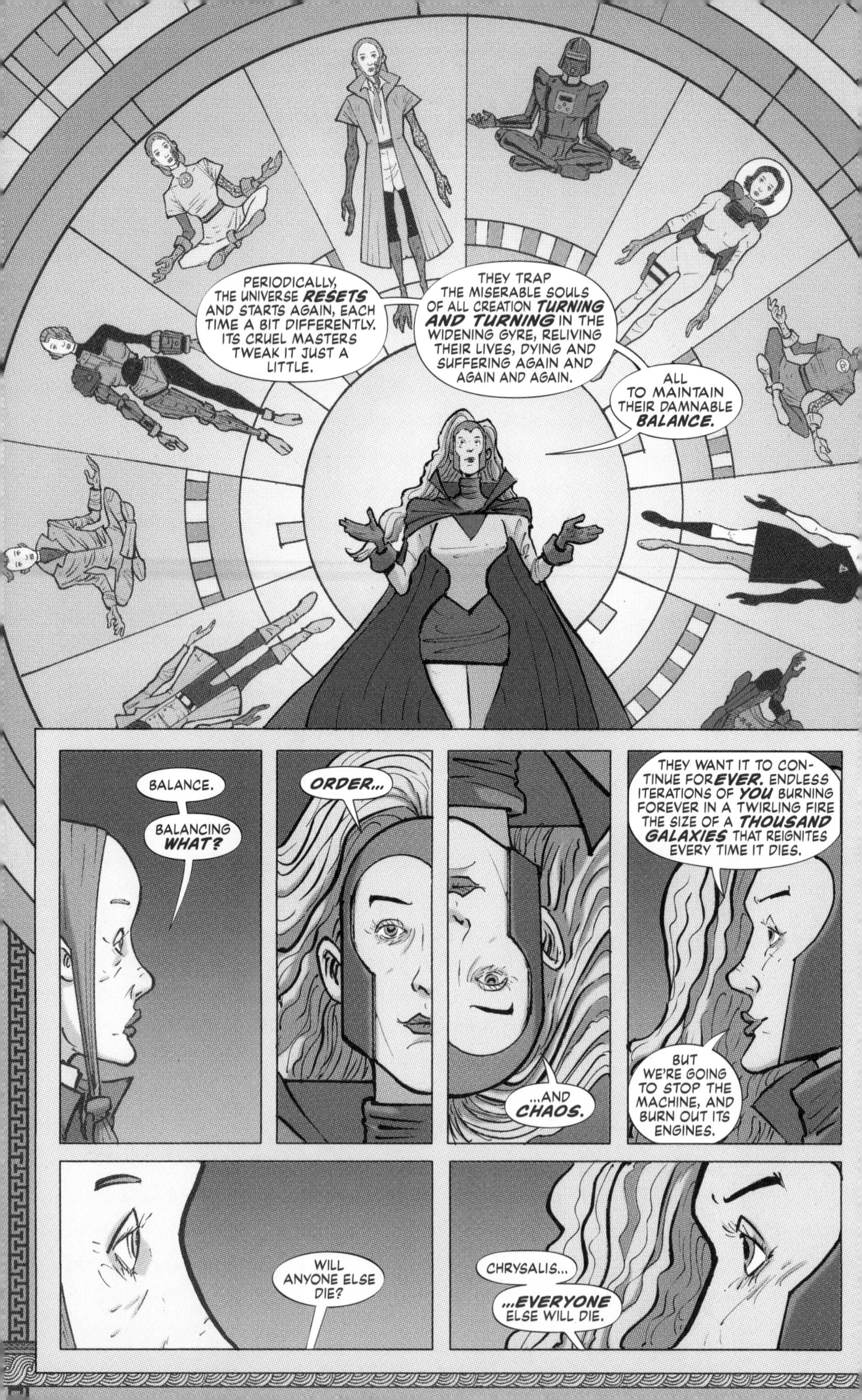
PERIODICALLY, THE UNIVERSE RESETS AND STARTS AGAIN, EACH TIME A BIT DIFFERENTLY. ITS CRUEL MASTERS TWEAK IT JUST A LITTLE.
THEY TRAP THE MISERABLE SOULS OF ALL CREATION TURNING AND TURNING IN THE WIDENING GYRE, RELIVING THEIR LIVES, DYING AND SUFFERING AGAIN AND AGAIN AND AGAIN.
ALL TO MAINTAIN THEIR DAMNABLE BALANCE.
BALANCE.
BALANCING WHAT?
ORDER...
...AND CHAOS.
THEY WANT IT TO CONTINUE FOREVER. ENDLESS ITERATIONS OF YOU BURNING FOREVER IN A TWIRLING FIRE THE SIZE OF A THOUSAND GALAXIES THAT REIGNITES EVERY TIME IT DIES.
BUT WE'RE GOING TO STOP THE MACHINE, AND BURN OUT ITS ENGINES.
WILL ANYONE ELSE DIE?
CHRYSALIS...
...EVERYONE ELSE WILL DIE.

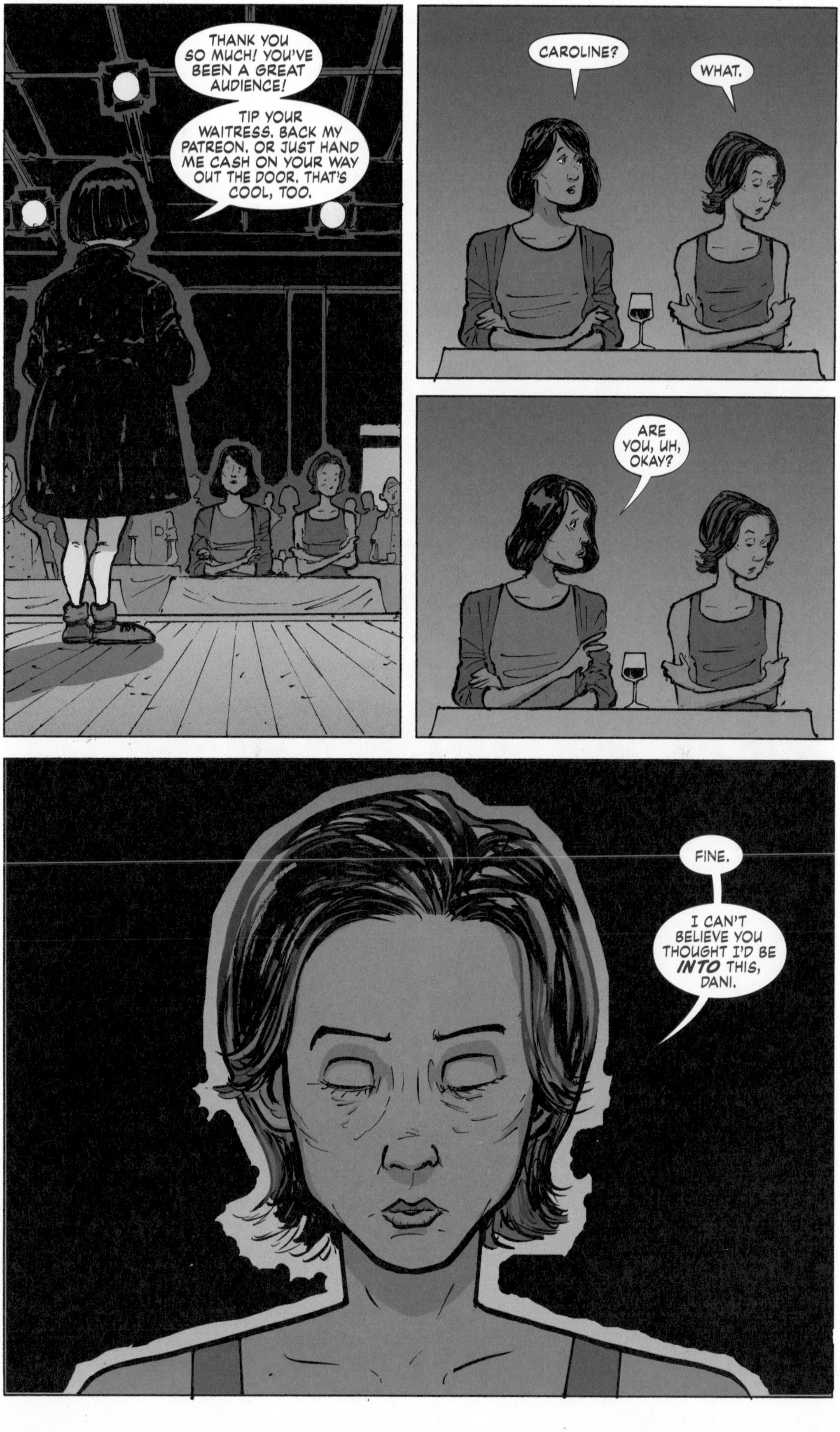
THANK YOU SO MUCH! YOU'VE BEEN A GREAT AUDIENCE!
TIP YOUR WAITRESS. BACK MY PATREON. OR JUST HAND ME CASH ON YOUR WAY OUT THE DOOR. THAT'S COOL, TOO.
CAROLINE?
WHAT.
ARE YOU, UH, OKAY?
FINE.
I CAN'T BELIEVE YOU THOUGHT I'D BE *INTO* THIS, DANI.

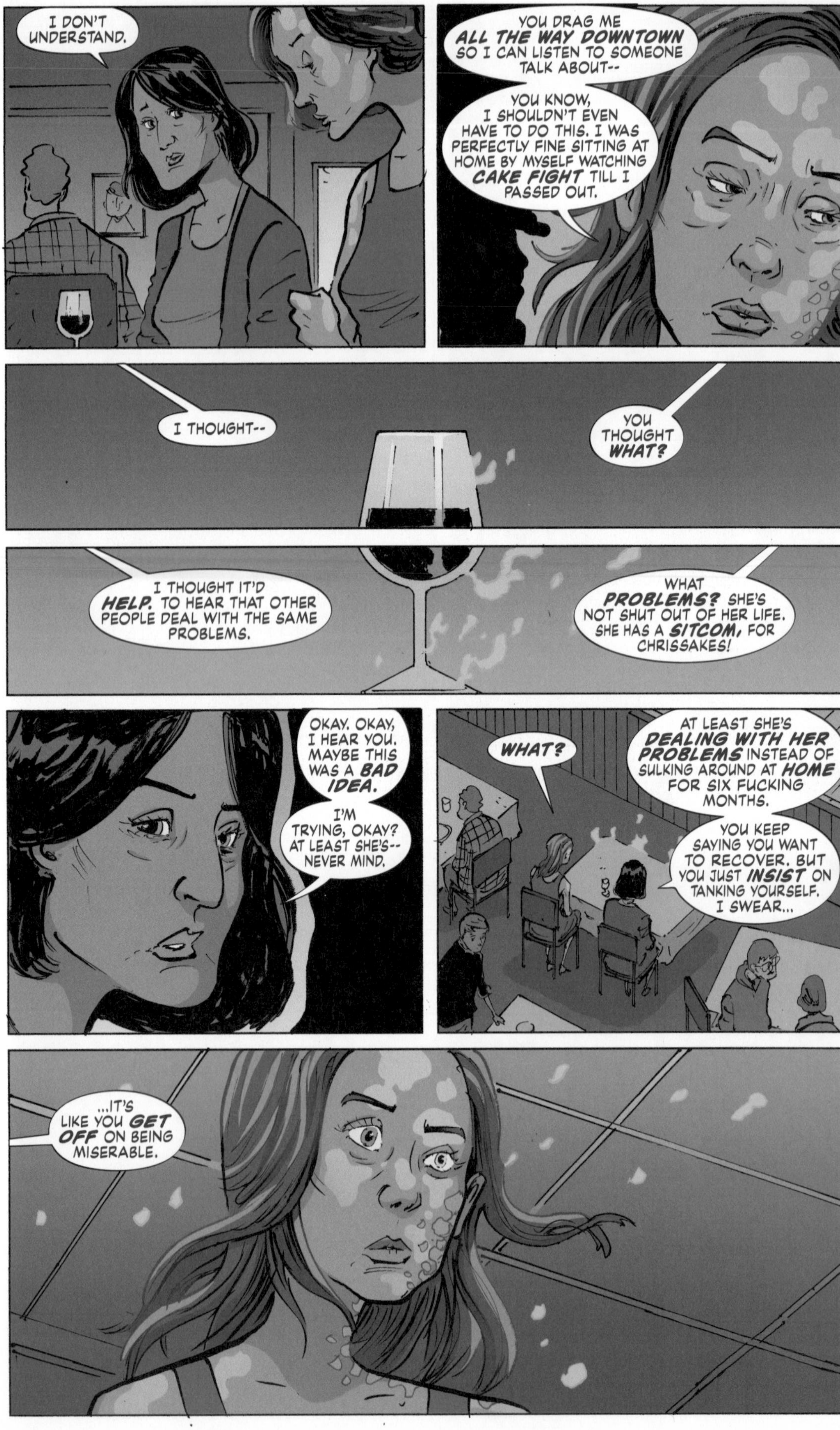
I DON'T UNDERSTAND.
YOU DRAG ME ALL THE WAY DOWNTOWN SO I CAN LISTEN TO SOMEONE TALK ABOUT--
YOU KNOW, I SHOULDN'T EVEN HAVE TO DO THIS. I WAS PERFECTLY FINE SITTING AT HOME BY MYSELF WATCHING CAKE FIGHT TILL I PASSED OUT.
I THOUGHT--
YOU THOUGHT WHAT?
I THOUGHT IT'D HELP. TO HEAR THAT OTHER PEOPLE DEAL WITH THE SAME PROBLEMS.
WHAT PROBLEMS? SHE'S NOT SHUT OUT OF HER LIFE. SHE HAS A SITCOM, FOR CHRISSAKES!
OKAY. OKAY, I HEAR YOU. MAYBE THIS WAS A BAD IDEA.
I'M TRYING, OKAY? AT LEAST SHE'S-- NEVER MIND.
WHAT?
AT LEAST SHE'S DEALING WITH HER PROBLEMS INSTEAD OF SULKING AROUND AT HOME FOR SIX FUCKING MONTHS.
YOU KEEP SAYING YOU WANT TO RECOVER. BUT YOU JUST INSIST ON TANKING YOURSELF. I SWEAR...
...IT'S LIKE YOU GET OFF ON BEING MISERABLE.

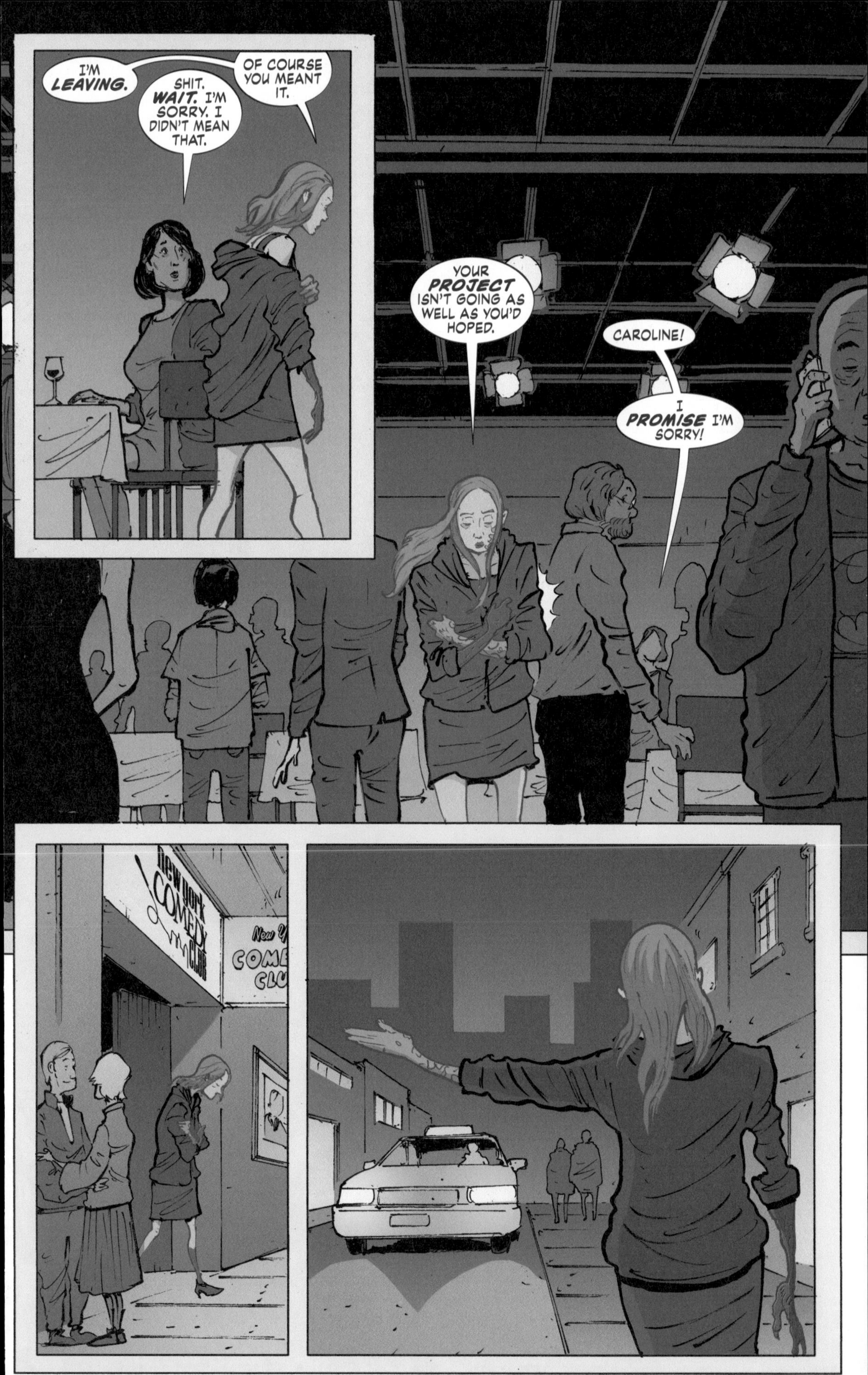
I'M **LEAVING.**
SHIT. **WAIT.** I'M SORRY. I DIDN'T MEAN THAT.
OF COURSE YOU MEANT IT.
YOUR **PROJECT** ISN'T GOING AS WELL AS YOU'D HOPED.
CAROLINE!
I **PROMISE** I'M SORRY!
New York COMEDY CLUB

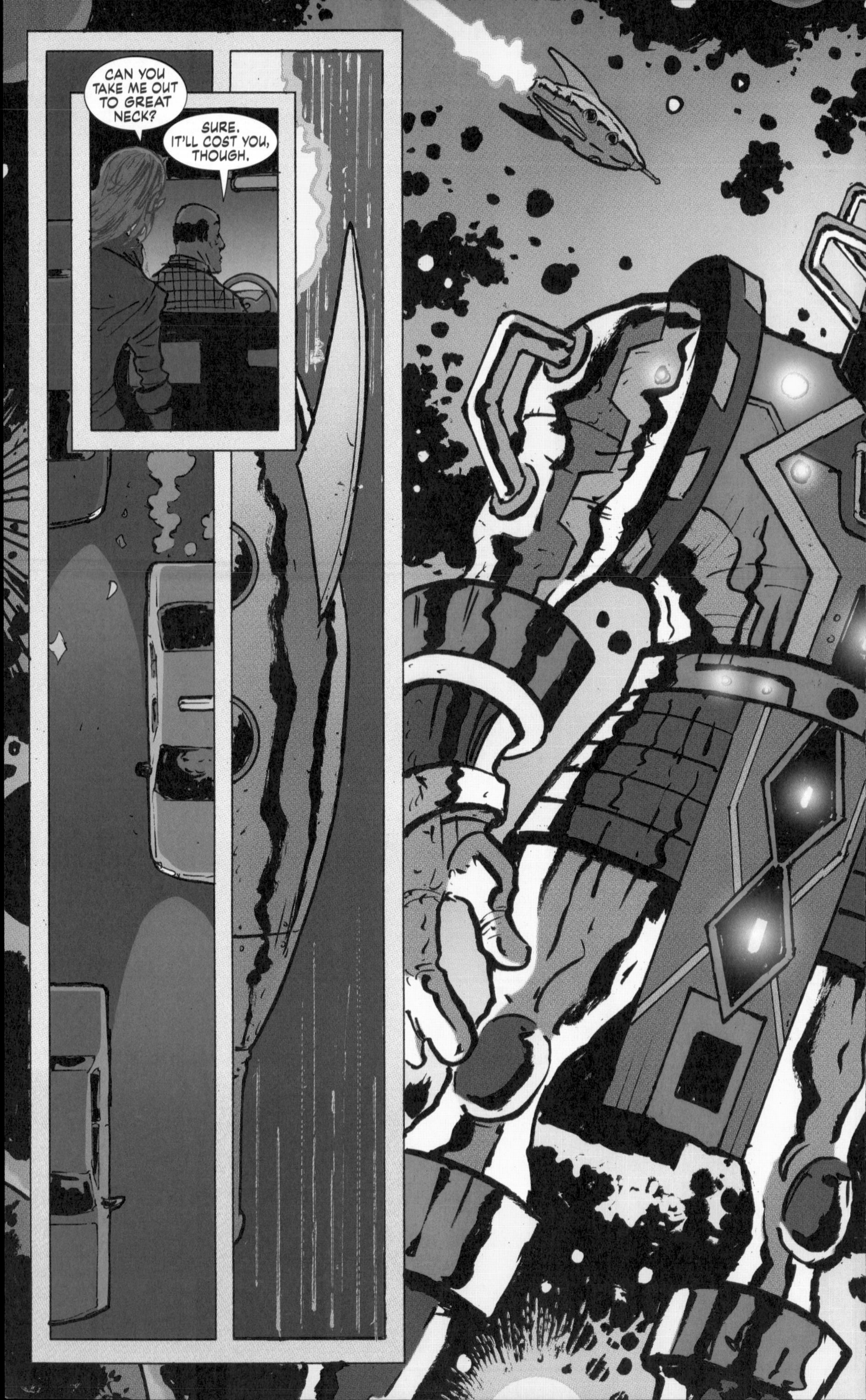
CAN YOU TAKE ME OUT TO GREAT NECK?
SURE. IT'LL COST YOU, THOUGH.

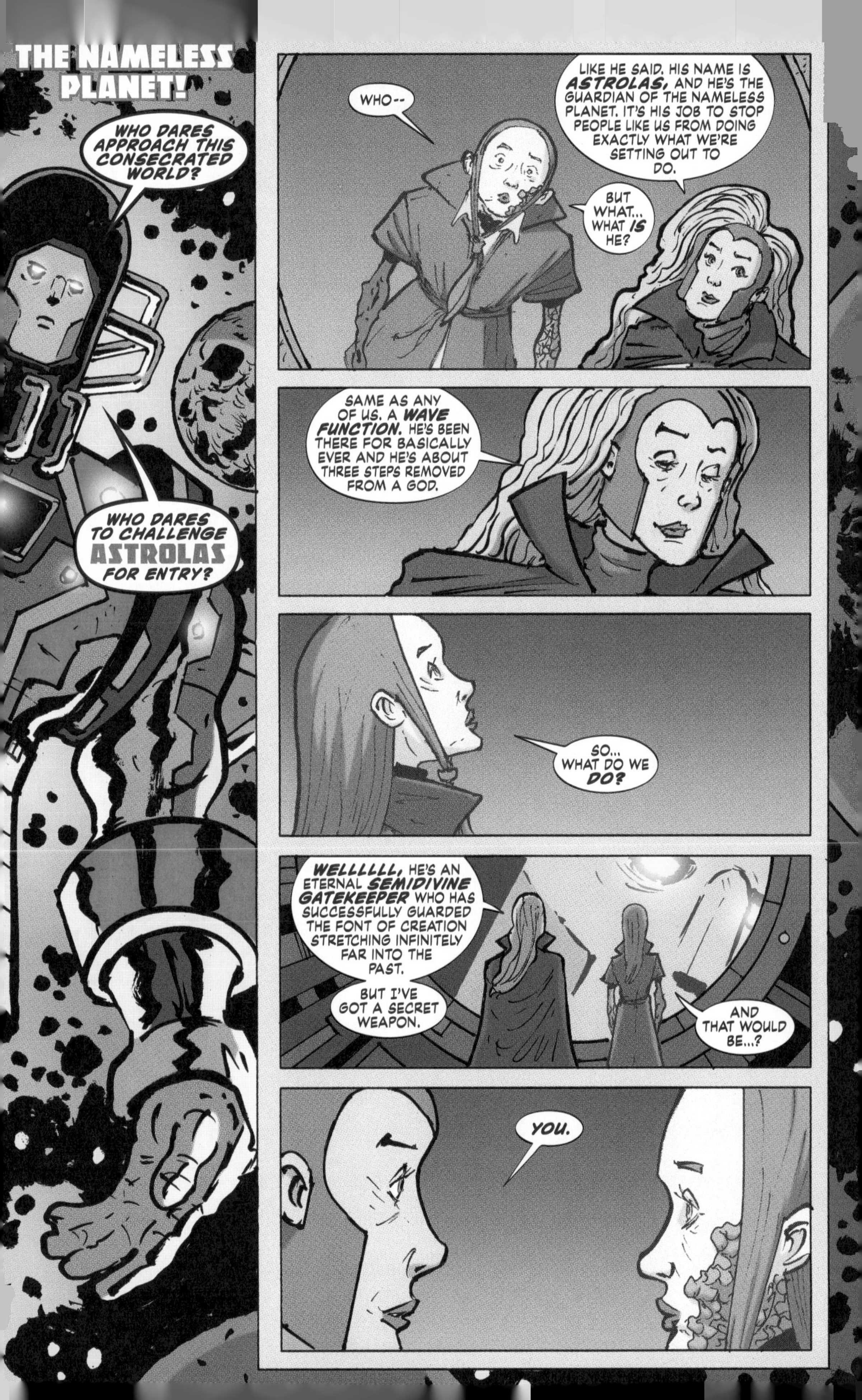
THE NAMELESS PLANET!
WHO DARES APPROACH THIS CONSECRATED WORLD?
WHO DARES TO CHALLENGE ASTROLAS FOR ENTRY?
WHO--
LIKE HE SAID, HIS NAME IS ASTROLAS, AND HE'S THE GUARDIAN OF THE NAMELESS PLANET. IT'S HIS JOB TO STOP PEOPLE LIKE US FROM DOING EXACTLY WHAT WE'RE SETTING OUT TO DO.
BUT WHAT... WHAT IS HE?
SAME AS ANY OF US. A WAVE FUNCTION. HE'S BEEN THERE FOR BASICALLY EVER AND HE'S ABOUT THREE STEPS REMOVED FROM A GOD.
SO... WHAT DO WE DO?
WELLLLLLL, HE'S AN ETERNAL SEMIDIVINE GATEKEEPER WHO HAS SUCCESSFULLY GUARDED THE FONT OF CREATION STRETCHING INFINITELY FAR INTO THE PAST.
BUT I'VE GOT A SECRET WEAPON.
AND THAT WOULD BE...?
YOU.

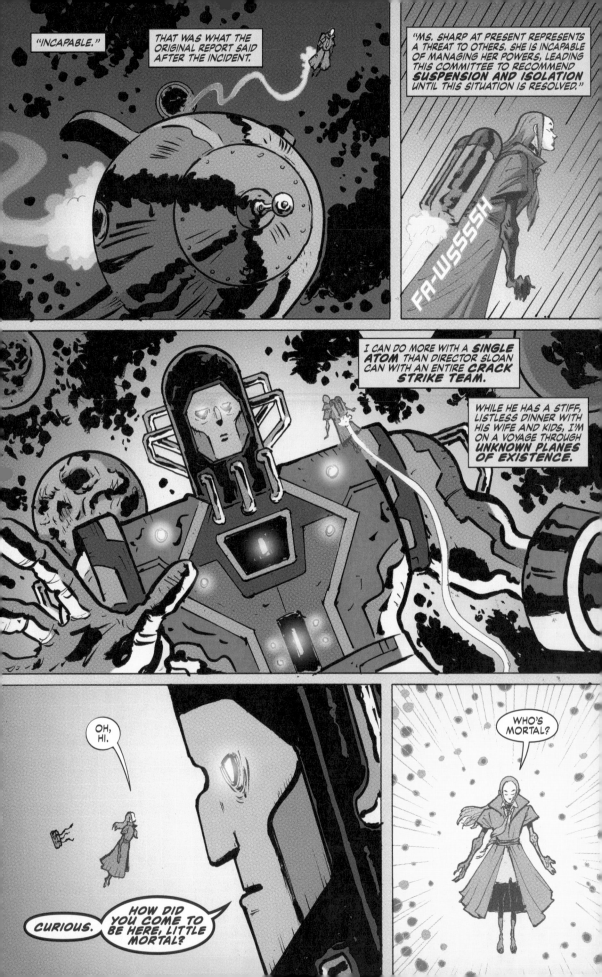

"INCAPABLE."

THAT WAS WHAT THE ORIGINAL REPORT SAID AFTER THE INCIDENT.

"MS. SHARP AT PRESENT REPRESENTS A THREAT TO OTHERS. SHE IS INCAPABLE OF MANAGING HER POWERS, LEADING THIS COMMITTEE TO RECOMMEND **SUSPENSION AND ISOLATION** UNTIL THIS SITUATION IS RESOLVED."

FA-WSSSSH

I CAN DO MORE WITH A **SINGLE ATOM** THAN DIRECTOR SLOAN CAN WITH AN ENTIRE **CRACK STRIKE TEAM.**

WHILE HE HAS A STIFF, LISTLESS DINNER WITH HIS WIFE AND KIDS, I'M ON A VOYAGE THROUGH **UNKNOWN PLANES OF EXISTENCE.**

OH, HI.

CURIOUS.

HOW DID YOU COME TO BE HERE, LITTLE MORTAL?

WHO'S MORTAL?

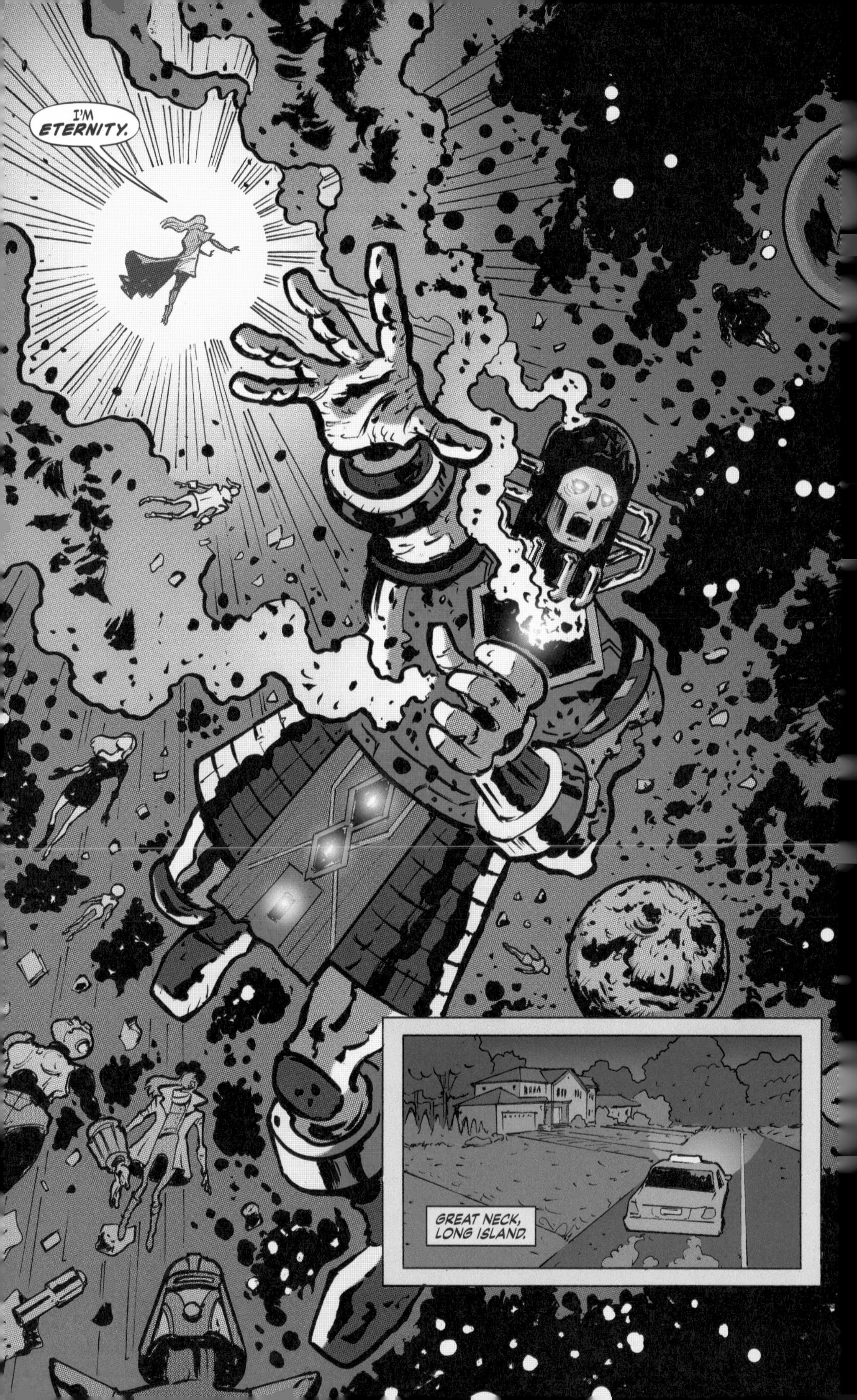
I'M ETERNITY.
GREAT NECK, LONG ISLAND.

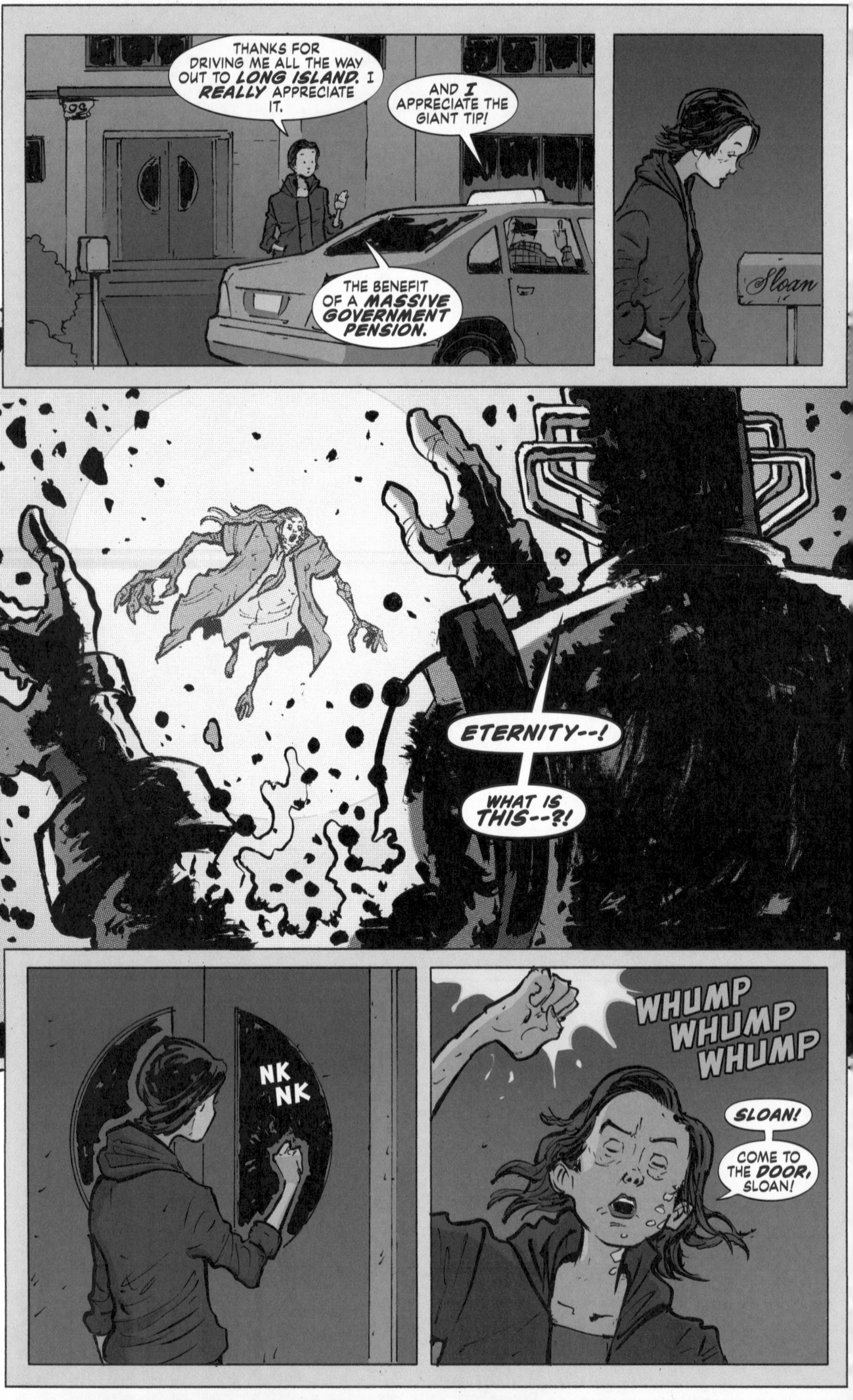
THANKS FOR DRIVING ME ALL THE WAY OUT TO LONG ISLAND. I REALLY APPRECIATE IT.
AND I APPRECIATE THE GIANT TIP!
THE BENEFIT OF A MASSIVE GOVERNMENT PENSION.
Sloan
ETERNITY--!
WHAT IS THIS--?!
NK NK
WHUMP WHUMP WHUMP
SLOAN!
COME TO THE DOOR, SLOAN!

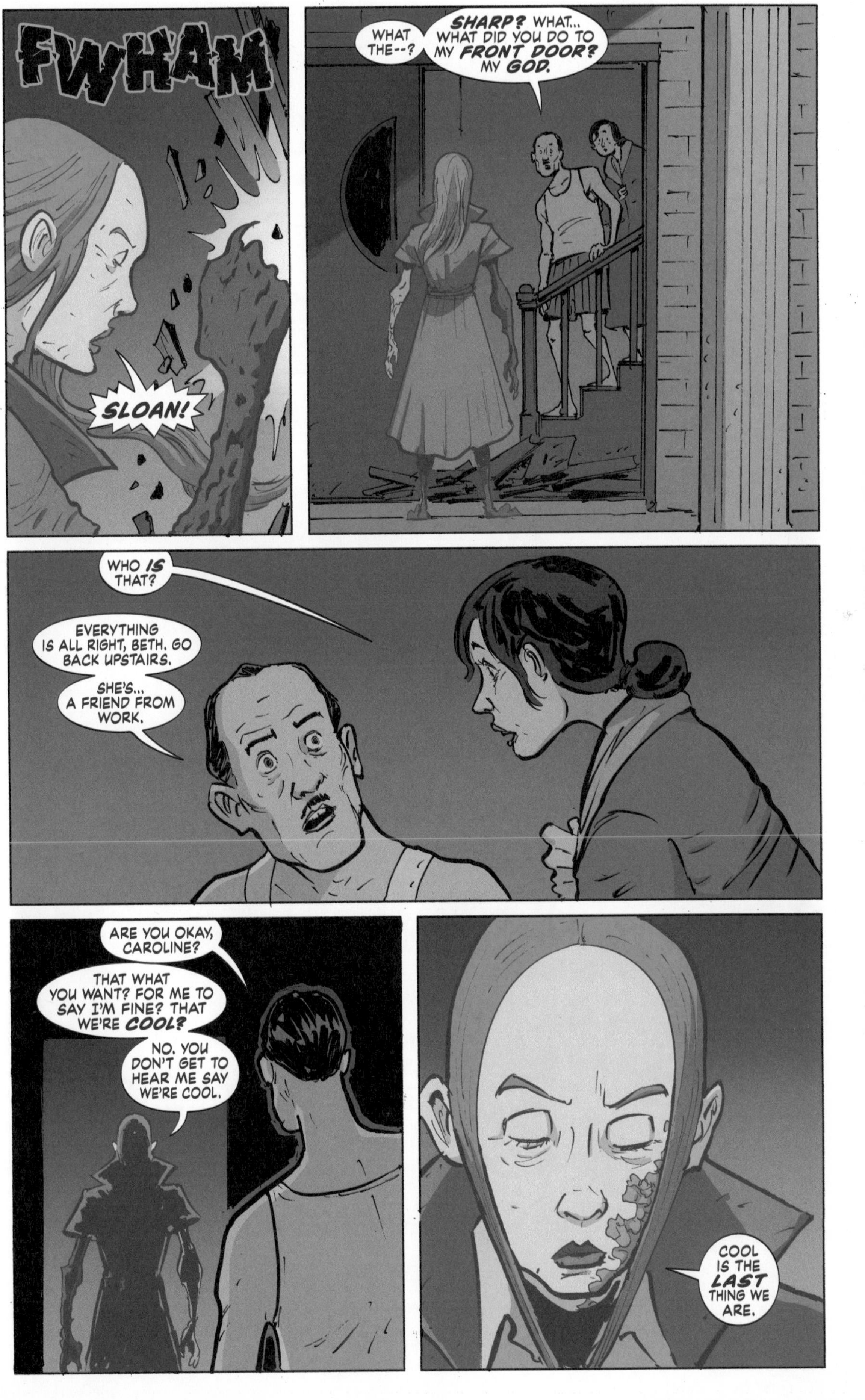
FWHAM
SLOAN!
WHAT THE--?
SHARP? WHAT... WHAT DID YOU DO TO MY FRONT DOOR? MY GOD.
WHO IS THAT?
EVERYTHING IS ALL RIGHT, BETH. GO BACK UPSTAIRS.
SHE'S... A FRIEND FROM WORK.
ARE YOU OKAY, CAROLINE?
THAT WHAT YOU WANT? FOR ME TO SAY I'M FINE? THAT WE'RE COOL?
NO. YOU DON'T GET TO HEAR ME SAY WE'RE COOL.
COOL IS THE LAST THING WE ARE.

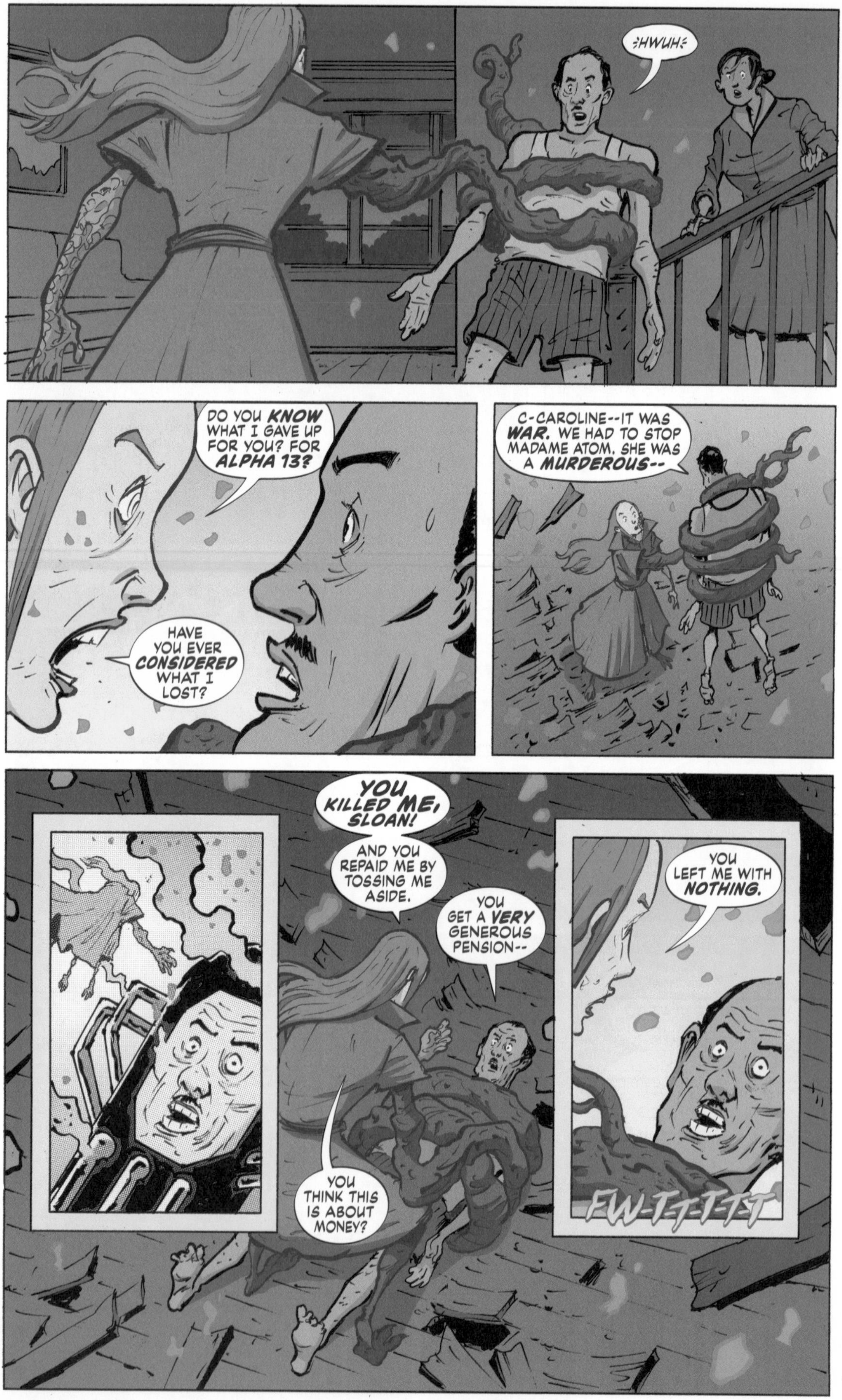
HWUH
DO YOU KNOW WHAT I GAVE UP FOR YOU? FOR ALPHA 13?
HAVE YOU EVER CONSIDERED WHAT I LOST?
C-CAROLINE--IT WAS WAR. WE HAD TO STOP MADAME ATOM. SHE WAS A MURDEROUS--
YOU KILLED ME, SLOAN!
AND YOU REPAID ME BY TOSSING ME ASIDE.
YOU GET A VERY GENEROUS PENSION--
YOU THINK THIS IS ABOUT MONEY?
YOU LEFT ME WITH NOTHING.
FW-T-T-T-T-T

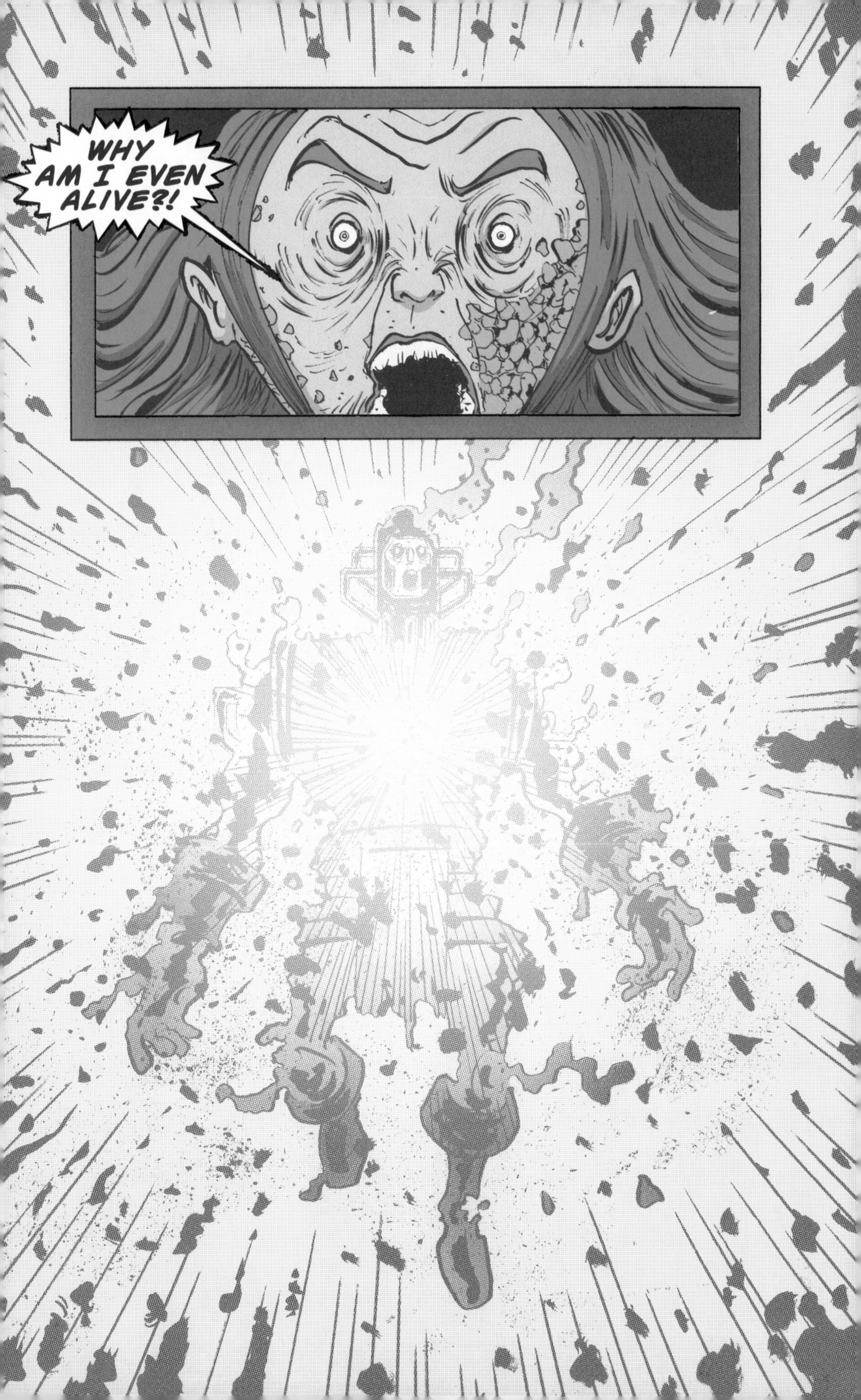
WHY AM I EVEN ALIVE?!

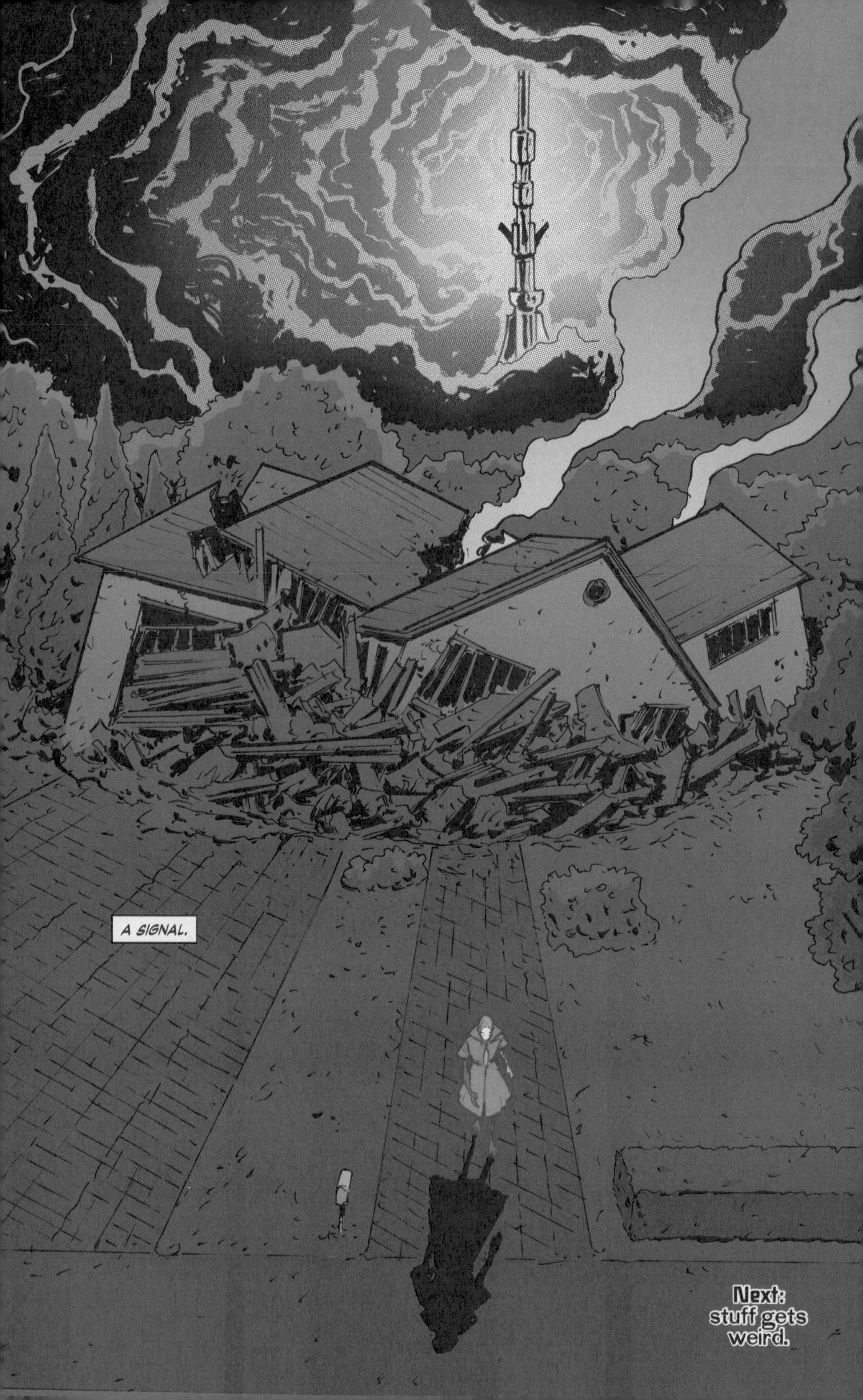
A SIGNAL.
Next: stuff gets weird.

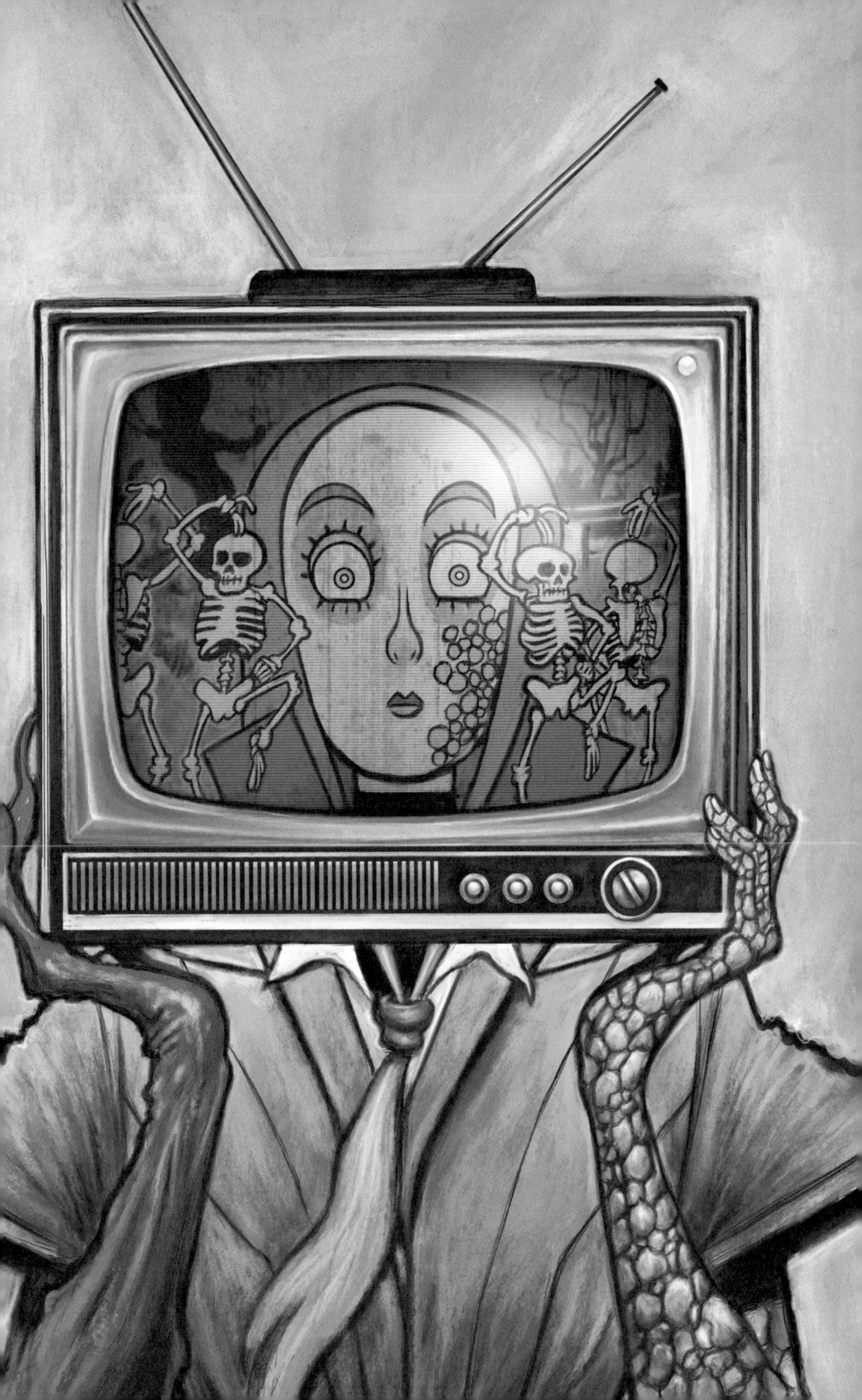

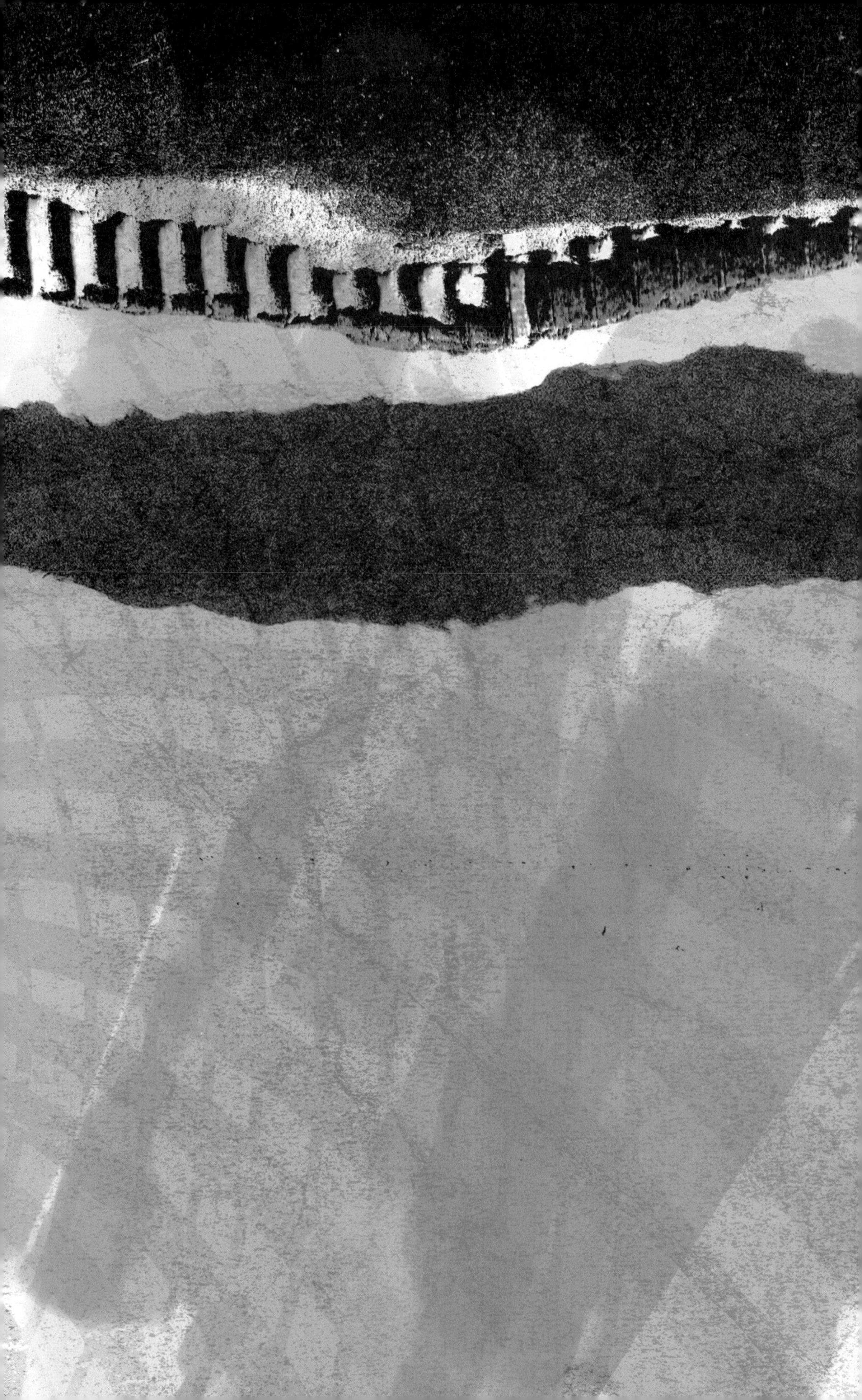

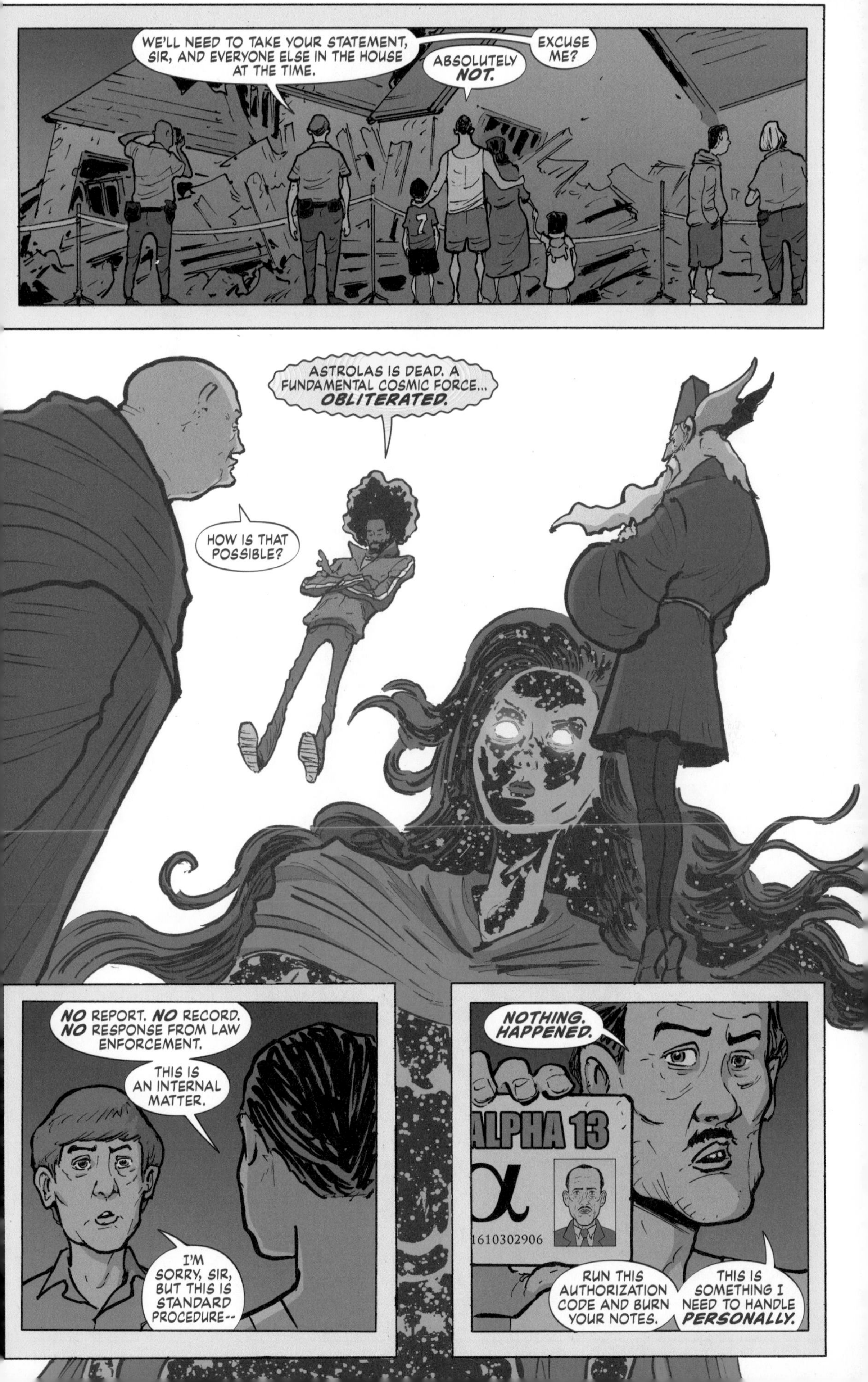
WE'LL NEED TO TAKE YOUR STATEMENT, SIR, AND EVERYONE ELSE IN THE HOUSE AT THE TIME.
EXCUSE ME?
ABSOLUTELY **NOT.**
ASTROLAS IS DEAD. A FUNDAMENTAL COSMIC FORCE... ***OBLITERATED.***
HOW IS THAT POSSIBLE?
NO REPORT. ***NO*** RECORD. ***NO*** RESPONSE FROM LAW ENFORCEMENT.
THIS IS AN INTERNAL MATTER.
I'M SORRY, SIR, BUT THIS IS STANDARD PROCEDURE--
NOTHING. HAPPENED.
ALPHA 13
α
1610302906
RUN THIS AUTHORIZATION CODE AND BURN YOUR NOTES.
THIS IS SOMETHING I NEED TO HANDLE ***PERSONALLY.***

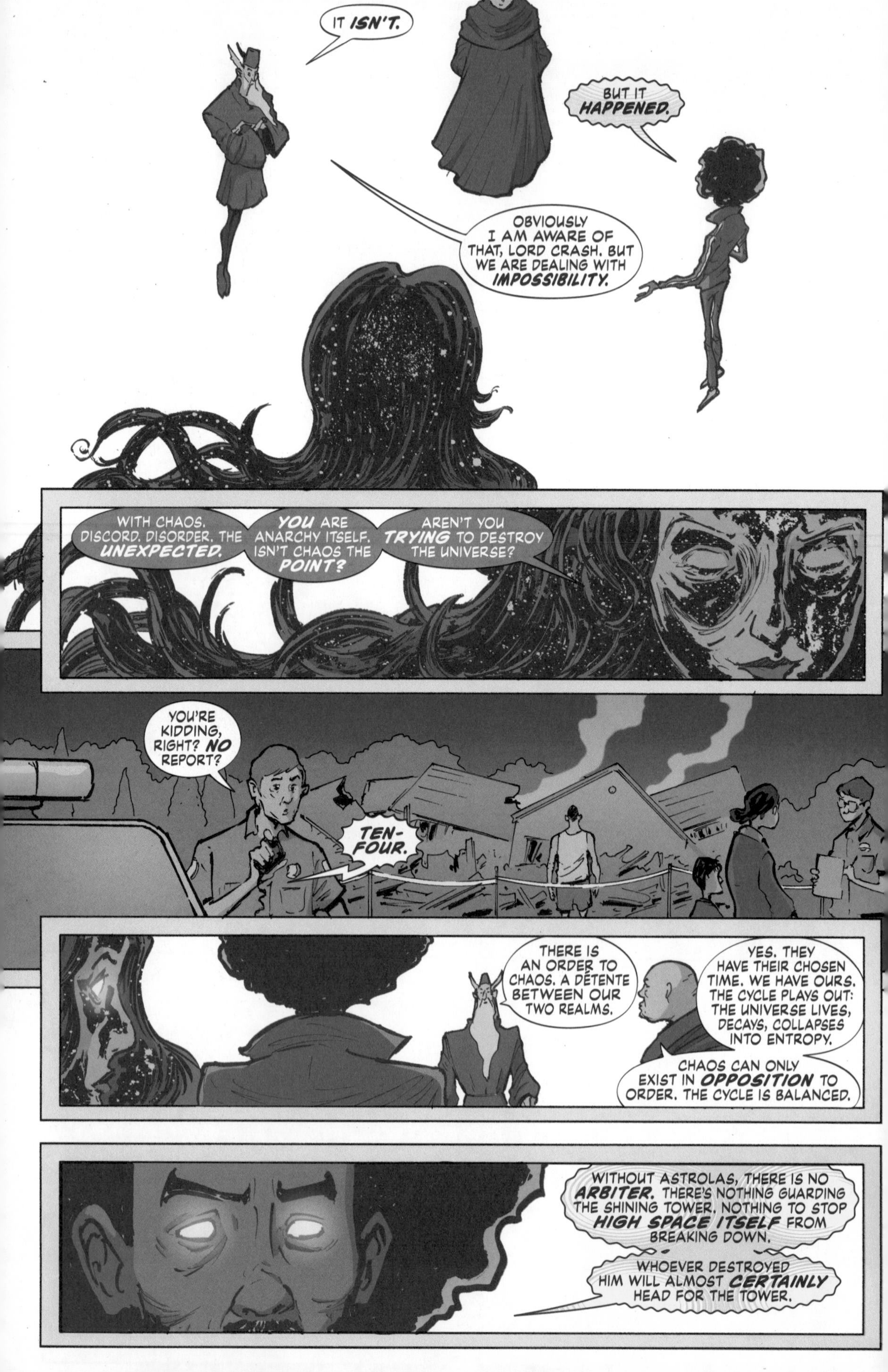
IT ISN'T.
BUT IT HAPPENED.
OBVIOUSLY I AM AWARE OF THAT, LORD CRASH. BUT WE ARE DEALING WITH IMPOSSIBILITY.
WITH CHAOS. DISCORD. DISORDER. THE UNEXPECTED.
YOU ARE ANARCHY ITSELF. ISN'T CHAOS THE POINT?
AREN'T YOU TRYING TO DESTROY THE UNIVERSE?
YOU'RE KIDDING, RIGHT? NO REPORT?
TEN-FOUR.
THERE IS AN ORDER TO CHAOS. A DÉTENTE BETWEEN OUR TWO REALMS.
YES. THEY HAVE THEIR CHOSEN TIME. WE HAVE OURS. THE CYCLE PLAYS OUT: THE UNIVERSE LIVES, DECAYS, COLLAPSES INTO ENTROPY.
CHAOS CAN ONLY EXIST IN OPPOSITION TO ORDER. THE CYCLE IS BALANCED.
WITHOUT ASTROLAS, THERE IS NO ARBITER. THERE'S NOTHING GUARDING THE SHINING TOWER. NOTHING TO STOP HIGH SPACE ITSELF FROM BREAKING DOWN.
WHOEVER DESTROYED HIM WILL ALMOST CERTAINLY HEAD FOR THE TOWER.

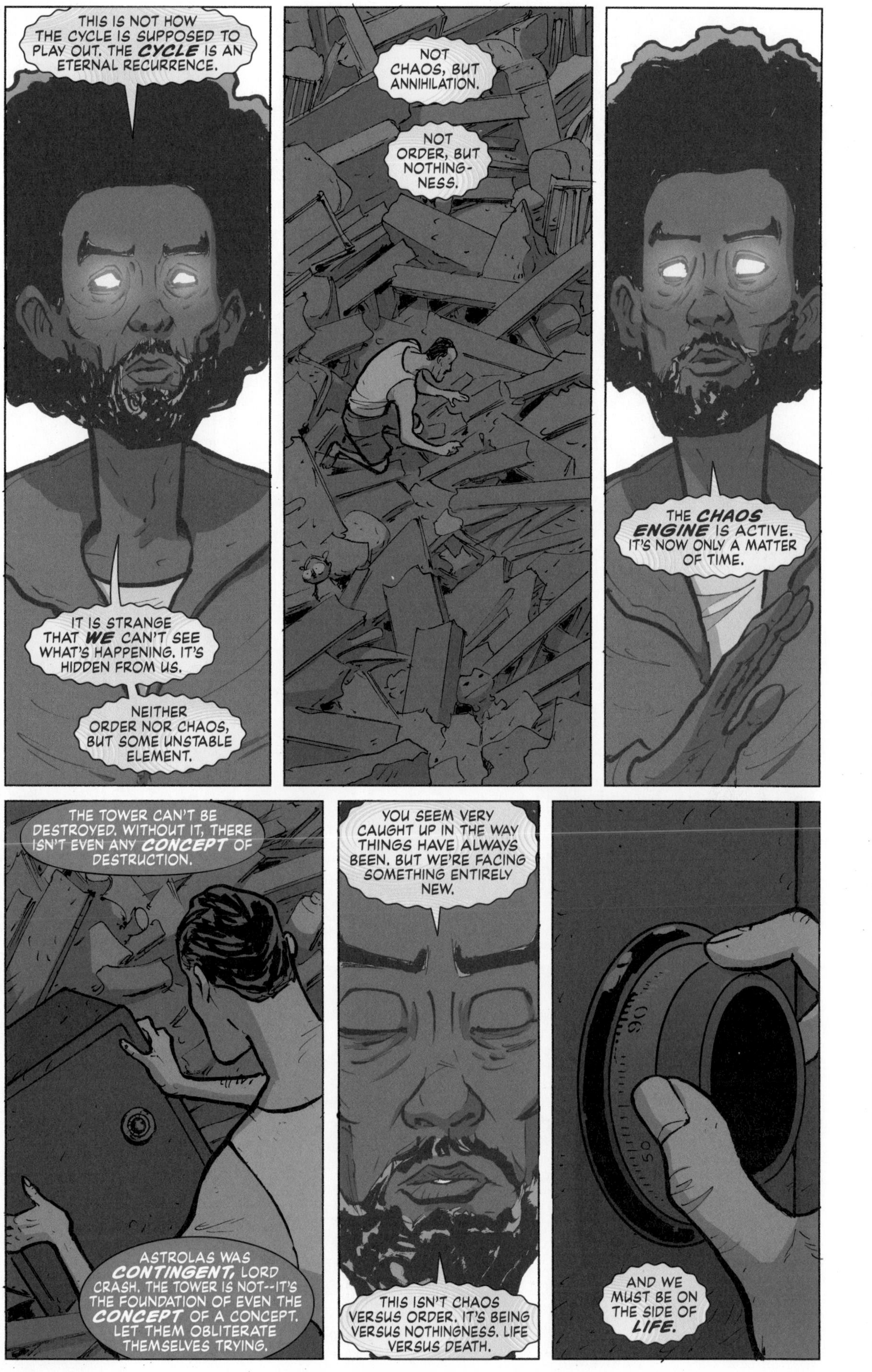
THIS IS NOT HOW THE CYCLE IS SUPPOSED TO PLAY OUT. THE CYCLE IS AN ETERNAL RECURRENCE.
IT IS STRANGE THAT WE CAN'T SEE WHAT'S HAPPENING. IT'S HIDDEN FROM US.
NEITHER ORDER NOR CHAOS, BUT SOME UNSTABLE ELEMENT.
NOT CHAOS, BUT ANNIHILATION.
NOT ORDER, BUT NOTHING-NESS.
THE CHAOS ENGINE IS ACTIVE. IT'S NOW ONLY A MATTER OF TIME.
THE TOWER CAN'T BE DESTROYED. WITHOUT IT, THERE ISN'T EVEN ANY CONCEPT OF DESTRUCTION.
ASTROLAS WAS CONTINGENT, LORD CRASH. THE TOWER IS NOT--IT'S THE FOUNDATION OF EVEN THE CONCEPT OF A CONCEPT. LET THEM OBLITERATE THEMSELVES TRYING.
YOU SEEM VERY CAUGHT UP IN THE WAY THINGS HAVE ALWAYS BEEN. BUT WE'RE FACING SOMETHING ENTIRELY NEW.
THIS ISN'T CHAOS VERSUS ORDER. IT'S BEING VERSUS NOTHINGNESS. LIFE VERSUS DEATH.
AND WE MUST BE ON THE SIDE OF LIFE.

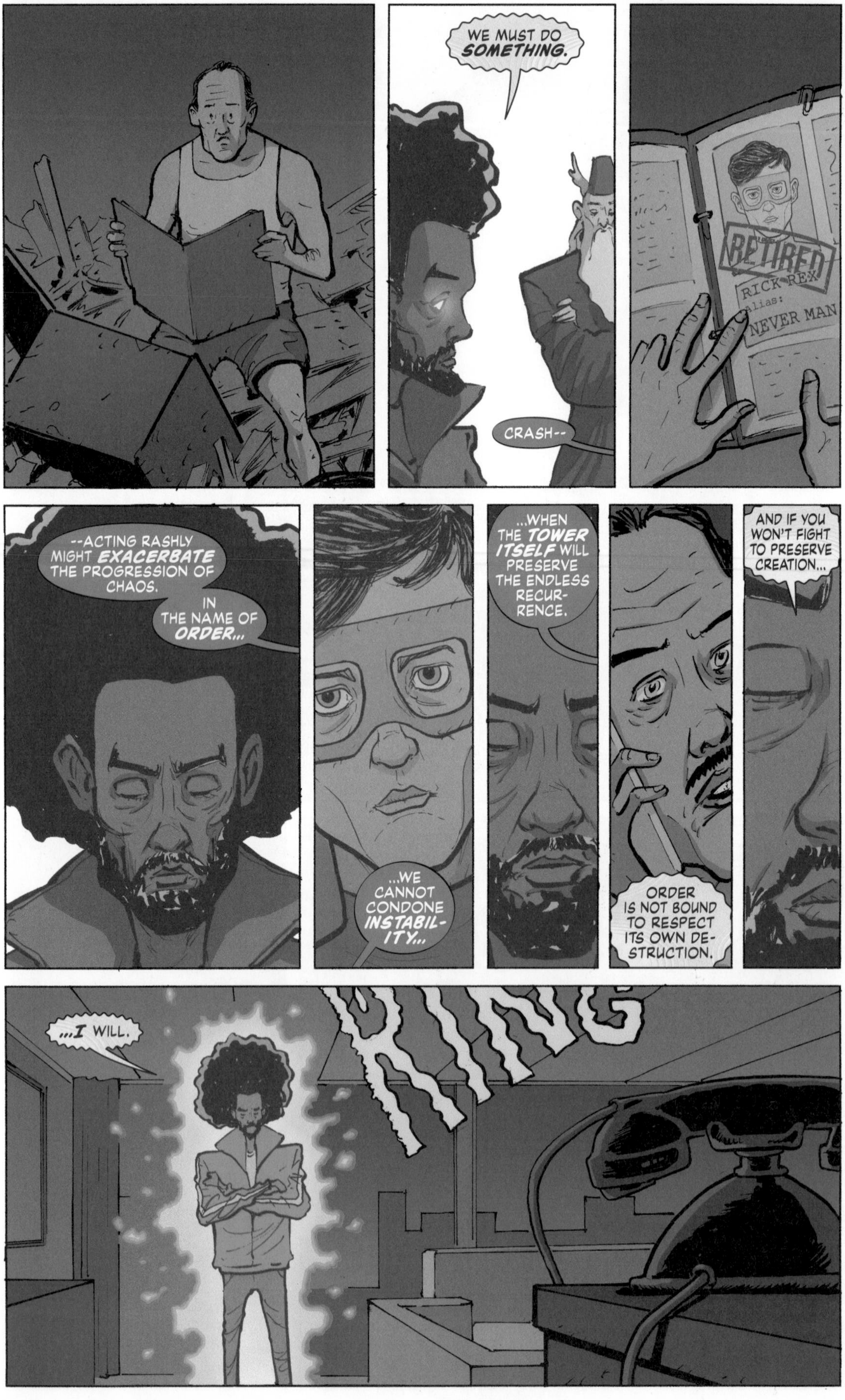

WE MUST DO SOMETHING.
CRASH--
RETIRED
RICK REX
alias:
NEVER MAN
--ACTING RASHLY MIGHT EXACERBATE THE PROGRESSION OF CHAOS.
IN THE NAME OF ORDER...
...WE CANNOT CONDONE INSTABIL-ITY...
...WHEN THE TOWER ITSELF WILL PRESERVE THE ENDLESS RECUR-RENCE.
ORDER IS NOT BOUND TO RESPECT ITS OWN DE-STRUCTION.
AND IF YOU WON'T FIGHT TO PRESERVE CREATION...
...I WILL.
RING

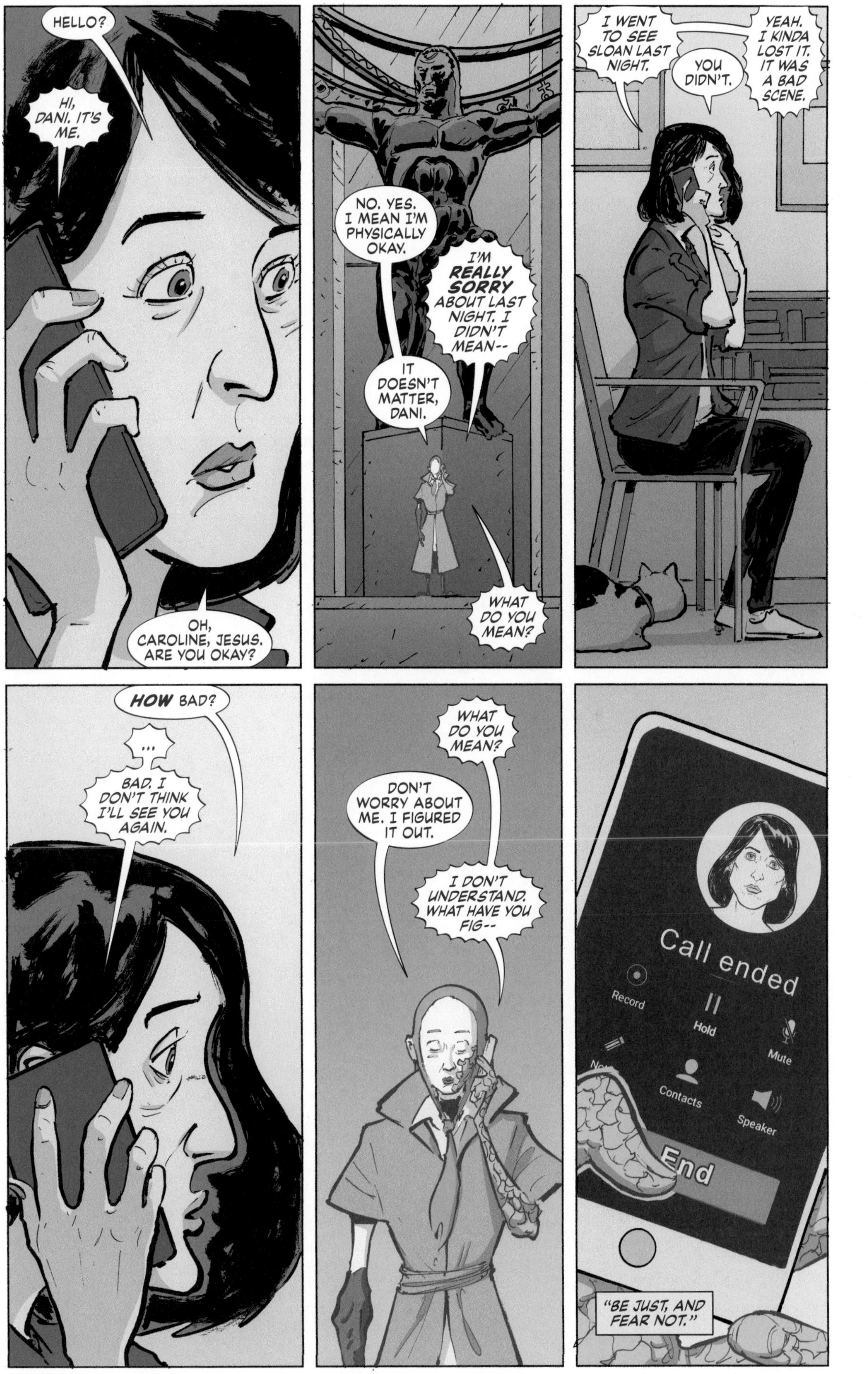
HELLO?
HI, DANI. IT'S ME.
OH, CAROLINE, JESUS. ARE YOU OKAY?
NO. YES. I MEAN I'M PHYSICALLY OKAY.
I'M REALLY SORRY ABOUT LAST NIGHT. I DIDN'T MEAN--
IT DOESN'T MATTER, DANI.
WHAT DO YOU MEAN?
I WENT TO SEE SLOAN LAST NIGHT.
YOU DIDN'T.
YEAH. I KINDA LOST IT. IT WAS A BAD SCENE.
HOW BAD?
...
BAD. I DON'T THINK I'LL SEE YOU AGAIN.
WHAT DO YOU MEAN?
DON'T WORRY ABOUT ME. I FIGURED IT OUT.
I DON'T UNDERSTAND. WHAT HAVE YOU FIG--
Call ended
Record
Hold
Mute
Contacts
Speaker
End
"BE JUST, AND FEAR NOT."

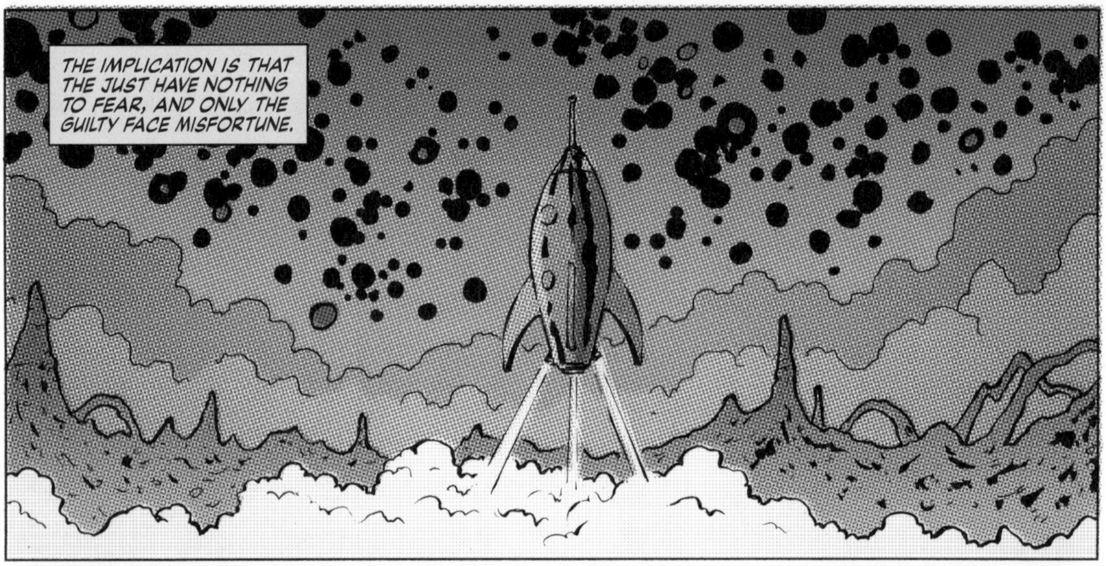
THE IMPLICATION IS THAT THE JUST HAVE NOTHING TO FEAR, AND ONLY THE GUILTY FACE MISFORTUNE.

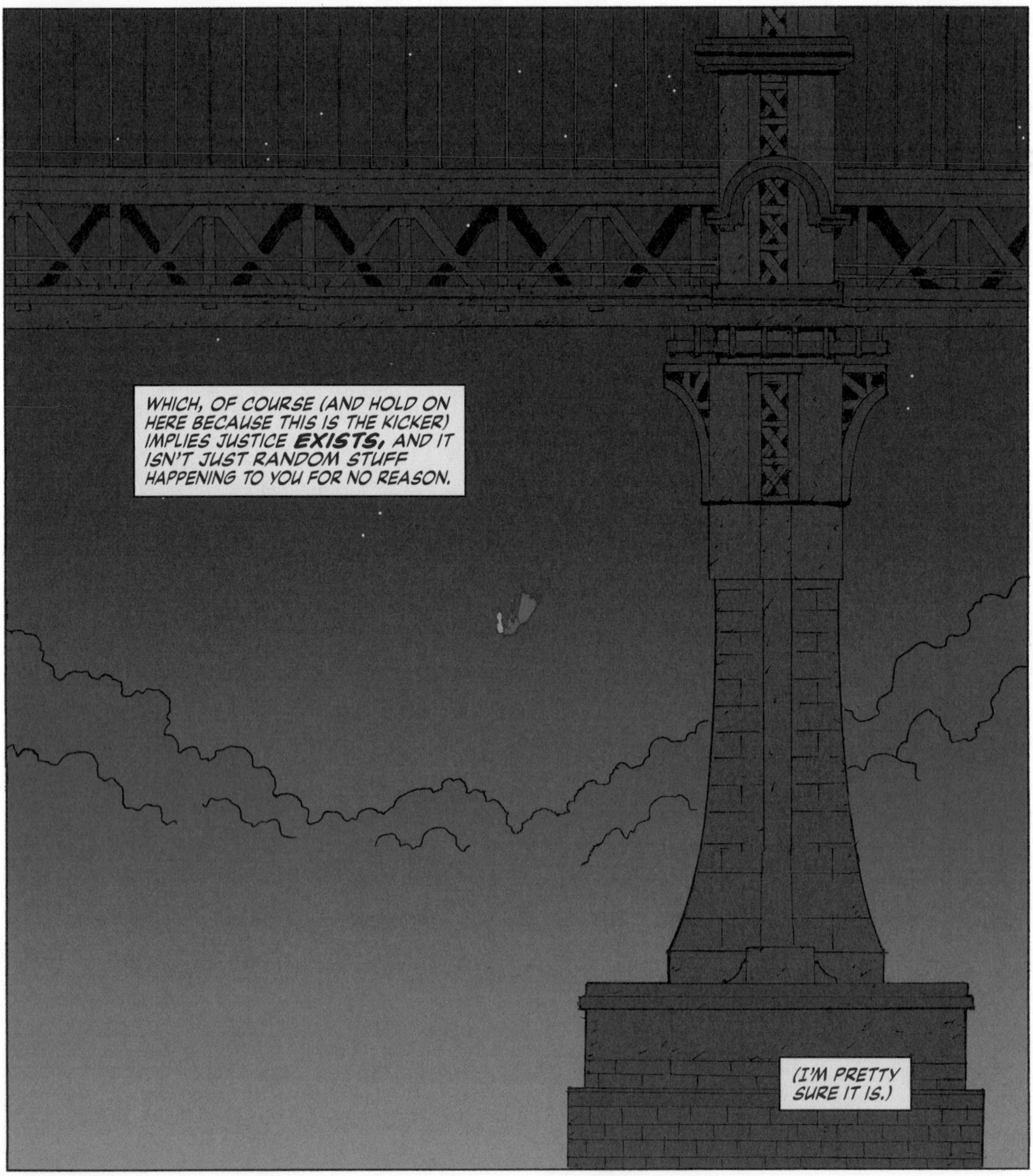
WHICH, OF COURSE (AND HOLD ON HERE BECAUSE THIS IS THE KICKER) IMPLIES JUSTICE EXISTS, AND IT ISN'T JUST RANDOM STUFF HAPPENING TO YOU FOR NO REASON.
(I'M PRETTY SURE IT IS.)

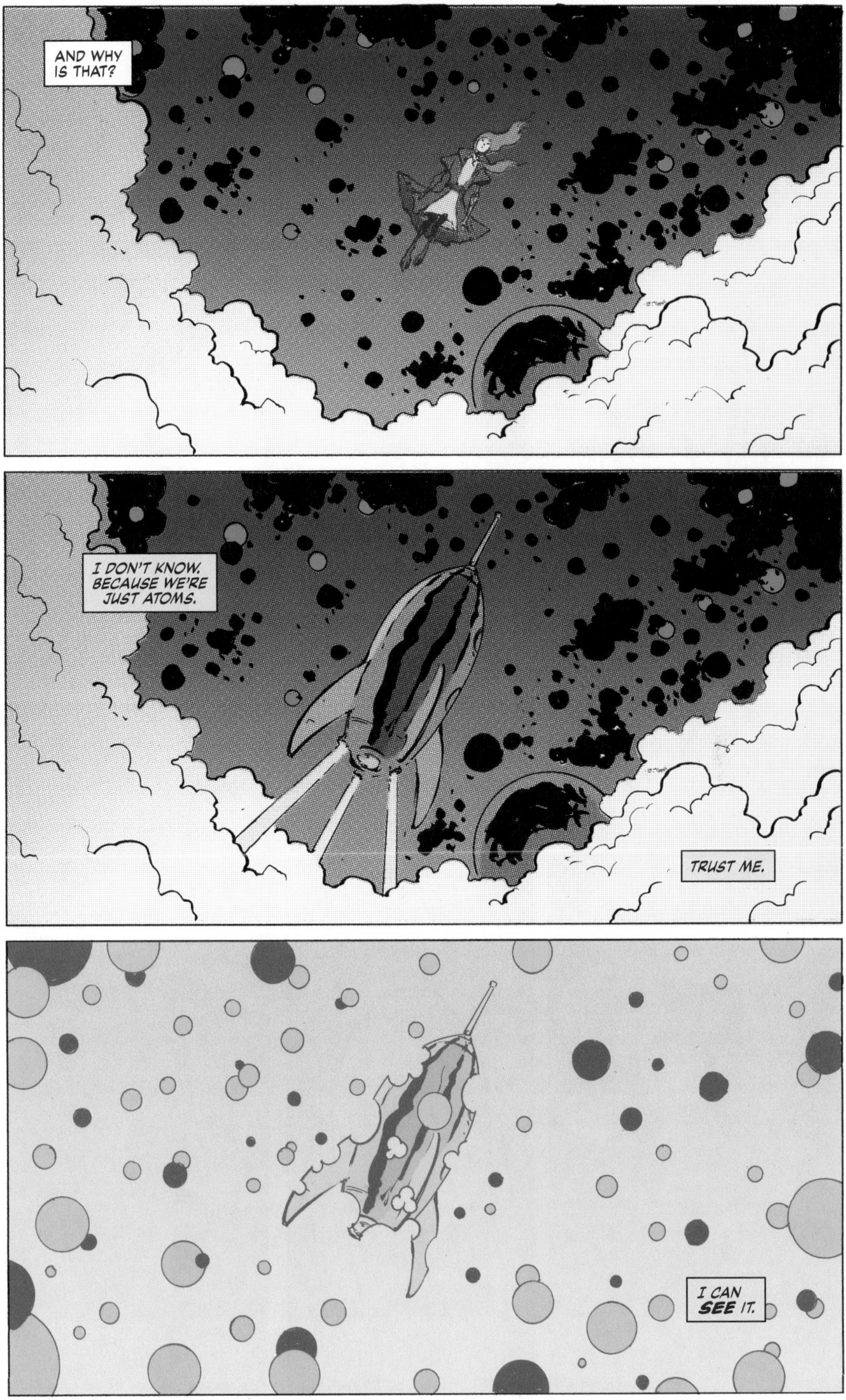
AND WHY IS THAT?
I DON'T KNOW. BECAUSE WE'RE JUST ATOMS.
TRUST ME.
I CAN SEE IT.

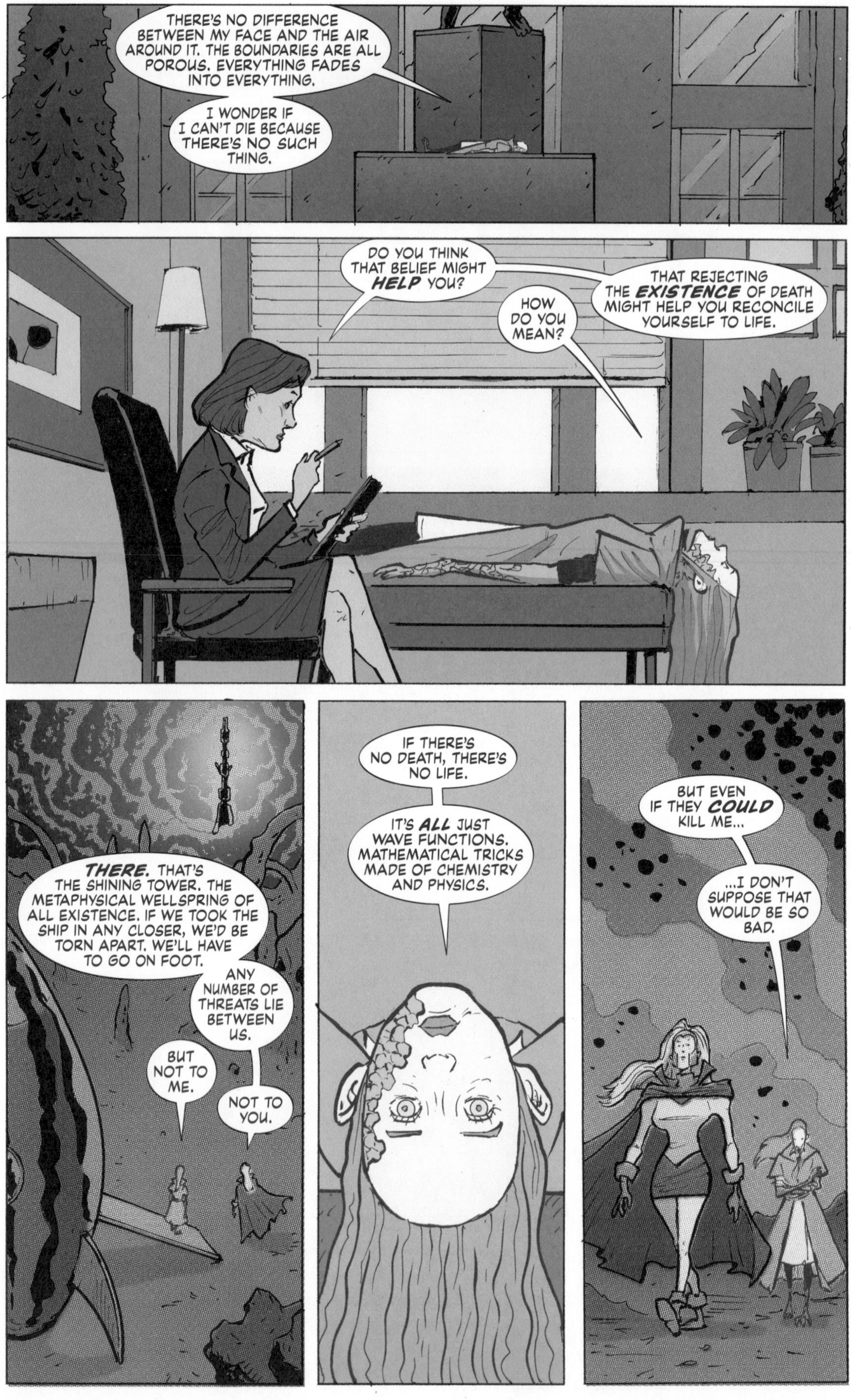
THERE'S NO DIFFERENCE BETWEEN MY FACE AND THE AIR AROUND IT. THE BOUNDARIES ARE ALL POROUS. EVERYTHING FADES INTO EVERYTHING.
I WONDER IF I CAN'T DIE BECAUSE THERE'S NO SUCH THING.
DO YOU THINK THAT BELIEF MIGHT **HELP** YOU?
HOW DO YOU MEAN?
THAT REJECTING THE **EXISTENCE** OF DEATH MIGHT HELP YOU RECONCILE YOURSELF TO LIFE.
THERE. THAT'S THE SHINING TOWER. THE METAPHYSICAL WELLSPRING OF ALL EXISTENCE. IF WE TOOK THE SHIP IN ANY CLOSER, WE'D BE TORN APART. WE'LL HAVE TO GO ON FOOT.
ANY NUMBER OF THREATS LIE BETWEEN US.
BUT NOT TO ME.
NOT TO YOU.
IF THERE'S NO DEATH, THERE'S NO LIFE.
IT'S **ALL** JUST WAVE FUNCTIONS. MATHEMATICAL TRICKS MADE OF CHEMISTRY AND PHYSICS.
BUT EVEN IF THEY **COULD** KILL ME...
...I DON'T SUPPOSE THAT WOULD BE SO BAD.

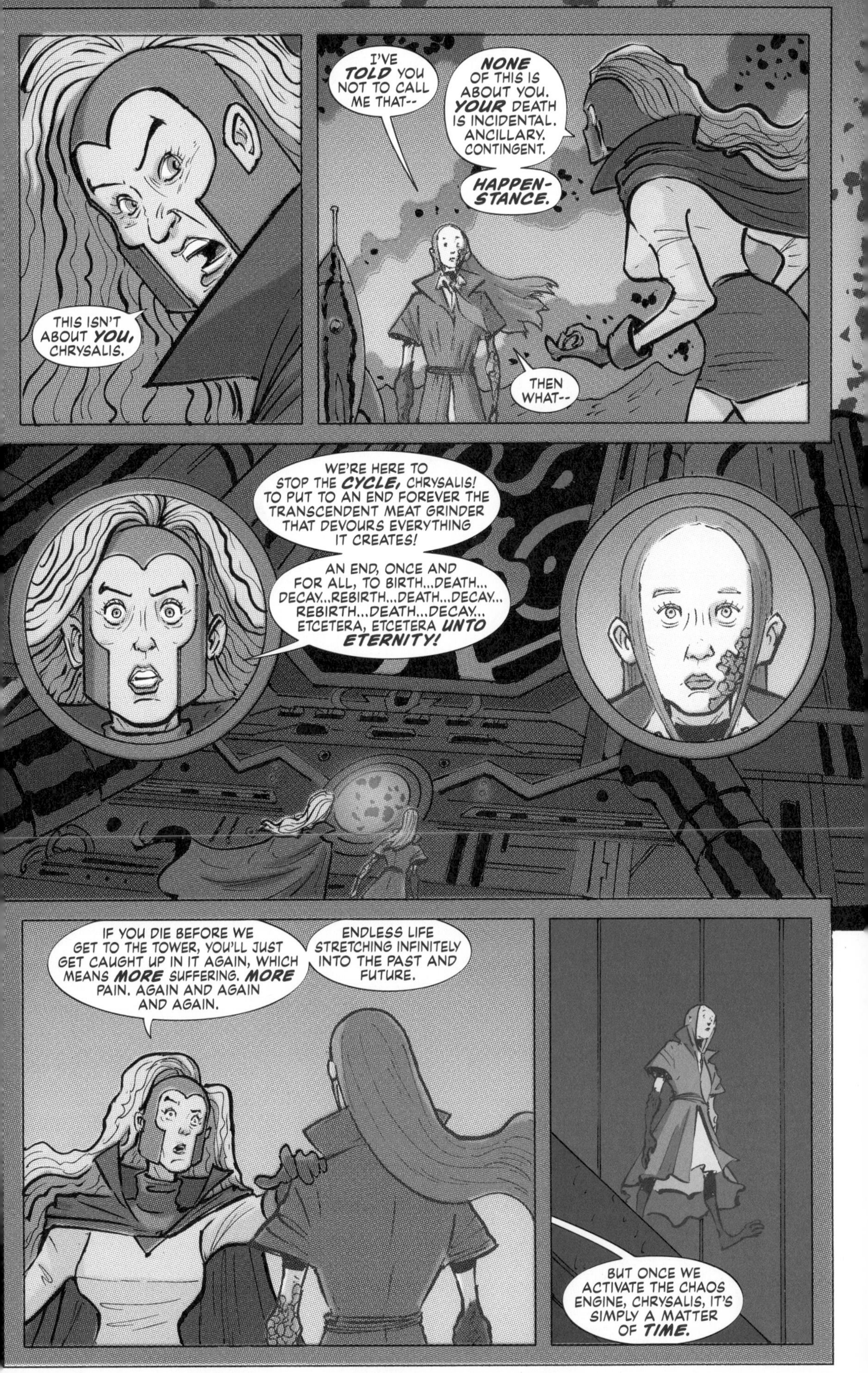

THIS ISN'T ABOUT YOU, CHRYSALIS.
I'VE TOLD YOU NOT TO CALL ME THAT--
NONE OF THIS IS ABOUT YOU. YOUR DEATH IS INCIDENTAL. ANCILLARY. CONTINGENT.
HAPPEN-STANCE.
THEN WHAT--
WE'RE HERE TO STOP THE CYCLE, CHRYSALIS! TO PUT TO AN END FOREVER THE TRANSCENDENT MEAT GRINDER THAT DEVOURS EVERYTHING IT CREATES!
AN END, ONCE AND FOR ALL, TO BIRTH...DEATH... DECAY...REBIRTH...DEATH...DECAY... REBIRTH...DEATH...DECAY... ETCETERA, ETCETERA UNTO ETERNITY!
IF YOU DIE BEFORE WE GET TO THE TOWER, YOU'LL JUST GET CAUGHT UP IN IT AGAIN, WHICH MEANS MORE SUFFERING. MORE PAIN. AGAIN AND AGAIN AND AGAIN.
ENDLESS LIFE STRETCHING INFINITELY INTO THE PAST AND FUTURE.
BUT ONCE WE ACTIVATE THE CHAOS ENGINE, CHRYSALIS, IT'S SIMPLY A MATTER OF TIME.

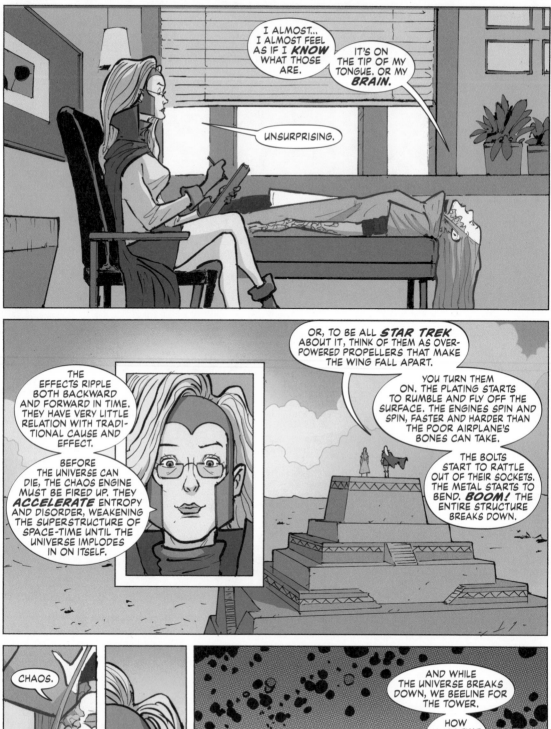

I ALMOST... I ALMOST FEEL AS IF I *KNOW* WHAT THOSE ARE.

IT'S ON THE TIP OF MY TONGUE. OR MY *BRAIN.*

UNSURPRISING.

THE EFFECTS RIPPLE BOTH BACKWARD AND FORWARD IN TIME. THEY HAVE VERY LITTLE RELATION WITH TRADITIONAL CAUSE AND EFFECT.

BEFORE THE UNIVERSE CAN DIE, THE CHAOS ENGINE MUST BE FIRED UP. THEY *ACCELERATE* ENTROPY AND DISORDER, WEAKENING THE SUPERSTRUCTURE OF SPACE-TIME UNTIL THE UNIVERSE IMPLODES IN ON ITSELF.

OR, TO BE ALL *STAR TREK* ABOUT IT, THINK OF THEM AS OVER-POWERED PROPELLERS THAT MAKE THE WING FALL APART.

YOU TURN THEM ON. THE PLATING STARTS TO RUMBLE AND FLY OFF THE SURFACE. THE ENGINES SPIN AND SPIN, FASTER AND HARDER THAN THE POOR AIRPLANE'S BONES CAN TAKE.

THE BOLTS START TO RATTLE OUT OF THEIR SOCKETS, THE METAL STARTS TO BEND. *BOOM!* THE ENTIRE STRUCTURE BREAKS DOWN.

CHAOS.

EXACTLY.

AND WHILE THE UNIVERSE BREAKS DOWN, WE BEELINE FOR THE TOWER.

HOW MUCH TIME WILL WE HAVE?

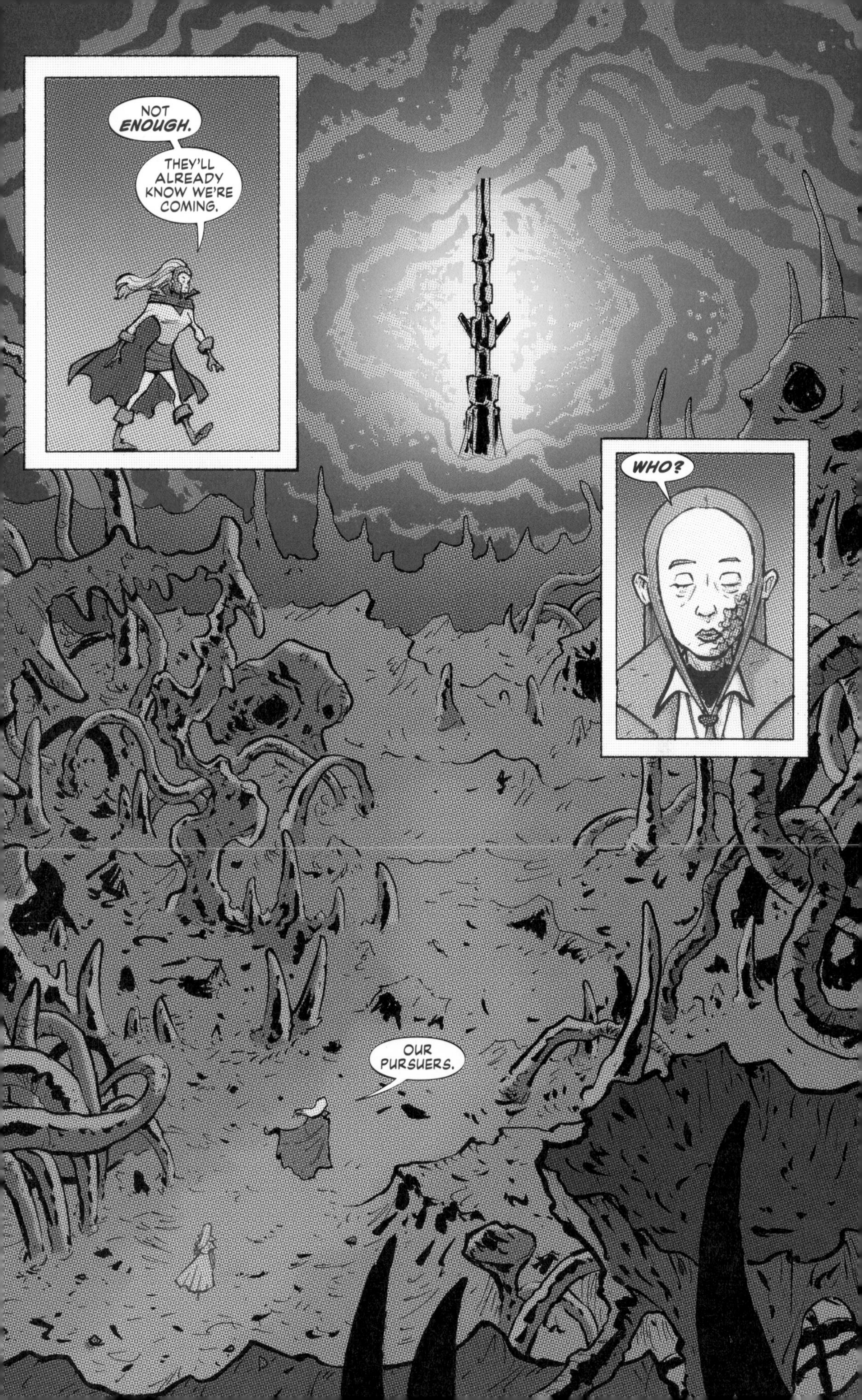
NOT *ENOUGH.*
THEY'LL ALREADY KNOW WE'RE COMING.
WHO?
OUR PURSUERS.

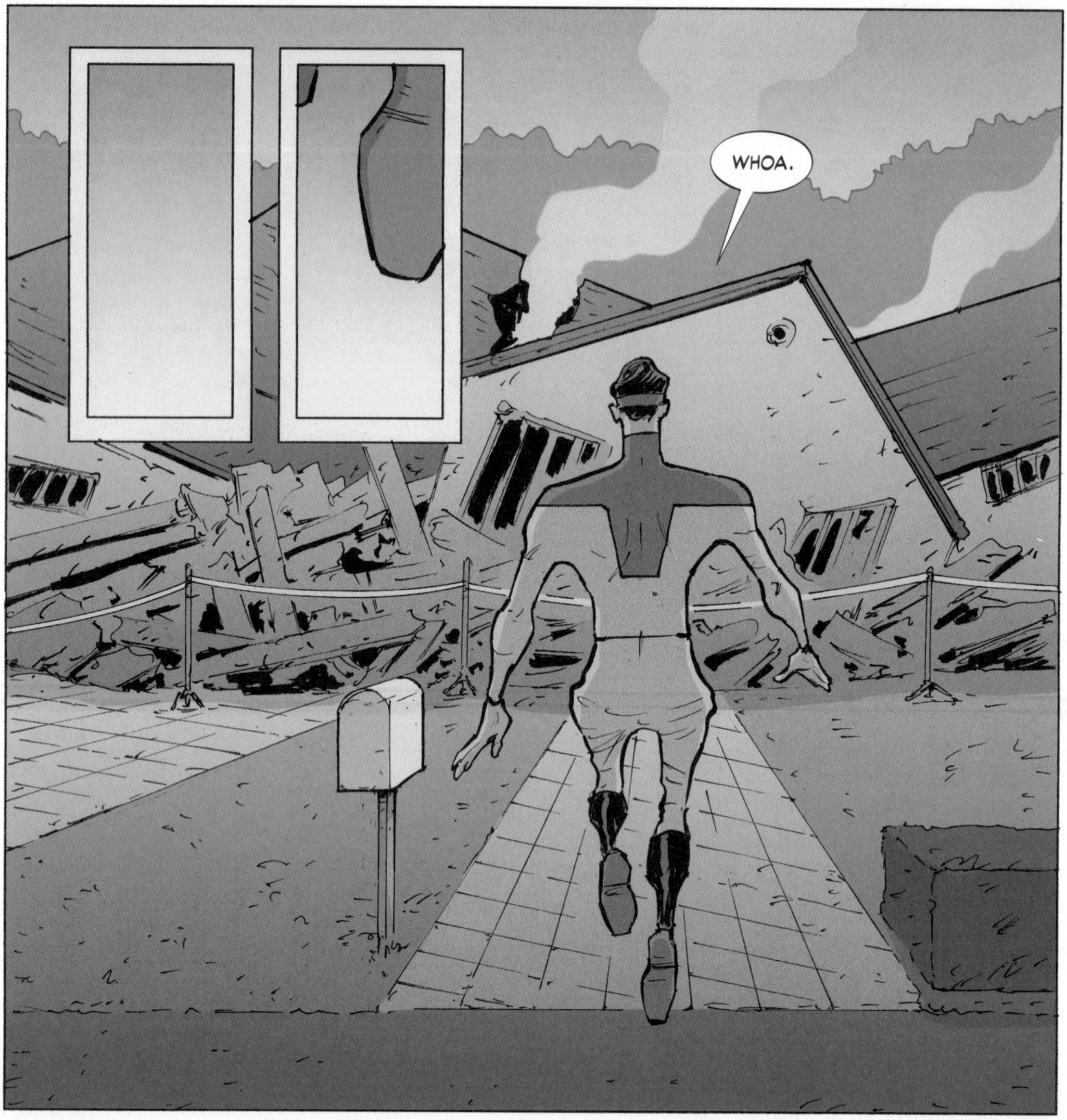
WHOA.

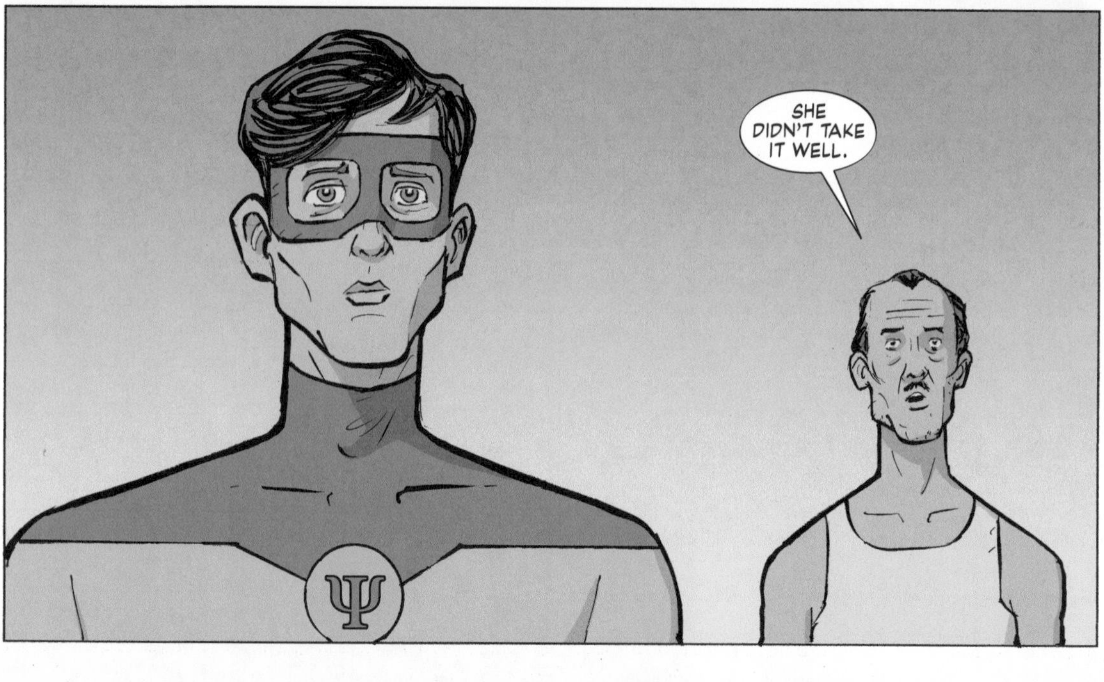
SHE DIDN'T TAKE IT WELL.

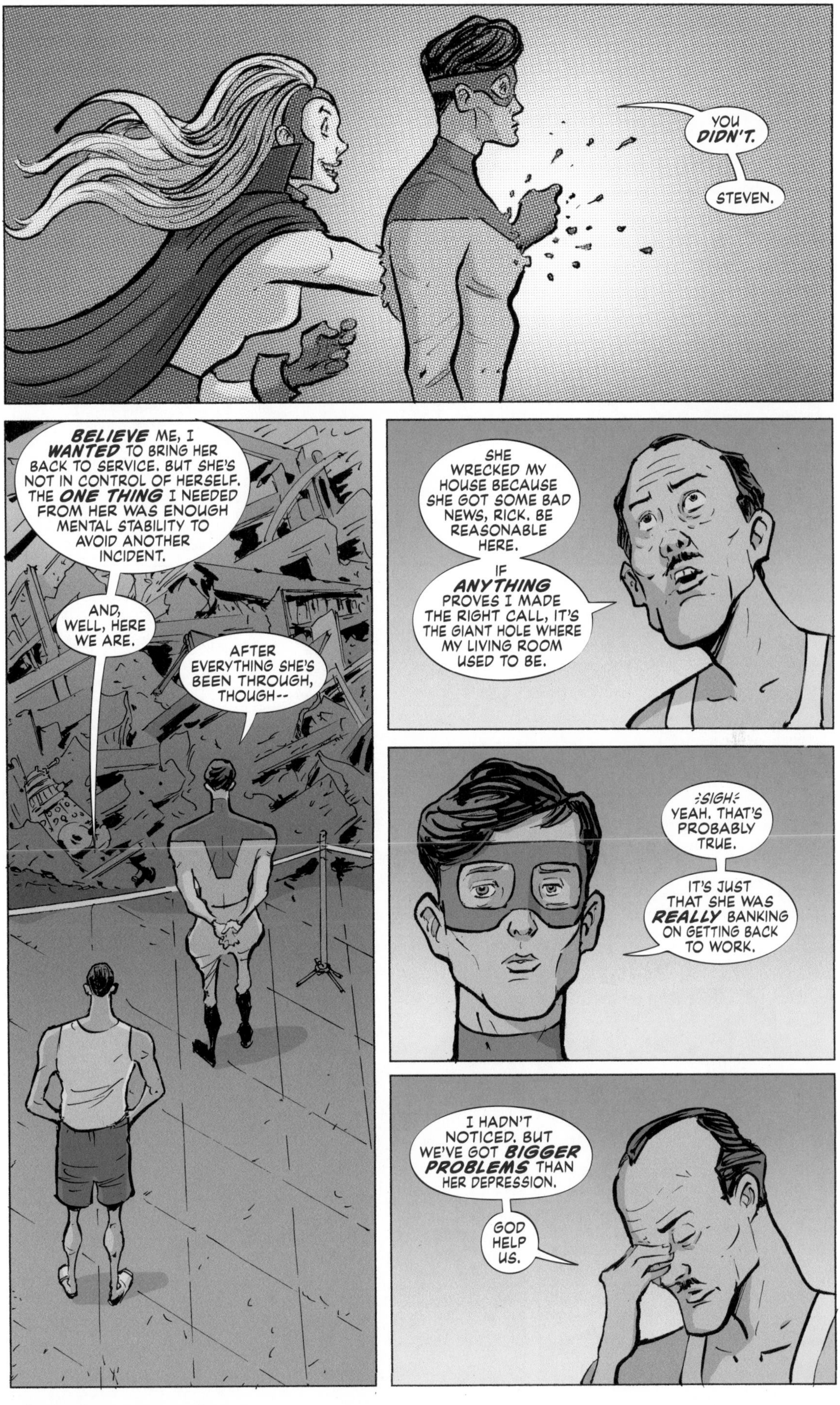
YOU DIDN'T.
STEVEN.
BELIEVE ME, I WANTED TO BRING HER BACK TO SERVICE. BUT SHE'S NOT IN CONTROL OF HERSELF. THE ONE THING I NEEDED FROM HER WAS ENOUGH MENTAL STABILITY TO AVOID ANOTHER INCIDENT.
AND, WELL, HERE WE ARE.
AFTER EVERYTHING SHE'S BEEN THROUGH, THOUGH--
SHE WRECKED MY HOUSE BECAUSE SHE GOT SOME BAD NEWS, RICK. BE REASONABLE HERE.
IF ANYTHING PROVES I MADE THE RIGHT CALL, IT'S THE GIANT HOLE WHERE MY LIVING ROOM USED TO BE.
SIGH
YEAH. THAT'S PROBABLY TRUE.
IT'S JUST THAT SHE WAS REALLY BANKING ON GETTING BACK TO WORK.
I HADN'T NOTICED. BUT WE'VE GOT BIGGER PROBLEMS THAN HER DEPRESSION.
GOD HELP US.

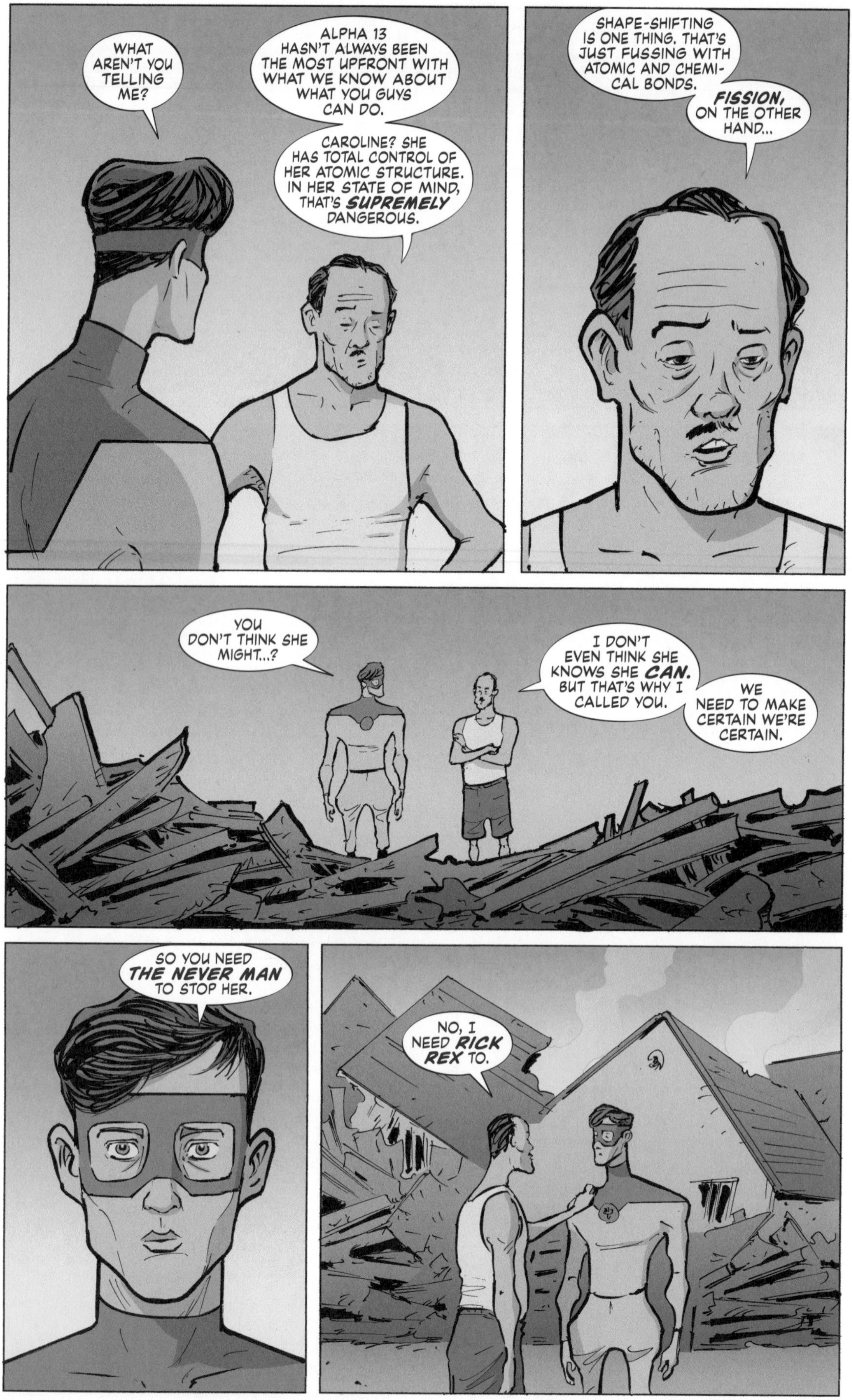
WHAT AREN'T YOU TELLING ME?
ALPHA 13 HASN'T ALWAYS BEEN THE MOST UPFRONT WITH WHAT WE KNOW ABOUT WHAT YOU GUYS CAN DO.
CAROLINE? SHE HAS TOTAL CONTROL OF HER ATOMIC STRUCTURE. IN HER STATE OF MIND, THAT'S SUPREMELY DANGEROUS.
SHAPE-SHIFTING IS ONE THING. THAT'S JUST FUSSING WITH ATOMIC AND CHEMICAL BONDS.
FISSION, ON THE OTHER HAND...
YOU DON'T THINK SHE MIGHT...?
I DON'T EVEN THINK SHE KNOWS SHE CAN. BUT THAT'S WHY I CALLED YOU.
WE NEED TO MAKE CERTAIN WE'RE CERTAIN.
SO YOU NEED THE NEVER MAN TO STOP HER.
NO, I NEED RICK REX TO.

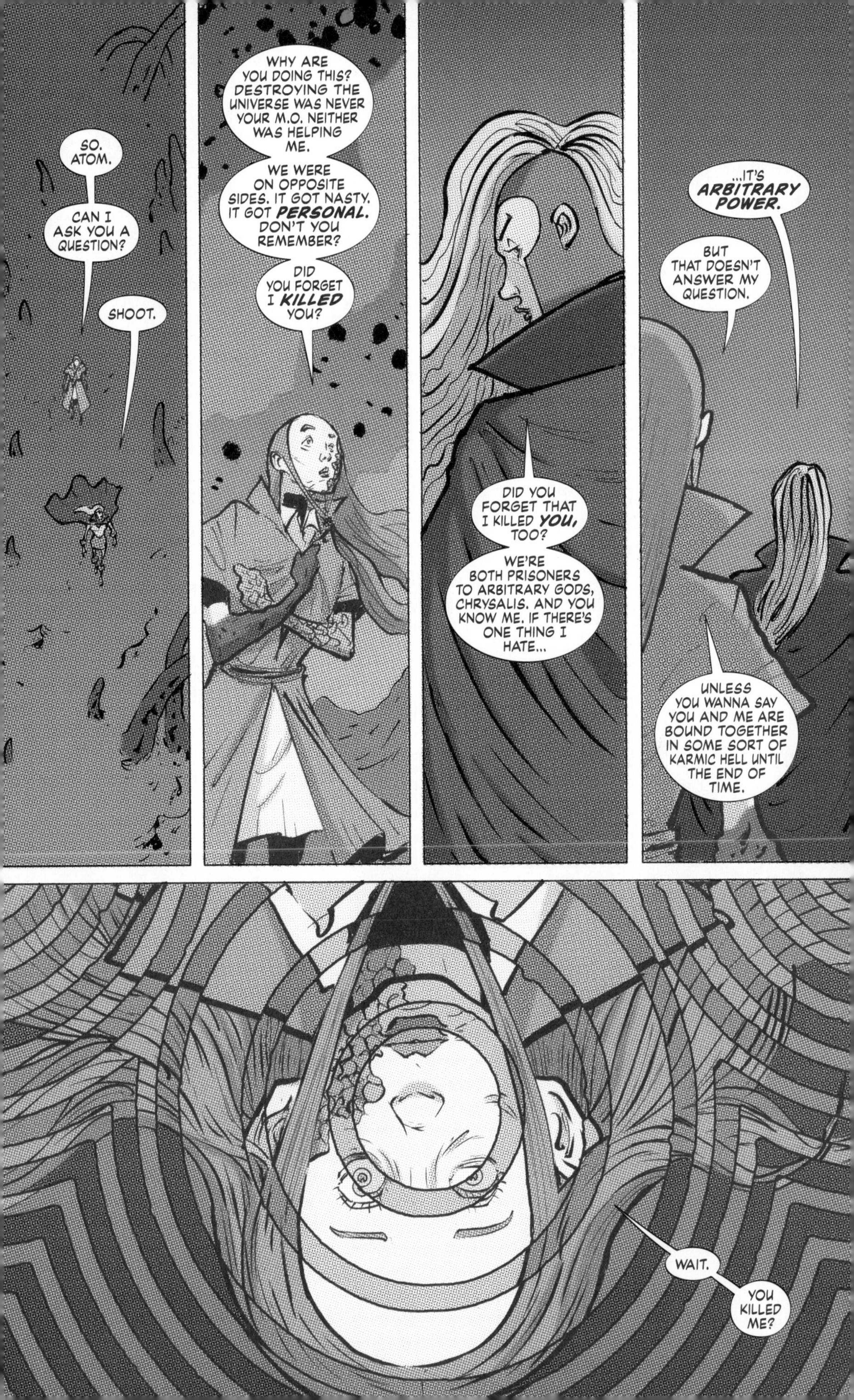
SO. ATOM.
CAN I ASK YOU A QUESTION?
SHOOT.
WHY ARE YOU DOING THIS? DESTROYING THE UNIVERSE WAS NEVER YOUR M.O. NEITHER WAS HELPING ME.
WE WERE ON OPPOSITE SIDES. IT GOT NASTY. IT GOT PERSONAL. DON'T YOU REMEMBER?
DID YOU FORGET I KILLED YOU?
DID YOU FORGET THAT I KILLED YOU, TOO?
WE'RE BOTH PRISONERS TO ARBITRARY GODS, CHRYSALIS. AND YOU KNOW ME. IF THERE'S ONE THING I HATE...
...IT'S ARBITRARY POWER.
BUT THAT DOESN'T ANSWER MY QUESTION.
UNLESS YOU WANNA SAY YOU AND ME ARE BOUND TOGETHER IN SOME SORT OF KARMIC HELL UNTIL THE END OF TIME.
WAIT.
YOU KILLED ME?

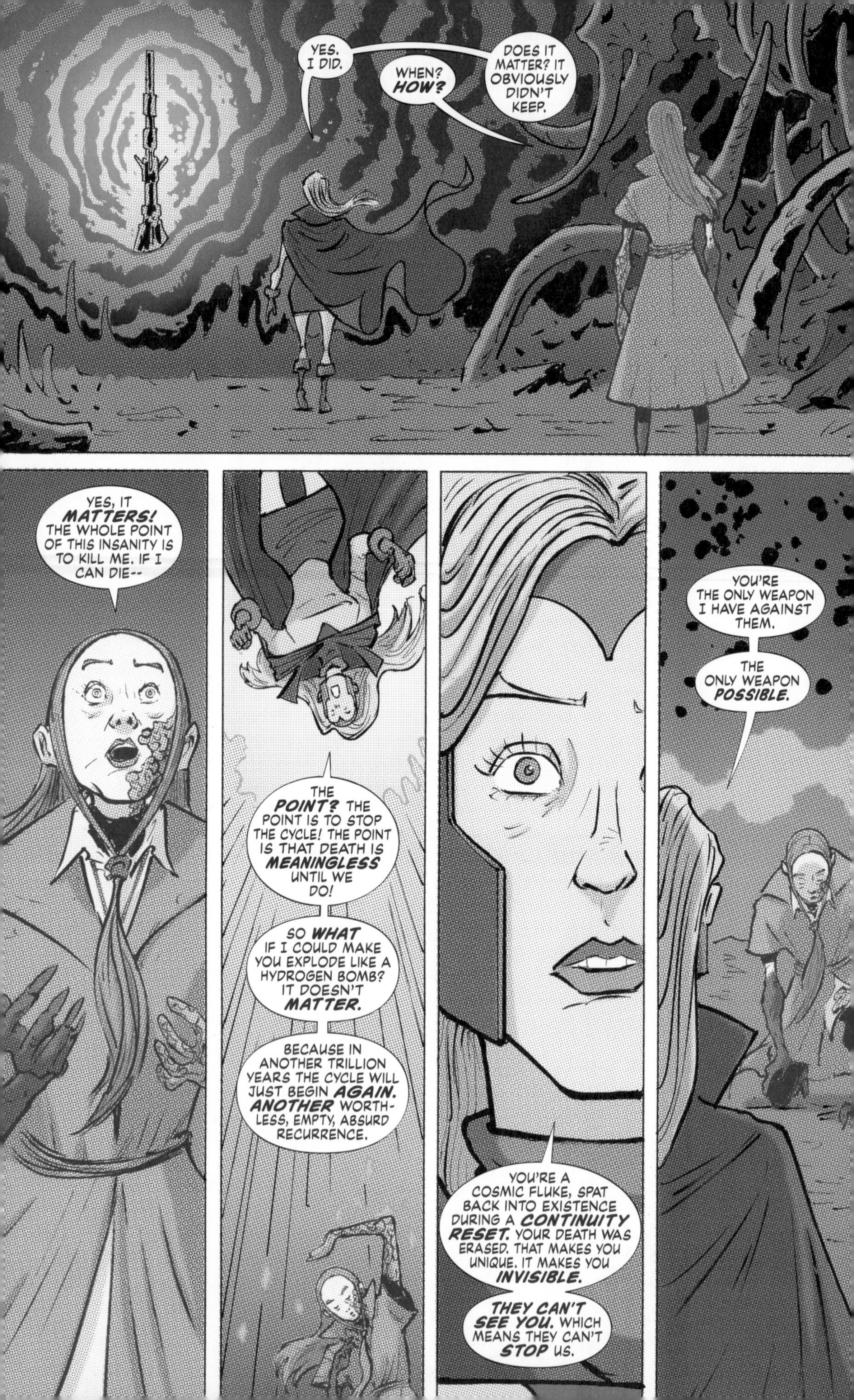
YES. I DID.
WHEN? HOW?
DOES IT MATTER? IT OBVIOUSLY DIDN'T KEEP.
YES, IT MATTERS! THE WHOLE POINT OF THIS INSANITY IS TO KILL ME. IF I CAN DIE--
THE POINT? THE POINT IS TO STOP THE CYCLE! THE POINT IS THAT DEATH IS MEANINGLESS UNTIL WE DO!
SO WHAT IF I COULD MAKE YOU EXPLODE LIKE A HYDROGEN BOMB? IT DOESN'T MATTER.
BECAUSE IN ANOTHER TRILLION YEARS THE CYCLE WILL JUST BEGIN AGAIN. ANOTHER WORTHLESS, EMPTY, ABSURD RECURRENCE.
YOU'RE A COSMIC FLUKE, SPAT BACK INTO EXISTENCE DURING A CONTINUITY RESET. YOUR DEATH WAS ERASED. THAT MAKES YOU UNIQUE. IT MAKES YOU INVISIBLE.
THEY CAN'T SEE YOU. WHICH MEANS THEY CAN'T STOP US.
YOU'RE THE ONLY WEAPON I HAVE AGAINST THEM.
THE ONLY WEAPON POSSIBLE.

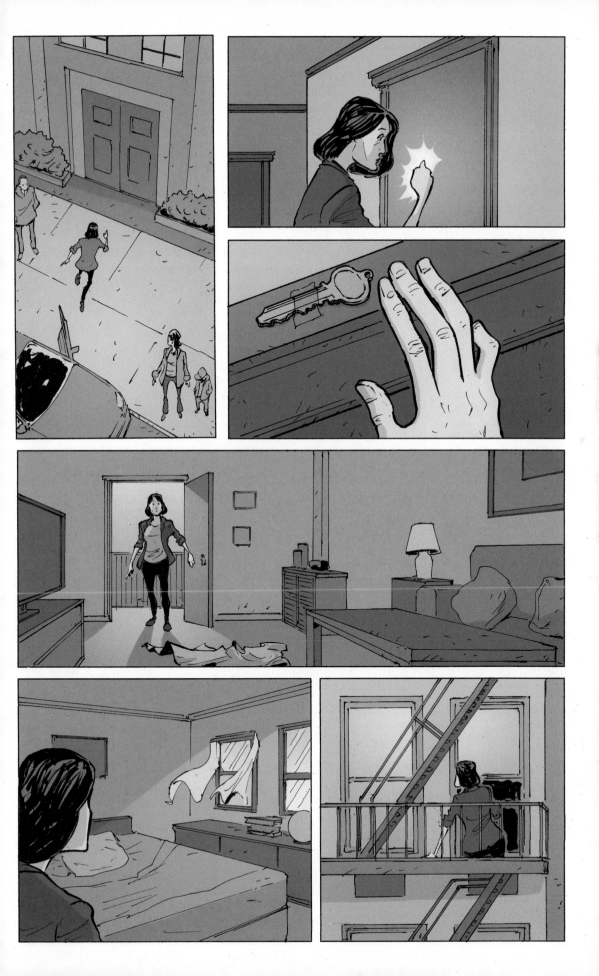

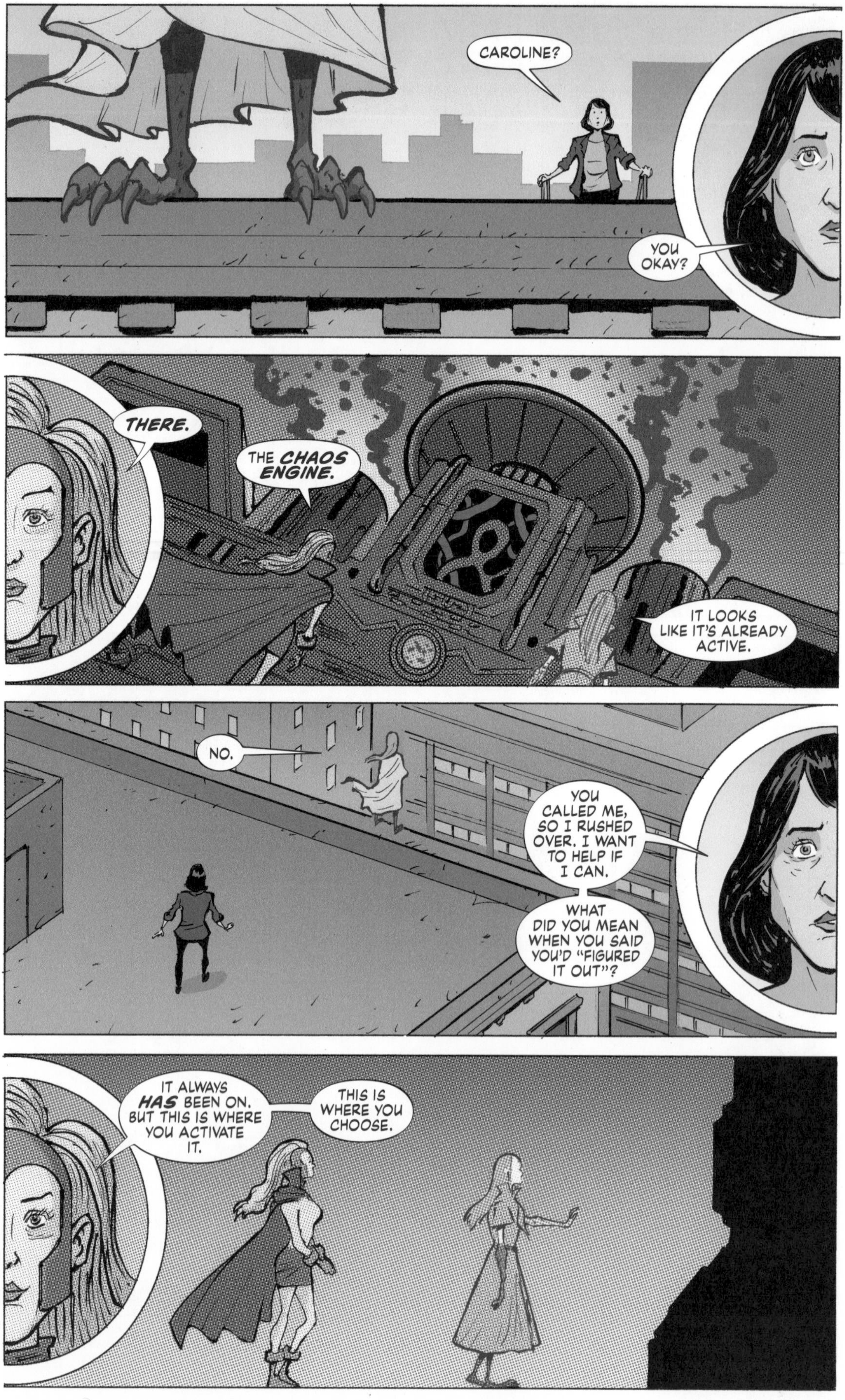
CAROLINE?
YOU OKAY?
THERE.
THE CHAOS ENGINE.
IT LOOKS LIKE IT'S ALREADY ACTIVE.
NO.
YOU CALLED ME, SO I RUSHED OVER. I WANT TO HELP IF I CAN.
WHAT DID YOU MEAN WHEN YOU SAID YOU'D "FIGURED IT OUT"?
IT ALWAYS HAS BEEN ON. BUT THIS IS WHERE YOU ACTIVATE IT.
THIS IS WHERE YOU CHOOSE.

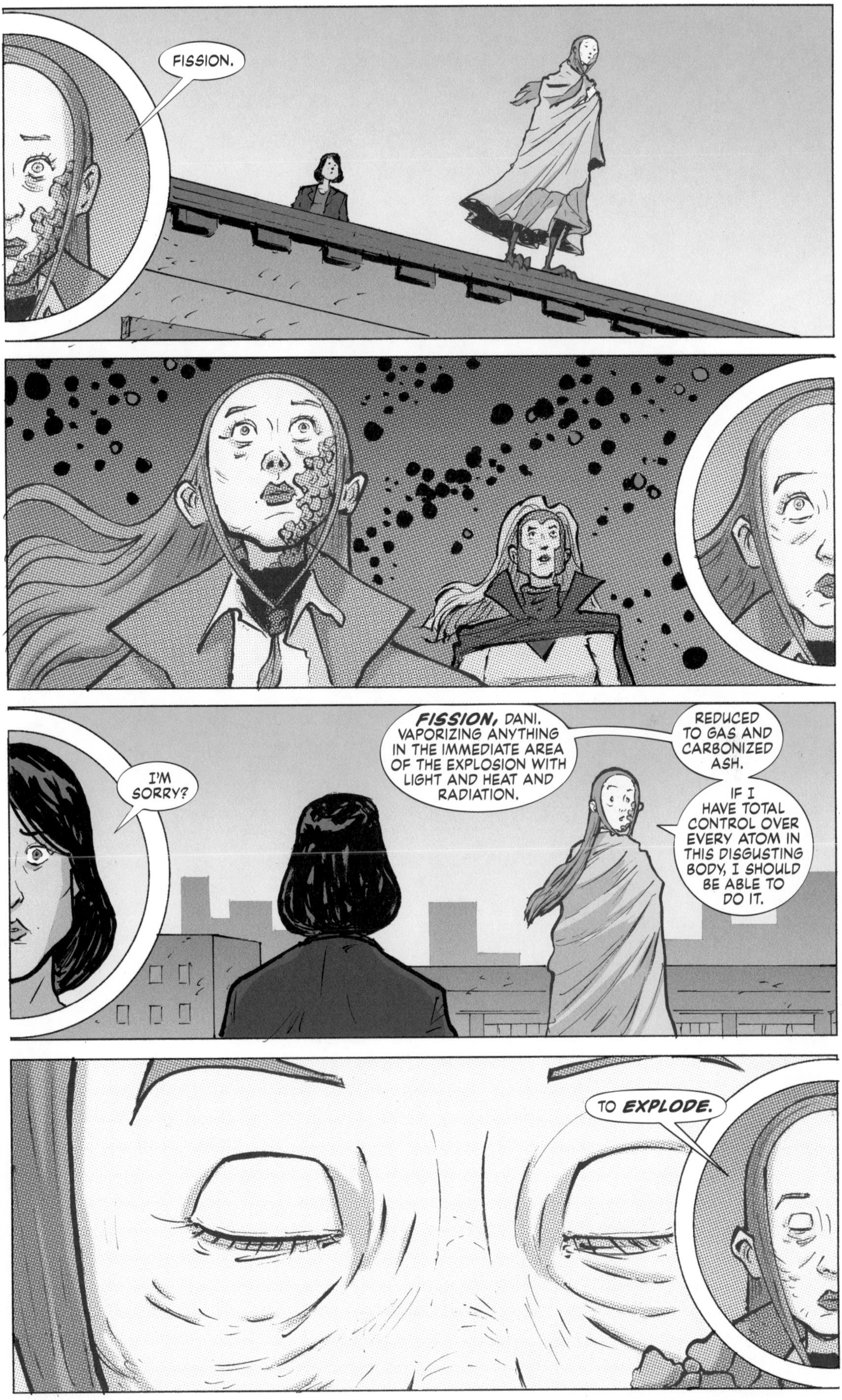
FISSION.
I'M SORRY?
FISSION, DANI. VAPORIZING ANYTHING IN THE IMMEDIATE AREA OF THE EXPLOSION WITH LIGHT AND HEAT AND RADIATION.
REDUCED TO GAS AND CARBONIZED ASH.
IF I HAVE TOTAL CONTROL OVER EVERY ATOM IN THIS DISGUSTING BODY, I SHOULD BE ABLE TO DO IT.
TO *EXPLODE.*

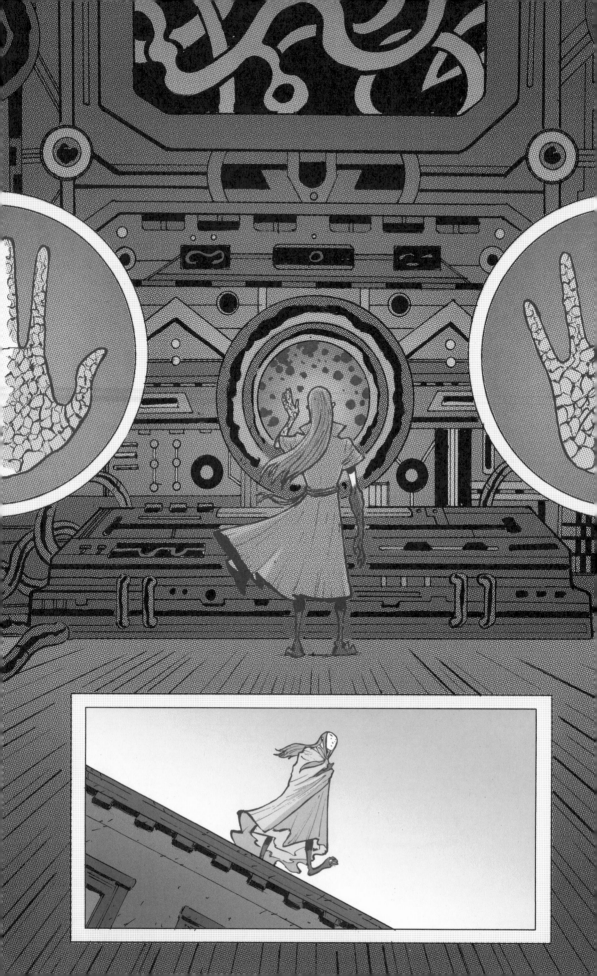

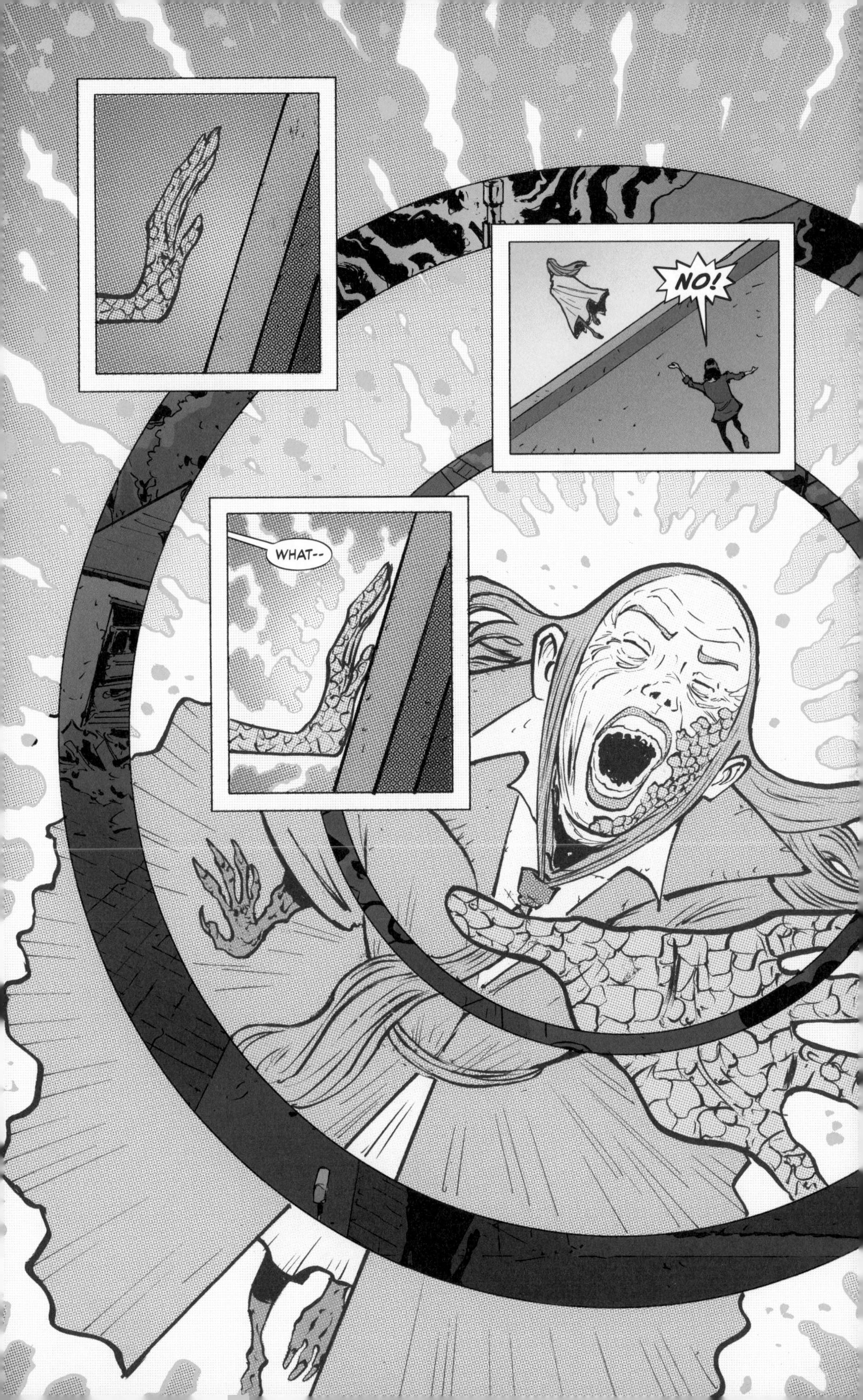
NO!
WHAT--

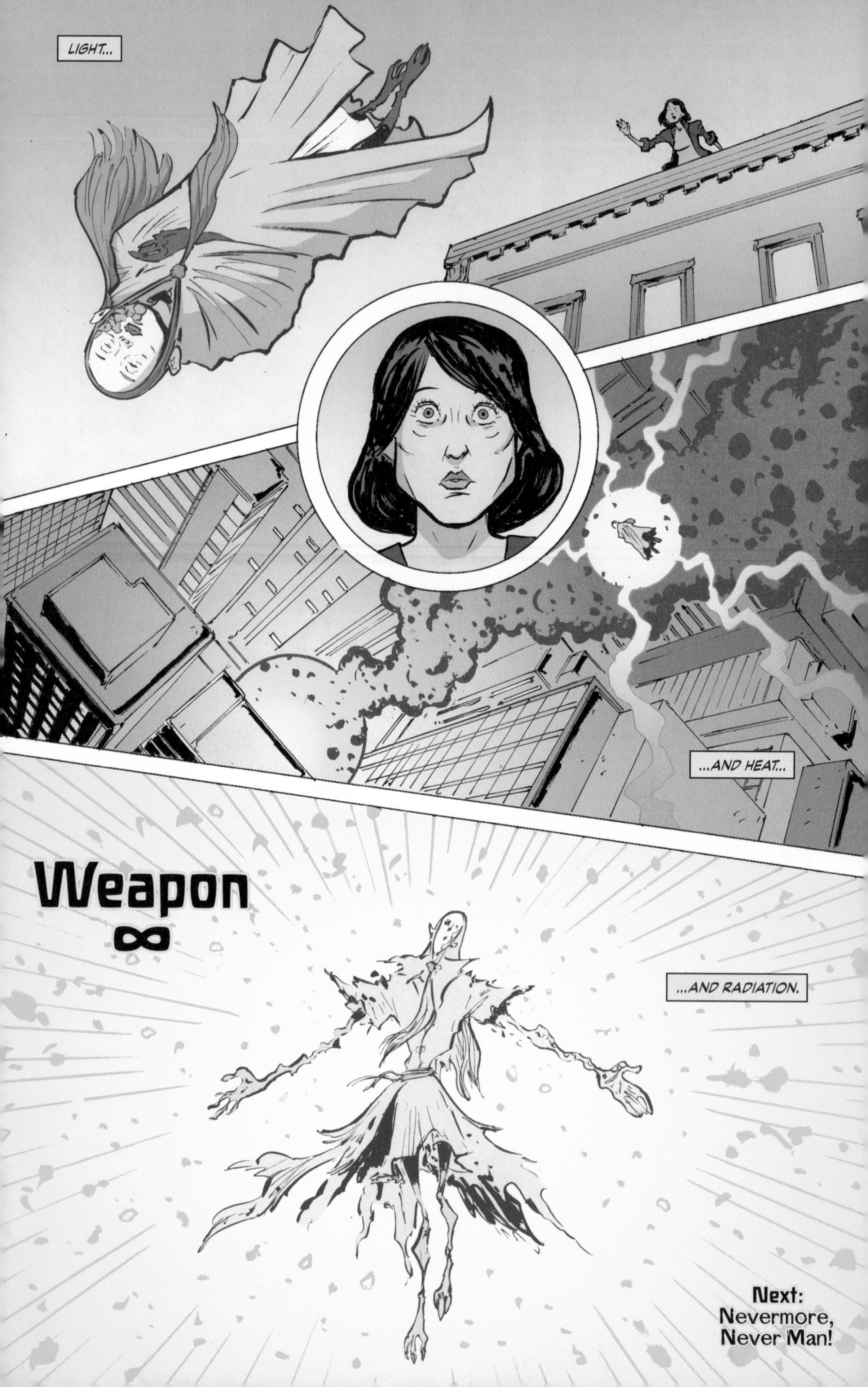
LIGHT...
...AND HEAT...
Weapon ∞
...AND RADIATION.
Next: Nevermore, Never Man!

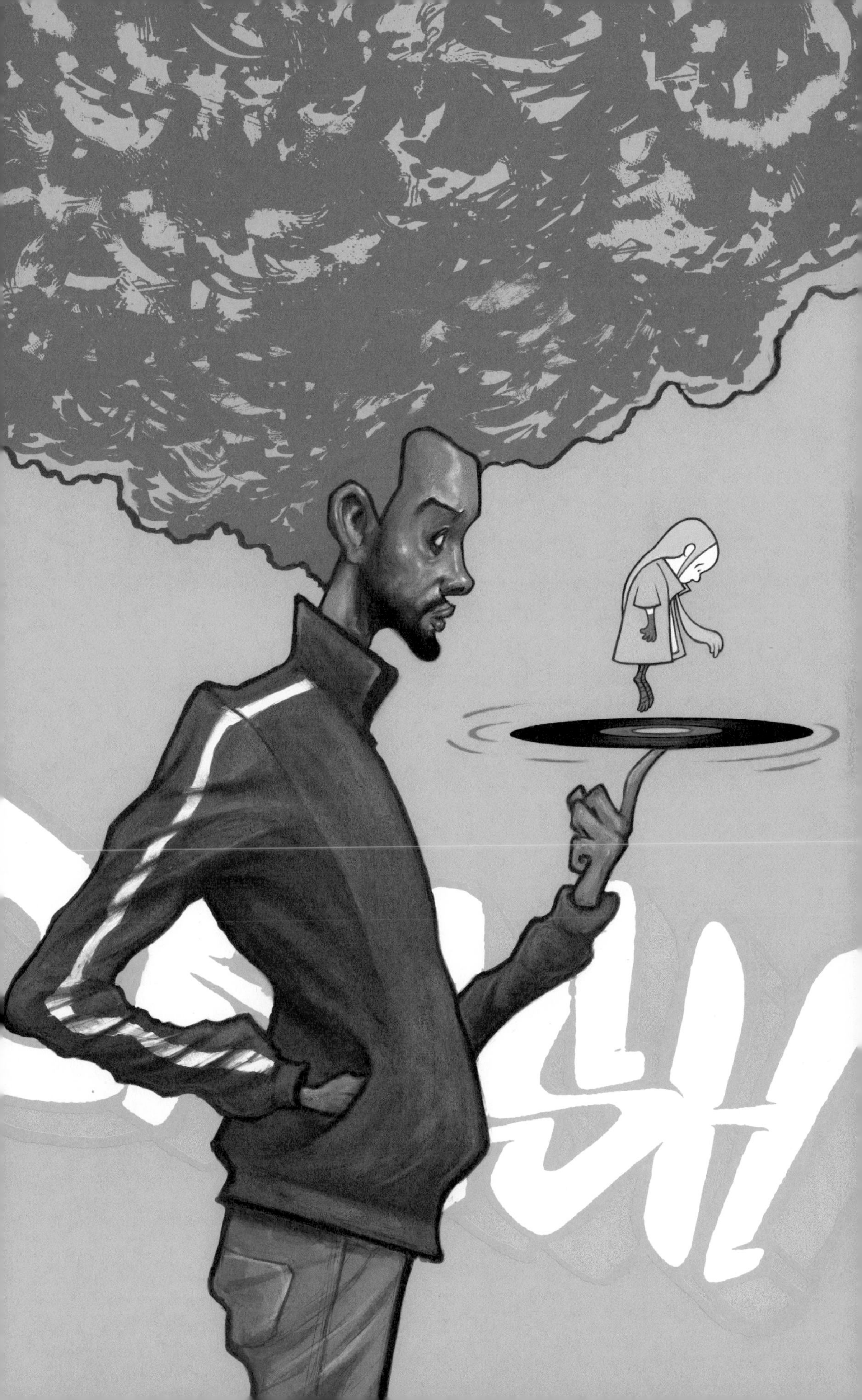

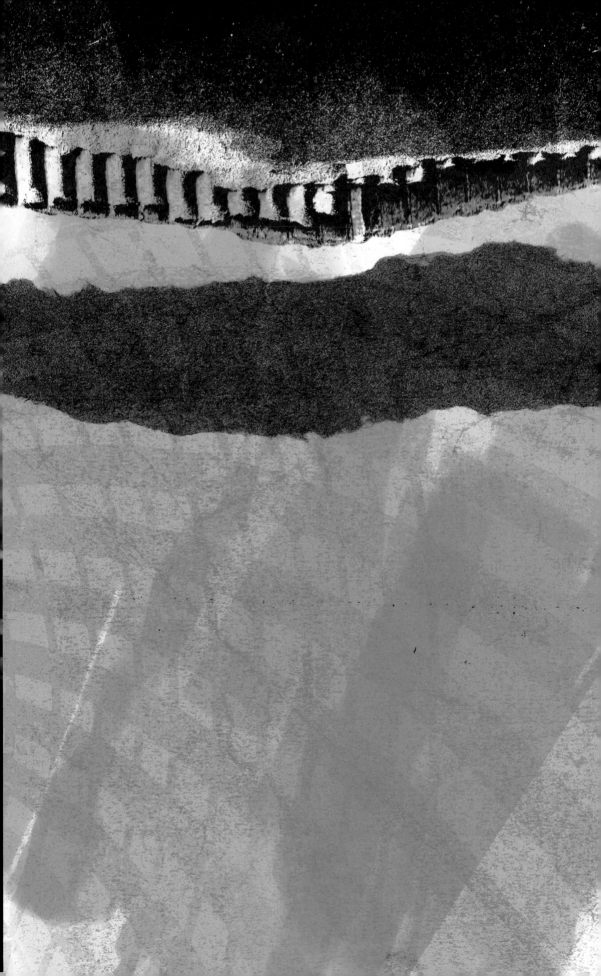

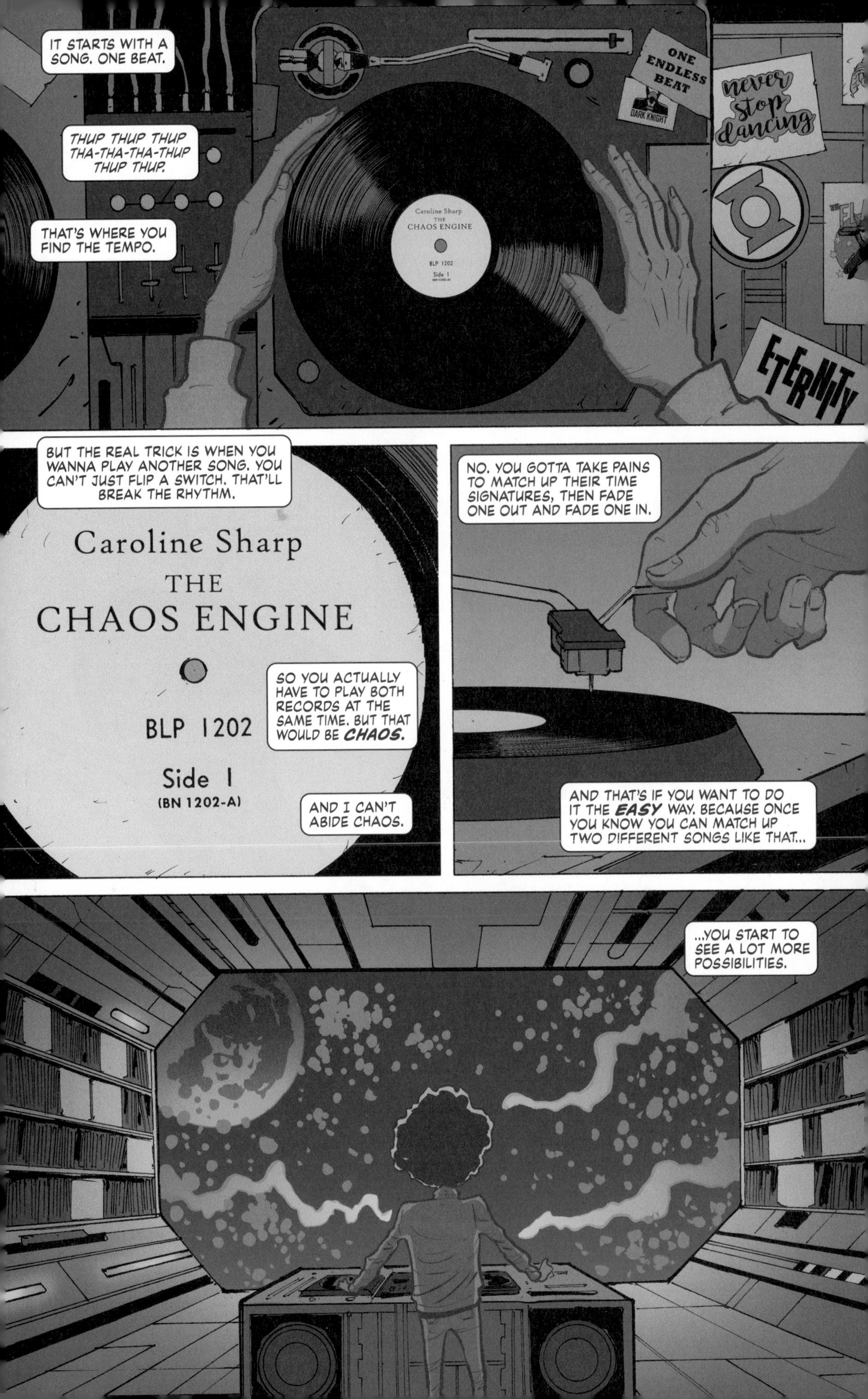
IT STARTS WITH A SONG. ONE BEAT.
ONE ENDLESS BEAT
DARK KNIGHT
never stop dancing
THUP THUP THUP THA-THA-THA-THUP THUP THUP.
Caroline Sharp THE CHAOS ENGINE BLP 1202 Side 1
THAT'S WHERE YOU FIND THE TEMPO.
ETERNITY
BUT THE REAL TRICK IS WHEN YOU WANNA PLAY ANOTHER SONG. YOU CAN'T JUST FLIP A SWITCH. THAT'LL BREAK THE RHYTHM.
Caroline Sharp
THE
CHAOS ENGINE
BLP 1202
Side 1
(BN 1202-A)
SO YOU ACTUALLY HAVE TO PLAY BOTH RECORDS AT THE SAME TIME. BUT THAT WOULD BE CHAOS.
AND I CAN'T ABIDE CHAOS.
NO. YOU GOTTA TAKE PAINS TO MATCH UP THEIR TIME SIGNATURES, THEN FADE ONE OUT AND FADE ONE IN.
AND THAT'S IF YOU WANT TO DO IT THE EASY WAY. BECAUSE ONCE YOU KNOW YOU CAN MATCH UP TWO DIFFERENT SONGS LIKE THAT...
...YOU START TO SEE A LOT MORE POSSIBILITIES.

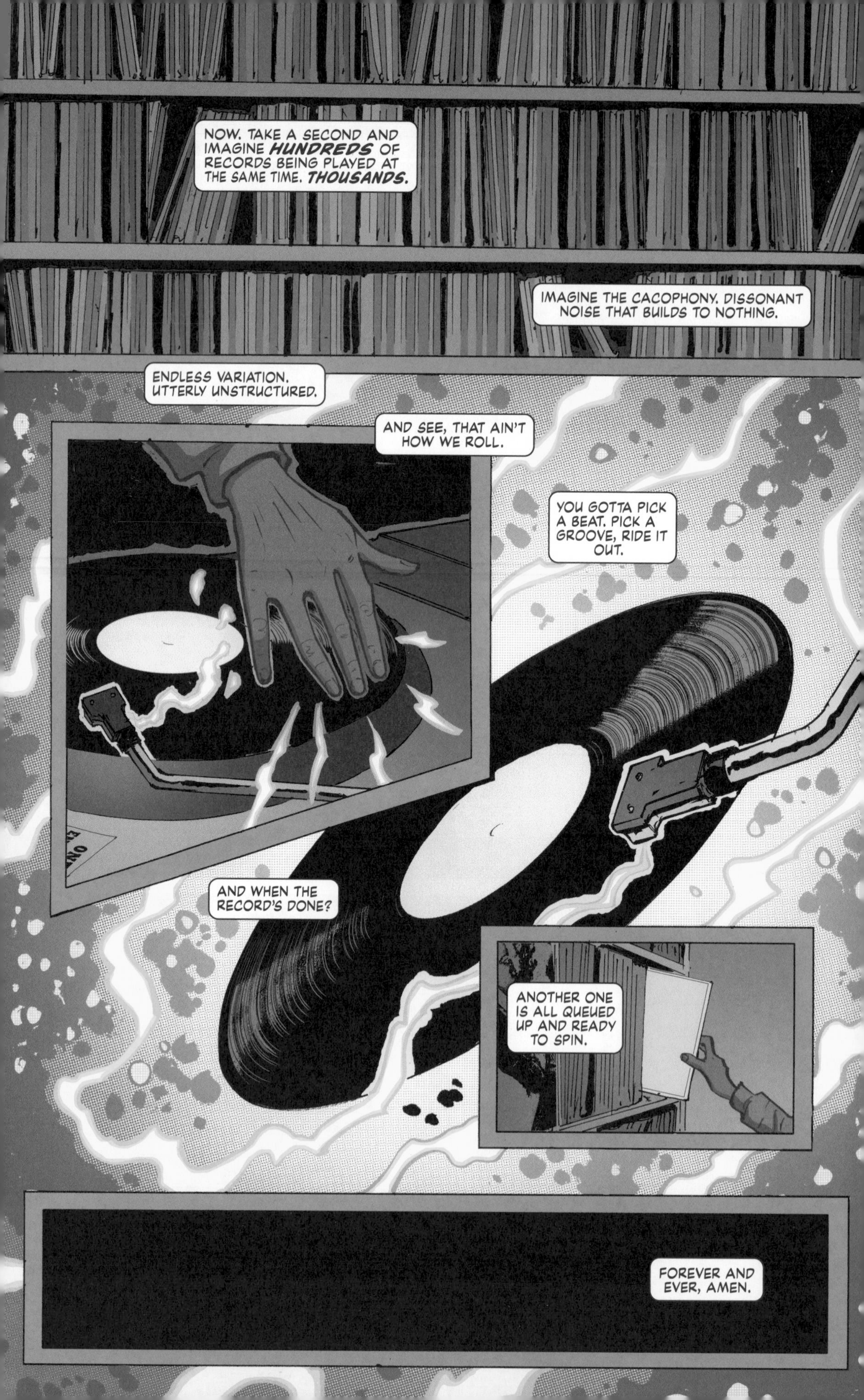
NOW. TAKE A SECOND AND IMAGINE HUNDREDS OF RECORDS BEING PLAYED AT THE SAME TIME. THOUSANDS.
IMAGINE THE CACOPHONY. DISSONANT NOISE THAT BUILDS TO NOTHING.
ENDLESS VARIATION. UTTERLY UNSTRUCTURED.
AND SEE, THAT AIN'T HOW WE ROLL.
YOU GOTTA PICK A BEAT. PICK A GROOVE, RIDE IT OUT.
AND WHEN THE RECORD'S DONE?
ANOTHER ONE IS ALL QUEUED UP AND READY TO SPIN.
FOREVER AND EVER, AMEN.

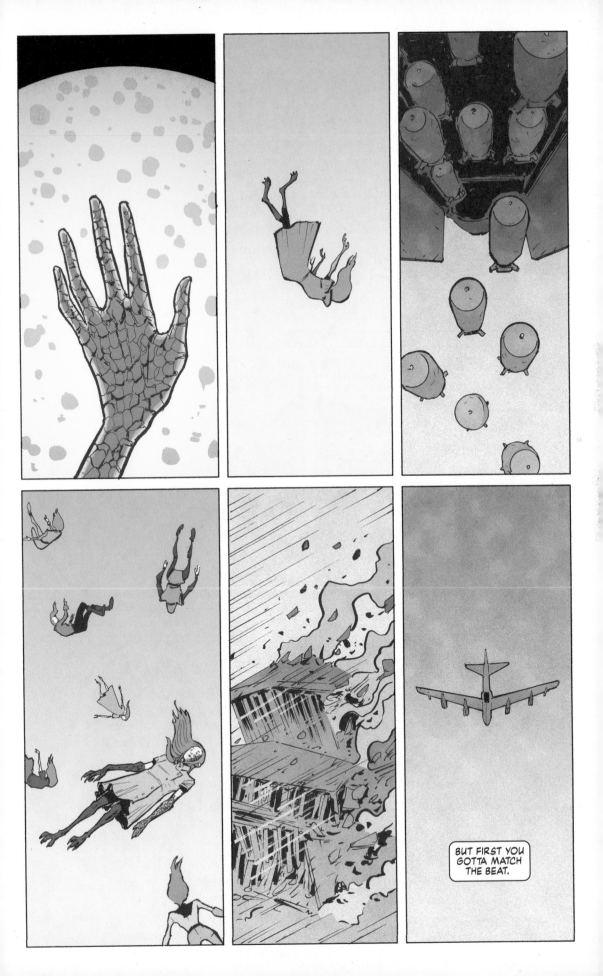

BUT FIRST YOU
GOTTA MATCH
THE BEAT.

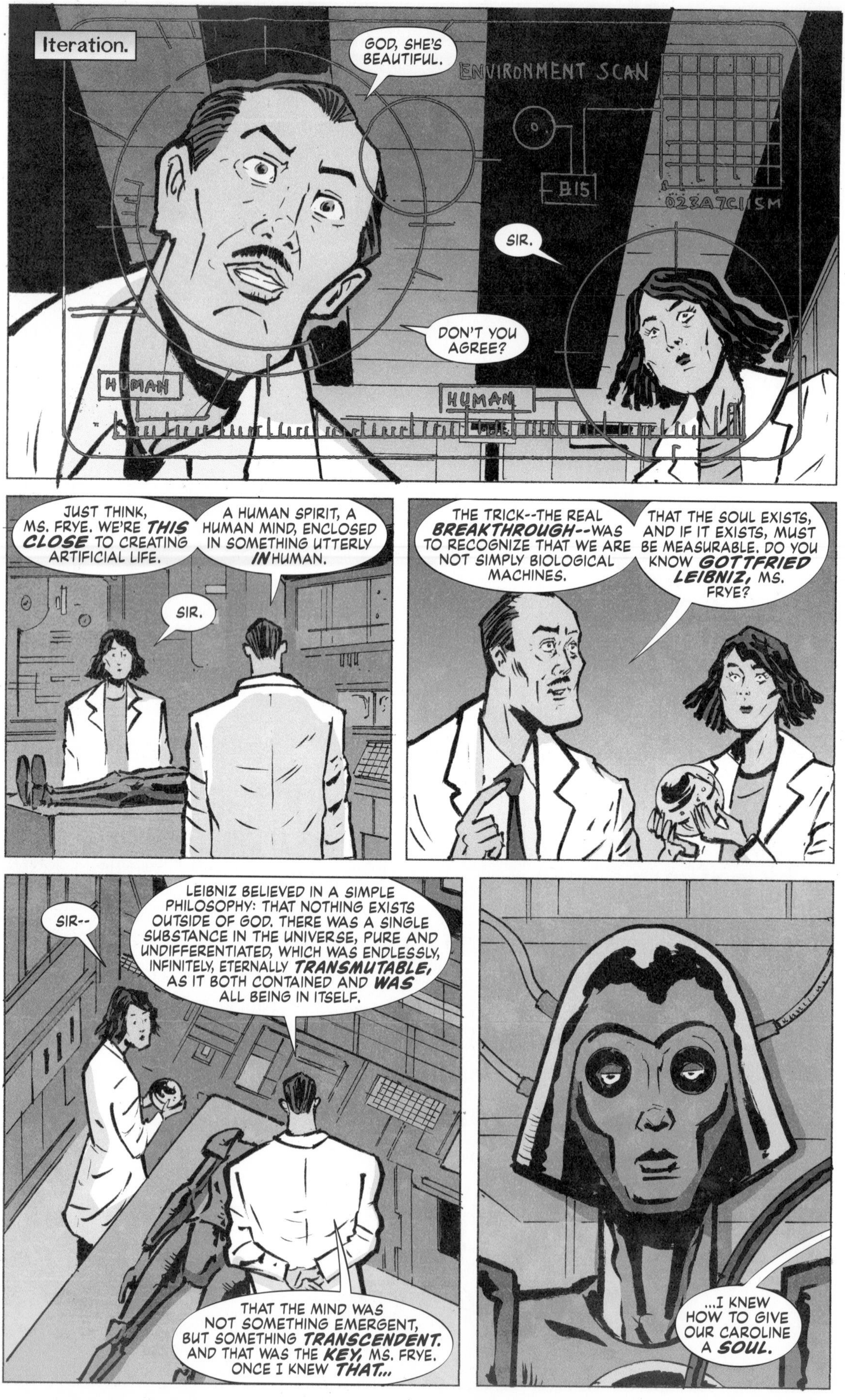
Iteration.
GOD, SHE'S BEAUTIFUL.
ENVIRONMENT SCAN
B15
023A7C115M
SIR.
DON'T YOU AGREE?
HUMAN
HUMAN
JUST THINK, MS. FRYE. WE'RE THIS CLOSE TO CREATING ARTIFICIAL LIFE.
A HUMAN SPIRIT, A HUMAN MIND, ENCLOSED IN SOMETHING UTTERLY INHUMAN.
SIR.
THE TRICK--THE REAL BREAKTHROUGH--WAS TO RECOGNIZE THAT WE ARE NOT SIMPLY BIOLOGICAL MACHINES.
THAT THE SOUL EXISTS, AND IF IT EXISTS, MUST BE MEASURABLE. DO YOU KNOW GOTTFRIED LEIBNIZ, MS. FRYE?
SIR--
LEIBNIZ BELIEVED IN A SIMPLE PHILOSOPHY: THAT NOTHING EXISTS OUTSIDE OF GOD. THERE WAS A SINGLE SUBSTANCE IN THE UNIVERSE, PURE AND UNDIFFERENTIATED, WHICH WAS ENDLESSLY, INFINITELY, ETERNALLY TRANSMUTABLE, AS IT BOTH CONTAINED AND WAS ALL BEING IN ITSELF.
THAT THE MIND WAS NOT SOMETHING EMERGENT, BUT SOMETHING TRANSCENDENT. AND THAT WAS THE KEY, MS. FRYE. ONCE I KNEW THAT...
...I KNEW HOW TO GIVE OUR CAROLINE A SOUL.

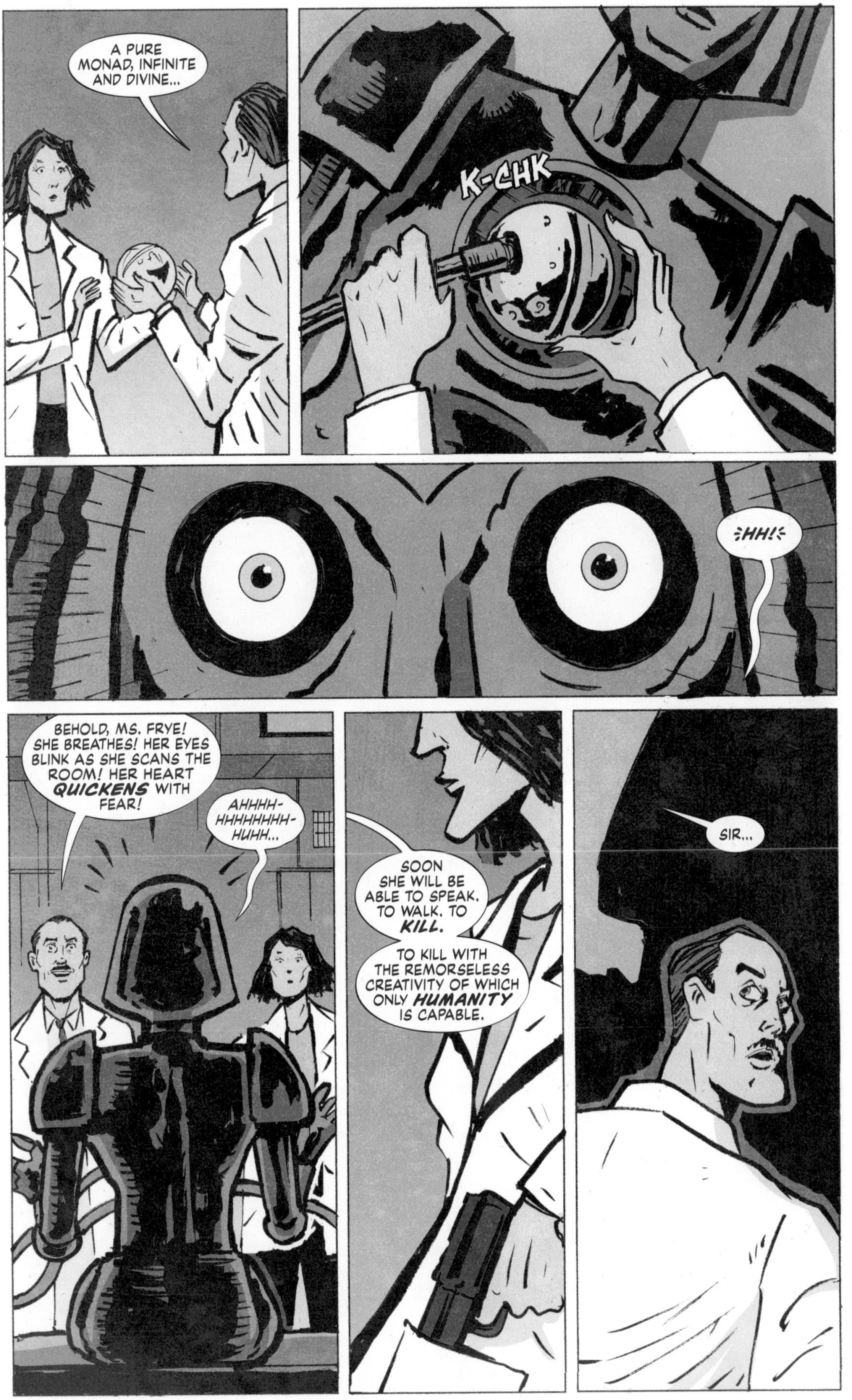

A PURE MONAD, INFINITE AND DIVINE...
K-CHK
HH!
BEHOLD, MS. FRYE! SHE BREATHES! HER EYES BLINK AS SHE SCANS THE ROOM! HER HEART QUICKENS WITH FEAR!
AHHHH-HHHHHHHH-HUHH...
SOON SHE WILL BE ABLE TO SPEAK. TO WALK. TO KILL.
TO KILL WITH THE REMORSELESS CREATIVITY OF WHICH ONLY HUMANITY IS CAPABLE.
SIR...

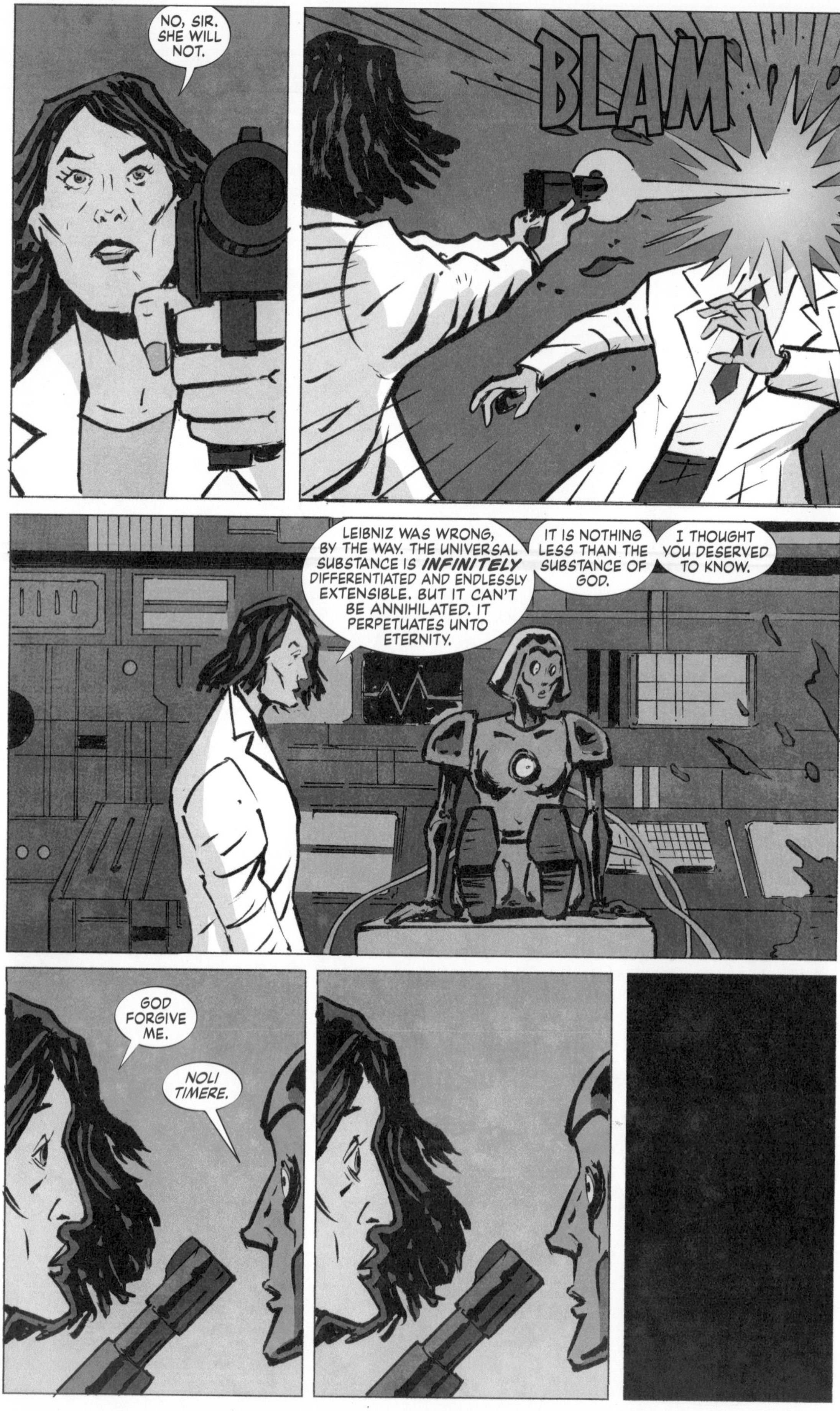
NO, SIR. SHE WILL NOT.
BLAM
LEIBNIZ WAS WRONG, BY THE WAY. THE UNIVERSAL SUBSTANCE IS INFINITELY DIFFERENTIATED AND ENDLESSLY EXTENSIBLE. BUT IT CAN'T BE ANNIHILATED. IT PERPETUATES UNTO ETERNITY.
IT IS NOTHING LESS THAN THE SUBSTANCE OF GOD.
I THOUGHT YOU DESERVED TO KNOW.
GOD FORGIVE ME.
NOLI TIMERE.

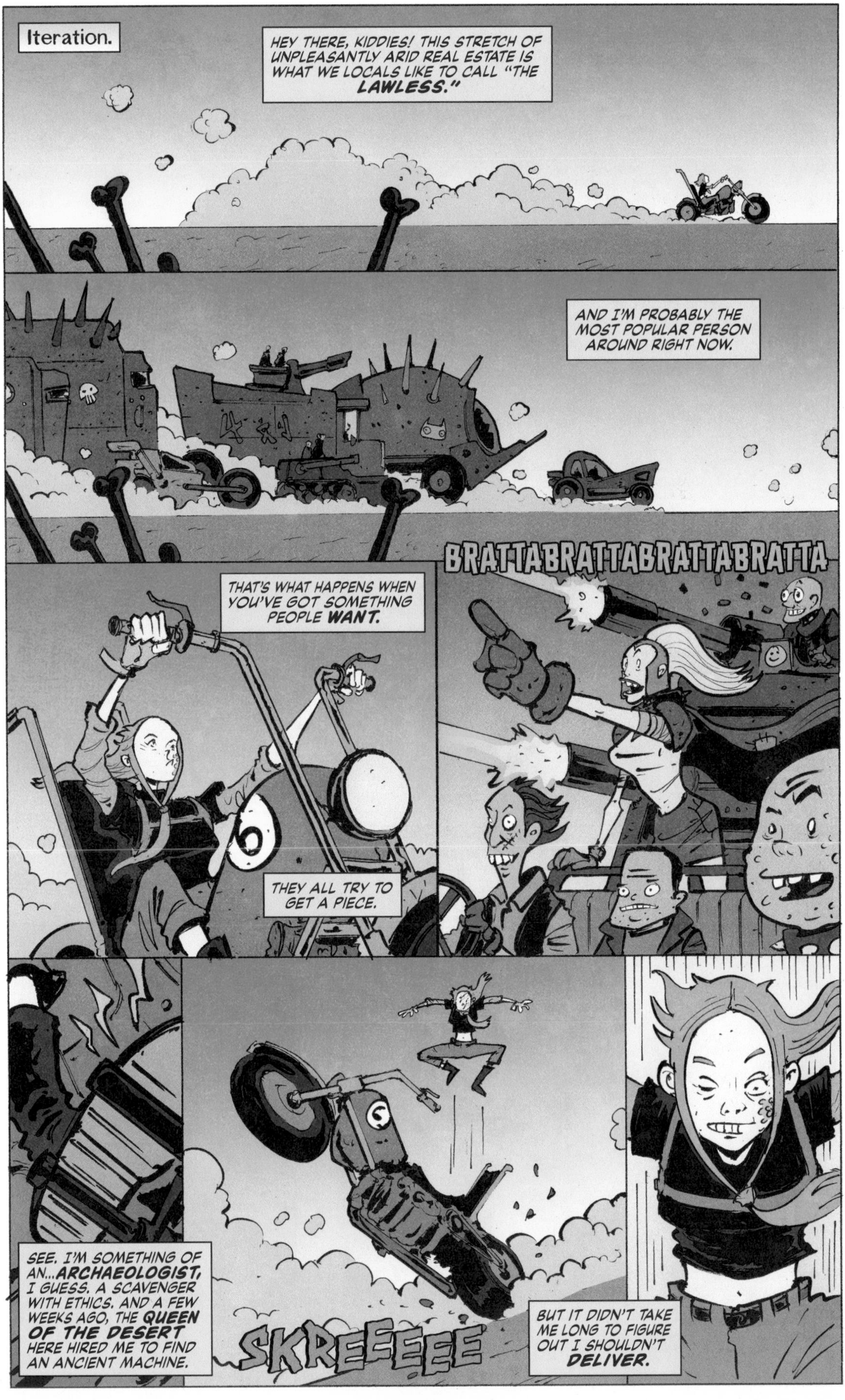
Iteration.
HEY THERE, KIDDIES! THIS STRETCH OF UNPLEASANTLY ARID REAL ESTATE IS WHAT WE LOCALS LIKE TO CALL "THE LAWLESS."
AND I'M PROBABLY THE MOST POPULAR PERSON AROUND RIGHT NOW.
THAT'S WHAT HAPPENS WHEN YOU'VE GOT SOMETHING PEOPLE WANT.
THEY ALL TRY TO GET A PIECE.
BRATTABRATTABRATTABRATTA
SEE. I'M SOMETHING OF AN...ARCHAEOLOGIST, I GUESS. A SCAVENGER WITH ETHICS. AND A FEW WEEKS AGO, THE QUEEN OF THE DESERT HERE HIRED ME TO FIND AN ANCIENT MACHINE.
SKREEEEEE
BUT IT DIDN'T TAKE ME LONG TO FIGURE OUT I SHOULDN'T DELIVER.

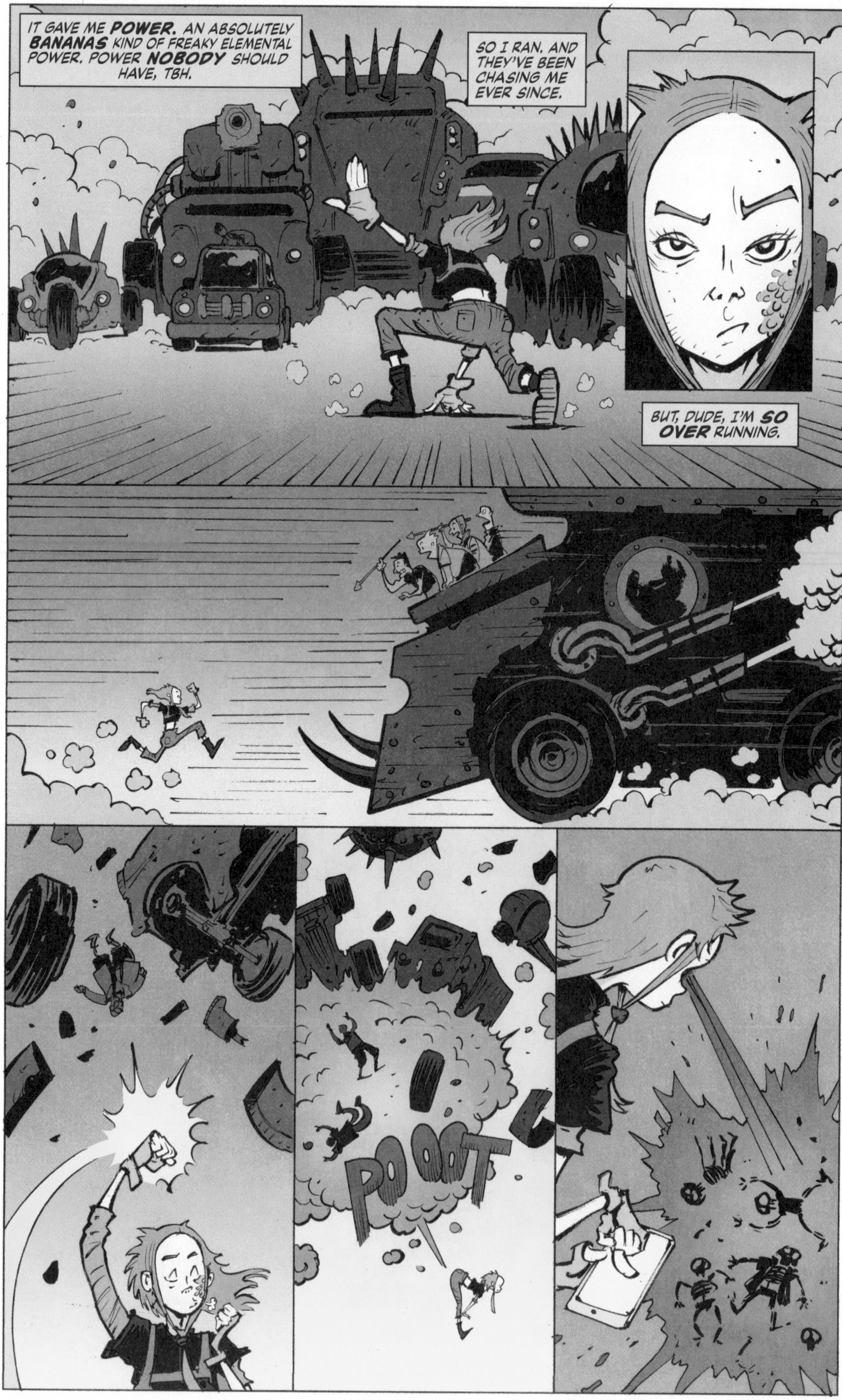
IT GAVE ME **POWER.** AN ABSOLUTELY **BANANAS** KIND OF FREAKY ELEMENTAL POWER. POWER **NOBODY** SHOULD HAVE, TBH.
SO I RAN. AND THEY'VE BEEN CHASING ME EVER SINCE.
BUT, DUDE, I'M **SO OVER** RUNNING.
POOOT

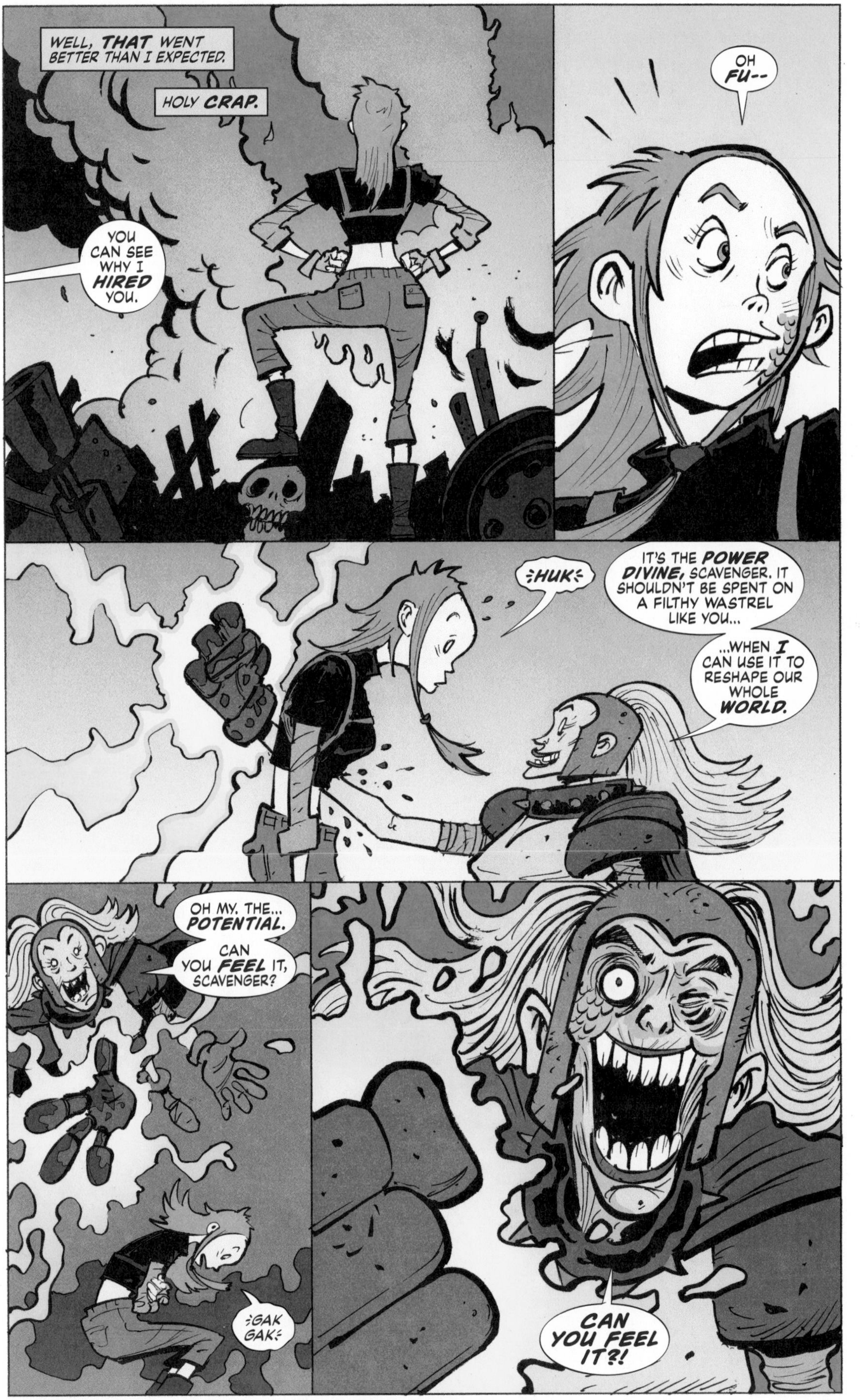
WELL, THAT WENT BETTER THAN I EXPECTED.
HOLY CRAP.
YOU CAN SEE WHY I HIRED YOU.
OH FU--
HUK
IT'S THE POWER DIVINE, SCAVENGER. IT SHOULDN'T BE SPENT ON A FILTHY WASTREL LIKE YOU...
...WHEN I CAN USE IT TO RESHAPE OUR WHOLE WORLD.
OH MY. THE... POTENTIAL.
CAN YOU FEEL IT, SCAVENGER?
GAK GAK
CAN YOU FEEL IT?!

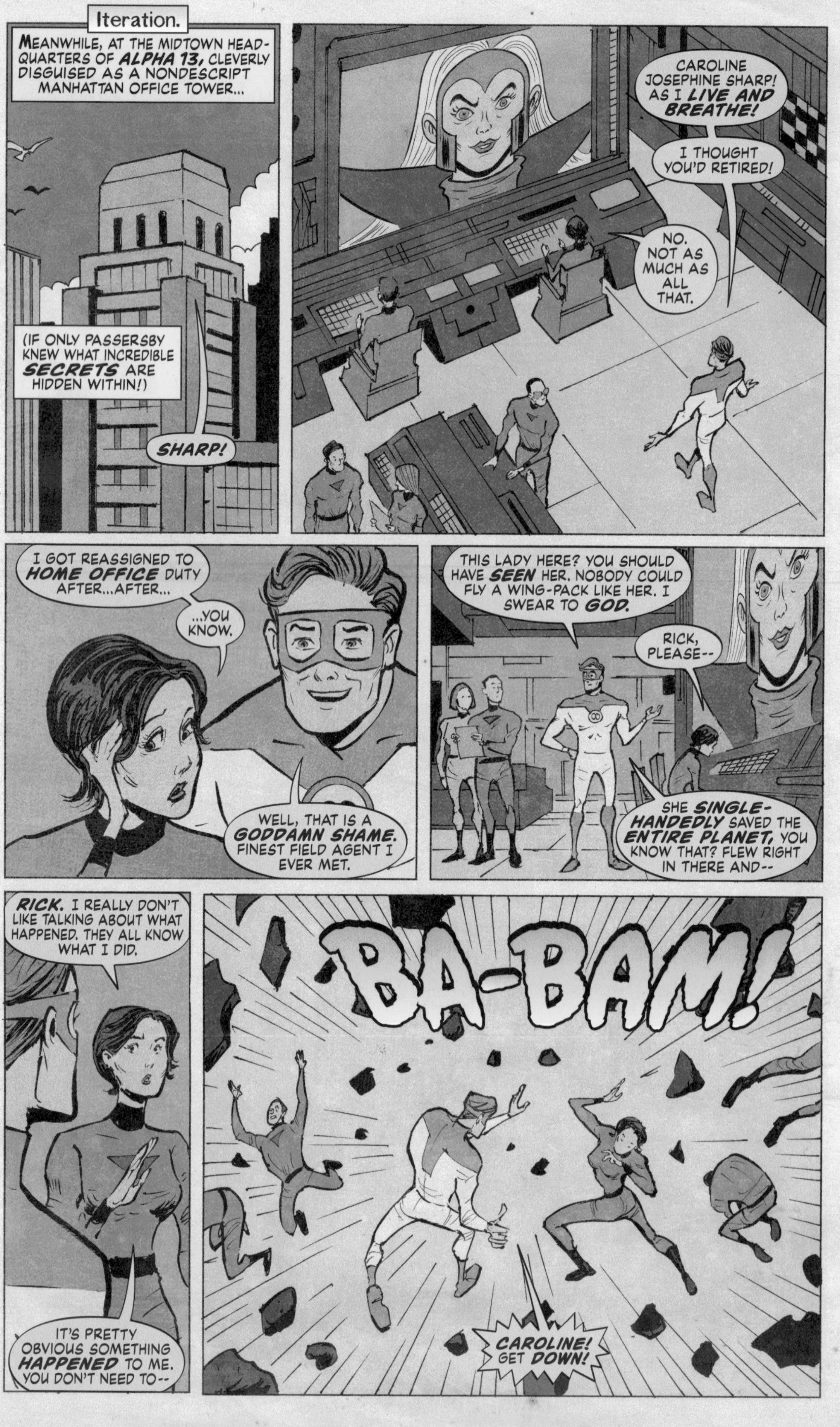
Iteration.
MEANWHILE, AT THE MIDTOWN HEADQUARTERS OF ALPHA 13, CLEVERLY DISGUISED AS A NONDESCRIPT MANHATTAN OFFICE TOWER...
(IF ONLY PASSERSBY KNEW WHAT INCREDIBLE SECRETS ARE HIDDEN WITHIN!)
SHARP!
CAROLINE JOSEPHINE SHARP! AS I LIVE AND BREATHE!
I THOUGHT YOU'D RETIRED!
NO. NOT AS MUCH AS ALL THAT.
I GOT REASSIGNED TO HOME OFFICE DUTY AFTER...AFTER...
...YOU KNOW.
WELL, THAT IS A GODDAMN SHAME. FINEST FIELD AGENT I EVER MET.
THIS LADY HERE? YOU SHOULD HAVE SEEN HER. NOBODY COULD FLY A WING-PACK LIKE HER. I SWEAR TO GOD.
RICK, PLEASE--
SHE SINGLE-HANDEDLY SAVED THE ENTIRE PLANET, YOU KNOW THAT? FLEW RIGHT IN THERE AND--
RICK. I REALLY DON'T LIKE TALKING ABOUT WHAT HAPPENED. THEY ALL KNOW WHAT I DID.
IT'S PRETTY OBVIOUS SOMETHING HAPPENED TO ME. YOU DON'T NEED TO--
BA-BAM!
CAROLINE! GET DOWN!

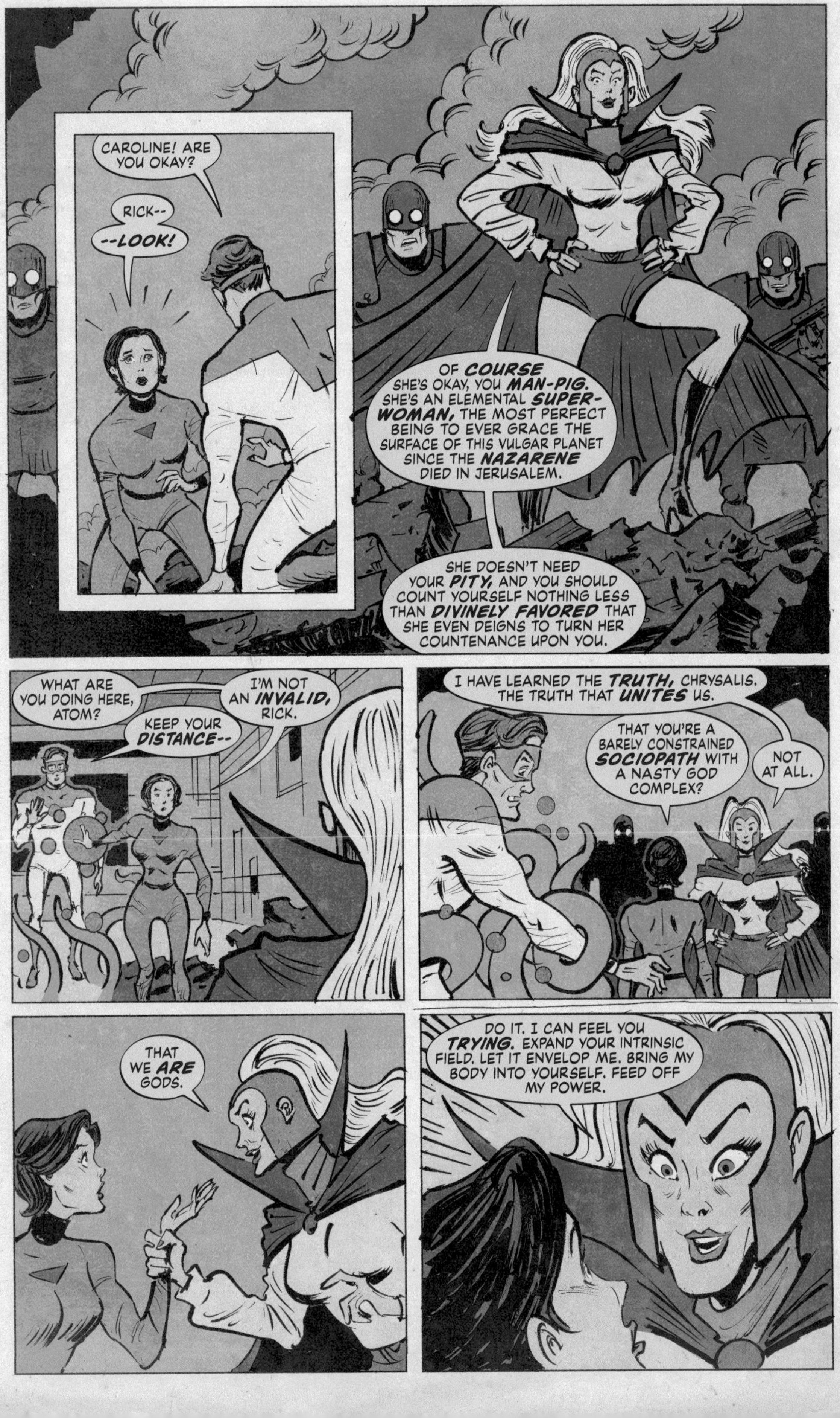
CAROLINE! ARE YOU OKAY?
RICK--
--LOOK!
OF COURSE SHE'S OKAY, YOU MAN-PIG. SHE'S AN ELEMENTAL SUPER-WOMAN, THE MOST PERFECT BEING TO EVER GRACE THE SURFACE OF THIS VULGAR PLANET SINCE THE NAZARENE DIED IN JERUSALEM.
SHE DOESN'T NEED YOUR PITY, AND YOU SHOULD COUNT YOURSELF NOTHING LESS THAN DIVINELY FAVORED THAT SHE EVEN DEIGNS TO TURN HER COUNTENANCE UPON YOU.
WHAT ARE YOU DOING HERE, ATOM?
KEEP YOUR DISTANCE--
I'M NOT AN INVALID, RICK.
I HAVE LEARNED THE TRUTH, CHRYSALIS. THE TRUTH THAT UNITES US.
THAT YOU'RE A BARELY CONSTRAINED SOCIOPATH WITH A NASTY GOD COMPLEX?
NOT AT ALL.
THAT WE ARE GODS.
DO IT. I CAN FEEL YOU TRYING. EXPAND YOUR INTRINSIC FIELD. LET IT ENVELOP ME. BRING MY BODY INTO YOURSELF. FEED OFF MY POWER.

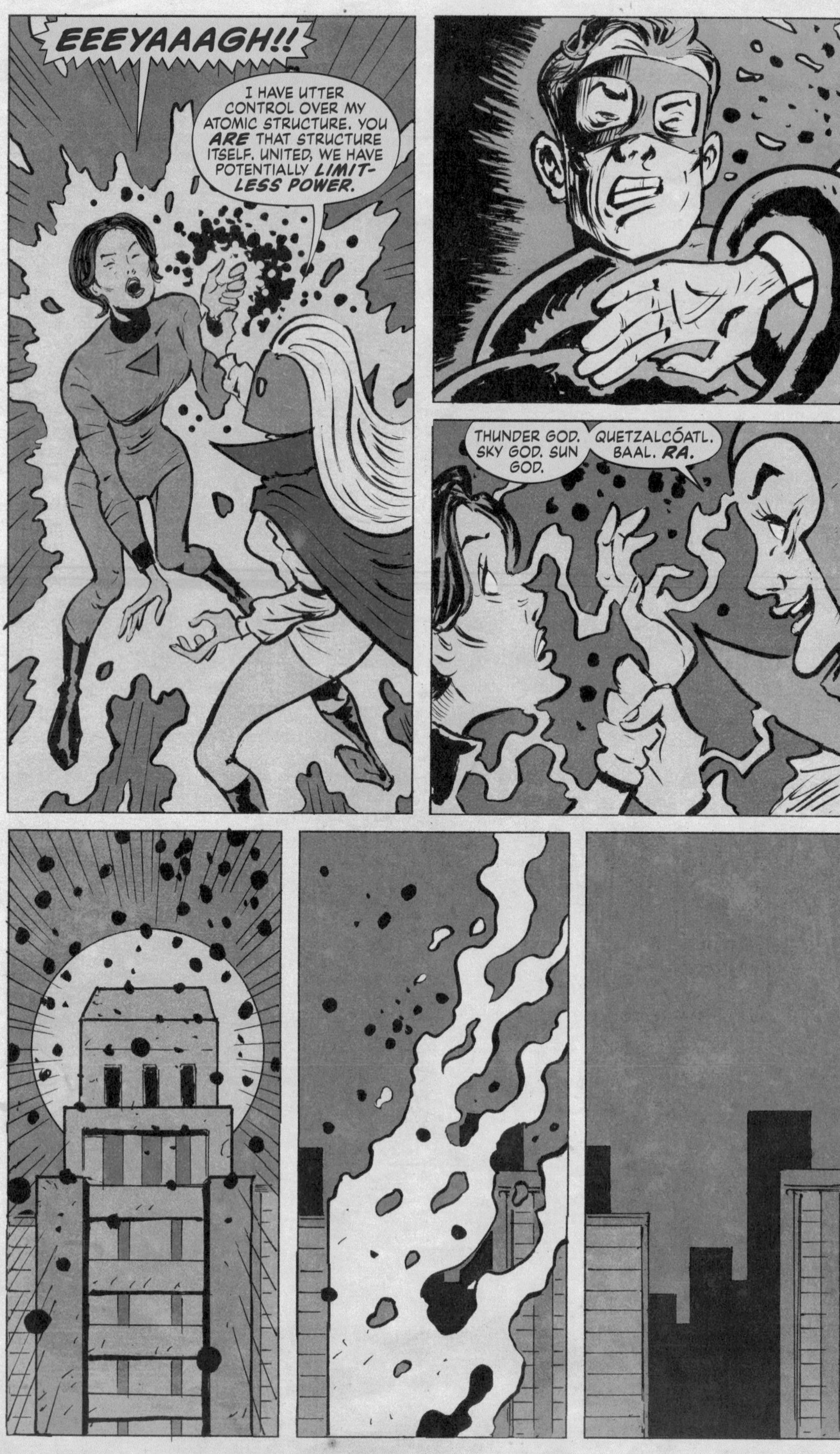
EEEYAAAGH!!
I HAVE UTTER CONTROL OVER MY ATOMIC STRUCTURE. YOU ARE THAT STRUCTURE ITSELF. UNITED, WE HAVE POTENTIALLY LIMITLESS POWER.
THUNDER GOD. SKY GOD. SUN GOD.
QUETZALCÓATL. BAAL. RA.

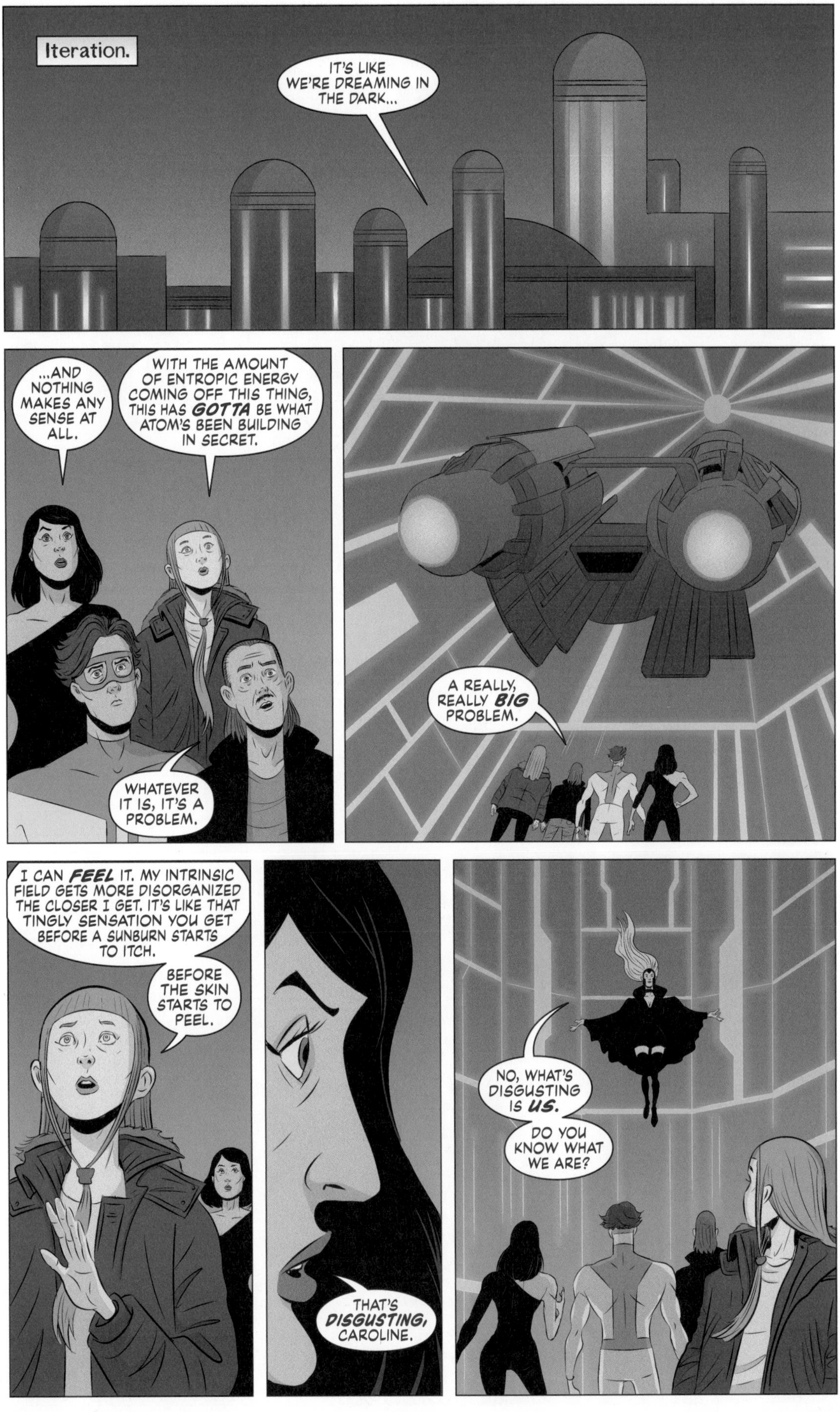
Iteration.
IT'S LIKE WE'RE DREAMING IN THE DARK...
...AND NOTHING MAKES ANY SENSE AT ALL.
WITH THE AMOUNT OF ENTROPIC ENERGY COMING OFF THIS THING, THIS HAS GOTTA BE WHAT ATOM'S BEEN BUILDING IN SECRET.
WHATEVER IT IS, IT'S A PROBLEM.
A REALLY, REALLY BIG PROBLEM.
I CAN FEEL IT. MY INTRINSIC FIELD GETS MORE DISORGANIZED THE CLOSER I GET. IT'S LIKE THAT TINGLY SENSATION YOU GET BEFORE A SUNBURN STARTS TO ITCH.
BEFORE THE SKIN STARTS TO PEEL.
THAT'S DISGUSTING, CAROLINE.
NO, WHAT'S DISGUSTING IS US.
DO YOU KNOW WHAT WE ARE?

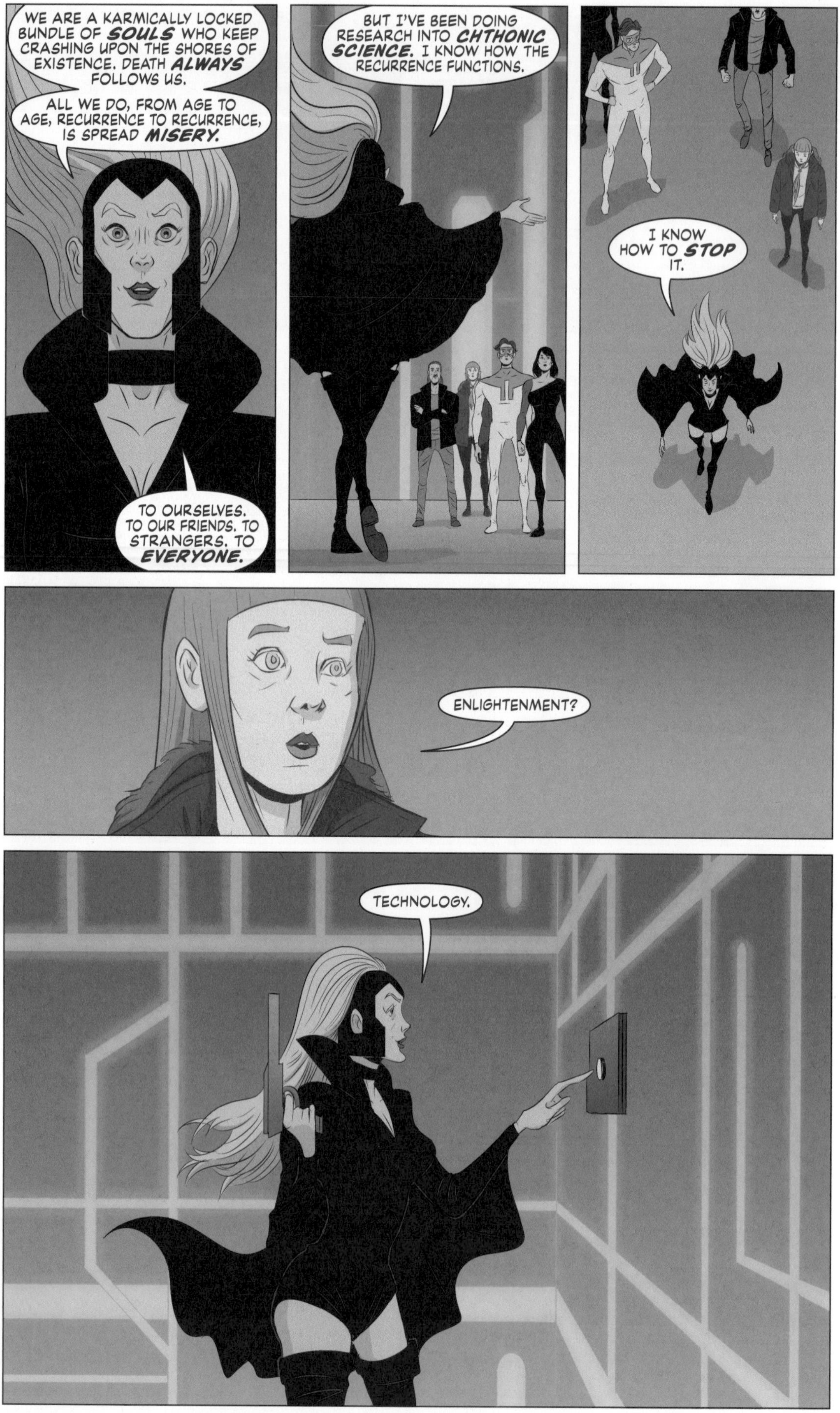
WE ARE A KARMICALLY LOCKED BUNDLE OF SOULS WHO KEEP CRASHING UPON THE SHORES OF EXISTENCE. DEATH ALWAYS FOLLOWS US.
ALL WE DO, FROM AGE TO AGE, RECURRENCE TO RECURRENCE, IS SPREAD MISERY.
TO OURSELVES. TO OUR FRIENDS. TO STRANGERS. TO EVERYONE.
BUT I'VE BEEN DOING RESEARCH INTO CHTHONIC SCIENCE. I KNOW HOW THE RECURRENCE FUNCTIONS.
I KNOW HOW TO STOP IT.
ENLIGHTENMENT?
TECHNOLOGY.

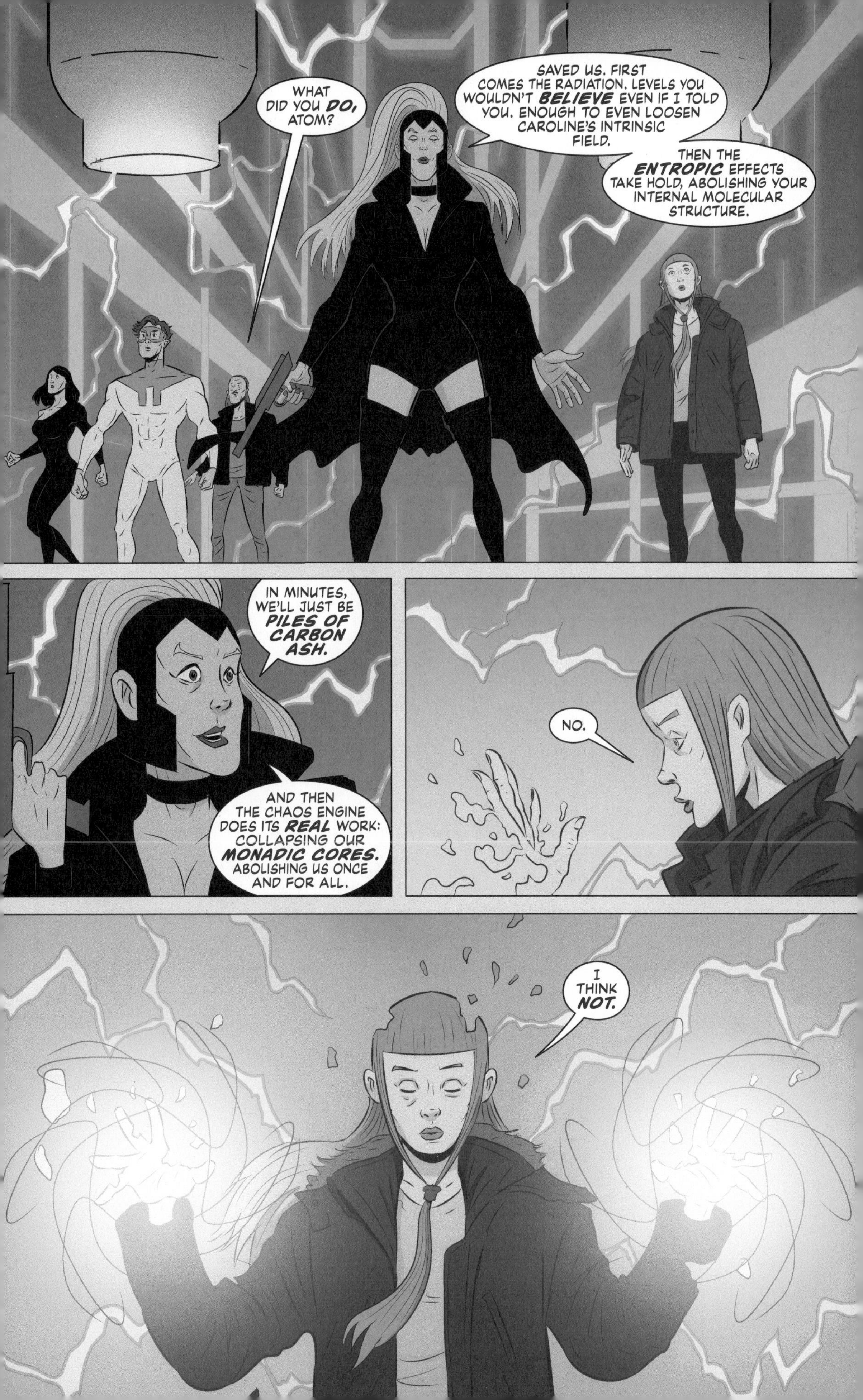
WHAT DID YOU DO, ATOM?
SAVED US. FIRST COMES THE RADIATION. LEVELS YOU WOULDN'T BELIEVE EVEN IF I TOLD YOU. ENOUGH TO EVEN LOOSEN CAROLINE'S INTRINSIC FIELD.
THEN THE ENTROPIC EFFECTS TAKE HOLD, ABOLISHING YOUR INTERNAL MOLECULAR STRUCTURE.
IN MINUTES, WE'LL JUST BE PILES OF CARBON ASH.
AND THEN THE CHAOS ENGINE DOES ITS REAL WORK: COLLAPSING OUR MONADIC CORES. ABOLISHING US ONCE AND FOR ALL.
NO.
I THINK NOT.

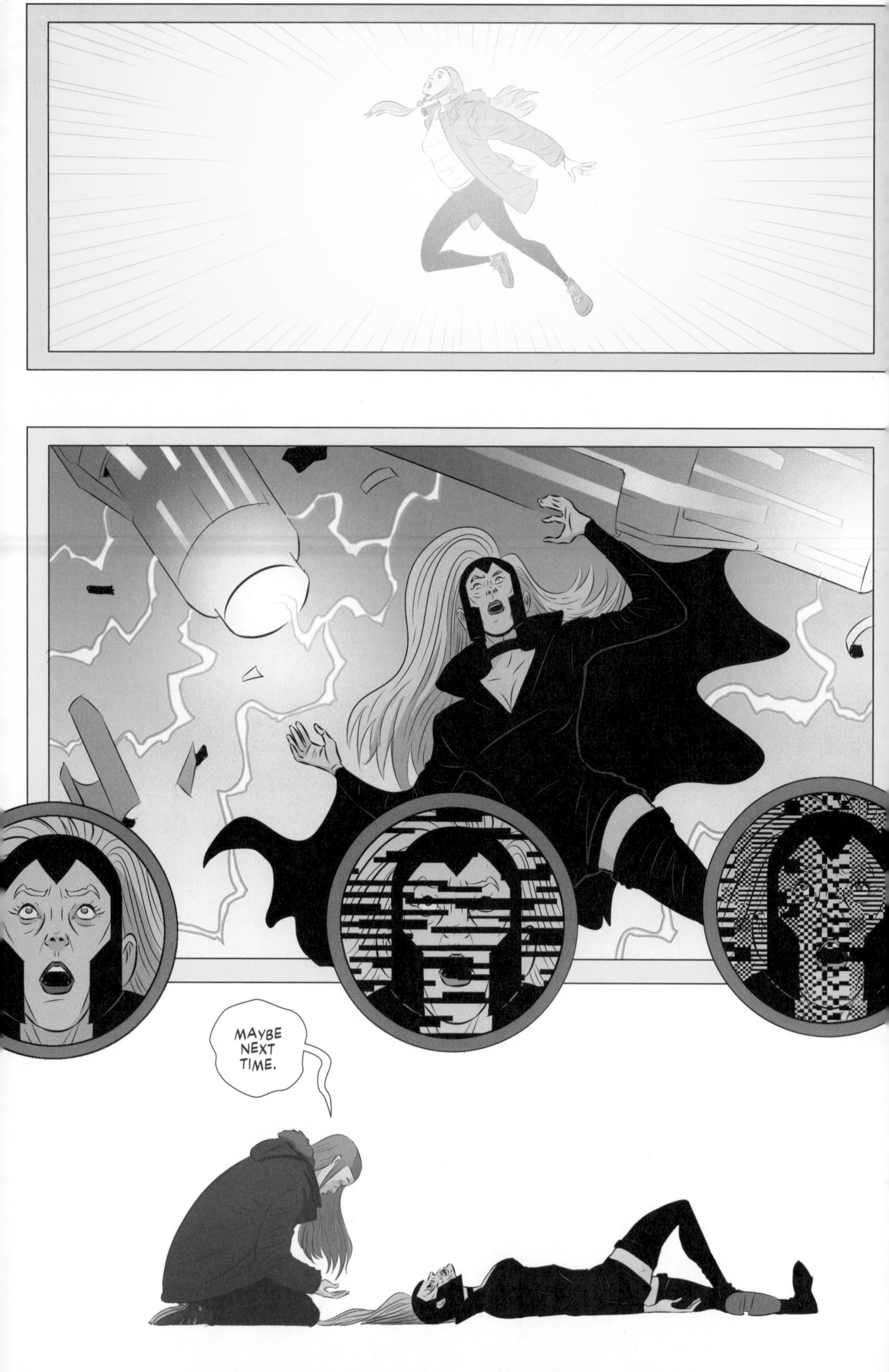
MAYBE NEXT TIME.

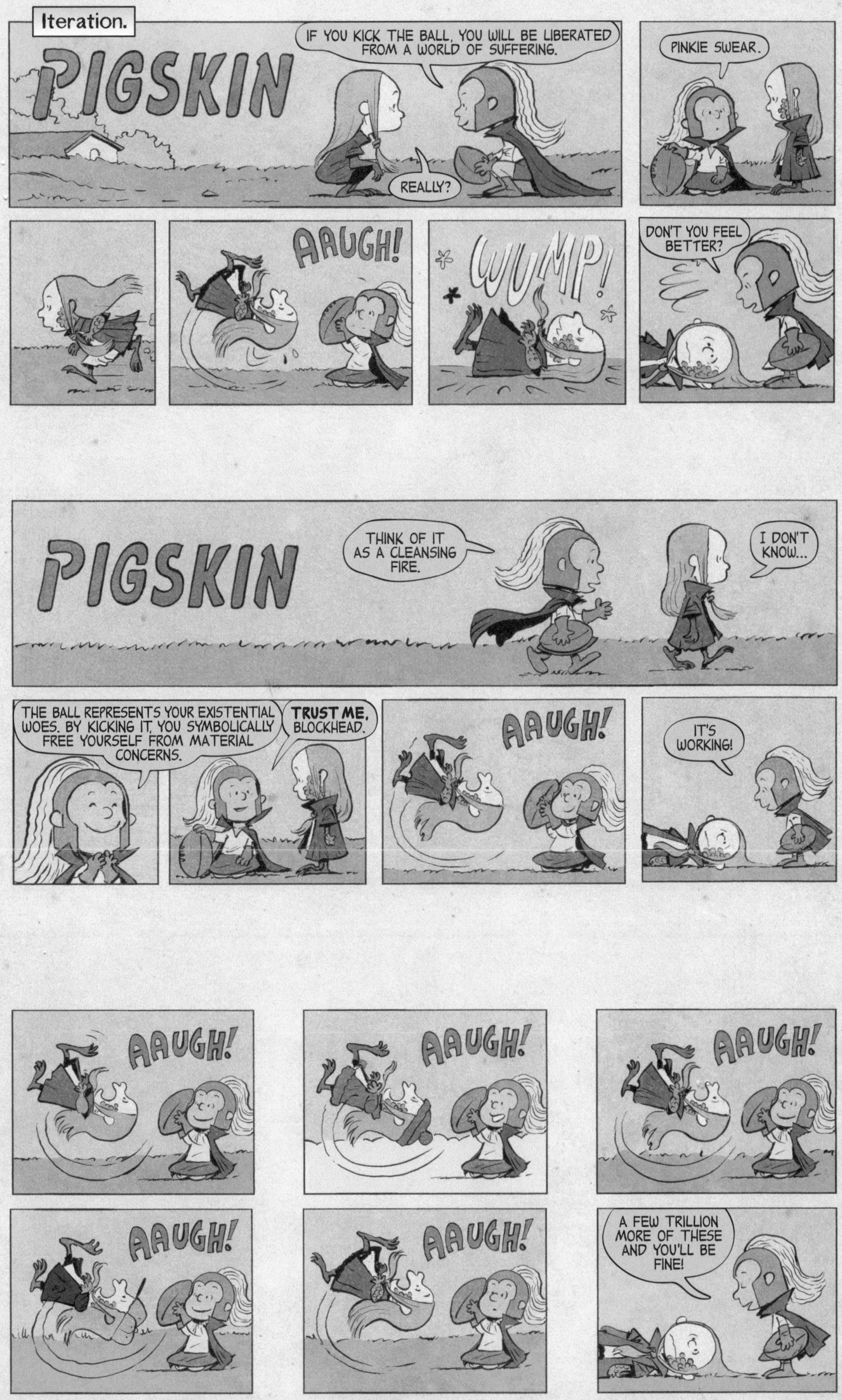
Iteration.
PIGSKIN
IF YOU KICK THE BALL, YOU WILL BE LIBERATED FROM A WORLD OF SUFFERING.
REALLY?
PINKIE SWEAR.
AAUGH!
WUMP!
DON'T YOU FEEL BETTER?
PIGSKIN
THINK OF IT AS A CLEANSING FIRE.
I DON'T KNOW...
THE BALL REPRESENTS YOUR EXISTENTIAL WOES. BY KICKING IT, YOU SYMBOLICALLY FREE YOURSELF FROM MATERIAL CONCERNS.
TRUST ME, BLOCKHEAD.
AAUGH!
IT'S WORKING!
AAUGH!
AAUGH!
AAUGH!
AAUGH!
AAUGH!
A FEW TRILLION MORE OF THESE AND YOU'LL BE FINE!

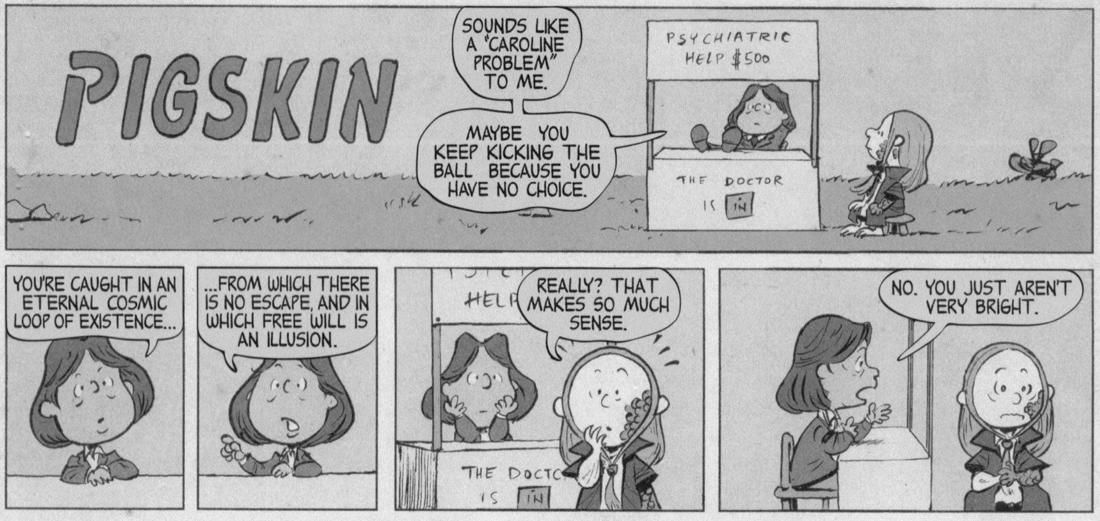
PIGSKIN
SOUNDS LIKE A "CAROLINE PROBLEM" TO ME.
MAYBE YOU KEEP KICKING THE BALL BECAUSE YOU HAVE NO CHOICE.
PSYCHIATRIC HELP $500
THE DOCTOR IS IN
YOU'RE CAUGHT IN AN ETERNAL COSMIC LOOP OF EXISTENCE...
...FROM WHICH THERE IS NO ESCAPE, AND IN WHICH FREE WILL IS AN ILLUSION.
REALLY? THAT MAKES SO MUCH SENSE.
NO. YOU JUST AREN'T VERY BRIGHT.

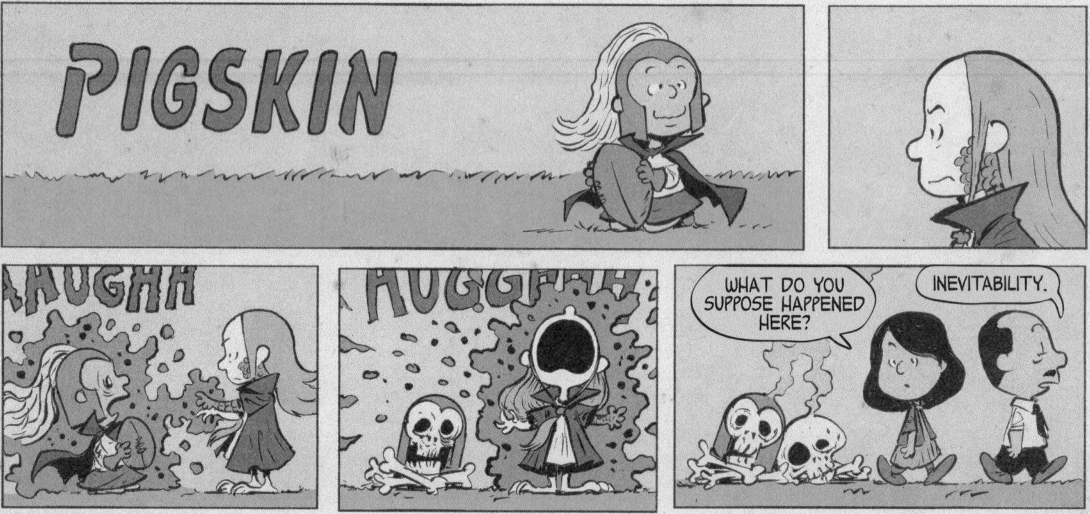
PIGSKIN
AUGHH
WHAT DO YOU SUPPOSE HAPPENED HERE?
INEVITABILITY.

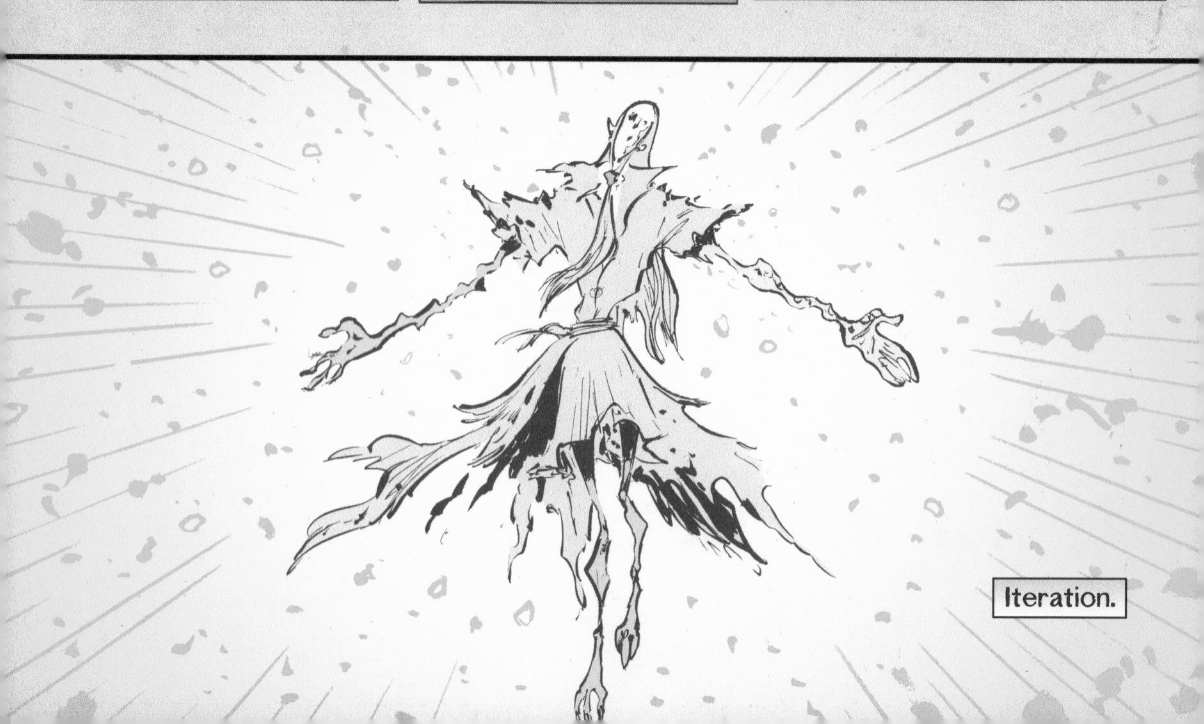
Iteration.

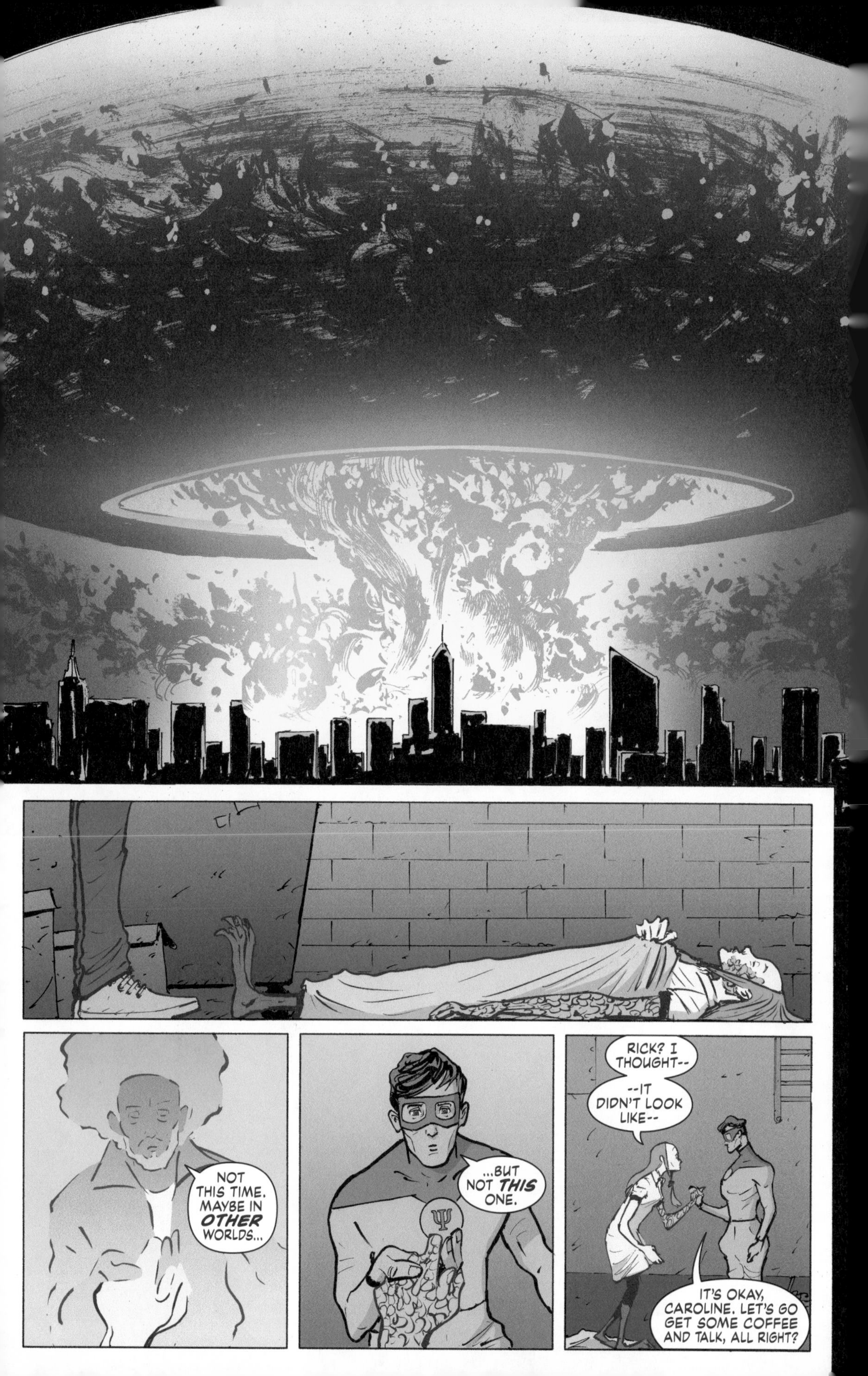
NOT THIS TIME. MAYBE IN **OTHER** WORLDS...
...BUT NOT **THIS** ONE.
RICK? I THOUGHT--
--IT DIDN'T LOOK LIKE--
IT'S OKAY, CAROLINE. LET'S GO GET SOME COFFEE AND TALK, ALL RIGHT?

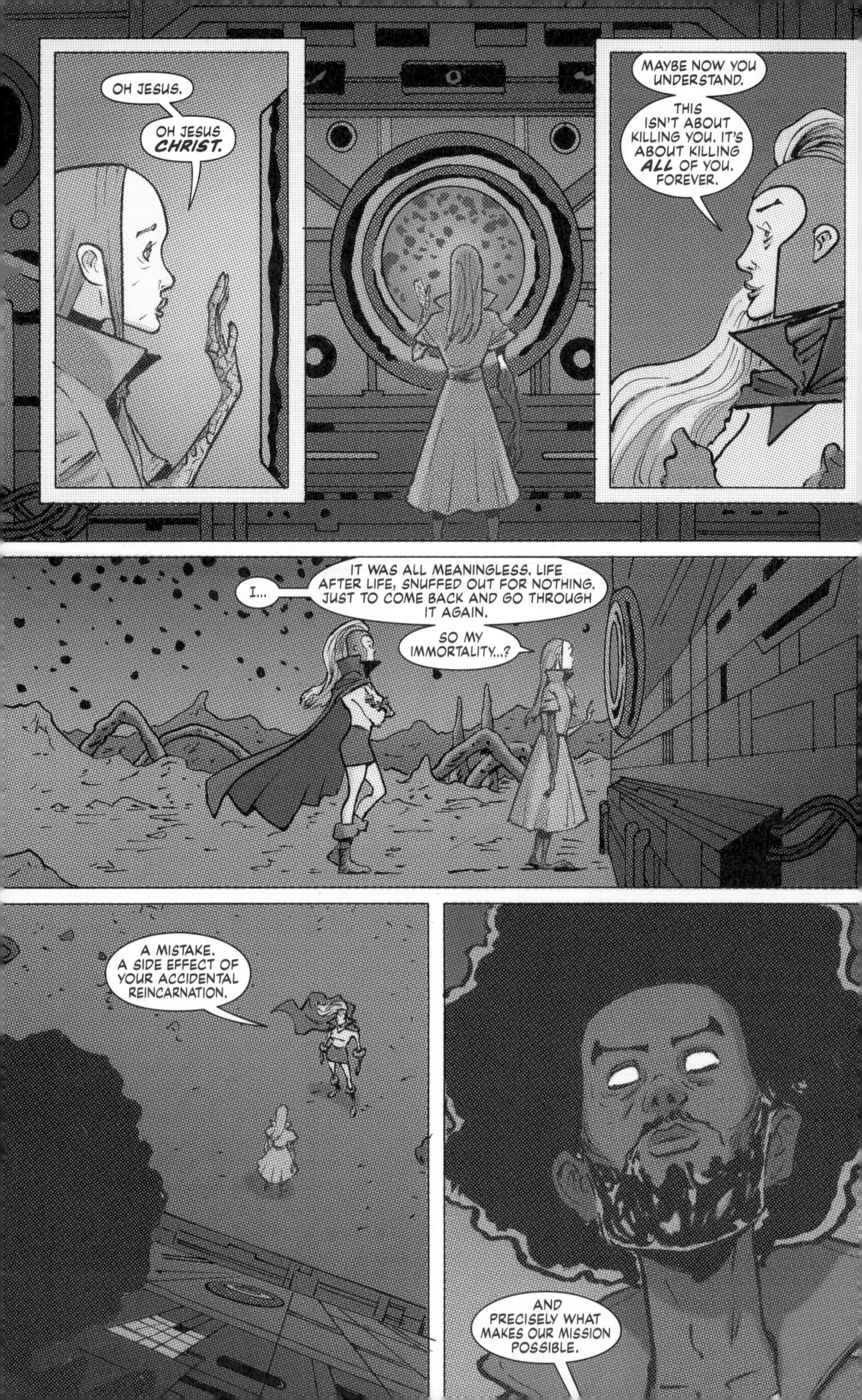
OH JESUS.
OH JESUS **CHRIST.**
MAYBE NOW YOU UNDERSTAND.
THIS ISN'T ABOUT KILLING YOU. IT'S ABOUT KILLING ***ALL*** OF YOU. FOREVER.
I...
IT WAS ALL MEANINGLESS. LIFE AFTER LIFE, SNUFFED OUT FOR NOTHING. JUST TO COME BACK AND GO THROUGH IT AGAIN.
SO MY IMMORTALITY...?
A MISTAKE. A SIDE EFFECT OF YOUR ACCIDENTAL REINCARNATION.
AND PRECISELY WHAT MAKES OUR MISSION POSSIBLE.

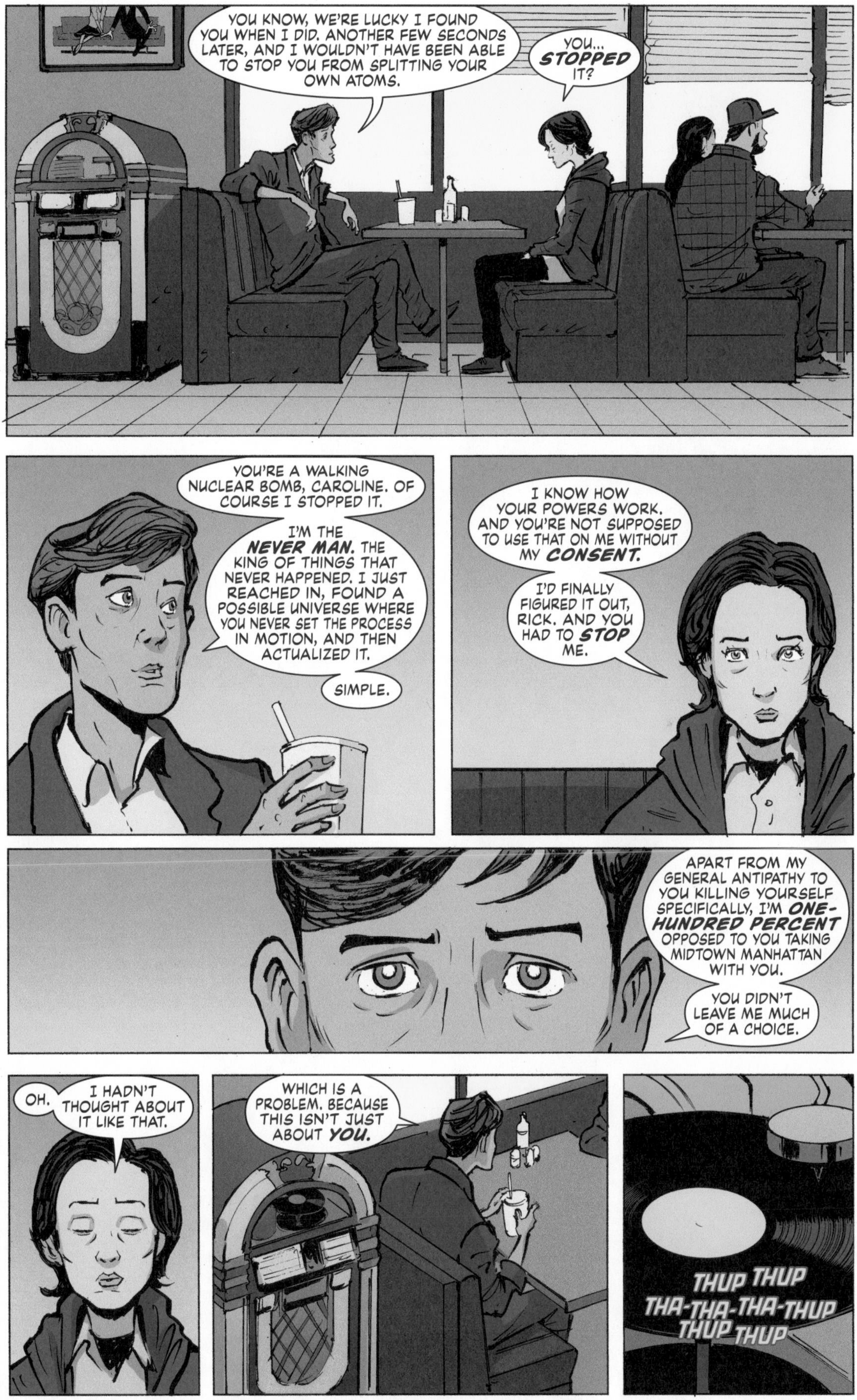
YOU KNOW, WE'RE LUCKY I FOUND YOU WHEN I DID. ANOTHER FEW SECONDS LATER, AND I WOULDN'T HAVE BEEN ABLE TO STOP YOU FROM SPLITTING YOUR OWN ATOMS.
YOU... STOPPED IT?
YOU'RE A WALKING NUCLEAR BOMB, CAROLINE. OF COURSE I STOPPED IT.
I'M THE NEVER MAN. THE KING OF THINGS THAT NEVER HAPPENED. I JUST REACHED IN, FOUND A POSSIBLE UNIVERSE WHERE YOU NEVER SET THE PROCESS IN MOTION, AND THEN ACTUALIZED IT.
SIMPLE.
I KNOW HOW YOUR POWERS WORK. AND YOU'RE NOT SUPPOSED TO USE THAT ON ME WITHOUT MY CONSENT.
I'D FINALLY FIGURED IT OUT, RICK. AND YOU HAD TO STOP ME.
APART FROM MY GENERAL ANTIPATHY TO YOU KILLING YOURSELF SPECIFICALLY, I'M ONE-HUNDRED PERCENT OPPOSED TO YOU TAKING MIDTOWN MANHATTAN WITH YOU.
YOU DIDN'T LEAVE ME MUCH OF A CHOICE.
OH.
I HADN'T THOUGHT ABOUT IT LIKE THAT.
WHICH IS A PROBLEM. BECAUSE THIS ISN'T JUST ABOUT YOU.
THUP THUP
THA-THA-THA-THUP
THUP THUP

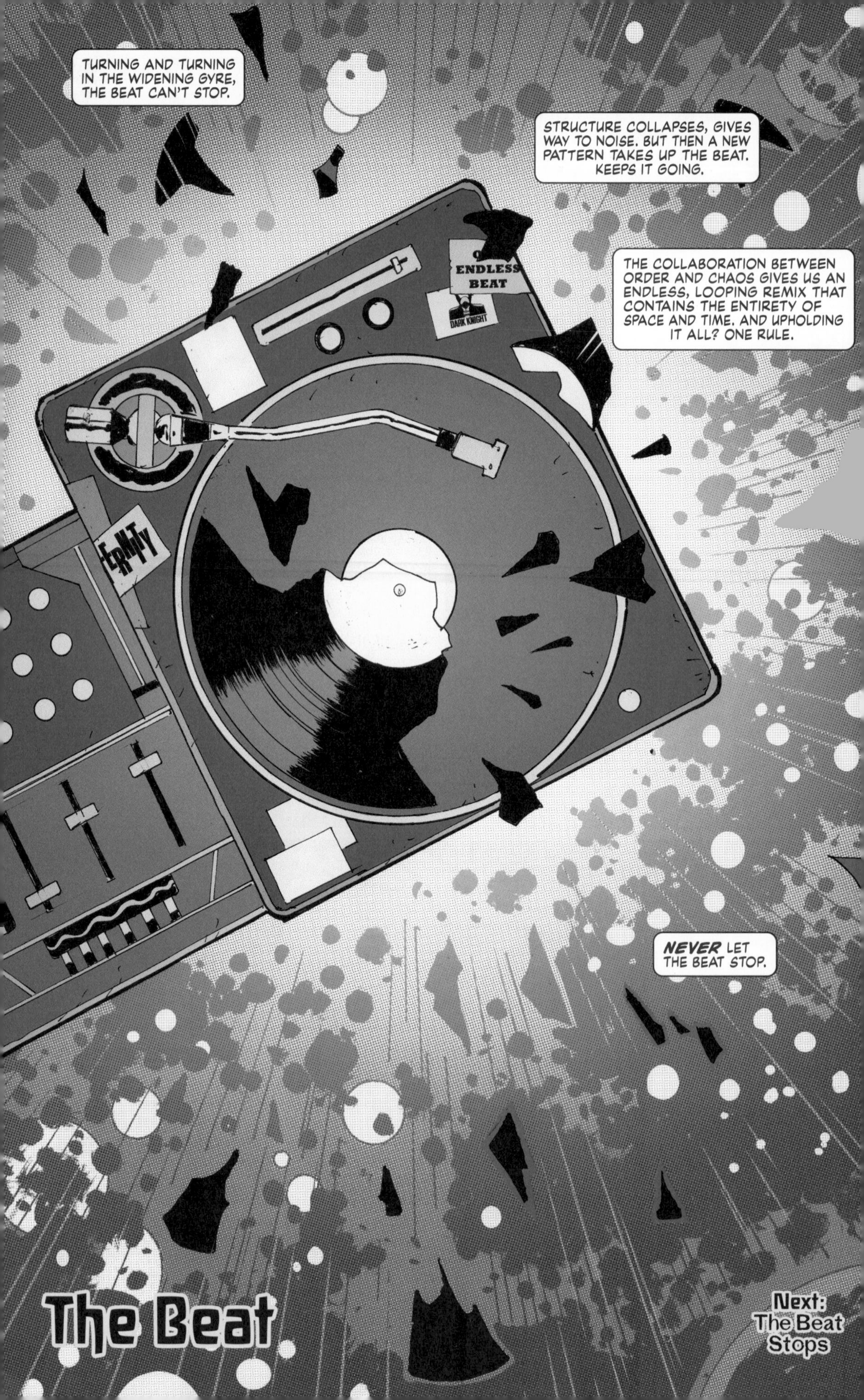
TURNING AND TURNING IN THE WIDENING GYRE, THE BEAT CAN'T STOP.
STRUCTURE COLLAPSES, GIVES WAY TO NOISE. BUT THEN A NEW PATTERN TAKES UP THE BEAT. KEEPS IT GOING.
ENDLESS BEAT
DARK KNIGHT
THE COLLABORATION BETWEEN ORDER AND CHAOS GIVES US AN ENDLESS, LOOPING REMIX THAT CONTAINS THE ENTIRETY OF SPACE AND TIME. AND UPHOLDING IT ALL? ONE RULE.
NEVER LET THE BEAT STOP.
The Beat
Next: The Beat Stops

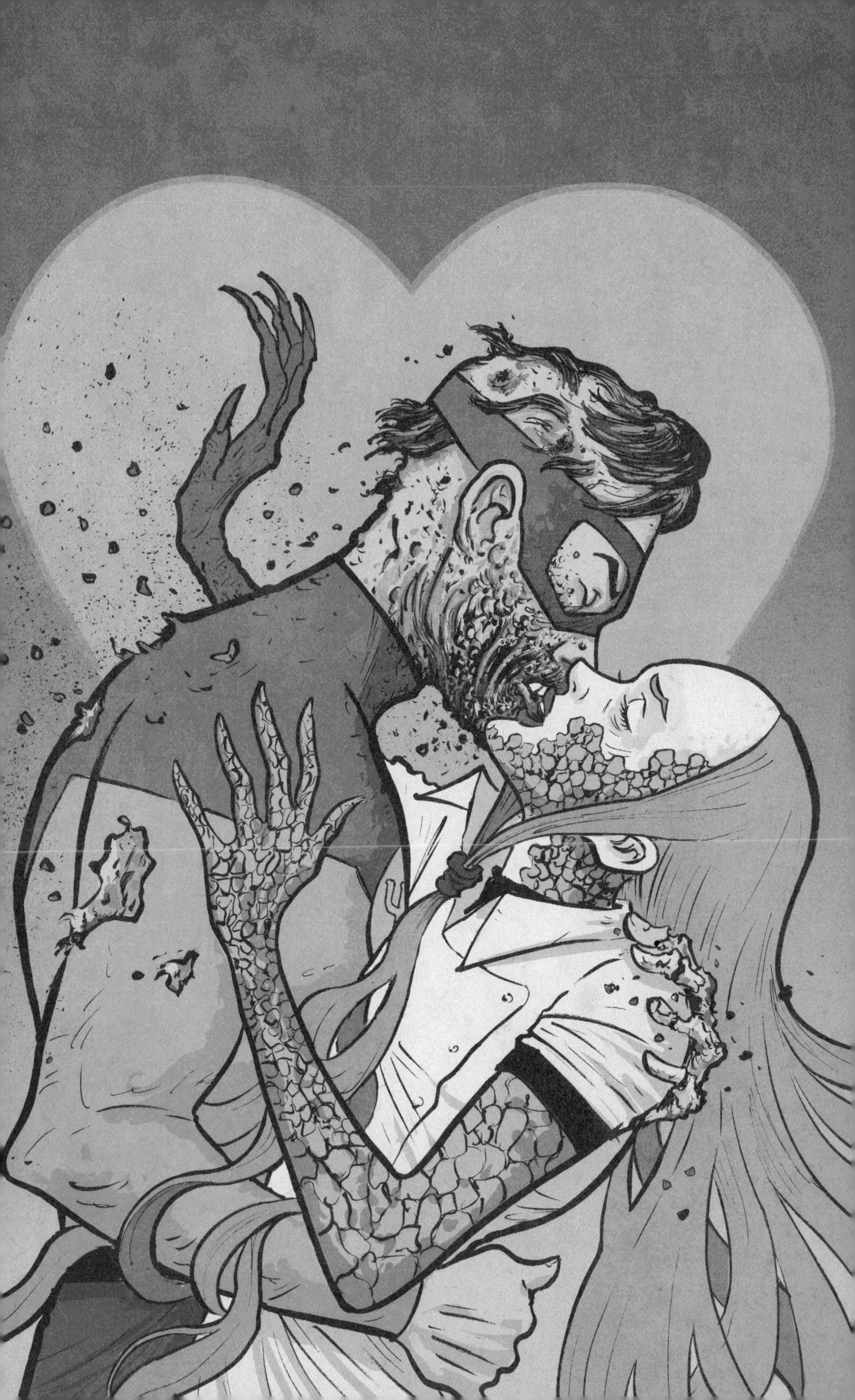

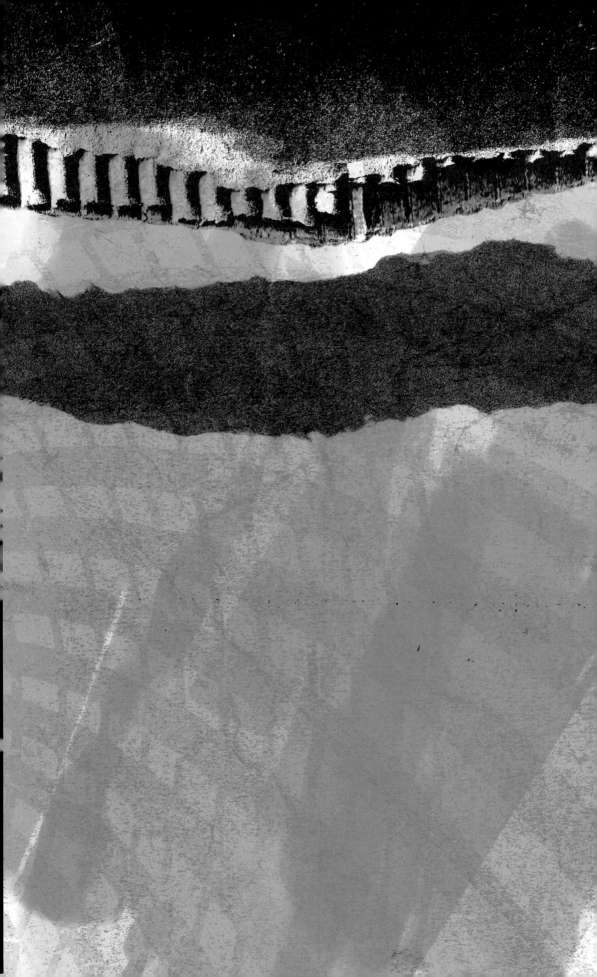

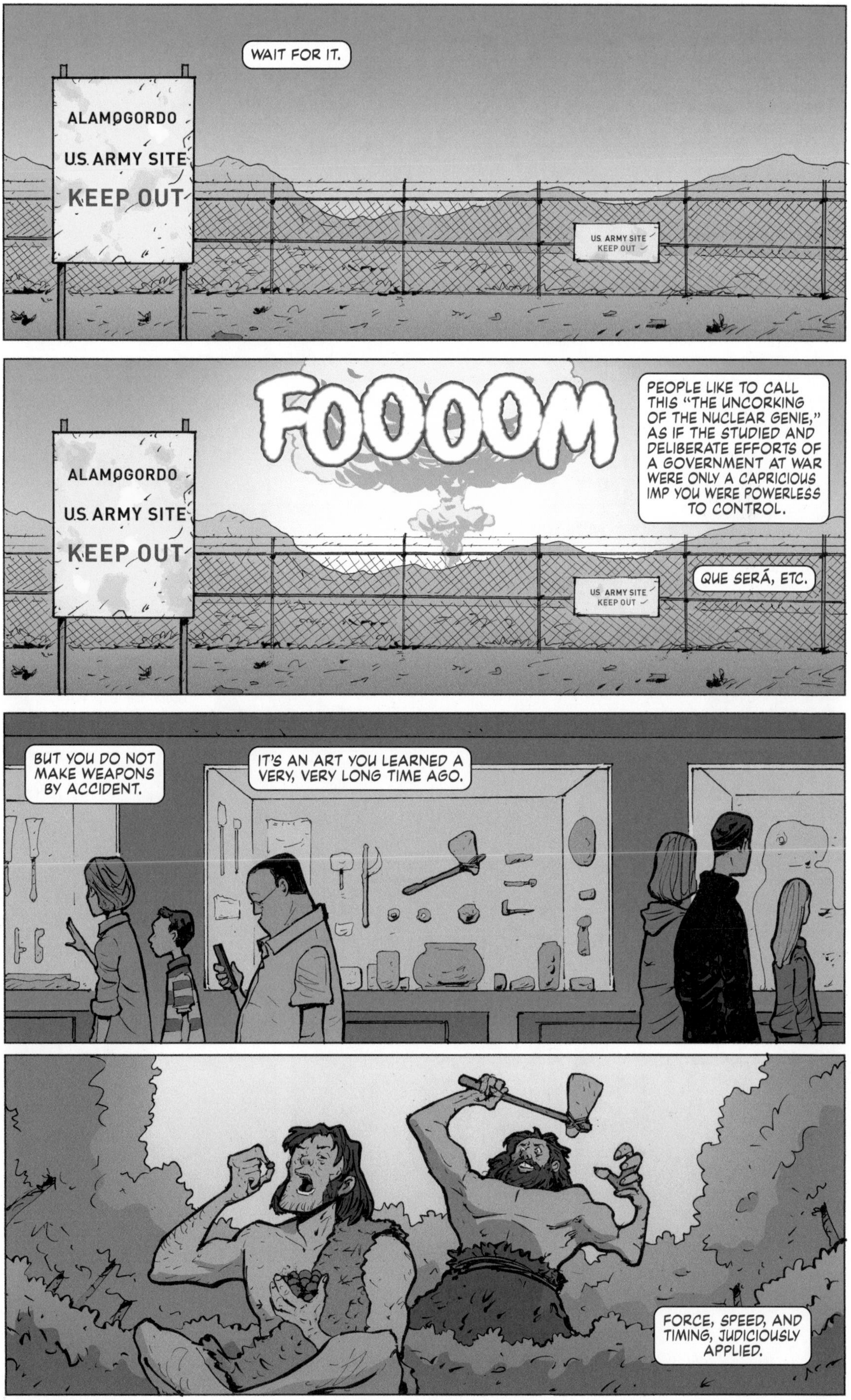
WAIT FOR IT.
ALAMOGORDO
U.S. ARMY SITE
KEEP OUT
U.S. ARMY SITE
KEEP OUT
FOOOOM
PEOPLE LIKE TO CALL THIS "THE UNCORKING OF THE NUCLEAR GENIE," AS IF THE STUDIED AND DELIBERATE EFFORTS OF A GOVERNMENT AT WAR WERE ONLY A CAPRICIOUS IMP YOU WERE POWERLESS TO CONTROL.
ALAMOGORDO
U.S. ARMY SITE
KEEP OUT
U.S. ARMY SITE
KEEP OUT
QUE SERÁ, ETC.
BUT YOU DO NOT MAKE WEAPONS BY ACCIDENT.
IT'S AN ART YOU LEARNED A VERY, VERY LONG TIME AGO.
FORCE, SPEED, AND TIMING, JUDICIOUSLY APPLIED.

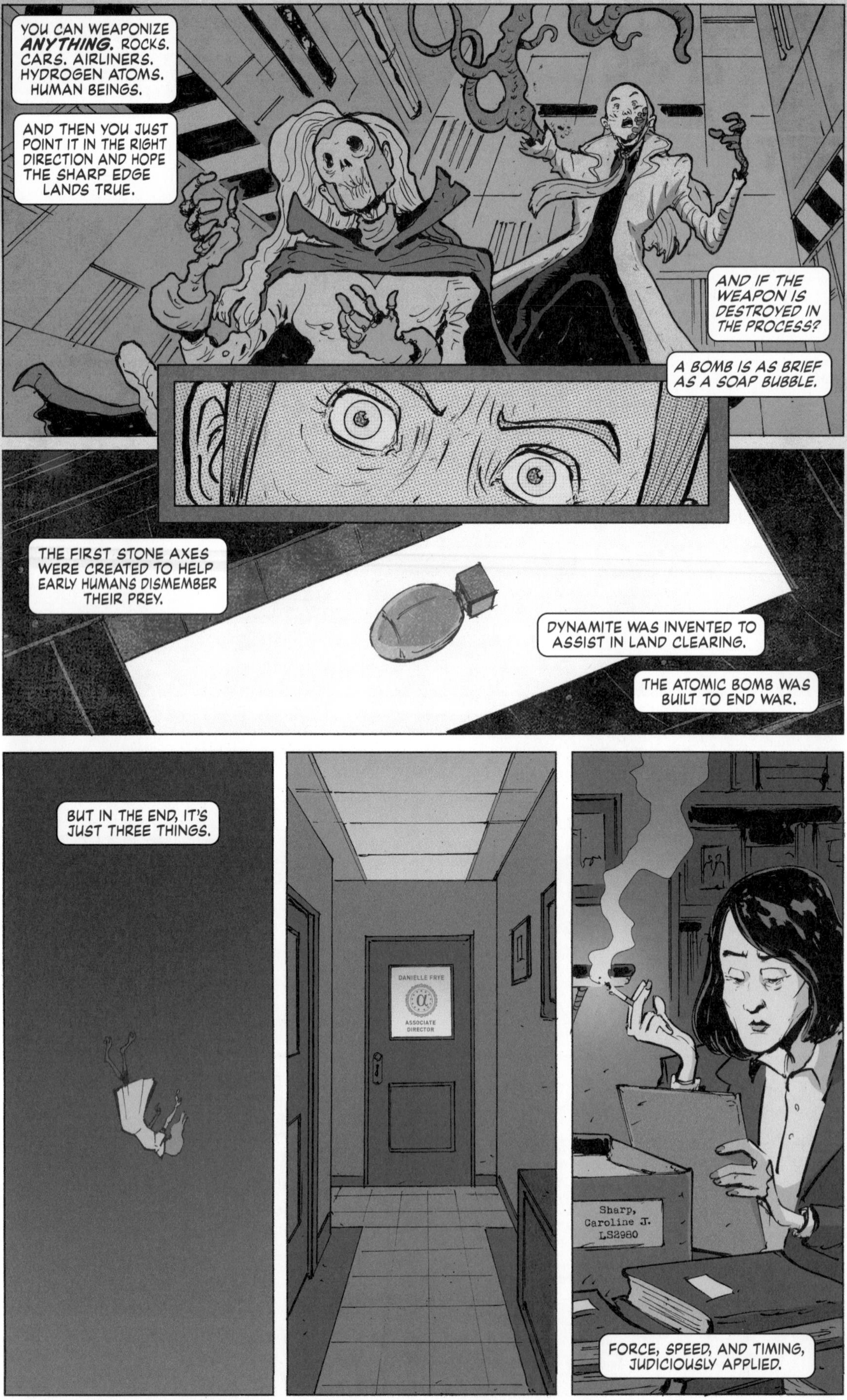
YOU CAN WEAPONIZE ANYTHING. ROCKS. CARS. AIRLINERS. HYDROGEN ATOMS. HUMAN BEINGS.
AND THEN YOU JUST POINT IT IN THE RIGHT DIRECTION AND HOPE THE SHARP EDGE LANDS TRUE.
AND IF THE WEAPON IS DESTROYED IN THE PROCESS?
A BOMB IS AS BRIEF AS A SOAP BUBBLE.
THE FIRST STONE AXES WERE CREATED TO HELP EARLY HUMANS DISMEMBER THEIR PREY.
DYNAMITE WAS INVENTED TO ASSIST IN LAND CLEARING.
THE ATOMIC BOMB WAS BUILT TO END WAR.
BUT IN THE END, IT'S JUST THREE THINGS.
DANIELLE FRYE
ASSOCIATE DIRECTOR
Sharp, Caroline J. LS2980
FORCE, SPEED, AND TIMING, JUDICIOUSLY APPLIED.

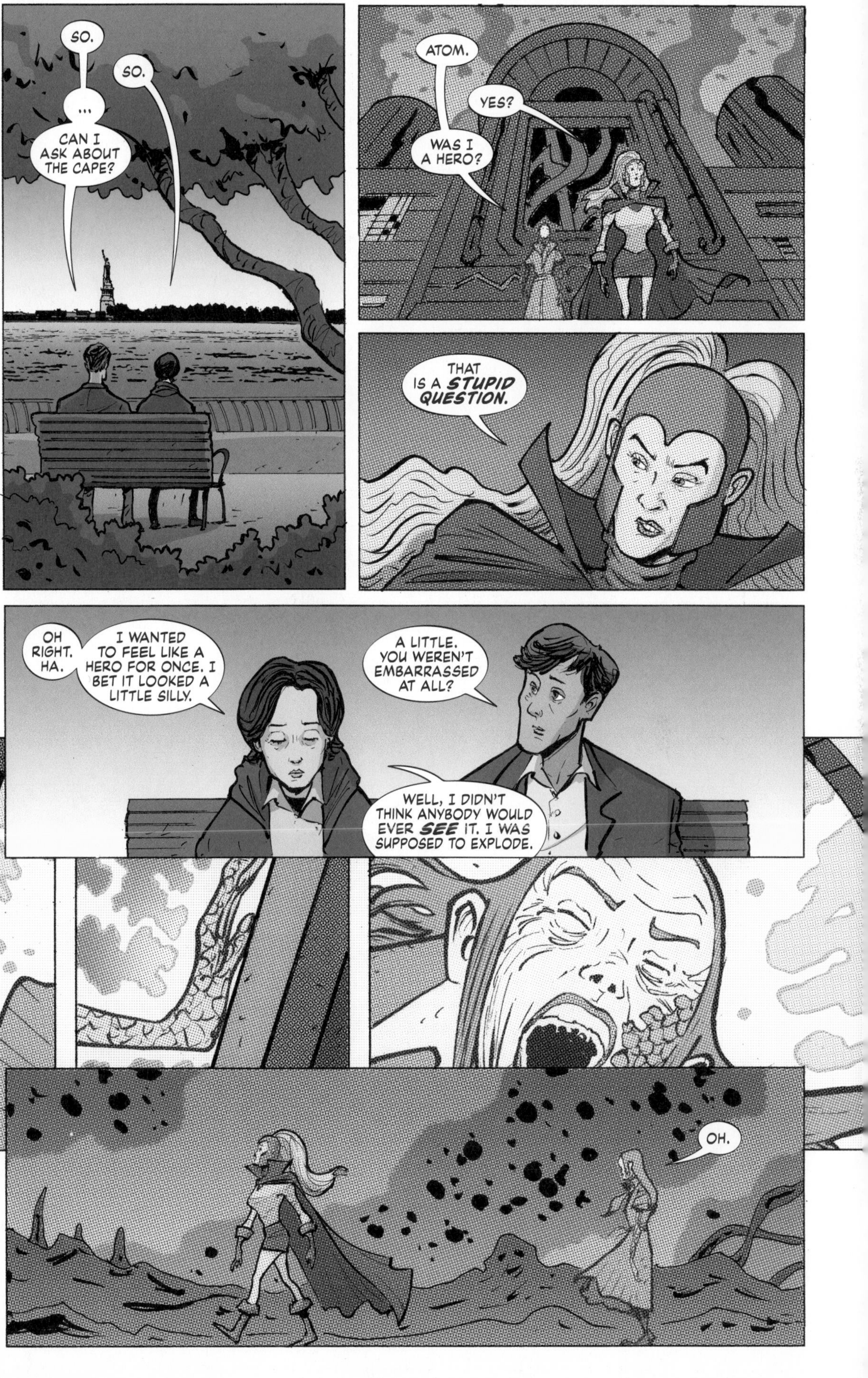
SO.
SO.
...
CAN I ASK ABOUT THE CAPE?
ATOM.
YES?
WAS I A HERO?
THAT IS A STUPID QUESTION.
OH RIGHT. HA.
I WANTED TO FEEL LIKE A HERO FOR ONCE. I BET IT LOOKED A LITTLE SILLY.
A LITTLE. YOU WEREN'T EMBARRASSED AT ALL?
WELL, I DIDN'T THINK ANYBODY WOULD EVER SEE IT. I WAS SUPPOSED TO EXPLODE.
OH.

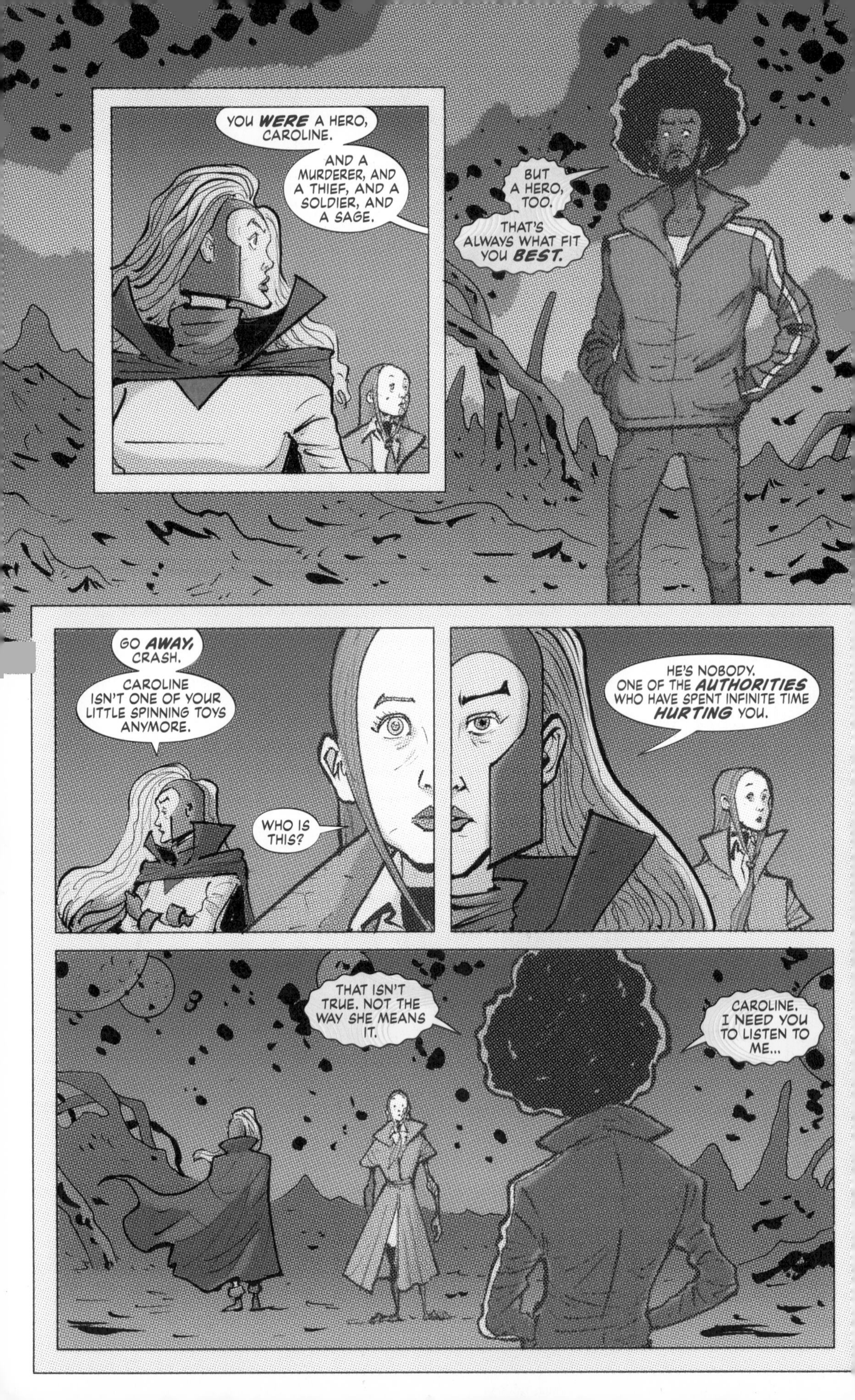
YOU WERE A HERO, CAROLINE.
AND A MURDERER, AND A THIEF, AND A SOLDIER, AND A SAGE.
BUT A HERO, TOO.
THAT'S ALWAYS WHAT FIT YOU BEST.
GO AWAY, CRASH.
CAROLINE ISN'T ONE OF YOUR LITTLE SPINNING TOYS ANYMORE.
WHO IS THIS?
HE'S NOBODY. ONE OF THE AUTHORITIES WHO HAVE SPENT INFINITE TIME HURTING YOU.
THAT ISN'T TRUE. NOT THE WAY SHE MEANS IT.
CAROLINE. I NEED YOU TO LISTEN TO ME...

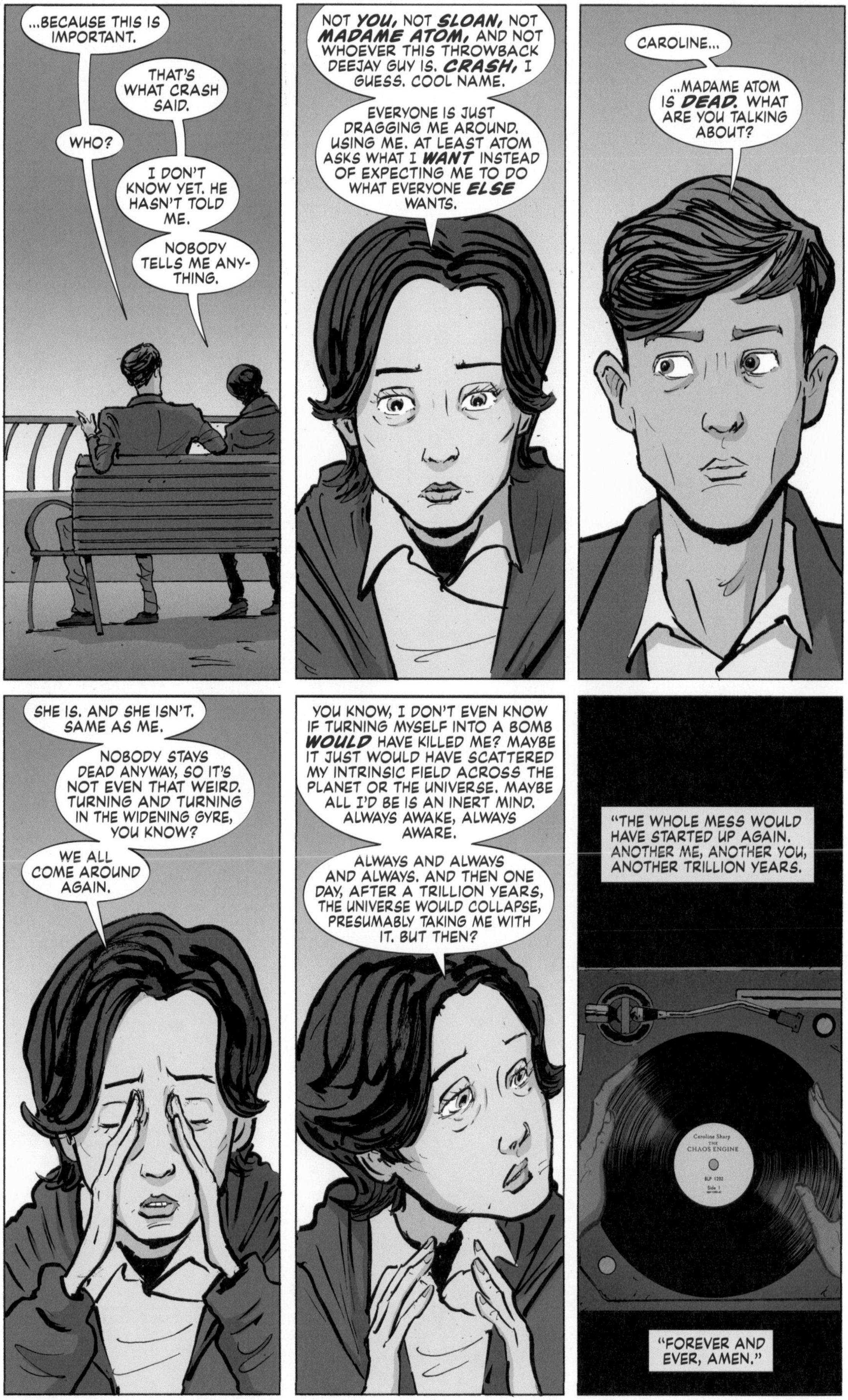
...BECAUSE THIS IS IMPORTANT.
THAT'S WHAT CRASH SAID.
WHO?
I DON'T KNOW YET. HE HASN'T TOLD ME.
NOBODY TELLS ME ANY-THING.
NOT YOU, NOT SLOAN, NOT MADAME ATOM, AND NOT WHOEVER THIS THROWBACK DEEJAY GUY IS. CRASH, I GUESS. COOL NAME.
EVERYONE IS JUST DRAGGING ME AROUND. USING ME. AT LEAST ATOM ASKS WHAT I WANT INSTEAD OF EXPECTING ME TO DO WHAT EVERYONE ELSE WANTS.
CAROLINE...
...MADAME ATOM IS DEAD. WHAT ARE YOU TALKING ABOUT?
SHE IS. AND SHE ISN'T. SAME AS ME.
NOBODY STAYS DEAD ANYWAY, SO IT'S NOT EVEN THAT WEIRD. TURNING AND TURNING IN THE WIDENING GYRE, YOU KNOW?
WE ALL COME AROUND AGAIN.
YOU KNOW, I DON'T EVEN KNOW IF TURNING MYSELF INTO A BOMB WOULD HAVE KILLED ME? MAYBE IT JUST WOULD HAVE SCATTERED MY INTRINSIC FIELD ACROSS THE PLANET OR THE UNIVERSE. MAYBE ALL I'D BE IS AN INERT MIND. ALWAYS AWAKE, ALWAYS AWARE.
ALWAYS AND ALWAYS AND ALWAYS. AND THEN ONE DAY, AFTER A TRILLION YEARS, THE UNIVERSE WOULD COLLAPSE, PRESUMABLY TAKING ME WITH IT. BUT THEN?
"THE WHOLE MESS WOULD HAVE STARTED UP AGAIN. ANOTHER ME, ANOTHER YOU, ANOTHER TRILLION YEARS.
Caroline Sharp
THE CHAOS ENGINE
BLP 1202
Side 1
"FOREVER AND EVER, AMEN."

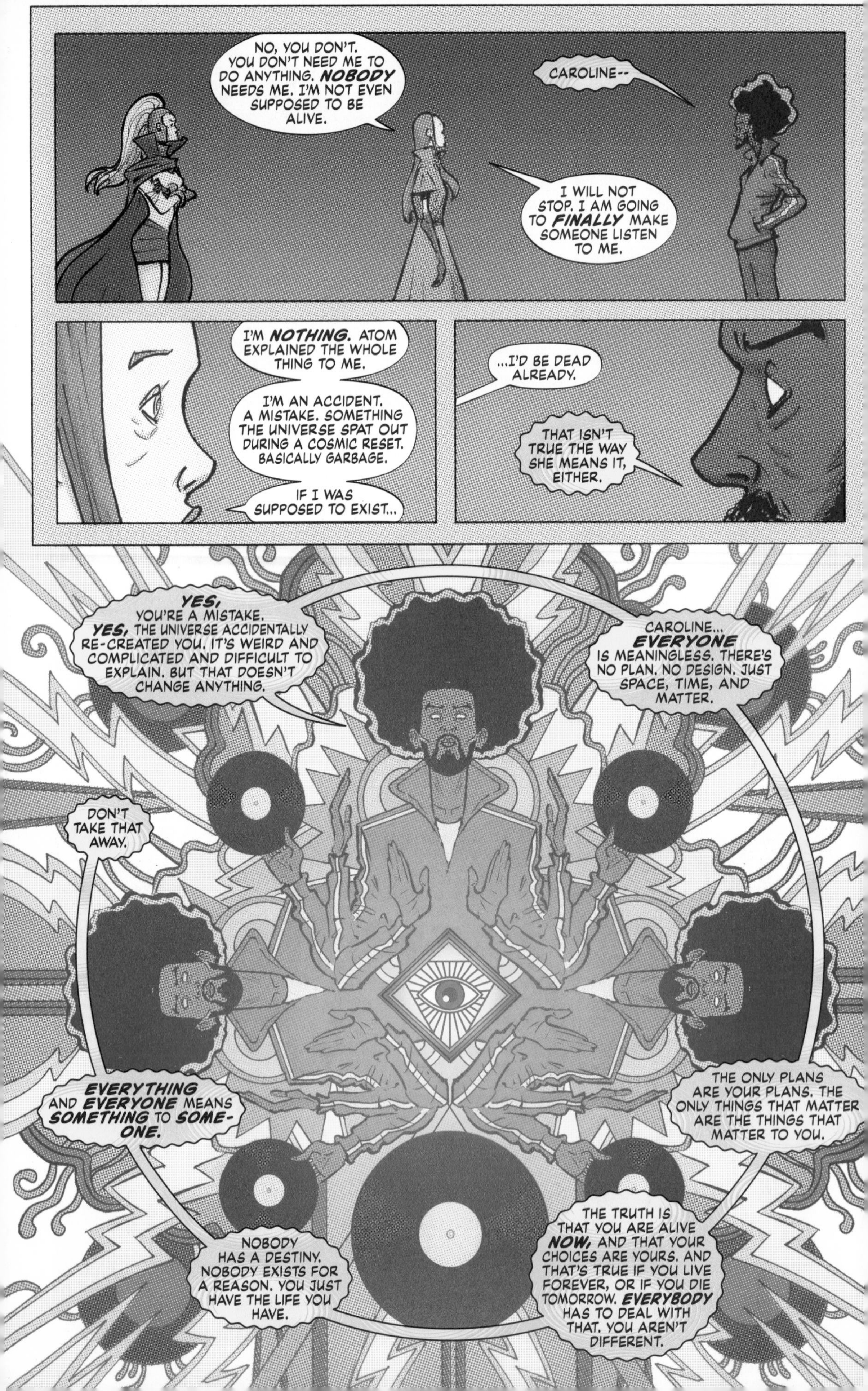
NO, YOU DON'T. YOU DON'T NEED ME TO DO ANYTHING. NOBODY NEEDS ME. I'M NOT EVEN SUPPOSED TO BE ALIVE.
CAROLINE--
I WILL NOT STOP. I AM GOING TO FINALLY MAKE SOMEONE LISTEN TO ME.
I'M NOTHING. ATOM EXPLAINED THE WHOLE THING TO ME.
I'M AN ACCIDENT. A MISTAKE. SOMETHING THE UNIVERSE SPAT OUT DURING A COSMIC RESET. BASICALLY GARBAGE.
IF I WAS SUPPOSED TO EXIST...
...I'D BE DEAD ALREADY.
THAT ISN'T TRUE THE WAY SHE MEANS IT, EITHER.
YES, YOU'RE A MISTAKE. YES, THE UNIVERSE ACCIDENTALLY RE-CREATED YOU. IT'S WEIRD AND COMPLICATED AND DIFFICULT TO EXPLAIN. BUT THAT DOESN'T CHANGE ANYTHING.
CAROLINE... EVERYONE IS MEANINGLESS. THERE'S NO PLAN. NO DESIGN. JUST SPACE, TIME, AND MATTER.
DON'T TAKE THAT AWAY.
EVERYTHING AND EVERYONE MEANS SOMETHING TO SOME-ONE.
THE ONLY PLANS ARE YOUR PLANS. THE ONLY THINGS THAT MATTER ARE THE THINGS THAT MATTER TO YOU.
NOBODY HAS A DESTINY. NOBODY EXISTS FOR A REASON. YOU JUST HAVE THE LIFE YOU HAVE.
THE TRUTH IS THAT YOU ARE ALIVE NOW, AND THAT YOUR CHOICES ARE YOURS. AND THAT'S TRUE IF YOU LIVE FOREVER, OR IF YOU DIE TOMORROW. EVERYBODY HAS TO DEAL WITH THAT. YOU AREN'T DIFFERENT.

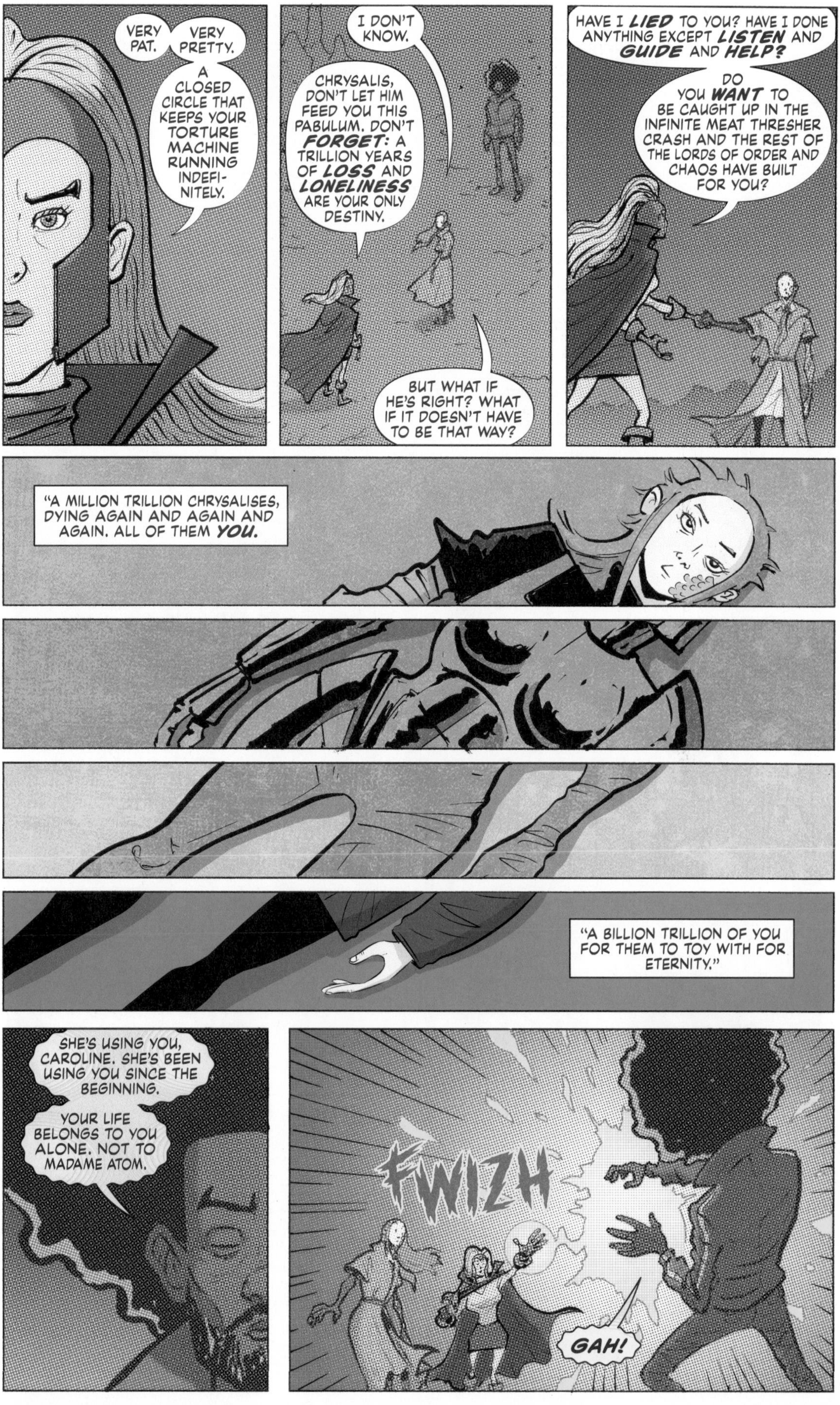
VERY PAT.
VERY PRETTY.
A CLOSED CIRCLE THAT KEEPS YOUR TORTURE MACHINE RUNNING INDEFI-NITELY.
I DON'T KNOW.
CHRYSALIS, DON'T LET HIM FEED YOU THIS PABULUM. DON'T FORGET: A TRILLION YEARS OF LOSS AND LONELINESS ARE YOUR ONLY DESTINY.
BUT WHAT IF HE'S RIGHT? WHAT IF IT DOESN'T HAVE TO BE THAT WAY?
HAVE I LIED TO YOU? HAVE I DONE ANYTHING EXCEPT LISTEN AND GUIDE AND HELP?
DO YOU WANT TO BE CAUGHT UP IN THE INFINITE MEAT THRESHER CRASH AND THE REST OF THE LORDS OF ORDER AND CHAOS HAVE BUILT FOR YOU?
"A MILLION TRILLION CHRYSALISES, DYING AGAIN AND AGAIN AND AGAIN. ALL OF THEM YOU.
"A BILLION TRILLION OF YOU FOR THEM TO TOY WITH FOR ETERNITY."
SHE'S USING YOU, CAROLINE. SHE'S BEEN USING YOU SINCE THE BEGINNING.
YOUR LIFE BELONGS TO YOU ALONE. NOT TO MADAME ATOM.
FWIZH
GAH!

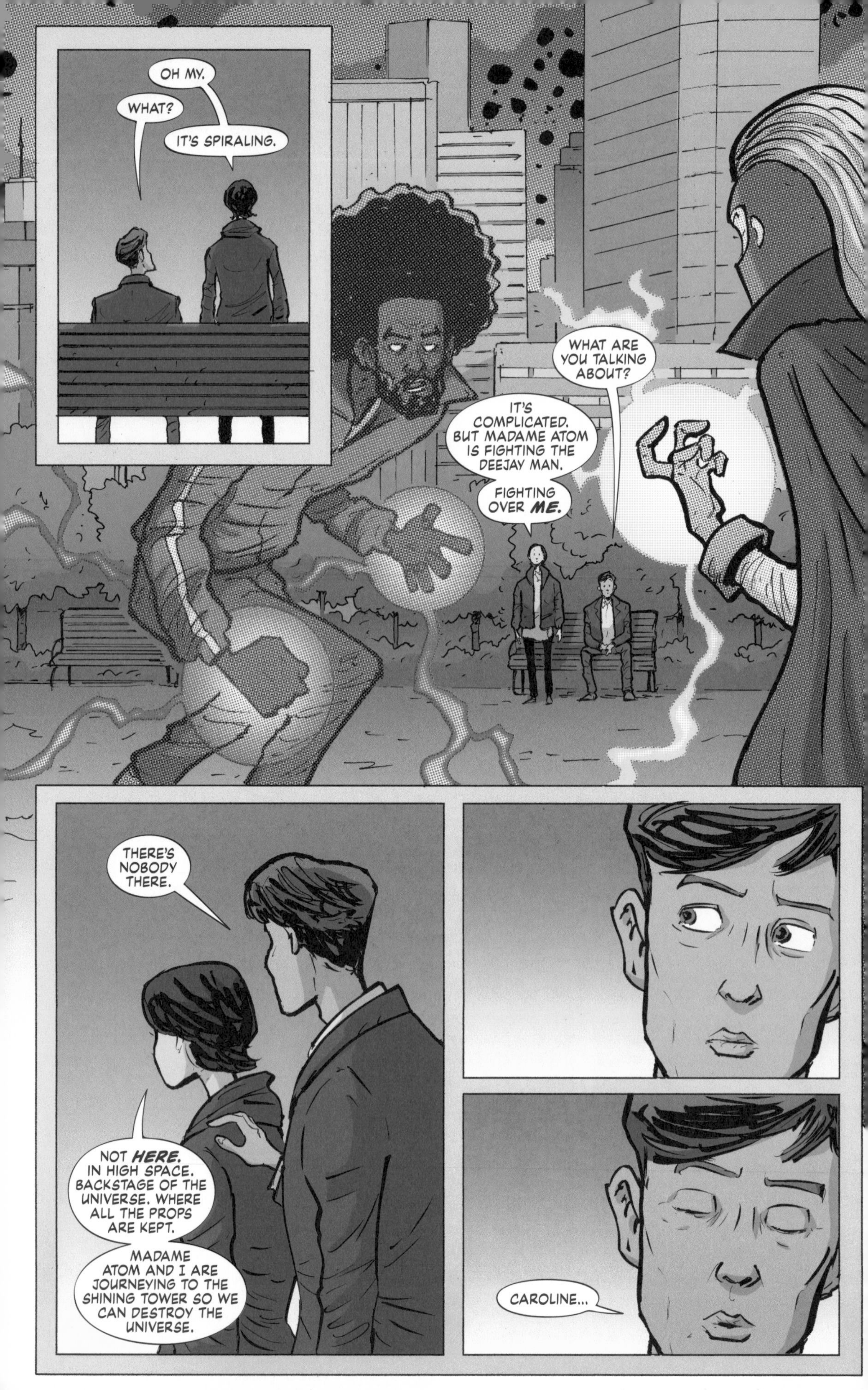
OH MY.
WHAT?
IT'S SPIRALING.
WHAT ARE YOU TALKING ABOUT?
IT'S COMPLICATED. BUT MADAME ATOM IS FIGHTING THE DEEJAY MAN.
FIGHTING OVER *ME.*
THERE'S NOBODY THERE.
NOT *HERE.* IN HIGH SPACE. BACKSTAGE OF THE UNIVERSE. WHERE ALL THE PROPS ARE KEPT.
MADAME ATOM AND I ARE JOURNEYING TO THE SHINING TOWER SO WE CAN DESTROY THE UNIVERSE.
CAROLINE...

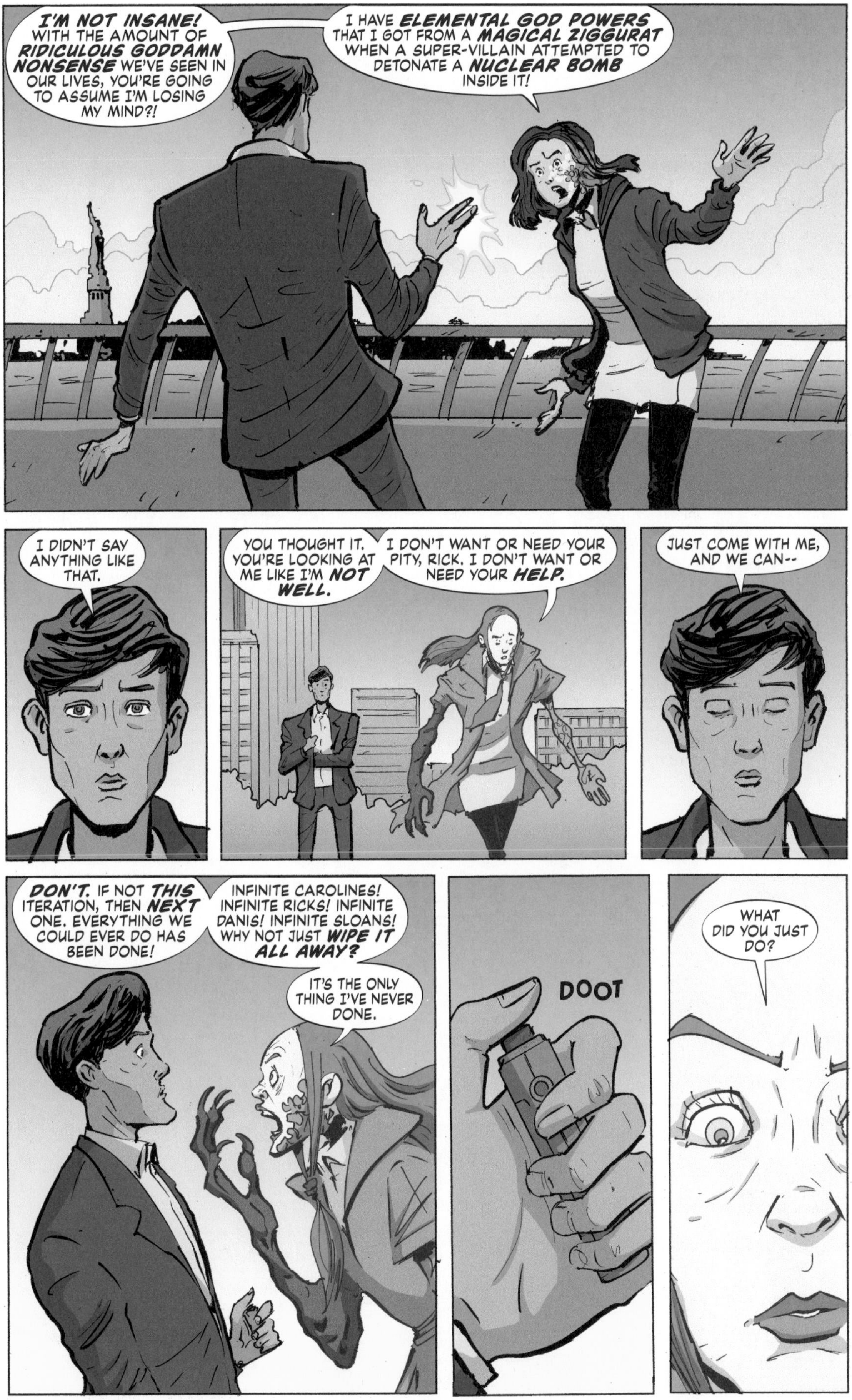
I'M NOT INSANE! WITH THE AMOUNT OF RIDICULOUS GODDAMN NONSENSE WE'VE SEEN IN OUR LIVES, YOU'RE GOING TO ASSUME I'M LOSING MY MIND?!
I HAVE ELEMENTAL GOD POWERS THAT I GOT FROM A MAGICAL ZIGGURAT WHEN A SUPER-VILLAIN ATTEMPTED TO DETONATE A NUCLEAR BOMB INSIDE IT!
I DIDN'T SAY ANYTHING LIKE THAT.
YOU THOUGHT IT. YOU'RE LOOKING AT ME LIKE I'M NOT WELL.
I DON'T WANT OR NEED YOUR PITY, RICK. I DON'T WANT OR NEED YOUR HELP.
JUST COME WITH ME, AND WE CAN--
DON'T. IF NOT THIS ITERATION, THEN NEXT ONE. EVERYTHING WE COULD EVER DO HAS BEEN DONE!
INFINITE CAROLINES! INFINITE RICKS! INFINITE DANIS! INFINITE SLOANS! WHY NOT JUST WIPE IT ALL AWAY?
IT'S THE ONLY THING I'VE NEVER DONE.
DOOT
WHAT DID YOU JUST DO?

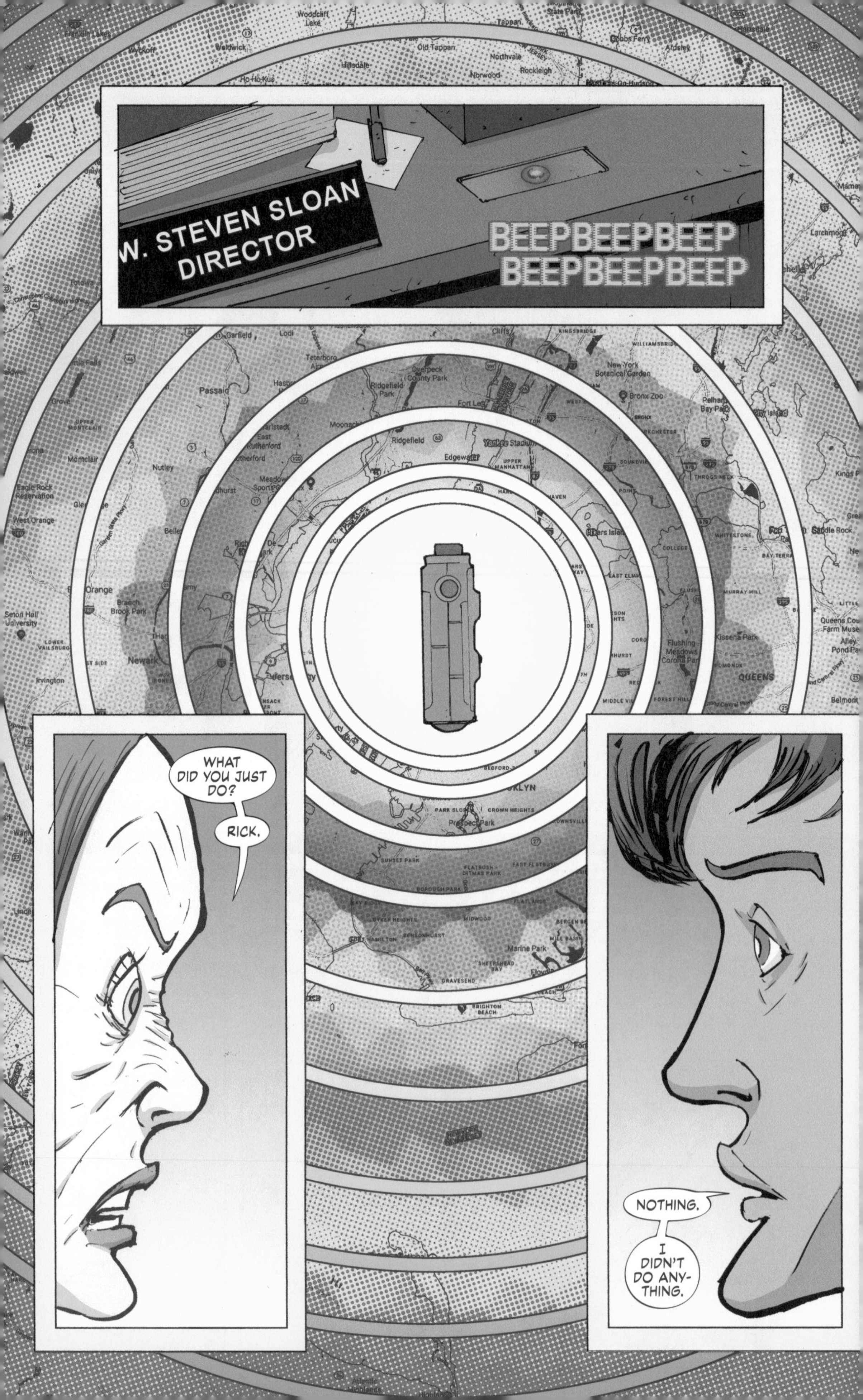
W. STEVEN SLOAN
DIRECTOR
BEEPBEEPBEEP
BEEPBEEPBEEP
WHAT DID YOU JUST DO?
RICK.
NOTHING.
I DIDN'T DO ANY-THING.

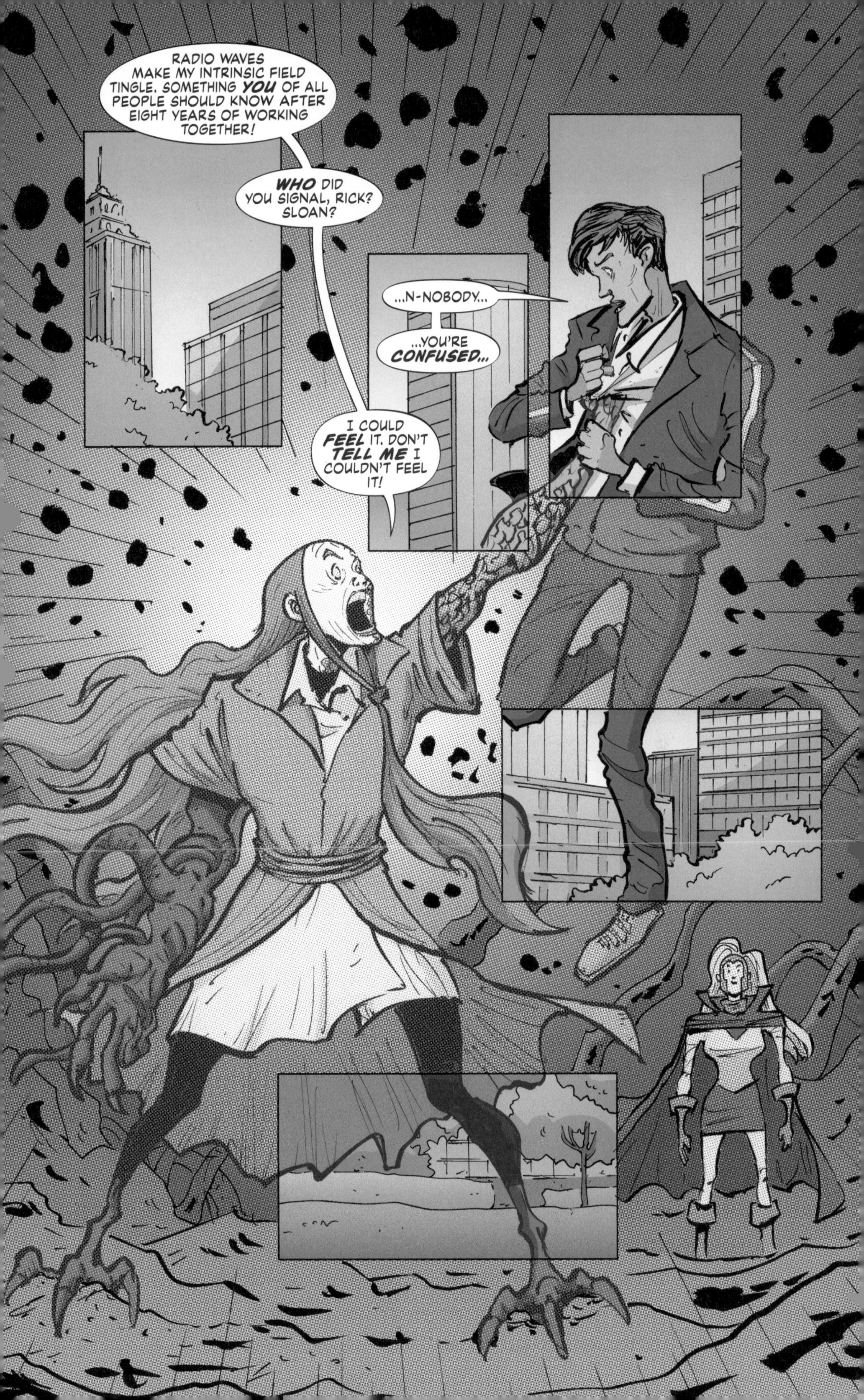
RADIO WAVES MAKE MY INTRINSIC FIELD TINGLE. SOMETHING YOU OF ALL PEOPLE SHOULD KNOW AFTER EIGHT YEARS OF WORKING TOGETHER!
WHO DID YOU SIGNAL, RICK? SLOAN?
...N-NOBODY...
...YOU'RE CONFUSED...
I COULD FEEL IT. DON'T TELL ME I COULDN'T FEEL IT!

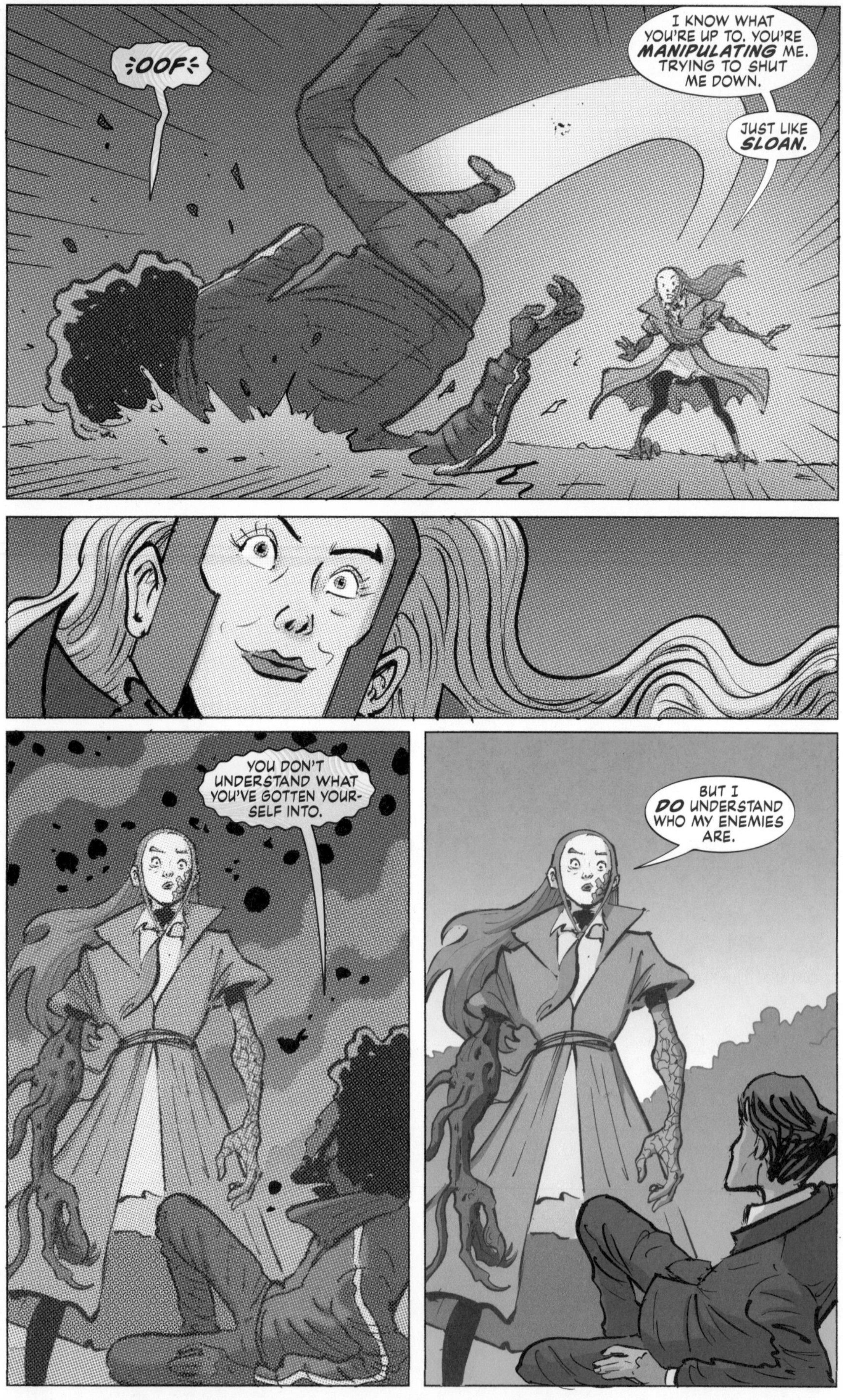
OOF
I KNOW WHAT YOU'RE UP TO. YOU'RE MANIPULATING ME. TRYING TO SHUT ME DOWN.
JUST LIKE SLOAN.
YOU DON'T UNDERSTAND WHAT YOU'VE GOTTEN YOUR-SELF INTO.
BUT I DO UNDERSTAND WHO MY ENEMIES ARE.

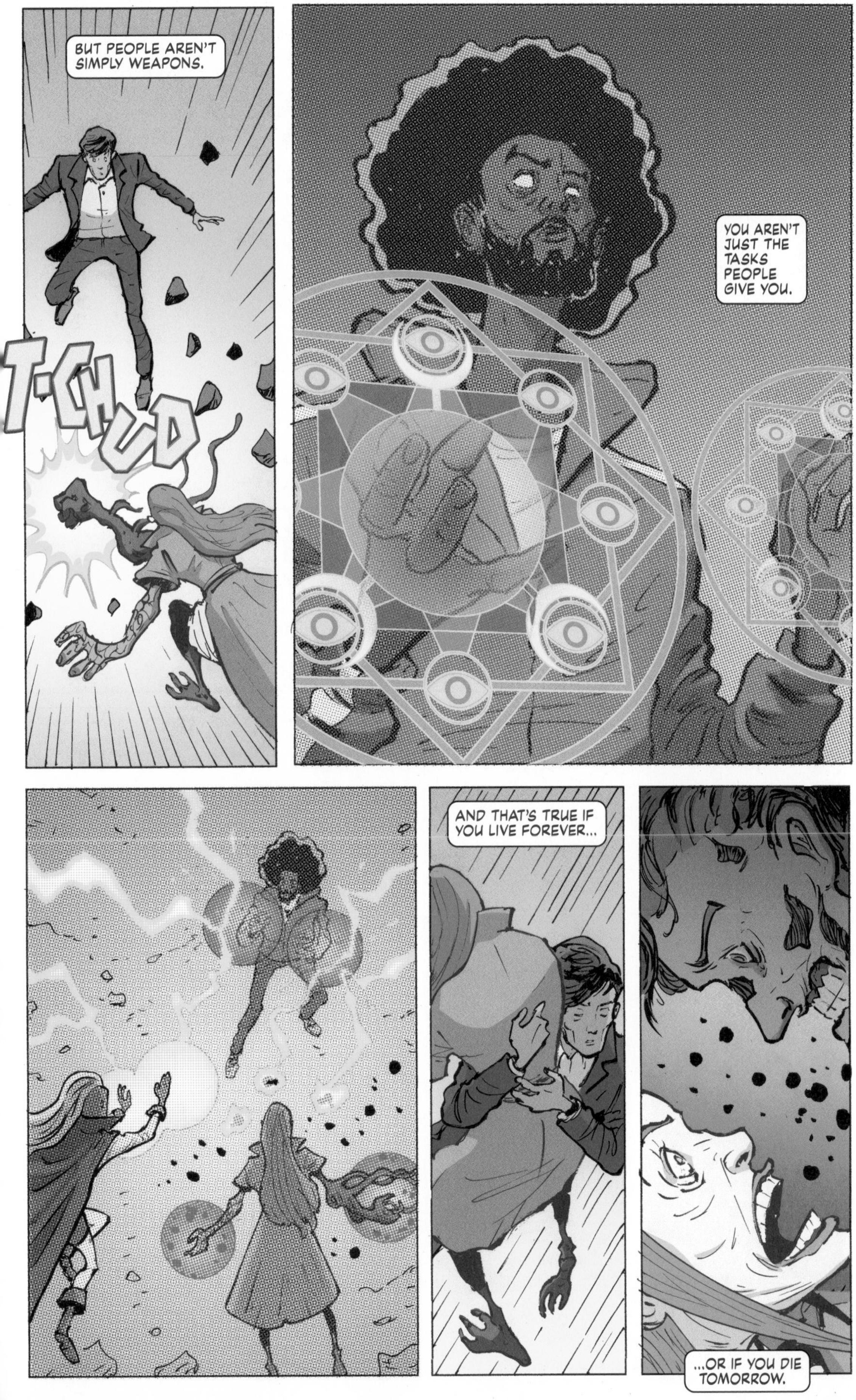
BUT PEOPLE AREN'T SIMPLY WEAPONS.
T-CHUD
YOU AREN'T JUST THE TASKS PEOPLE GIVE YOU.
AND THAT'S TRUE IF YOU LIVE FOREVER...
...OR IF YOU DIE TOMORROW.

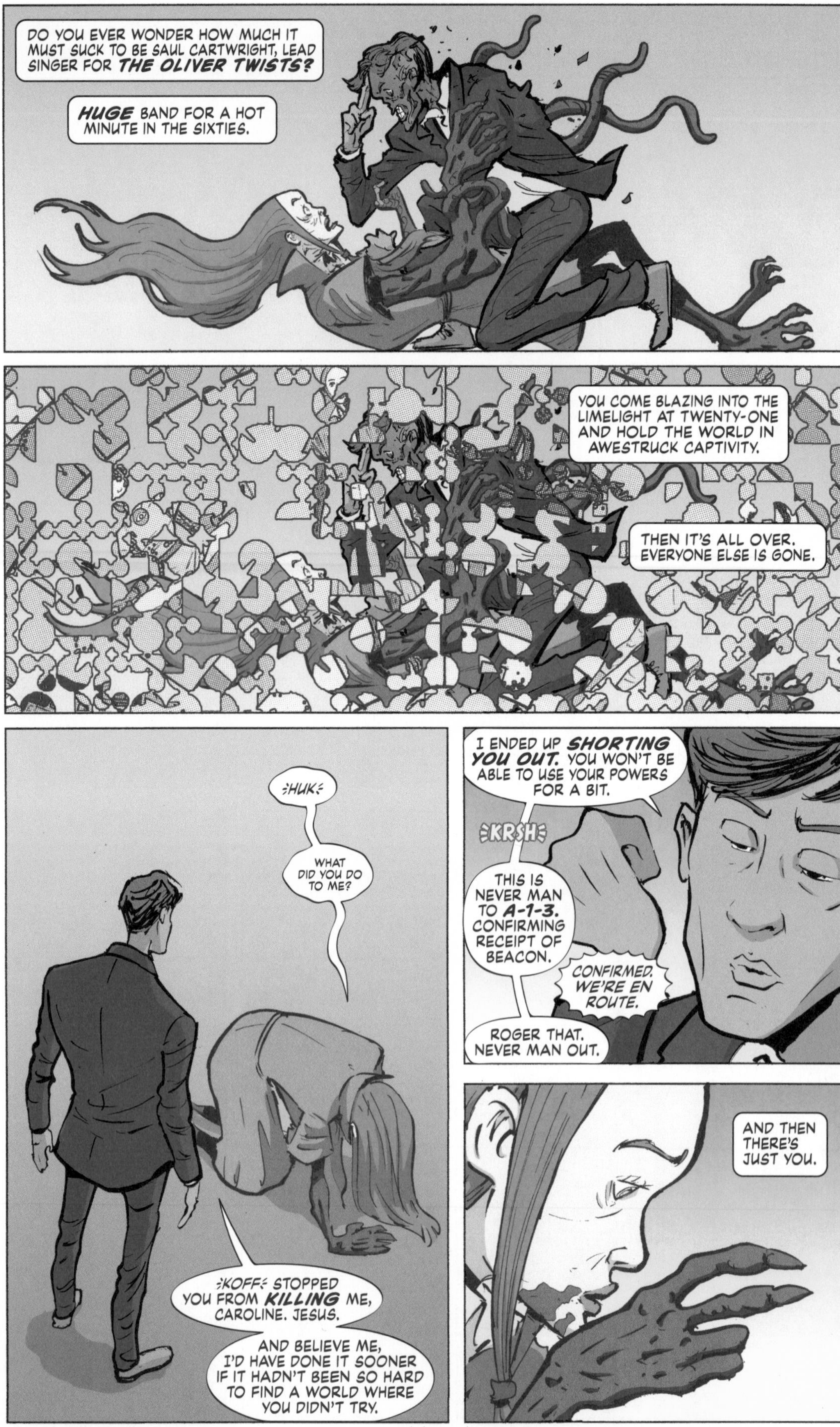
DO YOU EVER WONDER HOW MUCH IT MUST SUCK TO BE SAUL CARTWRIGHT, LEAD SINGER FOR THE OLIVER TWISTS?
HUGE BAND FOR A HOT MINUTE IN THE SIXTIES.
YOU COME BLAZING INTO THE LIMELIGHT AT TWENTY-ONE AND HOLD THE WORLD IN AWESTRUCK CAPTIVITY.
THEN IT'S ALL OVER. EVERYONE ELSE IS GONE.
HUK
WHAT DID YOU DO TO ME?
KOFF STOPPED YOU FROM KILLING ME, CAROLINE. JESUS.
AND BELIEVE ME, I'D HAVE DONE IT SOONER IF IT HADN'T BEEN SO HARD TO FIND A WORLD WHERE YOU DIDN'T TRY.
I ENDED UP SHORTING YOU OUT. YOU WON'T BE ABLE TO USE YOUR POWERS FOR A BIT.
KRSH
THIS IS NEVER MAN TO A-1-3. CONFIRMING RECEIPT OF BEACON.
CONFIRMED. WE'RE EN ROUTE.
ROGER THAT. NEVER MAN OUT.
AND THEN THERE'S JUST YOU.

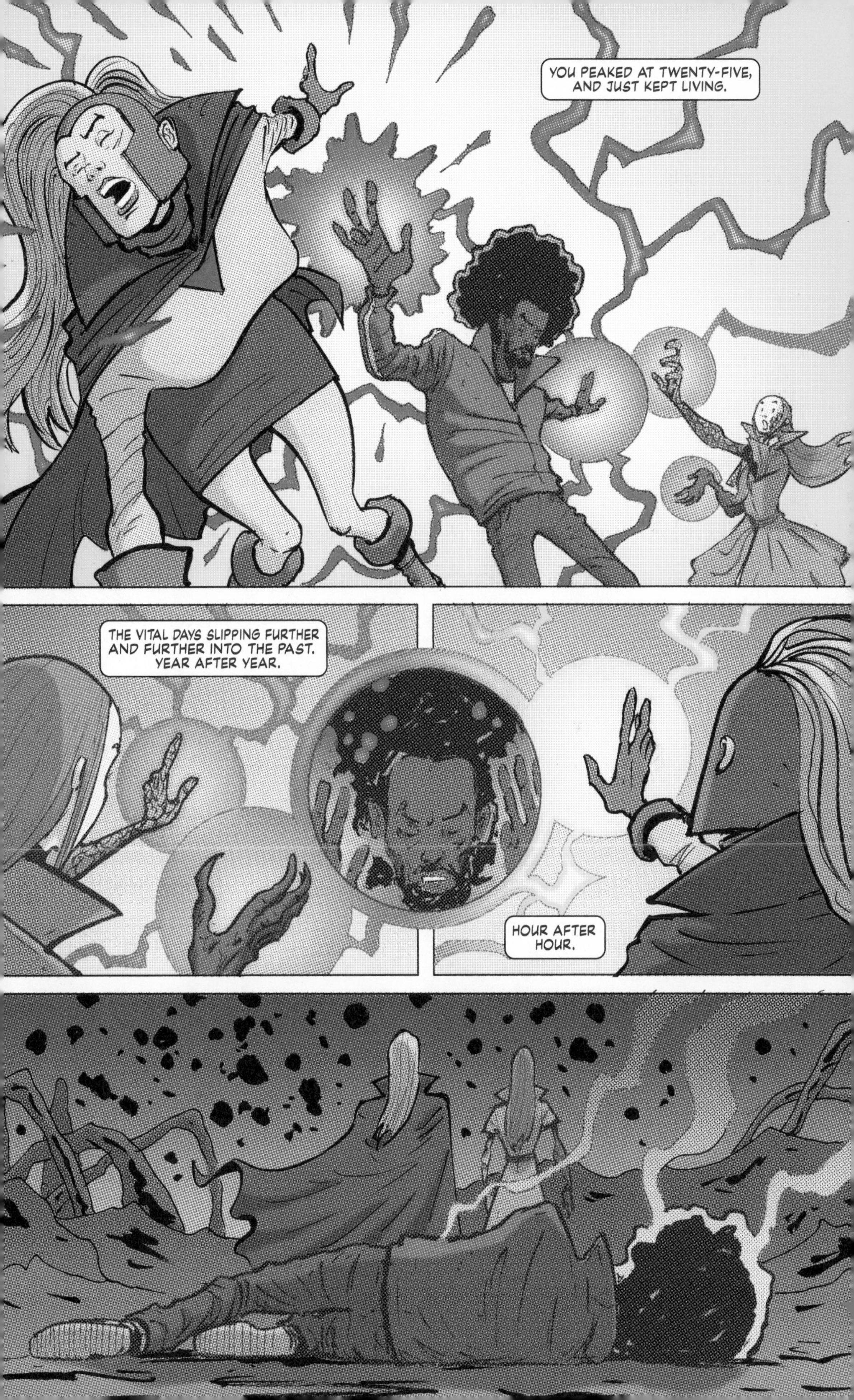
YOU PEAKED AT TWENTY-FIVE, AND JUST KEPT LIVING.
THE VITAL DAYS SLIPPING FURTHER AND FURTHER INTO THE PAST. YEAR AFTER YEAR.
HOUR AFTER HOUR.

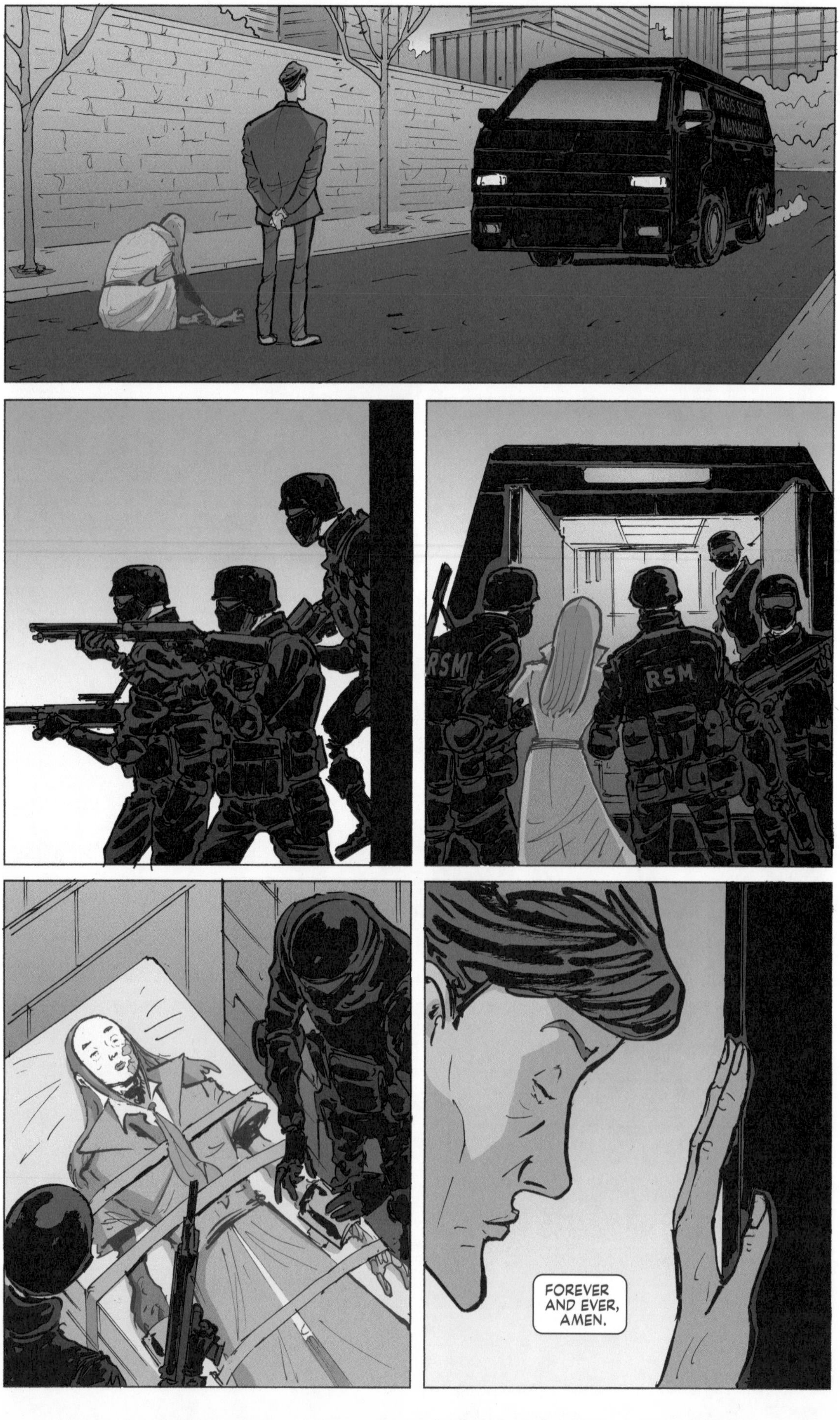
REGIS SECURITY
MANAGEMENT
RSM
RSM
FOREVER AND EVER, AMEN.

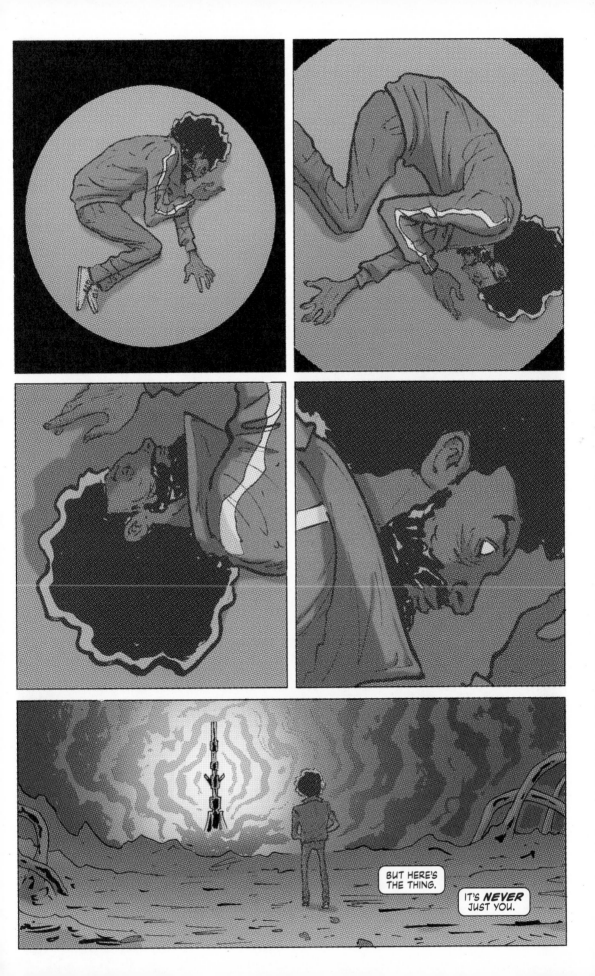

BUT HERE'S
THE THING.

IT'S **NEVER**
JUST YOU.

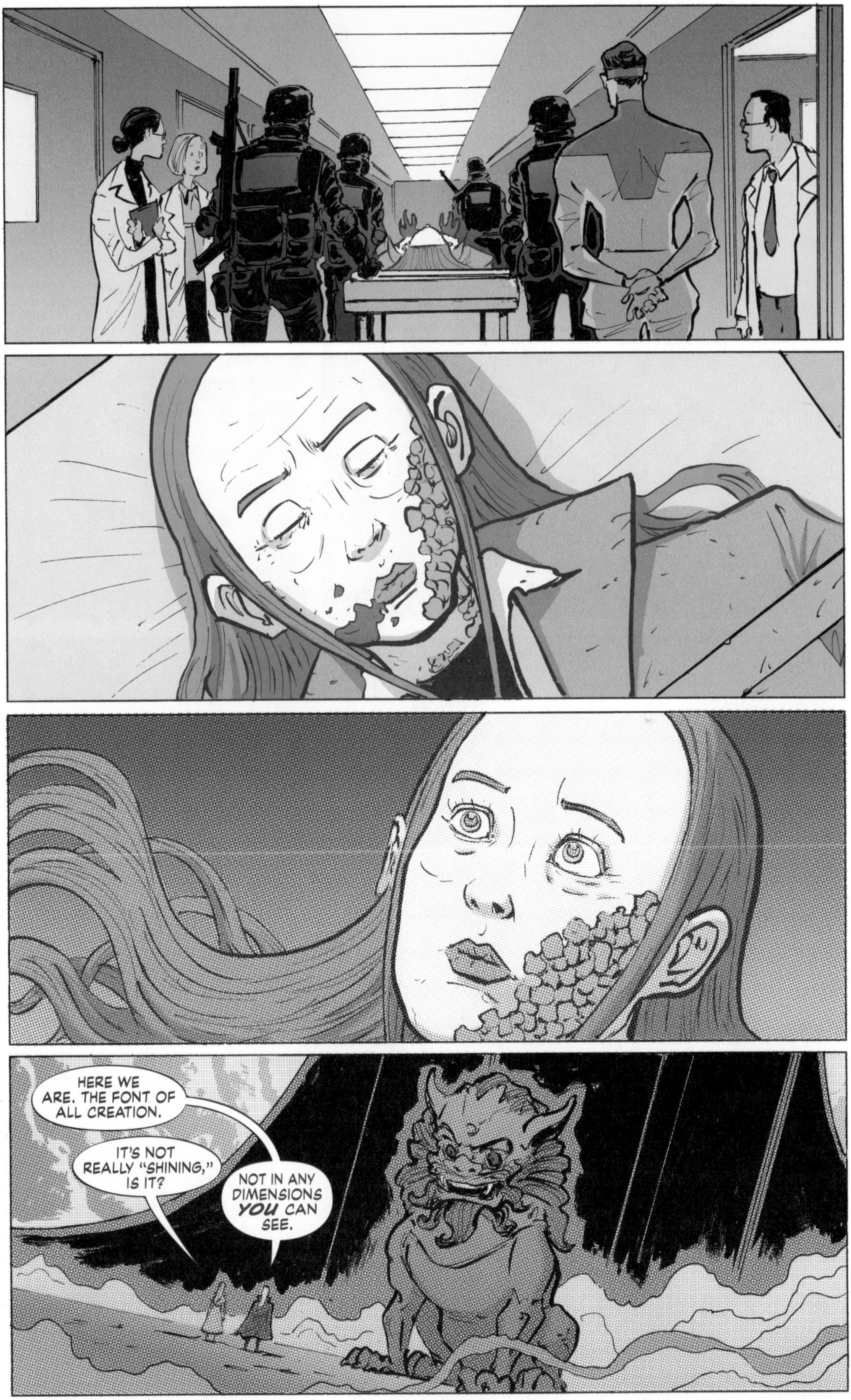
HERE WE ARE. THE FONT OF ALL CREATION.
IT'S NOT REALLY "SHINING," IS IT?
NOT IN ANY DIMENSIONS YOU CAN SEE.

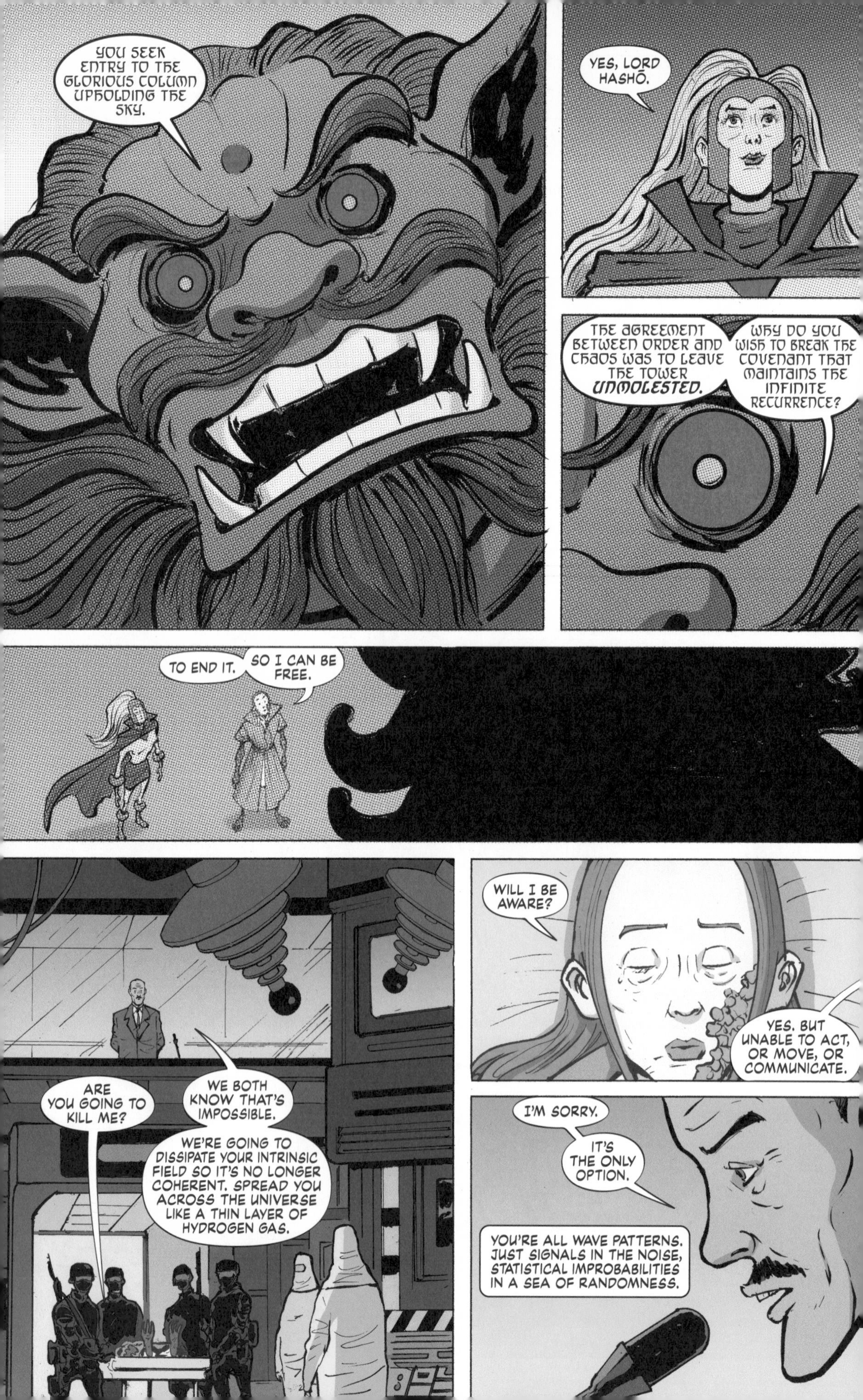
YOU SEEK ENTRY TO THE GLORIOUS COLUMN UPHOLDING THE SKY.
YES, LORD HASHŌ.
THE AGREEMENT BETWEEN ORDER AND CHAOS WAS TO LEAVE THE TOWER UNMOLESTED.
WHY DO YOU WISH TO BREAK THE COVENANT THAT MAINTAINS THE INFINITE RECURRENCE?
TO END IT.
SO I CAN BE FREE.
ARE YOU GOING TO KILL ME?
WE BOTH KNOW THAT'S IMPOSSIBLE.
WE'RE GOING TO DISSIPATE YOUR INTRINSIC FIELD SO IT'S NO LONGER COHERENT. SPREAD YOU ACROSS THE UNIVERSE LIKE A THIN LAYER OF HYDROGEN GAS.
WILL I BE AWARE?
YES. BUT UNABLE TO ACT, OR MOVE, OR COMMUNICATE.
I'M SORRY.
IT'S THE ONLY OPTION.
YOU'RE ALL WAVE PATTERNS. JUST SIGNALS IN THE NOISE, STATISTICAL IMPROBABILITIES IN A SEA OF RANDOMNESS.

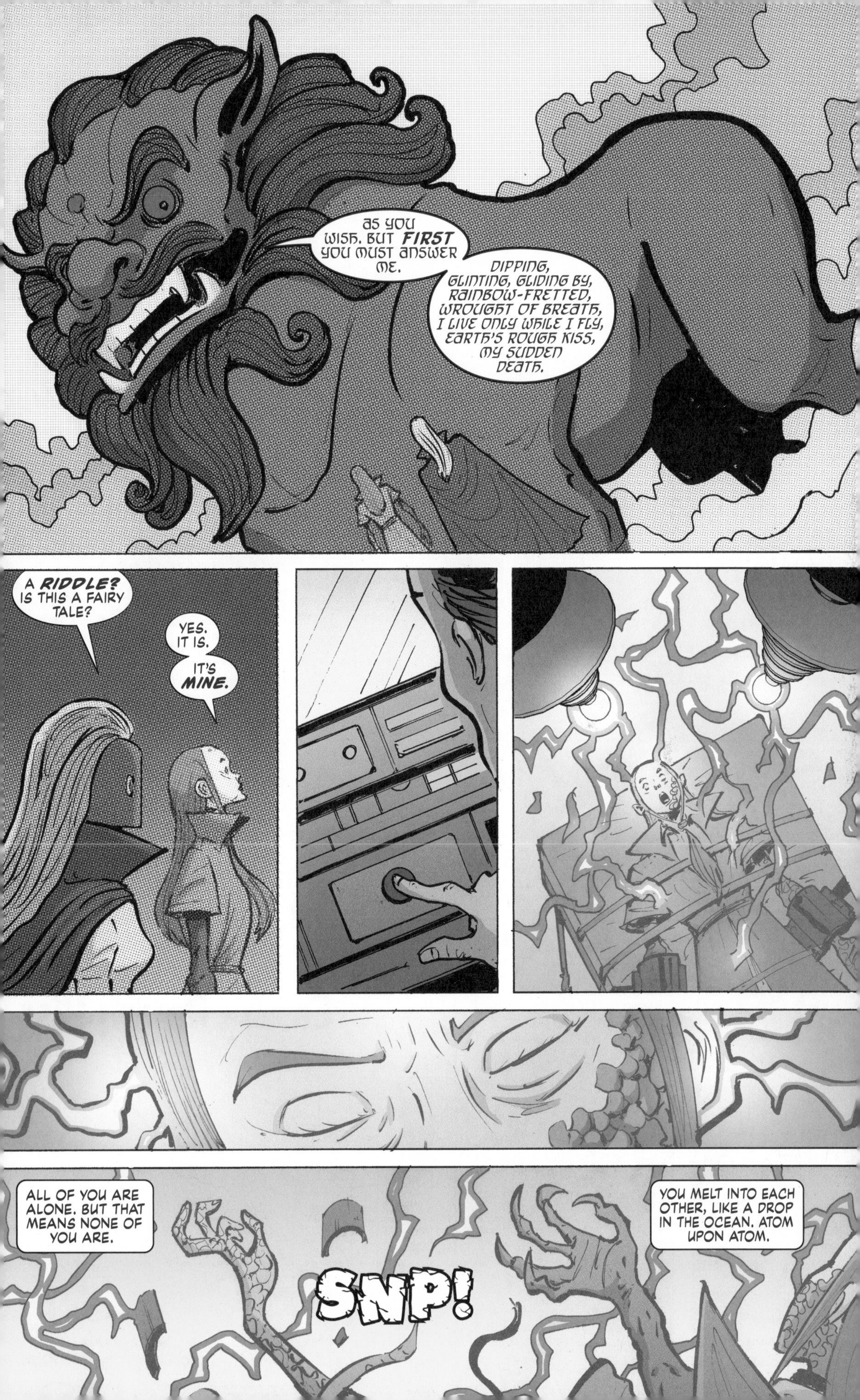

AS YOU WISH. BUT FIRST YOU MUST ANSWER ME.
DIPPING, GLINTING, GLIDING BY, RAINBOW-FRETTED, WROUGHT OF BREATH, I LIVE ONLY WHILE I FLY, EARTH'S ROUGH KISS, MY SUDDEN DEATH.
A RIDDLE? IS THIS A FAIRY TALE?
YES. IT IS.
IT'S MINE.
ALL OF YOU ARE ALONE. BUT THAT MEANS NONE OF YOU ARE.
YOU MELT INTO EACH OTHER, LIKE A DROP IN THE OCEAN. ATOM UPON ATOM.
SNP!

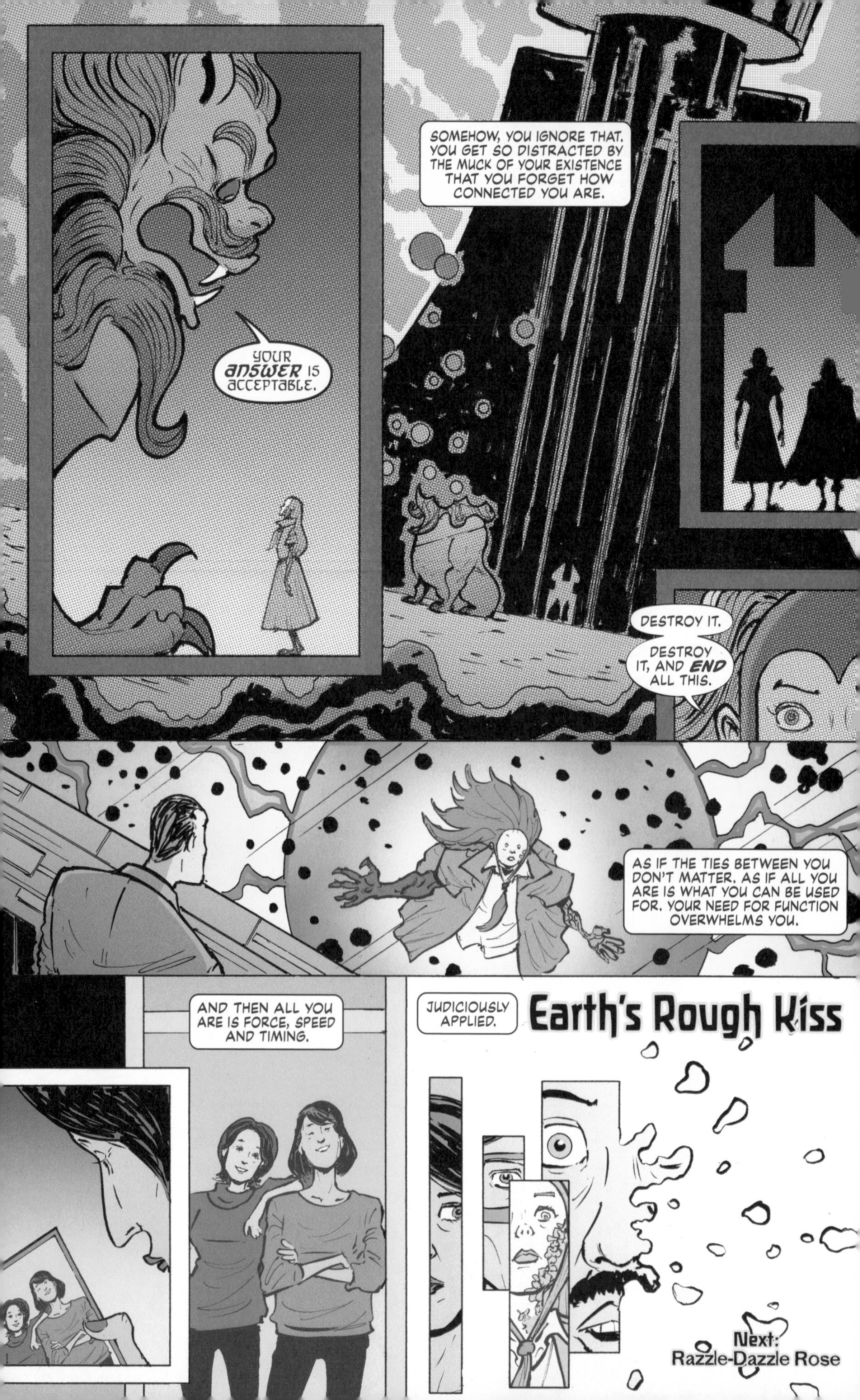
YOUR ANSWER IS ACCEPTABLE.
SOMEHOW, YOU IGNORE THAT. YOU GET SO DISTRACTED BY THE MUCK OF YOUR EXISTENCE THAT YOU FORGET HOW CONNECTED YOU ARE.
DESTROY IT.
DESTROY IT, AND END ALL THIS.
AS IF THE TIES BETWEEN YOU DON'T MATTER. AS IF ALL YOU ARE IS WHAT YOU CAN BE USED FOR. YOUR NEED FOR FUNCTION OVERWHELMS YOU.
AND THEN ALL YOU ARE IS FORCE, SPEED AND TIMING.
JUDICIOUSLY APPLIED.
Earth's Rough Kiss
Next:
Razzle-Dazzle Rose

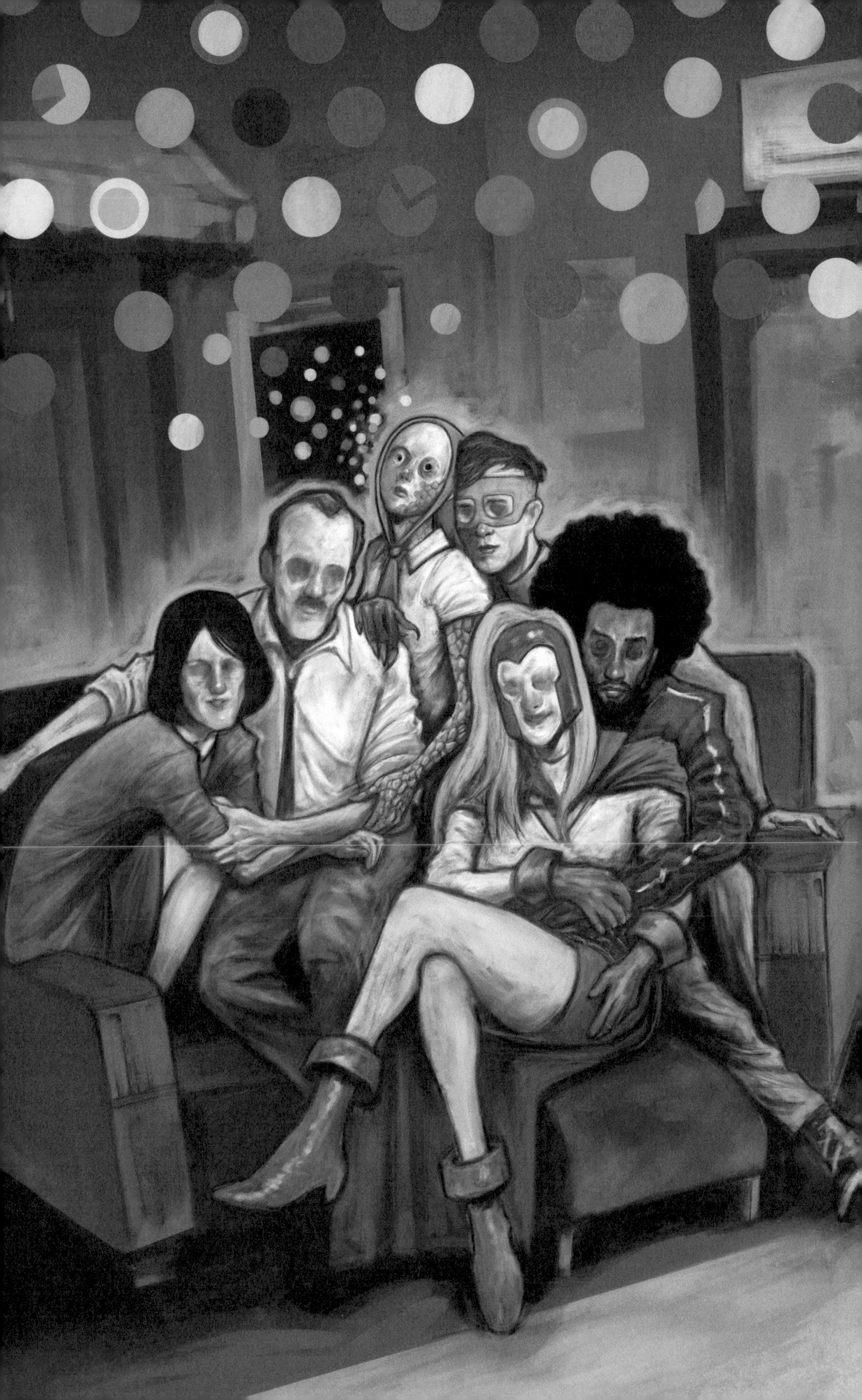

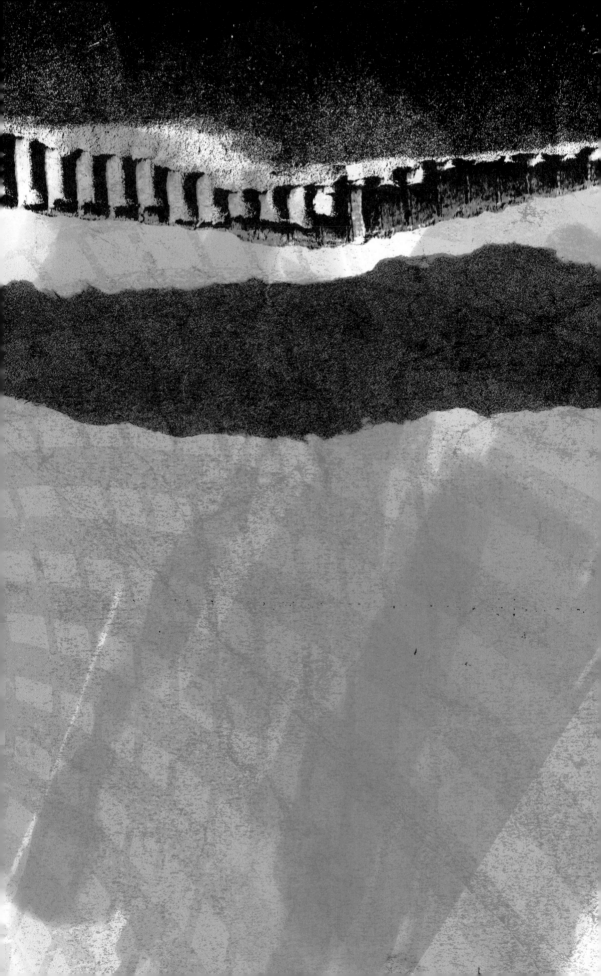

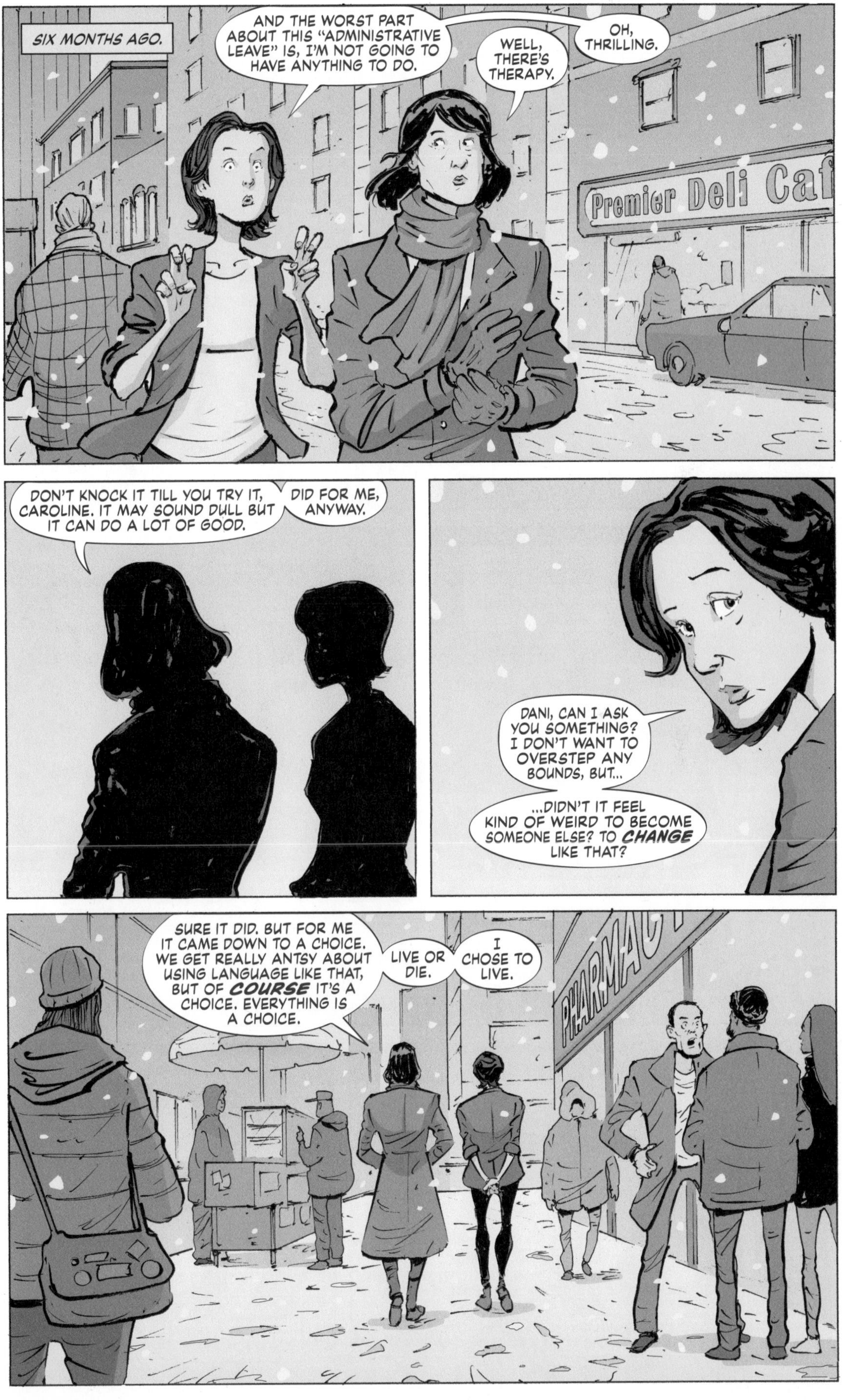
SIX MONTHS AGO.
AND THE WORST PART ABOUT THIS "ADMINISTRATIVE LEAVE" IS, I'M NOT GOING TO HAVE ANYTHING TO DO.
OH, THRILLING.
WELL, THERE'S THERAPY.
Premier Deli Caf
DON'T KNOCK IT TILL YOU TRY IT, CAROLINE. IT MAY SOUND DULL BUT IT CAN DO A LOT OF GOOD.
DID FOR ME, ANYWAY.
DANI, CAN I ASK YOU SOMETHING? I DON'T WANT TO OVERSTEP ANY BOUNDS, BUT...
...DIDN'T IT FEEL KIND OF WEIRD TO BECOME SOMEONE ELSE? TO ***CHANGE*** LIKE THAT?
SURE IT DID. BUT FOR ME IT CAME DOWN TO A CHOICE. WE GET REALLY ANTSY ABOUT USING LANGUAGE LIKE THAT, BUT OF ***COURSE*** IT'S A CHOICE. EVERYTHING IS A CHOICE.
LIVE OR DIE.
I CHOSE TO LIVE.

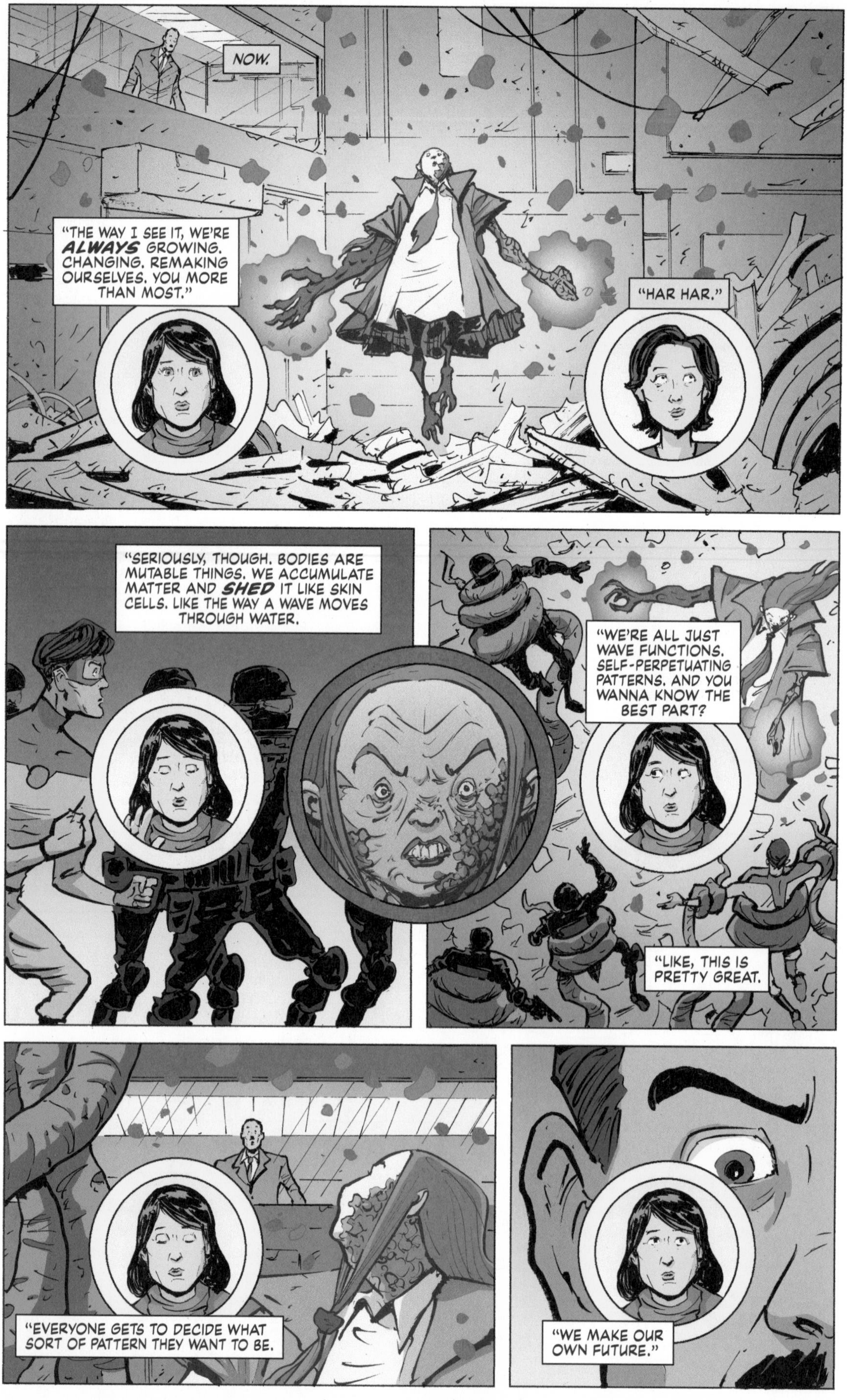
NOW.
"THE WAY I SEE IT, WE'RE ALWAYS GROWING. CHANGING. REMAKING OURSELVES. YOU MORE THAN MOST."
"HAR HAR."
"SERIOUSLY, THOUGH. BODIES ARE MUTABLE THINGS. WE ACCUMULATE MATTER AND SHED IT LIKE SKIN CELLS. LIKE THE WAY A WAVE MOVES THROUGH WATER.
"WE'RE ALL JUST WAVE FUNCTIONS. SELF-PERPETUATING PATTERNS. AND YOU WANNA KNOW THE BEST PART?
"LIKE, THIS IS PRETTY GREAT.
"EVERYONE GETS TO DECIDE WHAT SORT OF PATTERN THEY WANT TO BE.
"WE MAKE OUR OWN FUTURE."

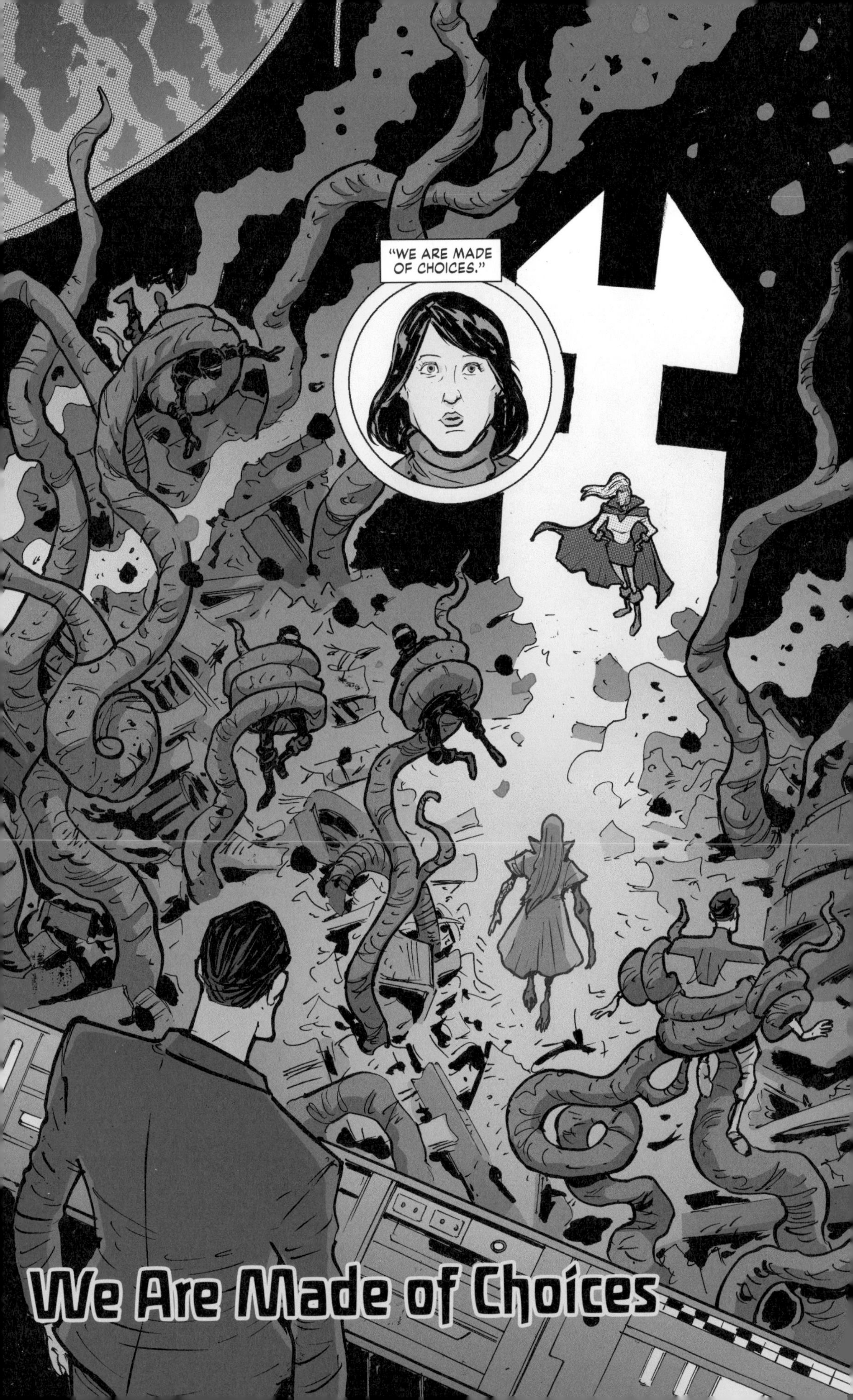
"WE ARE MADE OF CHOICES."
We Are Made of Choices

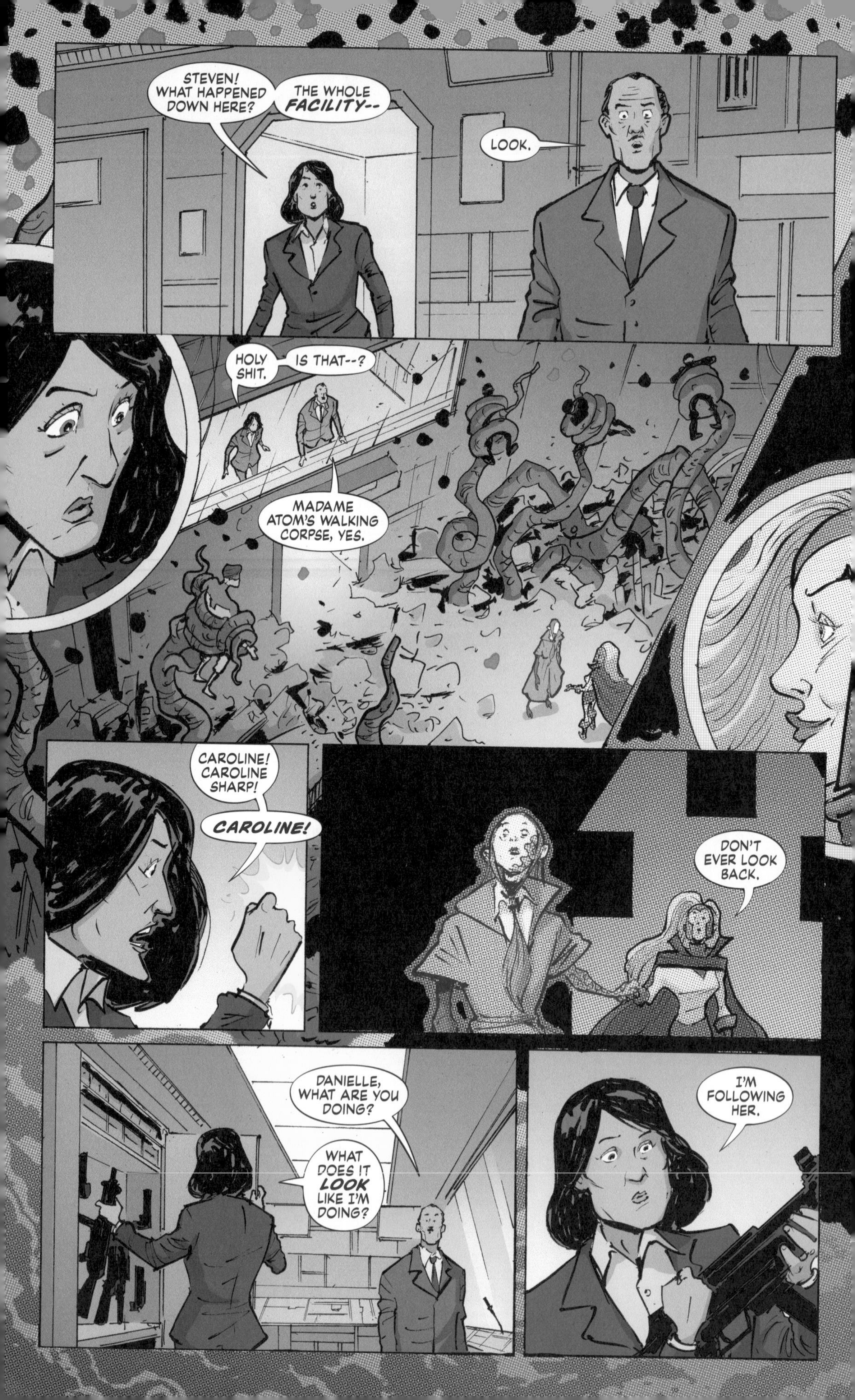

STEVEN! WHAT HAPPENED DOWN HERE?
THE WHOLE FACILITY--
LOOK.
HOLY SHIT.
IS THAT--?
MADAME ATOM'S WALKING CORPSE, YES.
CAROLINE! CAROLINE SHARP!
CAROLINE!
DON'T EVER LOOK BACK.
DANIELLE, WHAT ARE YOU DOING?
WHAT DOES IT LOOK LIKE I'M DOING?
I'M FOLLOWING HER.

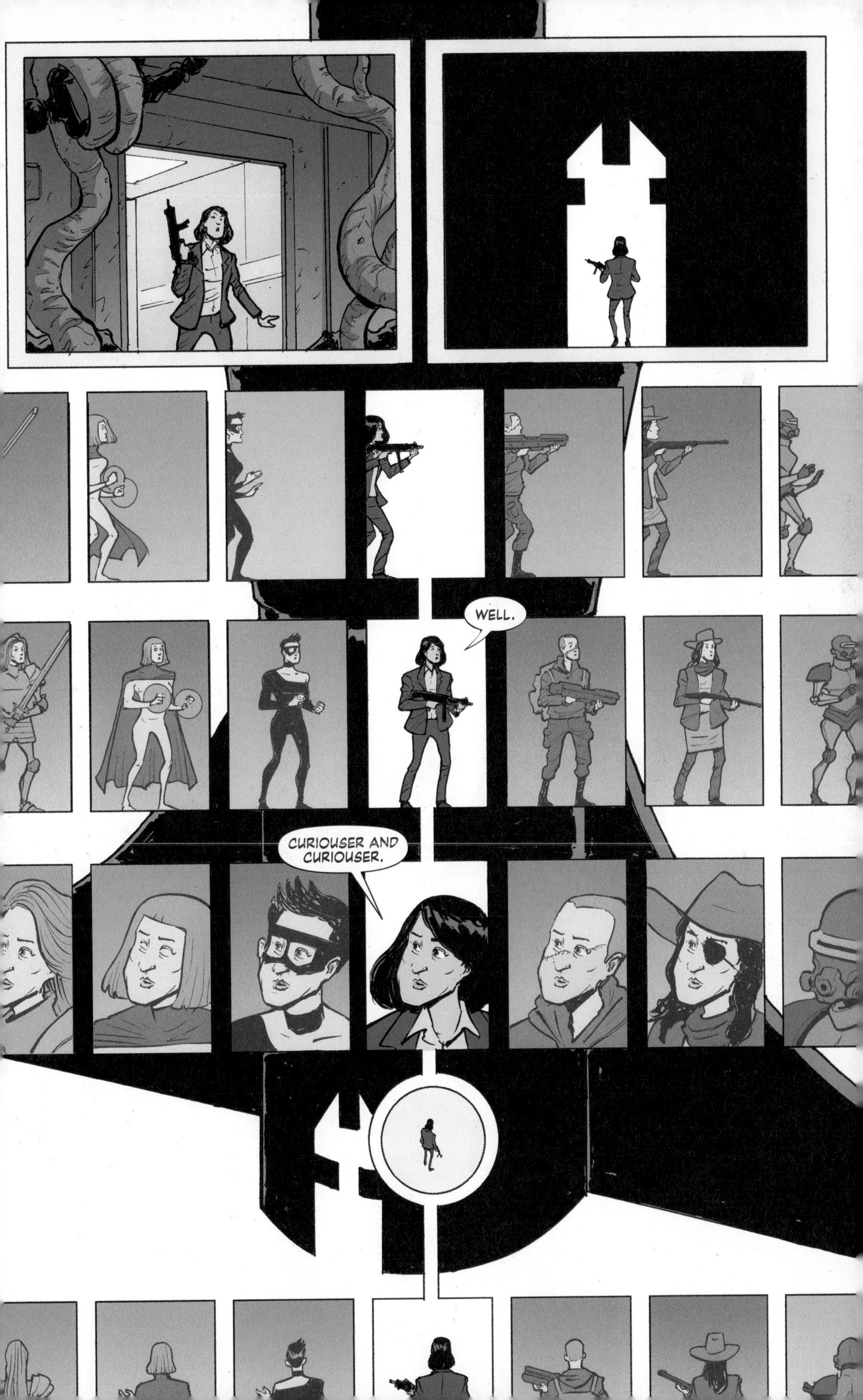
WELL.
CURIOUSER AND CURIOUSER.

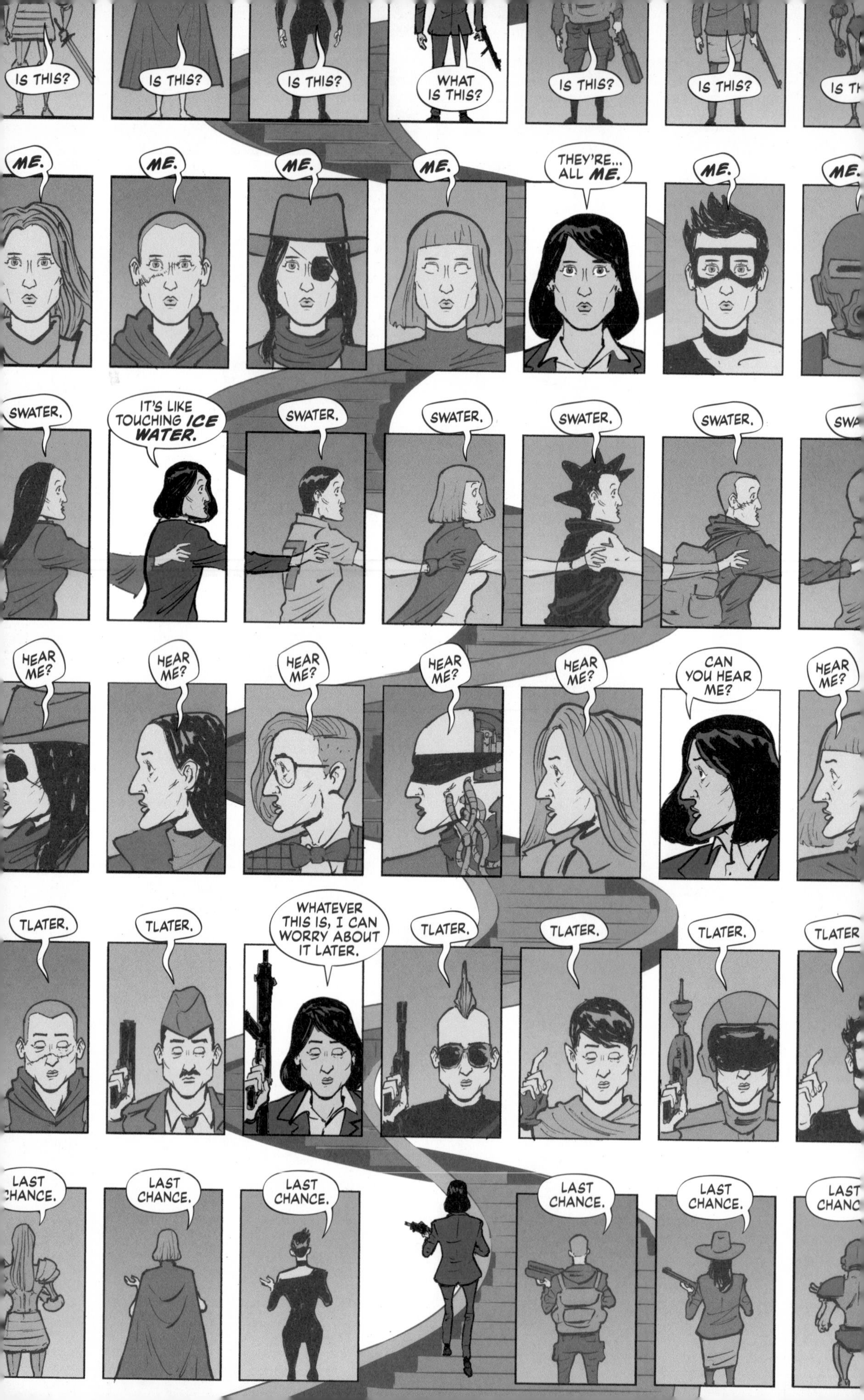
IS THIS?
IS THIS?
IS THIS?
WHAT IS THIS?
IS THIS?
IS THIS?
ME.
ME.
ME.
ME.
THEY'RE... ALL ME.
ME.
ME.
SWATER.
IT'S LIKE TOUCHING ICE WATER.
SWATER.
SWATER.
SWATER.
SWATER.
HEAR ME?
HEAR ME?
HEAR ME?
HEAR ME?
HEAR ME?
CAN YOU HEAR ME?
HEAR ME?
TLATER.
TLATER.
WHATEVER THIS IS, I CAN WORRY ABOUT IT LATER.
TLATER.
TLATER.
TLATER.
TLATER.
LAST CHANCE.
LAST CHANCE.
LAST CHANCE.
LAST CHANCE.
LAST CHANCE.

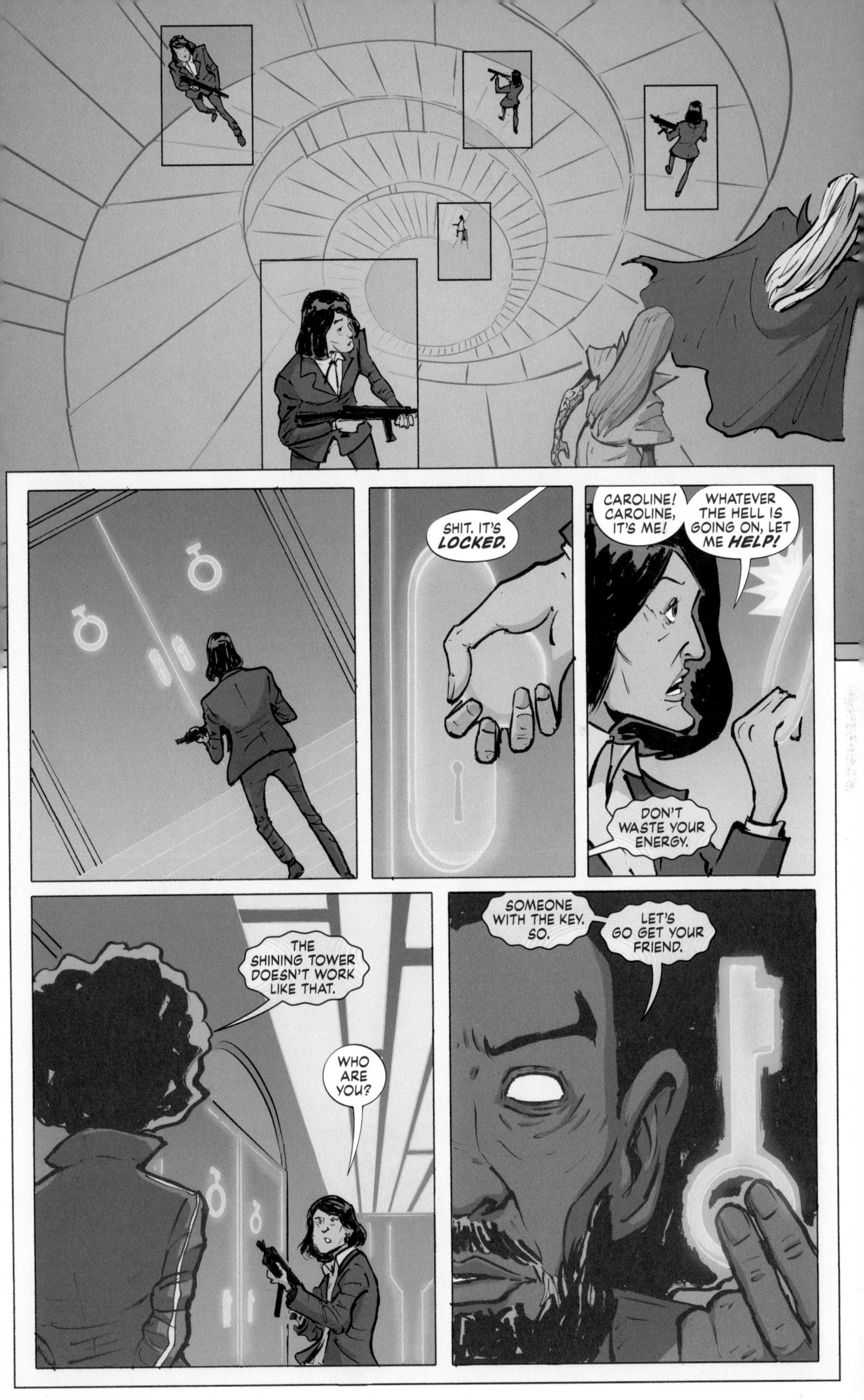
SHIT. IT'S
LOCKED.
CAROLINE! CAROLINE, IT'S ME!
WHATEVER THE HELL IS GOING ON, LET ME HELP!
DON'T WASTE YOUR ENERGY.
THE SHINING TOWER DOESN'T WORK LIKE THAT.
WHO ARE YOU?
SOMEONE WITH THE KEY. SO.
LET'S GO GET YOUR FRIEND.

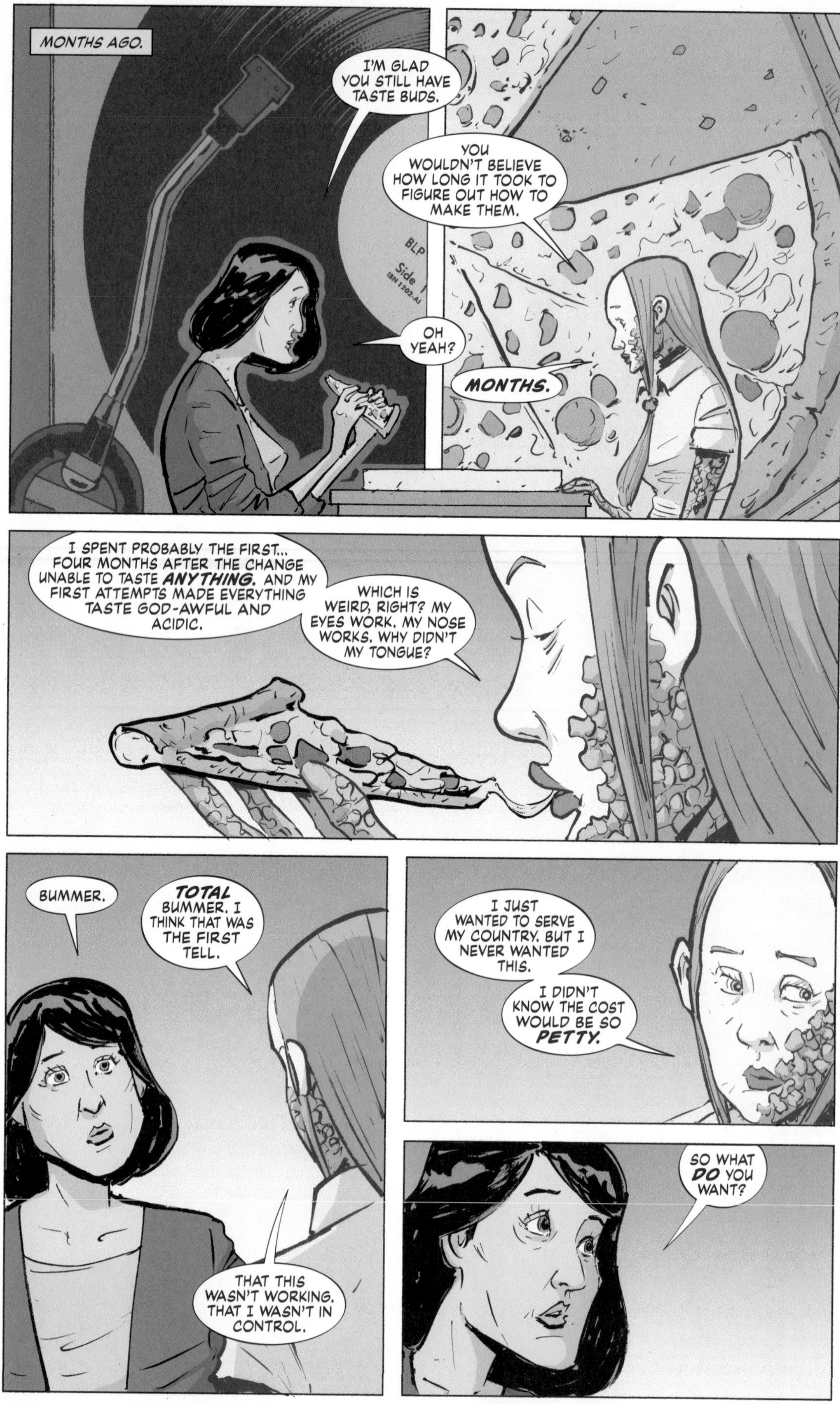
MONTHS AGO.
I'M GLAD YOU STILL HAVE TASTE BUDS.
YOU WOULDN'T BELIEVE HOW LONG IT TOOK TO FIGURE OUT HOW TO MAKE THEM.
BLP
Side 1
(BN 1202-A)
OH YEAH?
MONTHS.
I SPENT PROBABLY THE FIRST... FOUR MONTHS AFTER THE CHANGE UNABLE TO TASTE ANYTHING. AND MY FIRST ATTEMPTS MADE EVERYTHING TASTE GOD-AWFUL AND ACIDIC.
WHICH IS WEIRD, RIGHT? MY EYES WORK. MY NOSE WORKS. WHY DIDN'T MY TONGUE?
BUMMER.
TOTAL BUMMER. I THINK THAT WAS THE FIRST TELL.
THAT THIS WASN'T WORKING. THAT I WASN'T IN CONTROL.
I JUST WANTED TO SERVE MY COUNTRY. BUT I NEVER WANTED THIS.
I DIDN'T KNOW THE COST WOULD BE SO PETTY.
SO WHAT DO YOU WANT?

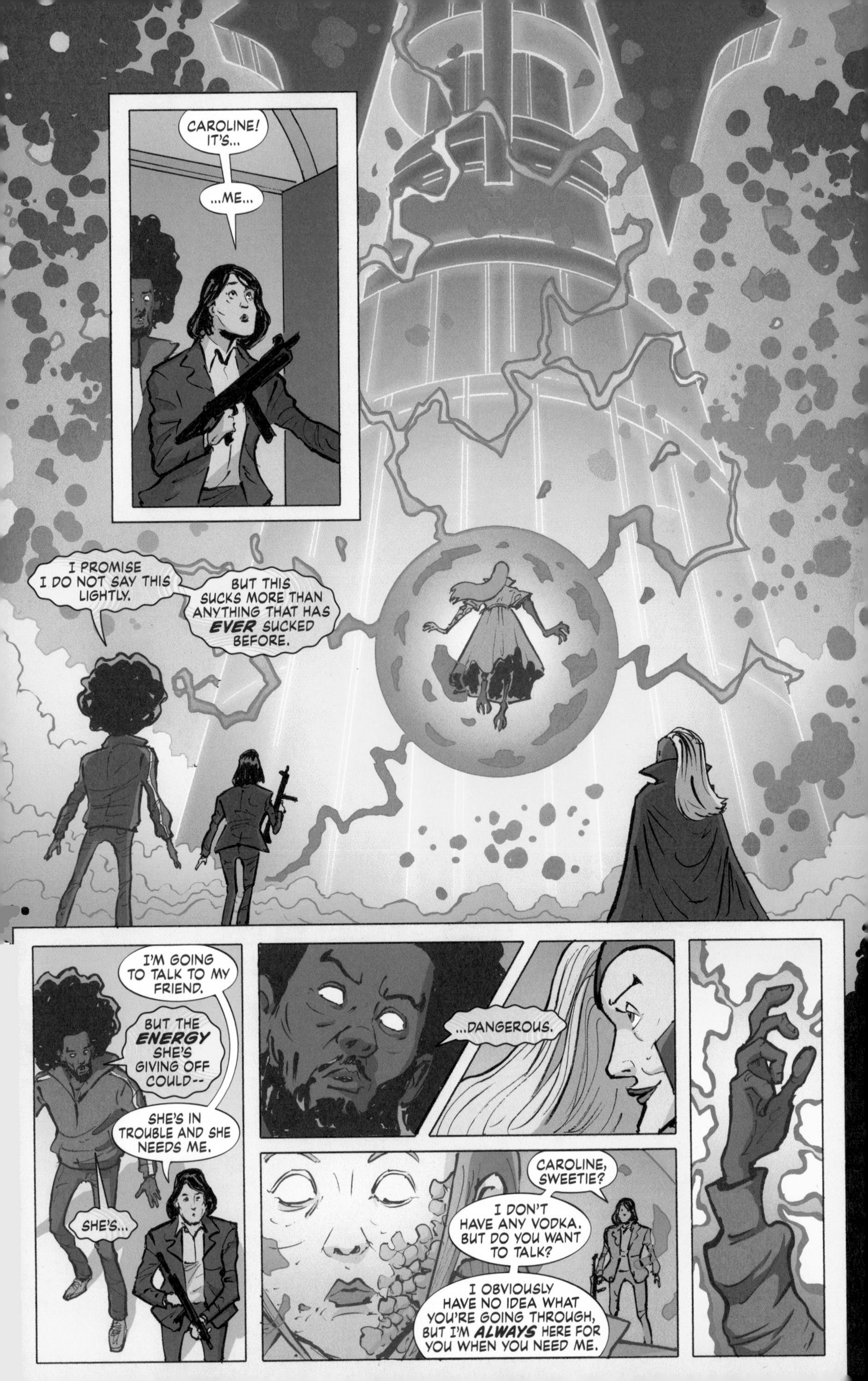
CAROLINE! IT'S...
...ME...
I PROMISE I DO NOT SAY THIS LIGHTLY.
BUT THIS SUCKS MORE THAN ANYTHING THAT HAS EVER SUCKED BEFORE.
I'M GOING TO TALK TO MY FRIEND.
BUT THE ENERGY SHE'S GIVING OFF COULD--
SHE'S IN TROUBLE AND SHE NEEDS ME.
SHE'S...
...DANGEROUS.
CAROLINE, SWEETIE?
I DON'T HAVE ANY VODKA. BUT DO YOU WANT TO TALK?
I OBVIOUSLY HAVE NO IDEA WHAT YOU'RE GOING THROUGH, BUT I'M ALWAYS HERE FOR YOU WHEN YOU NEED ME.

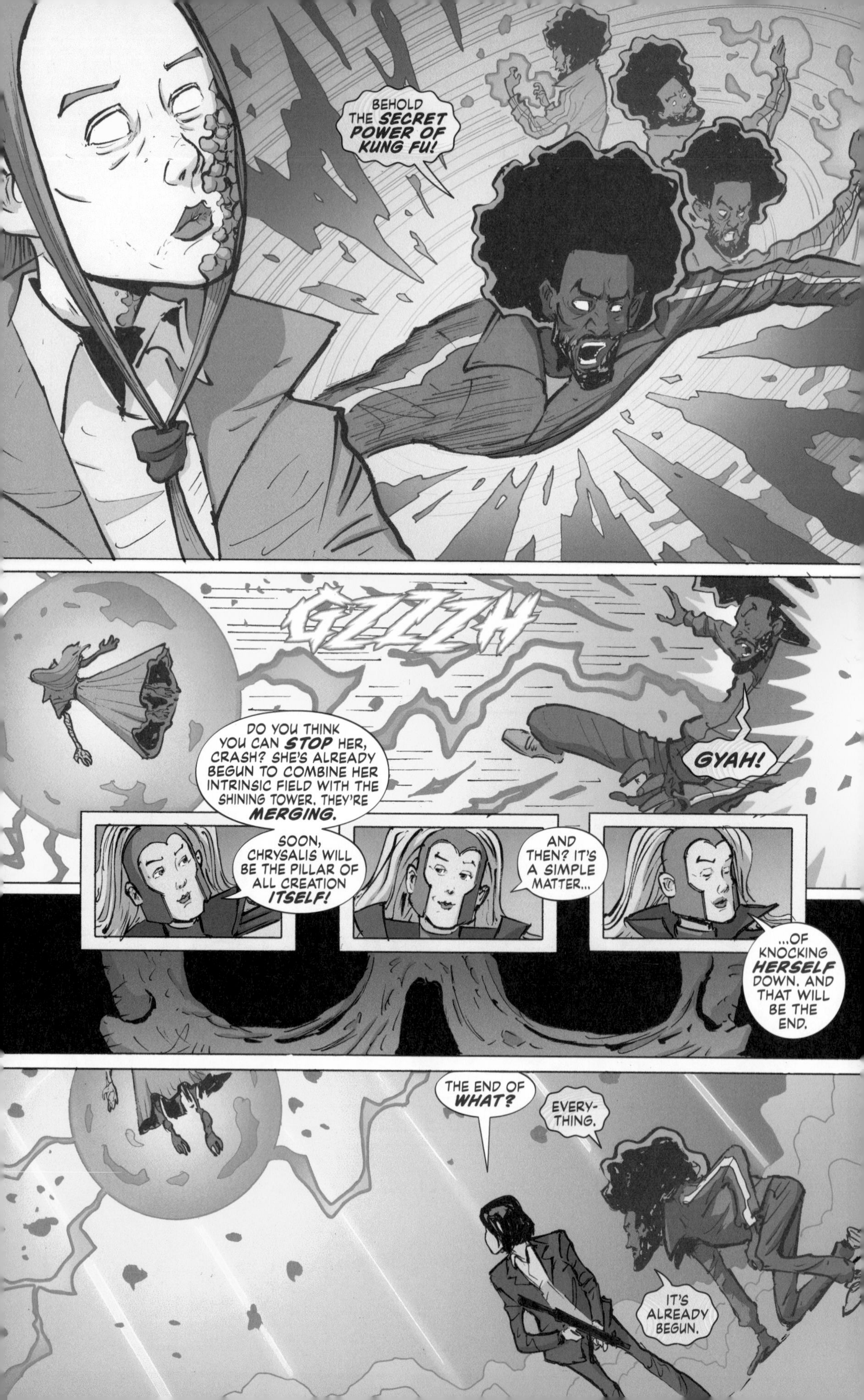
BEHOLD THE SECRET POWER OF KUNG FU!
GZZZH
GYAH!
DO YOU THINK YOU CAN STOP HER, CRASH? SHE'S ALREADY BEGUN TO COMBINE HER INTRINSIC FIELD WITH THE SHINING TOWER. THEY'RE MERGING.
SOON, CHRYSALIS WILL BE THE PILLAR OF ALL CREATION ITSELF!
AND THEN? IT'S A SIMPLE MATTER...
...OF KNOCKING HERSELF DOWN. AND THAT WILL BE THE END.
THE END OF WHAT?
EVERY-THING.
IT'S ALREADY BEGUN.

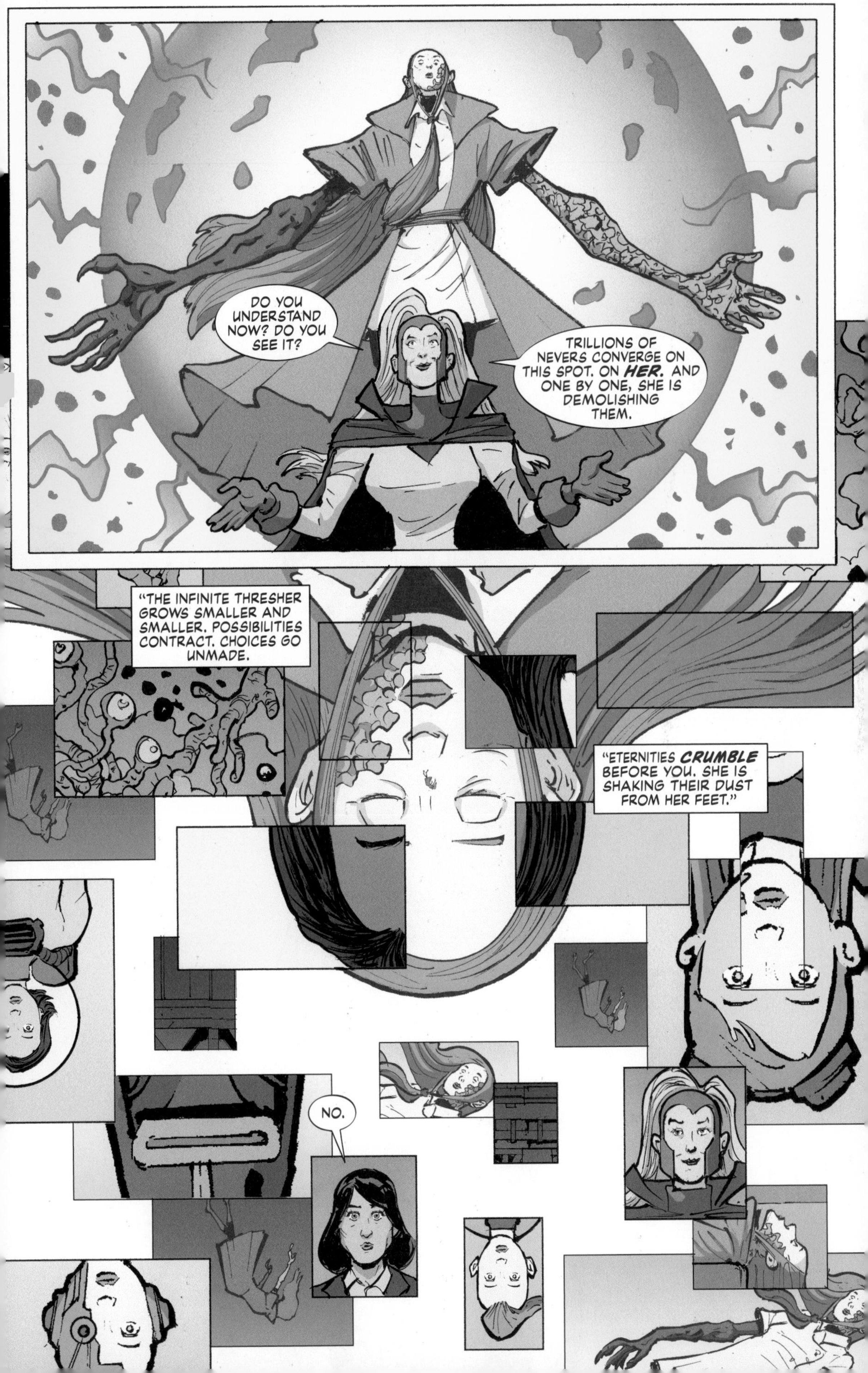
DO YOU UNDERSTAND NOW? DO YOU SEE IT?
TRILLIONS OF NEVERS CONVERGE ON THIS SPOT. ON HER. AND ONE BY ONE, SHE IS DEMOLISHING THEM.
"THE INFINITE THRESHER GROWS SMALLER AND SMALLER. POSSIBILITIES CONTRACT. CHOICES GO UNMADE.
"ETERNITIES CRUMBLE BEFORE YOU. SHE IS SHAKING THEIR DUST FROM HER FEET."
NO.

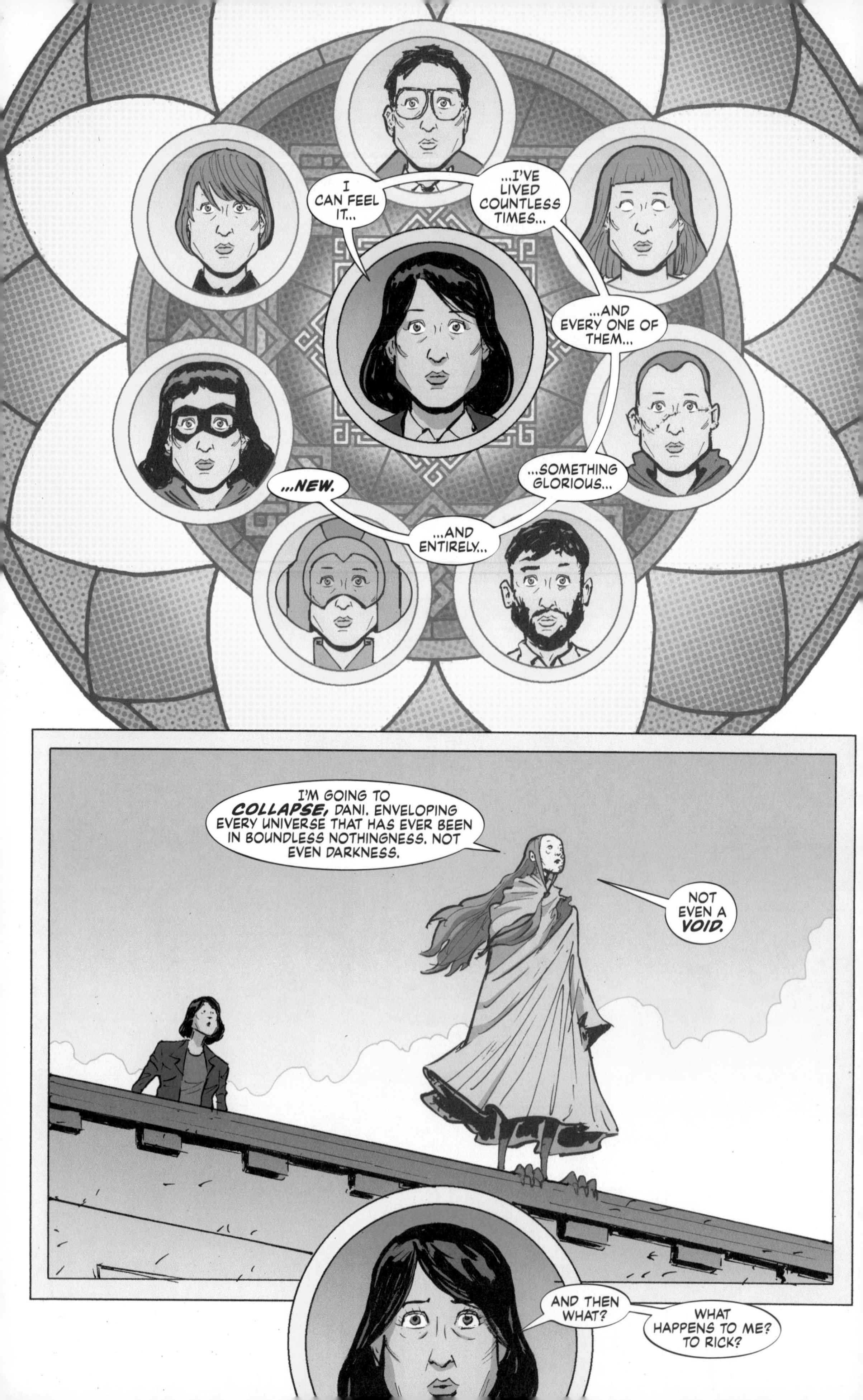
I CAN FEEL IT...
...I'VE LIVED COUNTLESS TIMES...
...AND EVERY ONE OF THEM...
...SOMETHING GLORIOUS...
...AND ENTIRELY...
...NEW.
I'M GOING TO COLLAPSE, DANI. ENVELOPING EVERY UNIVERSE THAT HAS EVER BEEN IN BOUNDLESS NOTHINGNESS. NOT EVEN DARKNESS.
NOT EVEN A VOID.
AND THEN WHAT?
WHAT HAPPENS TO ME? TO RICK?

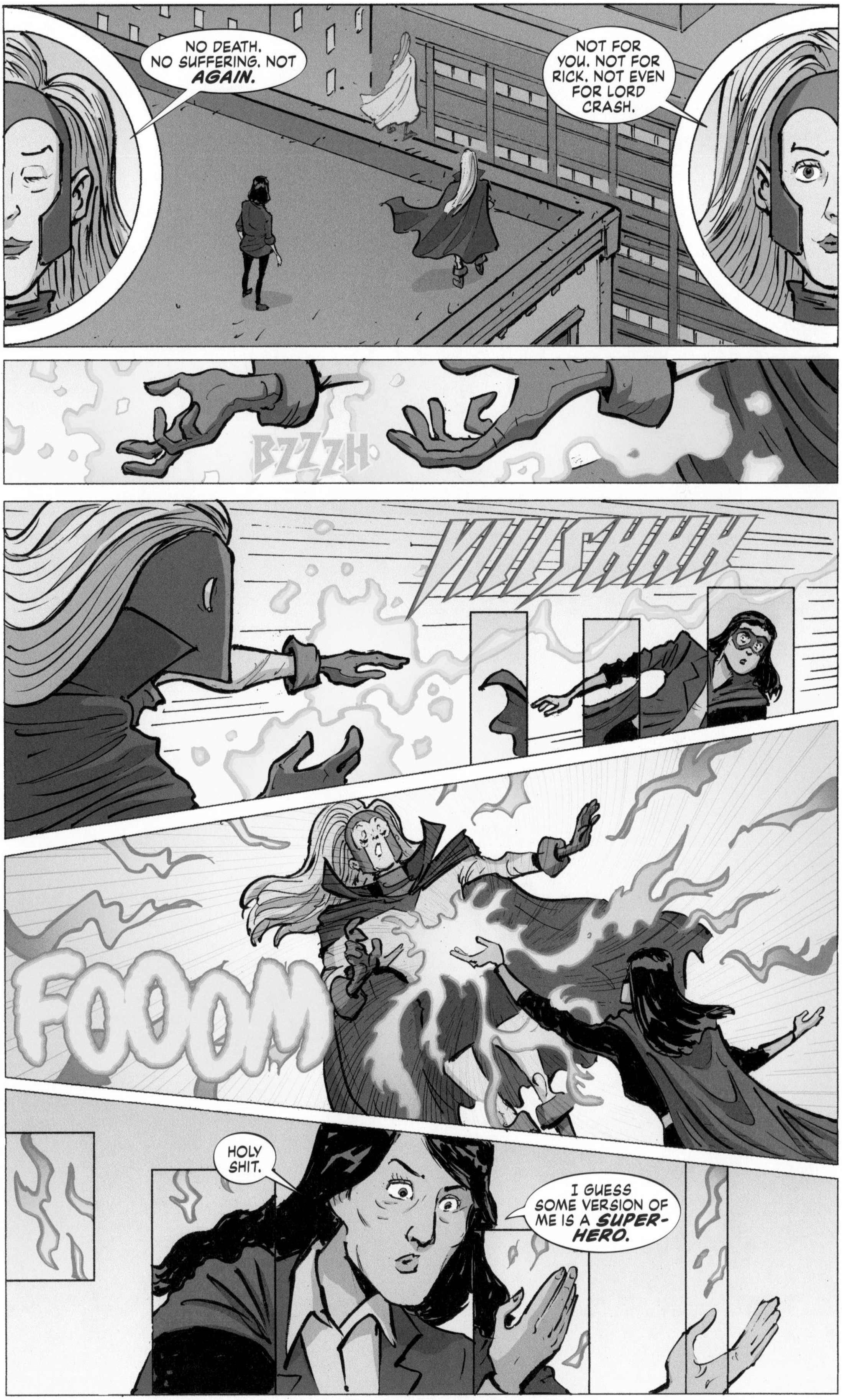
NO DEATH. NO SUFFERING. NOT **AGAIN.**
NOT FOR YOU. NOT FOR RICK. NOT EVEN FOR LORD CRASH.
BZZZH
VHUSHHH
FOOOM
HOLY SHIT.
I GUESS SOME VERSION OF ME IS A **SUPER-HERO.**

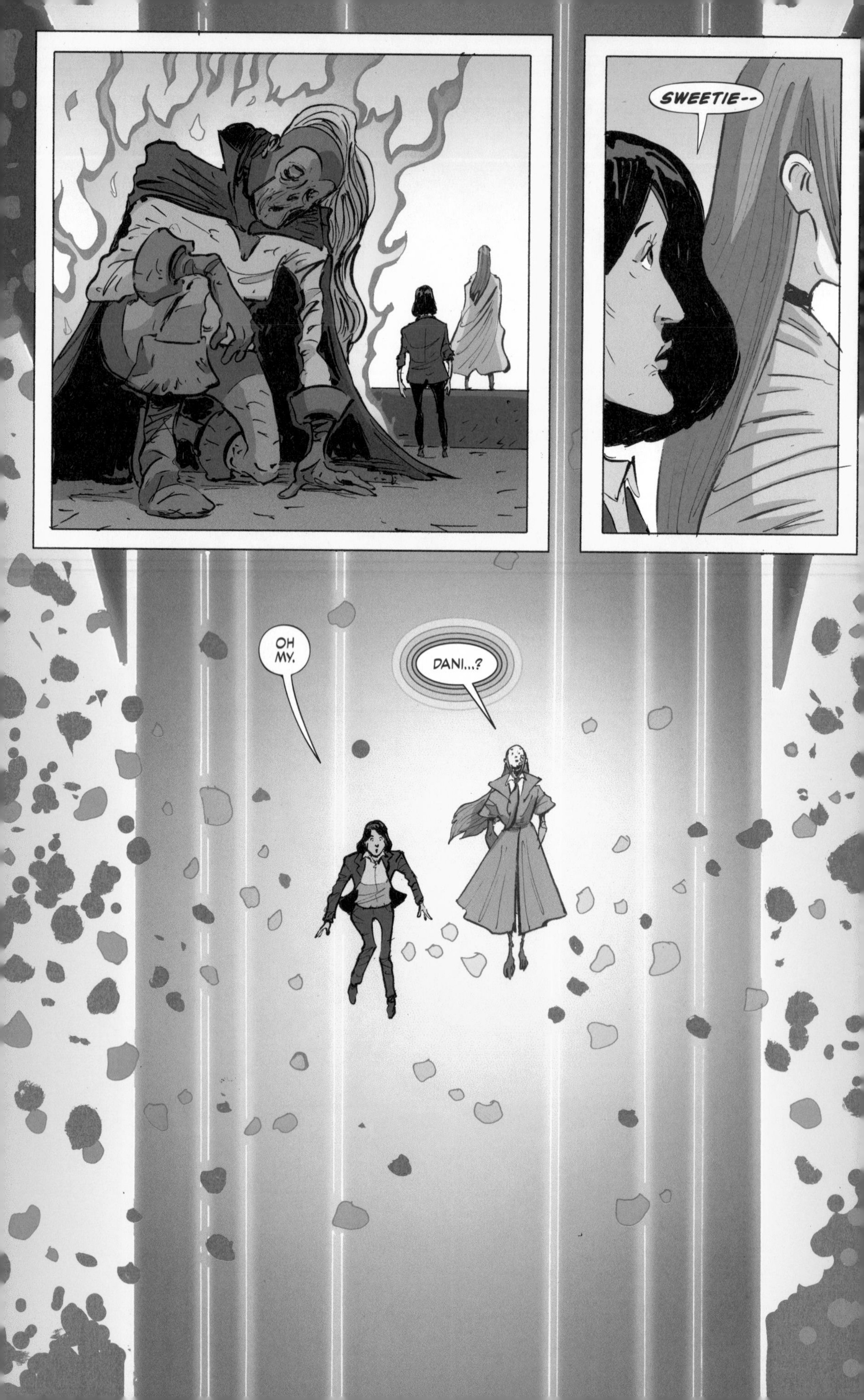
SWEETIE--
OH MY.
DANI...?

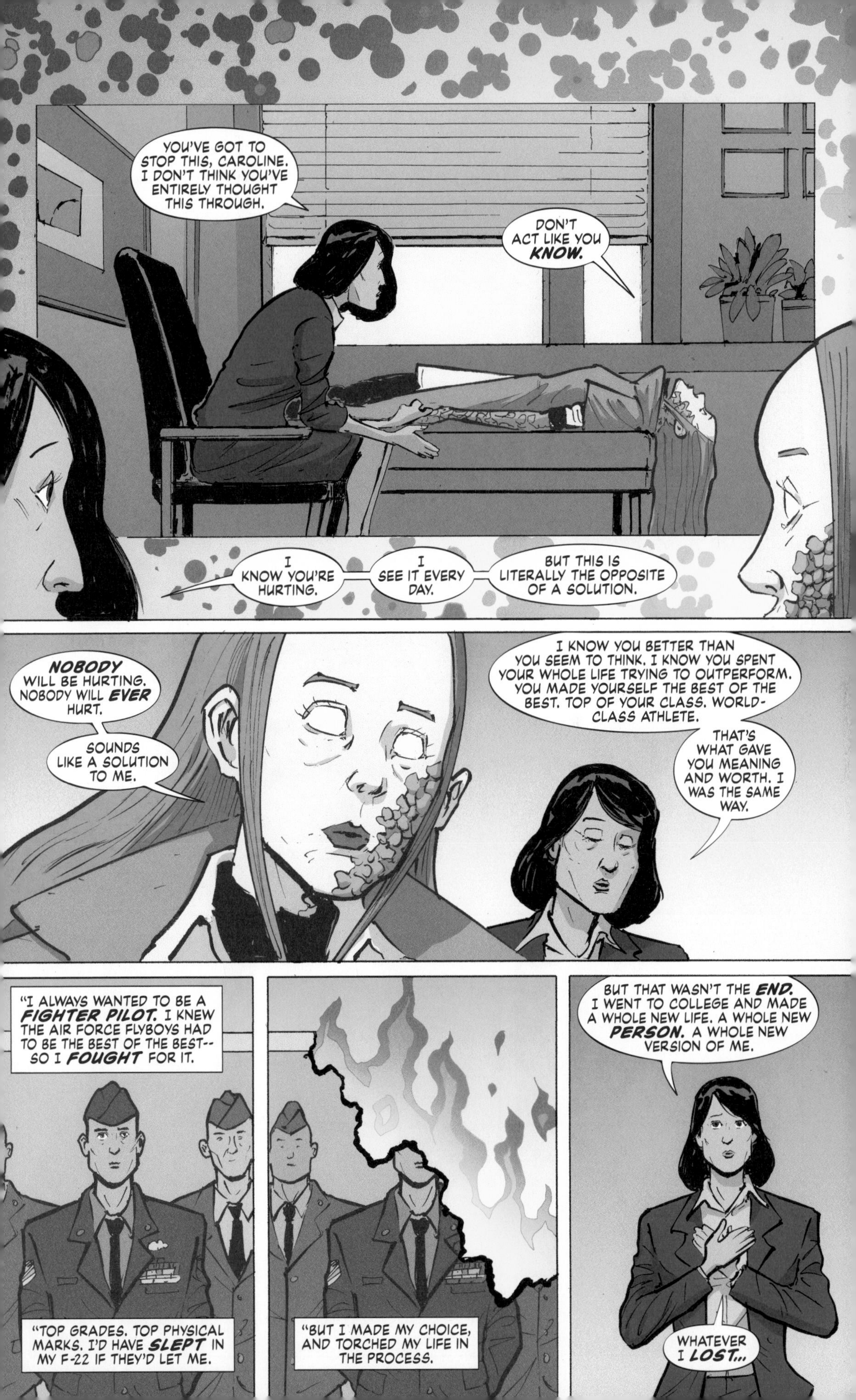
YOU'VE GOT TO STOP THIS, CAROLINE. I DON'T THINK YOU'VE ENTIRELY THOUGHT THIS THROUGH.
DON'T ACT LIKE YOU KNOW.
I KNOW YOU'RE HURTING.
I SEE IT EVERY DAY.
BUT THIS IS LITERALLY THE OPPOSITE OF A SOLUTION.
NOBODY WILL BE HURTING. NOBODY WILL EVER HURT.
SOUNDS LIKE A SOLUTION TO ME.
I KNOW YOU BETTER THAN YOU SEEM TO THINK. I KNOW YOU SPENT YOUR WHOLE LIFE TRYING TO OUTPERFORM. YOU MADE YOURSELF THE BEST OF THE BEST. TOP OF YOUR CLASS. WORLD-CLASS ATHLETE.
THAT'S WHAT GAVE YOU MEANING AND WORTH. I WAS THE SAME WAY.
"I ALWAYS WANTED TO BE A FIGHTER PILOT. I KNEW THE AIR FORCE FLYBOYS HAD TO BE THE BEST OF THE BEST-- SO I FOUGHT FOR IT.
"TOP GRADES. TOP PHYSICAL MARKS. I'D HAVE SLEPT IN MY F-22 IF THEY'D LET ME.
"BUT I MADE MY CHOICE, AND TORCHED MY LIFE IN THE PROCESS.
BUT THAT WASN'T THE END. I WENT TO COLLEGE AND MADE A WHOLE NEW LIFE. A WHOLE NEW PERSON. A WHOLE NEW VERSION OF ME.
WHATEVER I LOST...

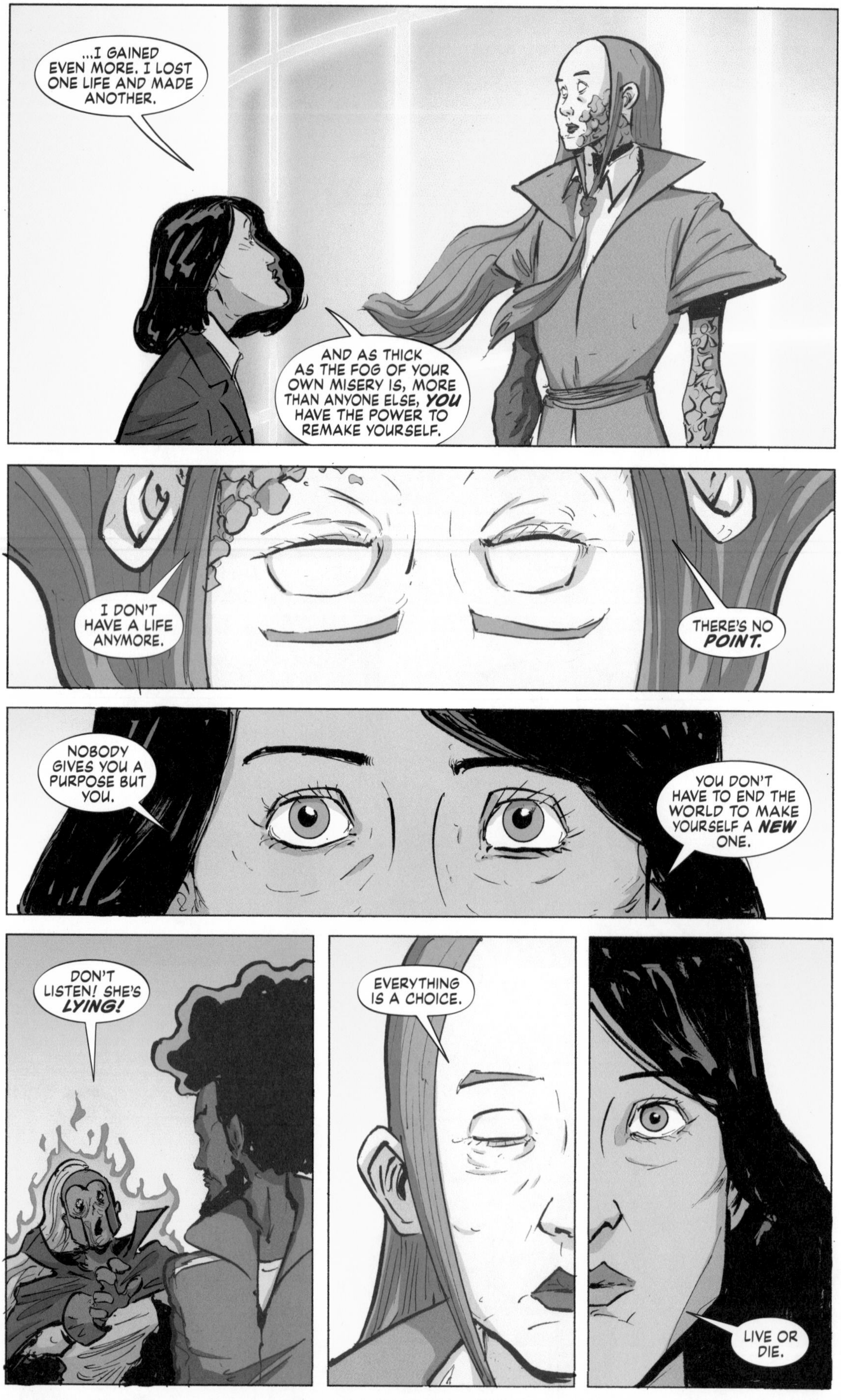
...I GAINED EVEN MORE. I LOST ONE LIFE AND MADE ANOTHER.
AND AS THICK AS THE FOG OF YOUR OWN MISERY IS, MORE THAN ANYONE ELSE, ***YOU*** HAVE THE POWER TO REMAKE YOURSELF.
I DON'T HAVE A LIFE ANYMORE.
THERE'S NO ***POINT.***
NOBODY GIVES YOU A PURPOSE BUT YOU.
YOU DON'T HAVE TO END THE WORLD TO MAKE YOURSELF A ***NEW*** ONE.
DON'T LISTEN! SHE'S ***LYING!***
EVERYTHING IS A CHOICE.
LIVE OR DIE.

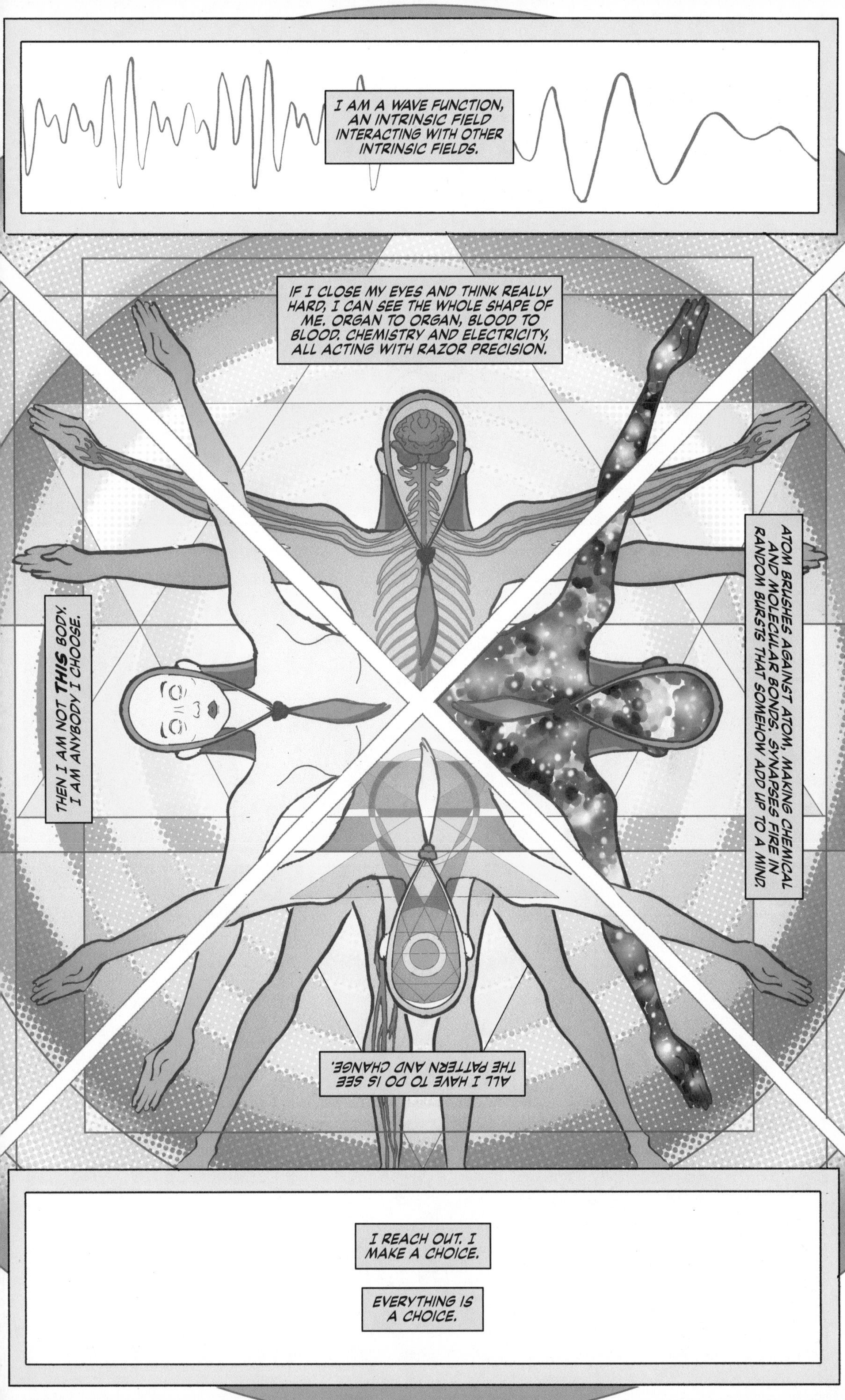

I AM A WAVE FUNCTION, AN INTRINSIC FIELD INTERACTING WITH OTHER INTRINSIC FIELDS.
IF I CLOSE MY EYES AND THINK REALLY HARD, I CAN SEE THE WHOLE SHAPE OF ME. ORGAN TO ORGAN, BLOOD TO BLOOD. CHEMISTRY AND ELECTRICITY, ALL ACTING WITH RAZOR PRECISION.
ATOM BRUSHES AGAINST ATOM, MAKING CHEMICAL AND MOLECULAR BONDS. SYNAPSES FIRE IN RANDOM BURSTS THAT SOMEHOW ADD UP TO A MIND.
ALL I HAVE TO DO IS SEE THE PATTERN AND CHANGE.
THEN I AM NOT **THIS** BODY. I AM ANYBODY I CHOOSE.
I REACH OUT. I MAKE A CHOICE.
EVERYTHING IS A CHOICE.

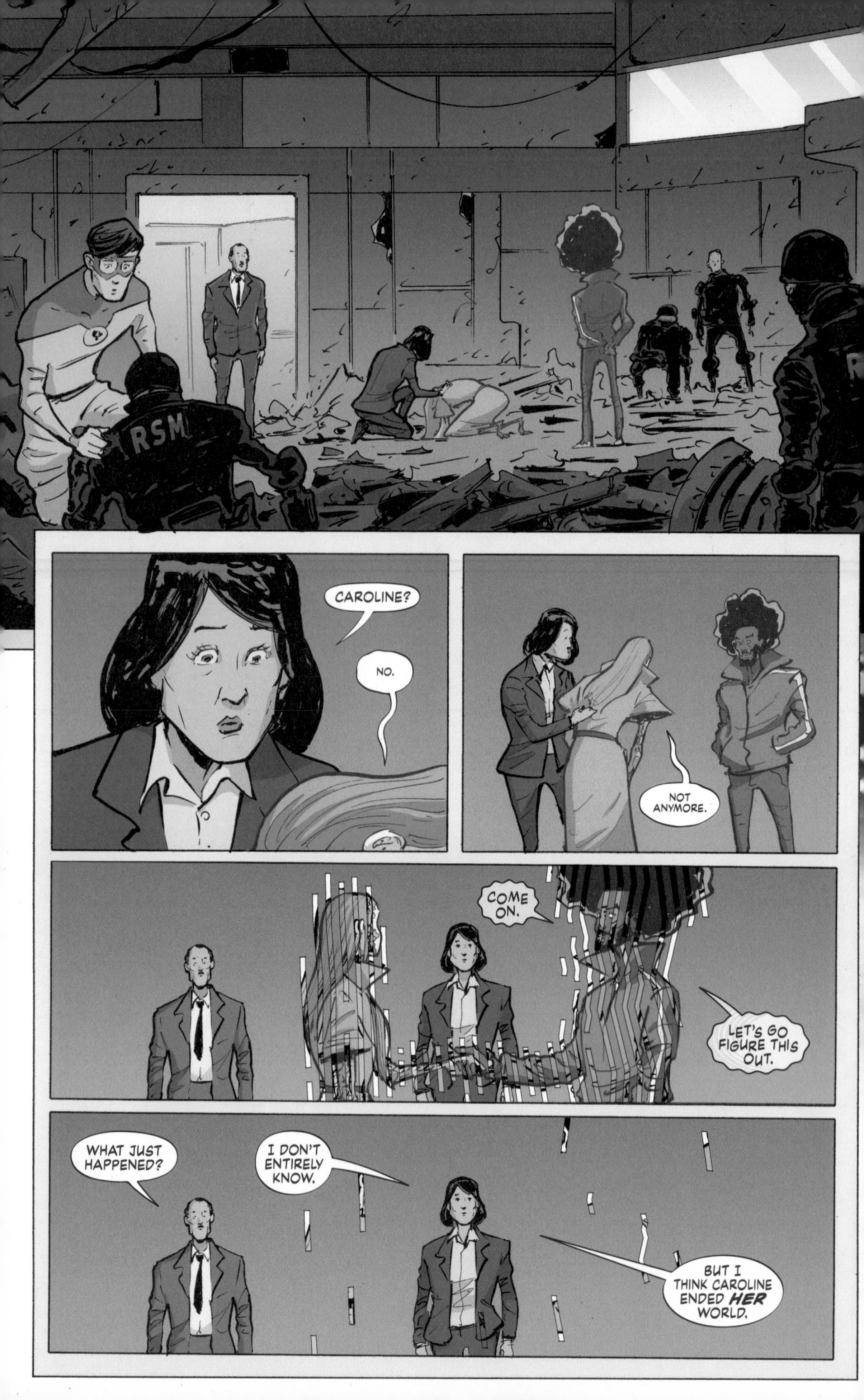
RSM
CAROLINE?
NO.
NOT ANYMORE.
COME ON.
LET'S GO FIGURE THIS OUT.
WHAT JUST HAPPENED?
I DON'T ENTIRELY KNOW.
BUT I THINK CAROLINE ENDED HER WORLD.

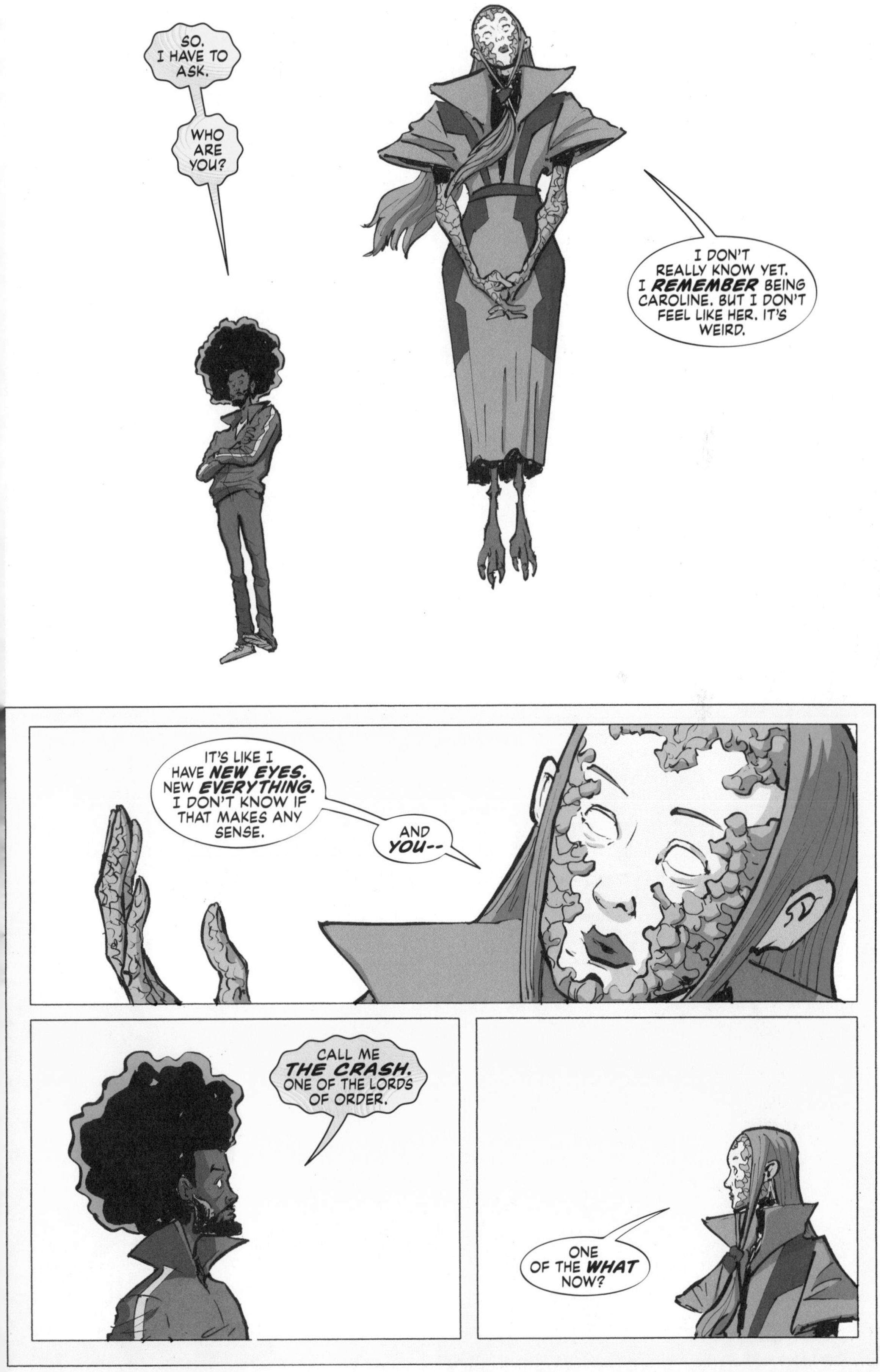
SO. I HAVE TO ASK.
WHO ARE YOU?
I DON'T REALLY KNOW YET. I REMEMBER BEING CAROLINE. BUT I DON'T FEEL LIKE HER. IT'S WEIRD.
IT'S LIKE I HAVE NEW EYES. NEW EVERYTHING. I DON'T KNOW IF THAT MAKES ANY SENSE.
AND YOU--
CALL ME THE CRASH. ONE OF THE LORDS OF ORDER.
ONE OF THE WHAT NOW?

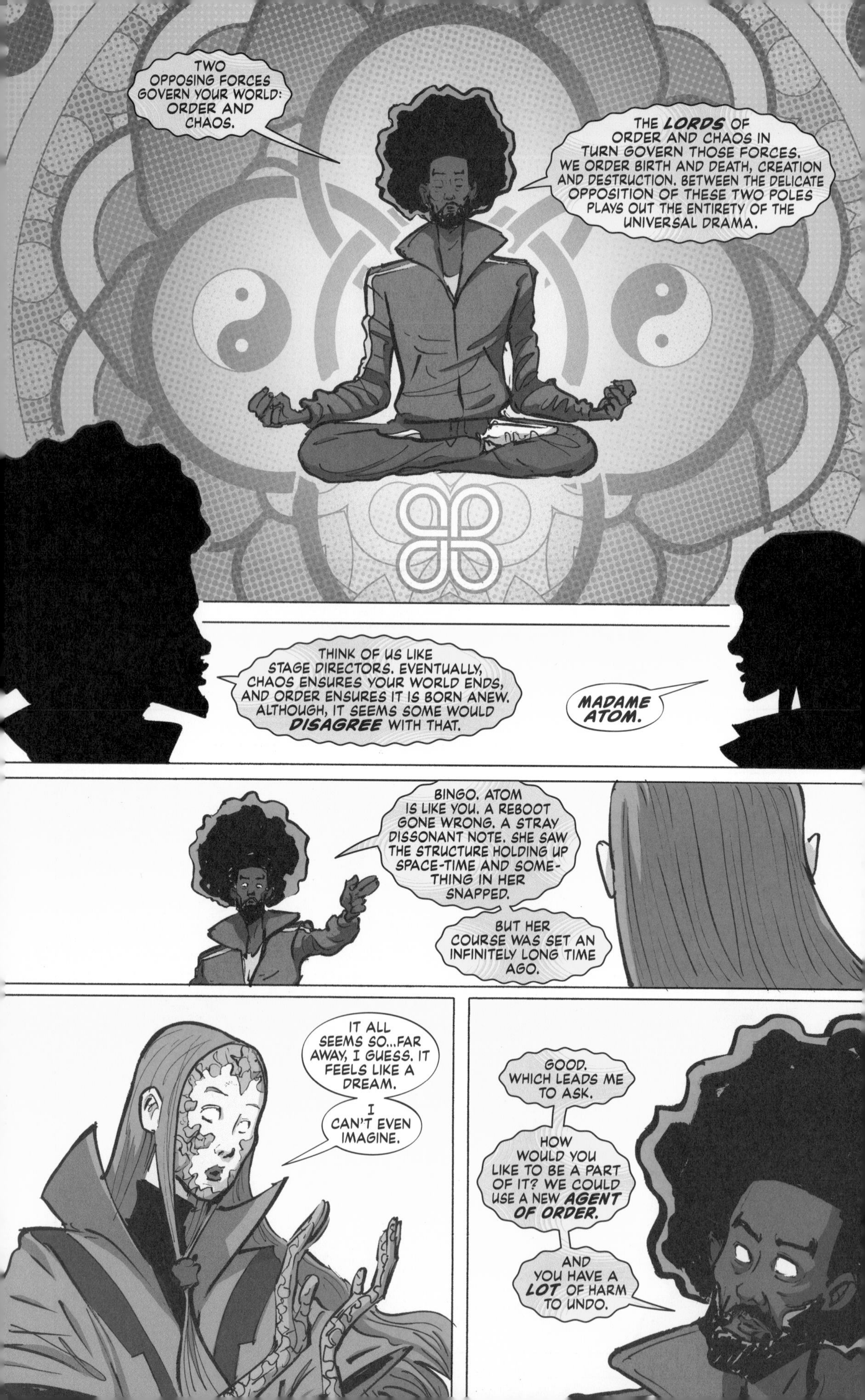
TWO OPPOSING FORCES GOVERN YOUR WORLD: ORDER AND CHAOS.
THE LORDS OF ORDER AND CHAOS IN TURN GOVERN THOSE FORCES. WE ORDER BIRTH AND DEATH, CREATION AND DESTRUCTION. BETWEEN THE DELICATE OPPOSITION OF THESE TWO POLES PLAYS OUT THE ENTIRETY OF THE UNIVERSAL DRAMA.
THINK OF US LIKE STAGE DIRECTORS. EVENTUALLY, CHAOS ENSURES YOUR WORLD ENDS, AND ORDER ENSURES IT IS BORN ANEW. ALTHOUGH, IT SEEMS SOME WOULD DISAGREE WITH THAT.
MADAME ATOM.
BINGO. ATOM IS LIKE YOU. A REBOOT GONE WRONG. A STRAY DISSONANT NOTE. SHE SAW THE STRUCTURE HOLDING UP SPACE-TIME AND SOME-THING IN HER SNAPPED.
BUT HER COURSE WAS SET AN INFINITELY LONG TIME AGO.
IT ALL SEEMS SO...FAR AWAY, I GUESS. IT FEELS LIKE A DREAM.
I CAN'T EVEN IMAGINE.
GOOD. WHICH LEADS ME TO ASK.
HOW WOULD YOU LIKE TO BE A PART OF IT? WE COULD USE A NEW AGENT OF ORDER.
AND YOU HAVE A LOT OF HARM TO UNDO.

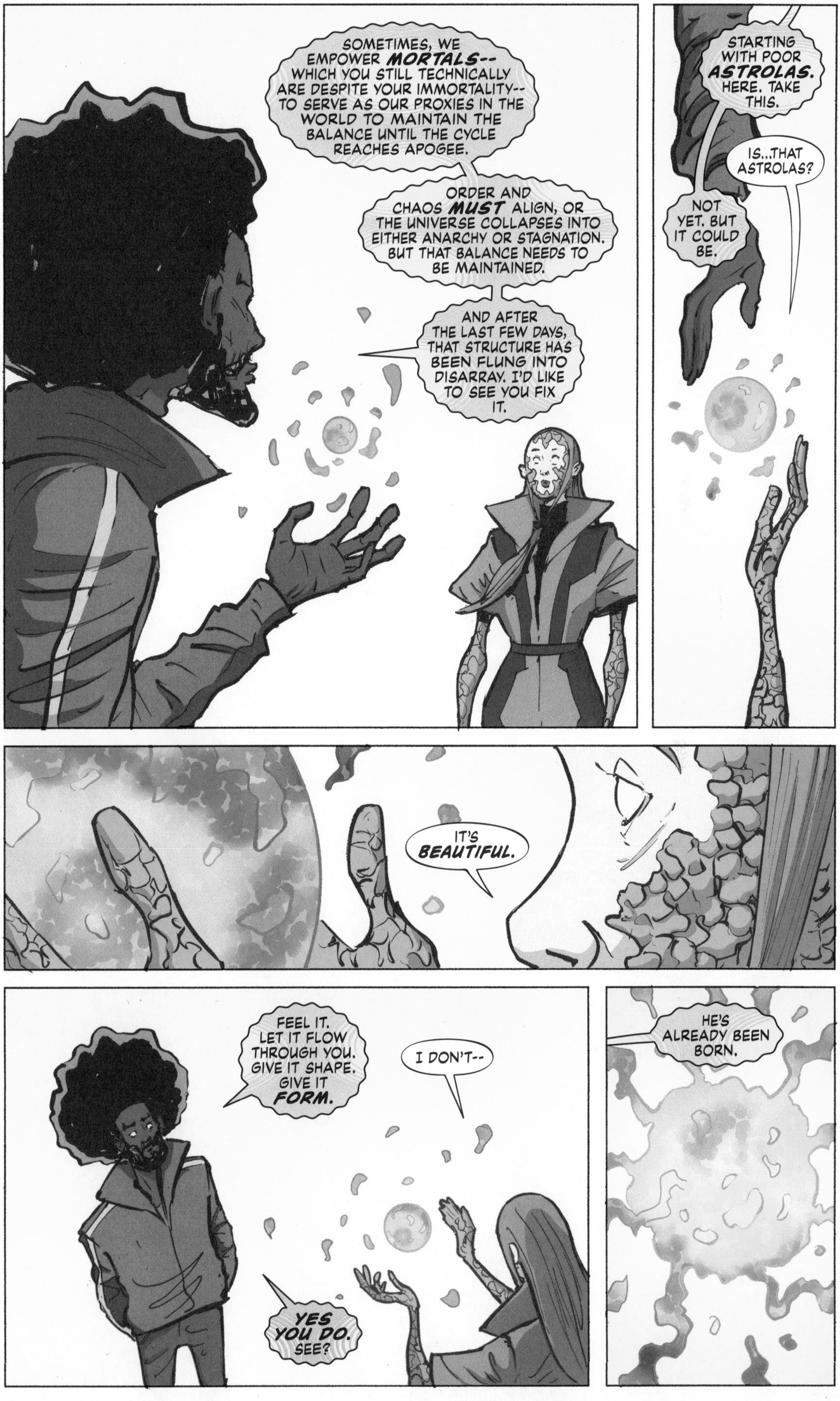
SOMETIMES, WE EMPOWER MORTALS-- WHICH YOU STILL TECHNICALLY ARE DESPITE YOUR IMMORTALITY-- TO SERVE AS OUR PROXIES IN THE WORLD TO MAINTAIN THE BALANCE UNTIL THE CYCLE REACHES APOGEE.
ORDER AND CHAOS MUST ALIGN, OR THE UNIVERSE COLLAPSES INTO EITHER ANARCHY OR STAGNATION. BUT THAT BALANCE NEEDS TO BE MAINTAINED.
AND AFTER THE LAST FEW DAYS, THAT STRUCTURE HAS BEEN FLUNG INTO DISARRAY. I'D LIKE TO SEE YOU FIX IT.
STARTING WITH POOR ASTROLAS. HERE. TAKE THIS.
IS...THAT ASTROLAS?
NOT YET. BUT IT COULD BE.
IT'S BEAUTIFUL.
FEEL IT. LET IT FLOW THROUGH YOU. GIVE IT SHAPE. GIVE IT FORM.
I DON'T--
YES YOU DO. SEE?
HE'S ALREADY BEEN BORN.

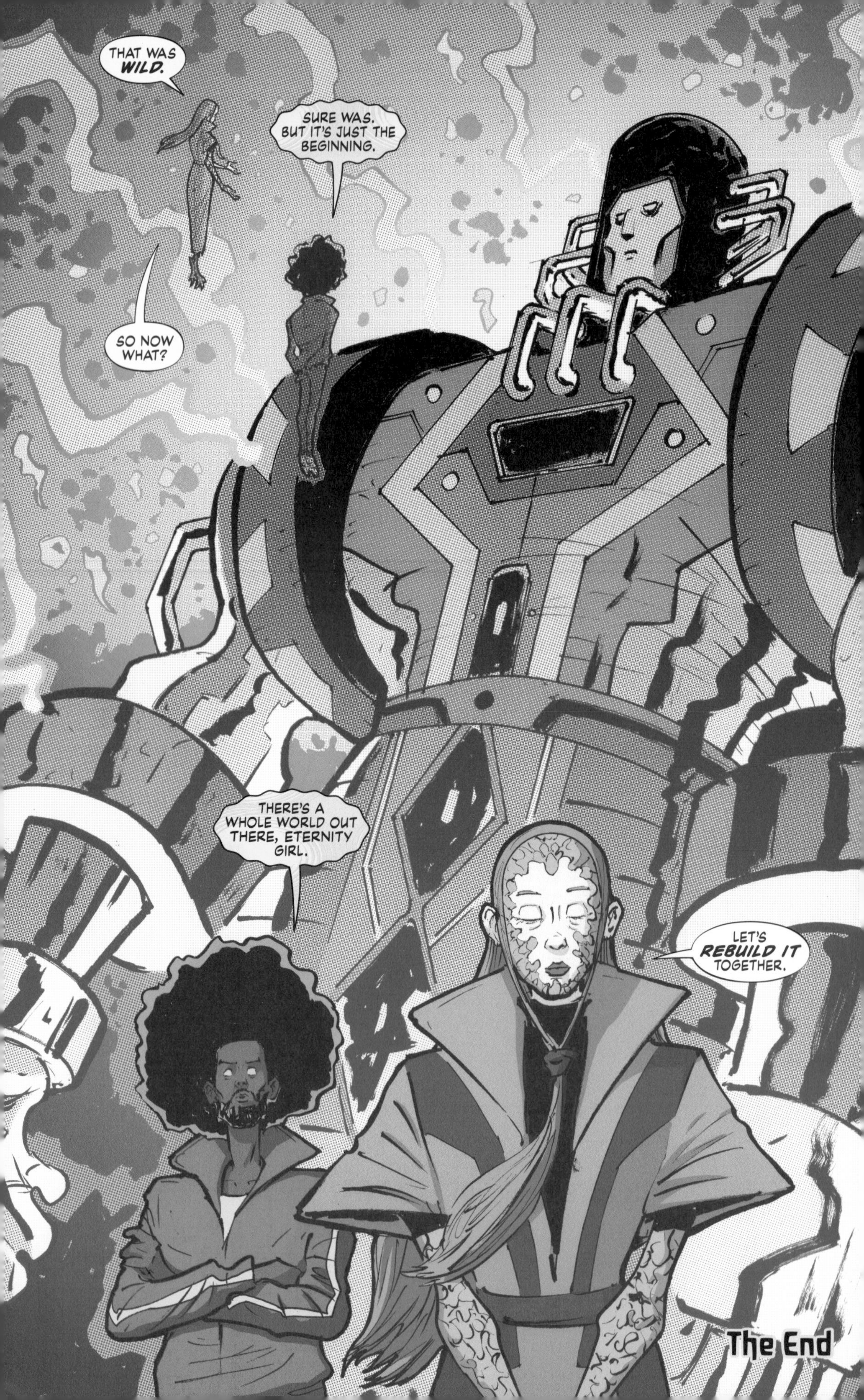
THAT WAS *WILD.*
SURE WAS. BUT IT'S JUST THE BEGINNING.
SO NOW WHAT?
THERE'S A WHOLE WORLD OUT THERE, ETERNITY GIRL.
LET'S *REBUILD IT* TOGETHER.
The End

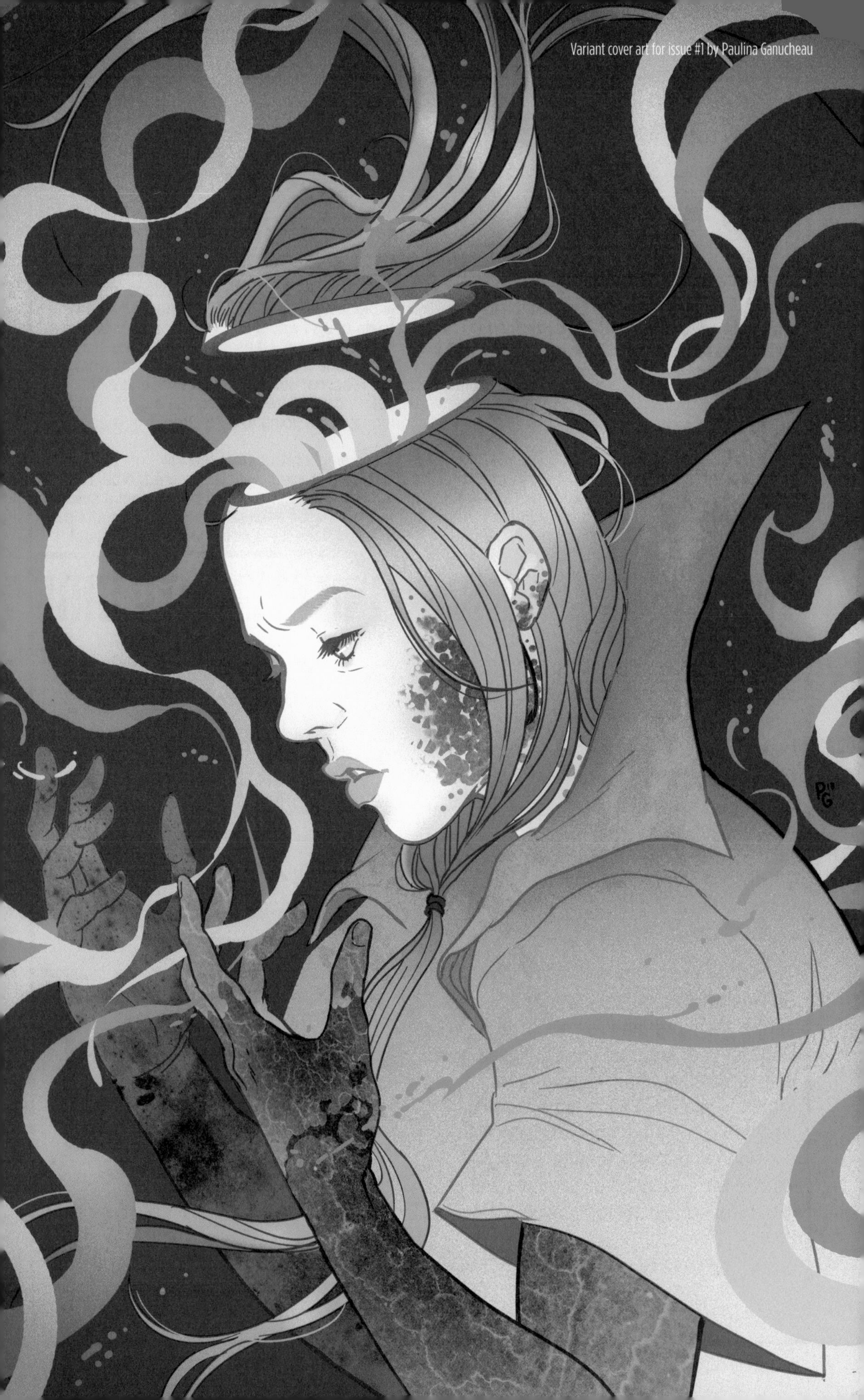

Variant cover art for issue #1 by Paulina Ganucheau

Who's Who

DC's Young Animal

PERSONAL DATA

NAME: Magdalene Visaggio
TWITTER: @MagsVisaggs
OCCUPATION: Writer
FIRST APPEARANCE:
SHADE THE CHANGING GIRL #4

HISTORY

I've really struggled with writing this. Shortly after college, my friend Steph told me that my biggest problem is that, whatever it was I decided I was going to do or be I would do or be for a year before giving up and trying something else. I was going to be a musician; I was going to be a Catholic priest (which didn't work out for what should be fairly obvious reasons, but I managed to spend eight months in seminary before they figured out I wasn't a guy); I was going to go into academia; I was going to be a Great Novelist.

The fact is that there is no single history that feels like my history; there's a whole host of lives I've lived, people I've tried to be, before I landed here at Young Animal writing this weird book about a suicidal immortal. And ultimately the lesson I've learned is not to be afraid of yourself. Live fearlessly, and honestly; this is the only life you get.

THE PROCESS OF WRITING ETERNITY GIRL

I think most people's process are pretty similar; a summary becomes an outline becomes a script, with various steps in between. I for one block out each page in big-picture terms before I ever get to full script, but even if the steps are different, the process generally has the same shape. I envy the crap out of writers who can sit down, look at a blank page, and just type "Page 1, Panel 1: Interior, the Batcave. Batman scowls," followed by an entire story.

So I just wanna say this: writing is about saying yes more than it is about saying no. Don't let your fear that your stuff isn't good enough stop you from listening to your instincts. You don't have to be a genius right when you start; spend time writing and figuring out what kind of writer you want to be, and then you'll know what ideas work and don't for what you are doing.

DC's
YOUNG ANIMAL
1 $3.99 MATURE READERS
ETERNITY GIRL
MAGDALENE VISAGGIO
SONNY LIEW
CHRIS CHUCKRY

Who's Who
DC's Young Animal

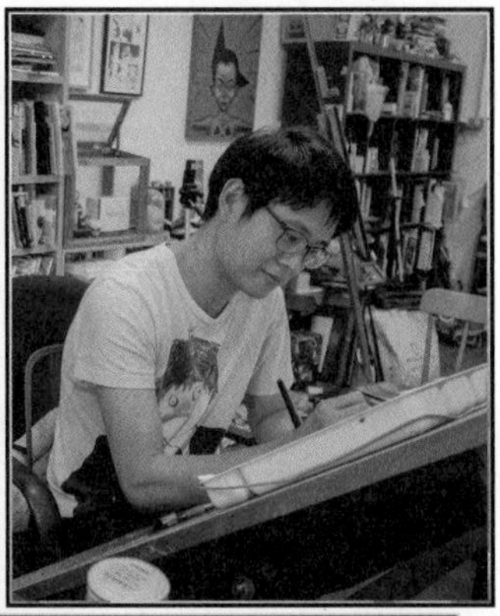

PERSONAL DATA

NAME: Sonny Liew
INSTAGRAM: @sonny_liew
OCCUPATION: Cartoonist
FIRST APPEARANCE:
JLA/DOOM PATROL SPECIAL #1

HISTORY

I was born, I'm alive for now, and one day will shuffle off the mortal coil. In between I hope to make some good comics, experience some minor epiphanies, and play some *Tabikaeru*.

THE PROCESS OF ILLUSTRATING ETERNITY GIRL

When I'm working on my own books like *The Art of Charlie Chan Hock Chye*, it's a more full-on process, with lots of reading and research required, worries about story structure and themes, narrative flow and much more. Collaborating with writers makes the work...well not exactly easier...but different–you're trying your best to flesh out someone else's vision for the most part, so it's a different kind of responsibility. Less personal, perhaps, and more about professionalism. But I suppose at some point there will be thumbnails, pencilling and inking.

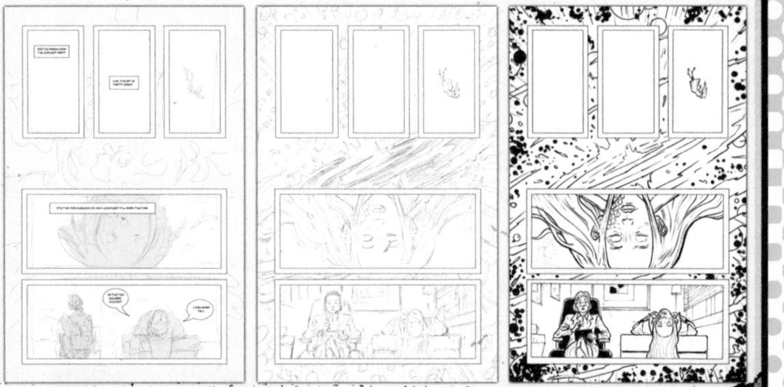

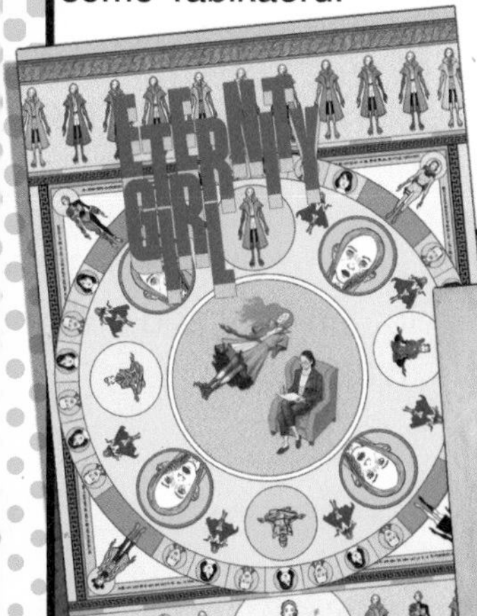
ETERNITY GIRL

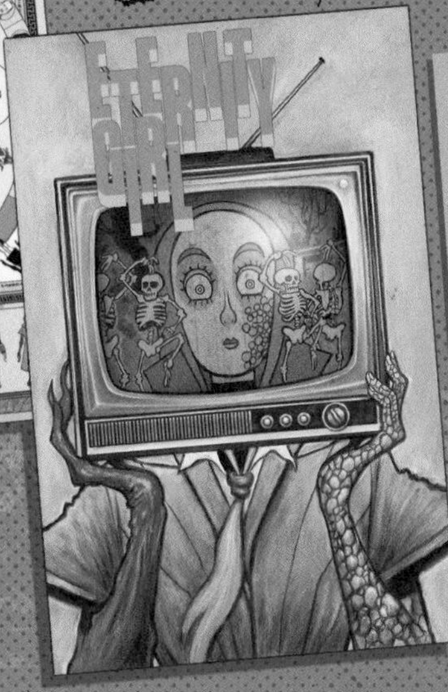
ETERNITY GIRL

Covers are always fun to do–in some ways you have more creative leeway with those. These are usually done digitally, just because it's so much easier to make adjustments, and speed is always good when you're swimming against deadline tides. For my inks I still think there's a kind of organic quality you can't quite duplicate on the computer, so I tend to do those with traditional brushes and pens. It's great that we get to pick and choose from both analog and digital tools these days, to get the best of both worlds, or at least whatever fits our idiosyncrasies.

Of course robots will be taking over everything soon enough, but for now, it's a pretty sweet spot.

Eternity Girl

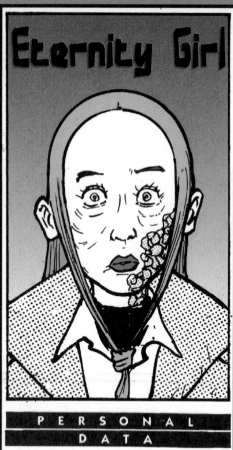

Who's Who
DC's Young Animal

PERSONAL DATA

Name: Caroline Sharp
Alias: Chrysalis, Eternity Girl
Age: 35
Height: Short for an elemental superwoman
Species: Sentient intrinsic field, former human

HISTORY

Like literally everyone, Caroline Sharp is the latest incarnation of a universal constant stretching infinitely far backward and forward in time. A chronic overachiever, she was recruited into the secret ops organization known only as ALPHA 13 out of college. On an early assignment, she was dispatched into the Iraqi desert to stop international terrorist super-villain Madame Atom from obtaining an ancient magical power, but inadvertently acquired it for herself.

Suddenly, Sharp found herself profoundly deformed and given immense power over her own matter and that within a thirty-foot radius, turning her into so much more than a shape-shifter. Under the code-name Chrysalis, she became Madame Atom's most powerful enemy. That is, until Madame Atom attempted to strip the power away from her--making it go haywire in the process.

Caroline was temporarily reassigned to the ALPHA 13 home office where she lost control of her abilities, causing significant structural damage to the building and costing one operative her arm, at which point she was removed from active service entirely and ordered into mandatory psychological evaluation.

It is not going well.